Guile Reference Manual 2/2

A catalogue record for this book is available from the Hong Kong Public Libraries.

Published in Hong Kong by Samurai Media Limited.

Email: info@samuraimedia.org

ISBN 978-988-8381-90-6

Table of Contents

7 Guile Modules

7.1 SLIB

SLIB is a portable library of Scheme packages which can be used with Guile and other Scheme implementations. SLIB is not included in the Guile distribution, but can be installed separately (see Section 7.1.1 [SLIB installation], page 467). It is available from `http://people.csail.mit.edu/jaffer/SLIB.html`.

After SLIB is installed, the following Scheme expression must be executed before the SLIB facilities can be used:

```
(use-modules (ice-9 slib))
```

`require` can then be used in the usual way (see Section "Require" in *The SLIB Manual*). For example,

```
(use-modules (ice-9 slib))
(require 'primes)
(prime? 13)
⇒ #t
```

A few Guile core functions are overridden by the SLIB setups; for example the SLIB version of `delete-file` returns a boolean indicating success or failure, whereas the Guile core version throws an error for failure. In general (and as might be expected) when SLIB is loaded it's the SLIB specifications that are followed.

7.1.1 SLIB installation

The following procedure works, e.g., with SLIB version 3a3 (see Section "Installation" in *The SLIB Portable Scheme Library*):

1. Unpack SLIB and install it using `make install` from its directory. By default, this will install SLIB in `/usr/local/lib/slib/`. Running `make install-info` installs its documentation, by default under `/usr/local/info/`.

2. Define the `SCHEME_LIBRARY_PATH` environment variable:

   ```
   $ SCHEME_LIBRARY_PATH=/usr/local/lib/slib/
   $ export SCHEME_LIBRARY_PATH
   ```

   Alternatively, you can create a symlink in the Guile directory to SLIB, e.g.:

   ```
   ln -s /usr/local/lib/slib /usr/local/share/guile/2.0/slib
   ```

3. Use Guile to create the catalog file, e.g.,:

   ```
   # guile
   guile> (use-modules (ice-9 slib))
   guile> (require 'new-catalog)
   guile> (quit)
   ```

   The catalog data should now be in `/usr/local/share/guile/2.0/slibcat`.

   If instead you get an error such as:

   ```
   Unbound variable: scheme-implementation-type
   ```

   then a solution is to get a newer version of Guile, or to modify `ice-9/slib.scm` to use `define-public` for the offending variables.

7.1.2 JACAL

Jacal is a symbolic math package written in Scheme by Aubrey Jaffer. It is usually installed as an extra package in SLIB.

You can use Guile's interface to SLIB to invoke Jacal:

```
(use-modules (ice-9 slib))
(slib:load "math")
(math)
```

For complete documentation on Jacal, please read the Jacal manual. If it has been installed on line, you can look at Section "Jacal" in *JACAL Symbolic Mathematics System*. Otherwise you can find it on the web at http://www-swiss.ai.mit.edu/~jaffer/JACAL. html

7.2 POSIX System Calls and Networking

7.2.1 POSIX Interface Conventions

These interfaces provide access to operating system facilities. They provide a simple wrapping around the underlying C interfaces to make usage from Scheme more convenient. They are also used to implement the Guile port of scsh (see Section 7.17 [The Scheme shell (scsh)], page 693).

Generally there is a single procedure for each corresponding Unix facility. There are some exceptions, such as procedures implemented for speed and convenience in Scheme with no primitive Unix equivalent, e.g. copy-file.

The interfaces are intended as far as possible to be portable across different versions of Unix. In some cases procedures which can't be implemented on particular systems may become no-ops, or perform limited actions. In other cases they may throw errors.

General naming conventions are as follows:

- The Scheme name is often identical to the name of the underlying Unix facility.

- Underscores in Unix procedure names are converted to hyphens.

- Procedures which destructively modify Scheme data have exclamation marks appended, e.g., recv!.

- Predicates (returning only #t or #f) have question marks appended, e.g., access?.

- Some names are changed to avoid conflict with dissimilar interfaces defined by scsh, e.g., primitive-fork.

- Unix preprocessor names such as EPERM or R_OK are converted to Scheme variables of the same name (underscores are not replaced with hyphens).

Unexpected conditions are generally handled by raising exceptions. There are a few procedures which return a special value if they don't succeed, e.g., getenv returns #f if it the requested string is not found in the environment. These cases are noted in the documentation.

For ways to deal with exceptions, see Section 6.13.8 [Exceptions], page 303.

Errors which the C library would report by returning a null pointer or through some other means are reported by raising a system-error exception with scm-error (see Section 6.13.9

[Error Reporting], page 309). The *data* parameter is a list containing the Unix `errno` value
(an integer). For example,

```
(define (my-handler key func fmt fmtargs data)
  (display key) (newline)
  (display func) (newline)
  (apply format #t fmt fmtargs) (newline)
  (display data) (newline))

(catch 'system-error
  (lambda () (dup2 -123 -456))
  my-handler)

⊣
system-error
dup2
Bad file descriptor
(9)
```

system-error-errno *arglist*   [Function]

    Return the `errno` value from a list which is the arguments to an exception handler.
    If the exception is not a `system-error`, then the return is `#f`. For example,

```
(catch
 'system-error
 (lambda ()
   (mkdir "/this-ought-to-fail-if-I'm-not-root"))
 (lambda stuff
   (let ((errno (system-error-errno stuff)))
     (cond
      ((= errno EACCES)
       (display "You're not allowed to do that."))
      ((= errno EEXIST)
       (display "Already exists."))
      (#t
       (display (strerror errno))))
     (newline)))))
```

7.2.2 Ports and File Descriptors

Conventions generally follow those of scsh, Section 7.17 [The Scheme shell (scsh)], page 693.

    File ports are implemented using low-level operating system I/O facilities, with optional
buffering to improve efficiency; see Section 6.14.9.1 [File Ports], page 326.

    Note that some procedures (e.g., `recv!`) will accept ports as arguments, but will actually
operate directly on the file descriptor underlying the port. Any port buffering is ignored,
including the buffer which implements `peek-char` and `unread-char`.

    The `force-output` and `drain-input` procedures can be used to clear the buffers.

Each open file port has an associated operating system file descriptor. File descriptors are generally not useful in Scheme programs; however they may be needed when interfacing with foreign code and the Unix environment.

A file descriptor can be extracted from a port and a new port can be created from a file descriptor. However a file descriptor is just an integer and the garbage collector doesn't recognize it as a reference to the port. If all other references to the port were dropped, then it's likely that the garbage collector would free the port, with the side-effect of closing the file descriptor prematurely.

To assist the programmer in avoiding this problem, each port has an associated *revealed count* which can be used to keep track of how many times the underlying file descriptor has been stored in other places. If a port's revealed count is greater than zero, the file descriptor will not be closed when the port is garbage collected. A programmer can therefore ensure that the revealed count will be greater than zero if the file descriptor is needed elsewhere.

For the simple case where a file descriptor is "imported" once to become a port, it does not matter if the file descriptor is closed when the port is garbage collected. There is no need to maintain a revealed count. Likewise when "exporting" a file descriptor to the external environment, setting the revealed count is not required provided the port is kept open (i.e., is pointed to by a live Scheme binding) while the file descriptor is in use.

To correspond with traditional Unix behaviour, three file descriptors (0, 1, and 2) are automatically imported when a program starts up and assigned to the initial values of the current/standard input, output, and error ports, respectively. The revealed count for each is initially set to one, so that dropping references to one of these ports will not result in its garbage collection: it could be retrieved with `fdopen` or `fdes->ports`.

`port-revealed` *port*   [Scheme Procedure]
`scm_port_revealed` (*port*)   [C Function]
  Return the revealed count for *port*.

`set-port-revealed!` *port rcount*   [Scheme Procedure]
`scm_set_port_revealed_x` (*port*, *rcount*)   [C Function]
  Sets the revealed count for a *port* to *rcount*. The return value is unspecified.

`fileno` *port*   [Scheme Procedure]
`scm_fileno` (*port*)   [C Function]
  Return the integer file descriptor underlying *port*. Does not change its revealed count.

`port->fdes` *port*   [Scheme Procedure]
  Returns the integer file descriptor underlying *port*. As a side effect the revealed count of *port* is incremented.

`fdopen` *fdes modes*   [Scheme Procedure]
`scm_fdopen` (*fdes*, *modes*)   [C Function]
  Return a new port based on the file descriptor *fdes*. Modes are given by the string *modes*. The revealed count of the port is initialized to zero. The *modes* string is the same as that accepted by `open-file` (see Section 6.14.9.1 [File Ports], page 326).

`fdes->ports` *fdes*   [Scheme Procedure]
`scm_fdes_to_ports` (*fdes*)   [C Function]
> Return a list of existing ports which have *fdes* as an underlying file descriptor, without changing their revealed counts.

`fdes->inport` *fdes*   [Scheme Procedure]
> Returns an existing input port which has *fdes* as its underlying file descriptor, if one exists, and increments its revealed count. Otherwise, returns a new input port with a revealed count of 1.

`fdes->outport` *fdes*   [Scheme Procedure]
> Returns an existing output port which has *fdes* as its underlying file descriptor, if one exists, and increments its revealed count. Otherwise, returns a new output port with a revealed count of 1.

`primitive-move->fdes` *port fdes*   [Scheme Procedure]
`scm_primitive_move_to_fdes` (*port, fdes*)   [C Function]
> Moves the underlying file descriptor for *port* to the integer value *fdes* without changing the revealed count of *port*. Any other ports already using this descriptor will be automatically shifted to new descriptors and their revealed counts reset to zero. The return value is `#f` if the file descriptor already had the required value or `#t` if it was moved.

`move->fdes` *port fdes*   [Scheme Procedure]
> Moves the underlying file descriptor for *port* to the integer value *fdes* and sets its revealed count to one. Any other ports already using this descriptor will be automatically shifted to new descriptors and their revealed counts reset to zero. The return value is unspecified.

`release-port-handle` *port*   [Scheme Procedure]
> Decrements the revealed count for a port.

`fsync` *port_or_fd*   [Scheme Procedure]
`scm_fsync` (*port_or_fd*)   [C Function]
> Copies any unwritten data for the specified output file descriptor to disk. If *port_or_fd* is a port, its buffer is flushed before the underlying file descriptor is fsync'd. The return value is unspecified.

`open` *path flags* [*mode*]   [Scheme Procedure]
`scm_open` (*path, flags, mode*)   [C Function]
> Open the file named by *path* for reading and/or writing. *flags* is an integer specifying how the file should be opened. *mode* is an integer specifying the permission bits of the file, if it needs to be created, before the umask (see Section 7.2.7 [Processes], page 490) is applied. The default is 666 (Unix itself has no default).
>
> *flags* can be constructed by combining variables using `logior`. Basic flags are:

> `O_RDONLY`   [Variable]
> > Open the file read-only.

O_WRONLY   [Variable]

> Open the file write-only.

O_RDWR   [Variable]

> Open the file read/write.

O_APPEND   [Variable]

> Append to the file instead of truncating.

O_CREAT   [Variable]

> Create the file if it does not already exist.

See Section "File Status Flags" in *The GNU C Library Reference Manual*, for additional flags.

open-fdes *path flags* [*mode*]   [Scheme Procedure]
scm_open_fdes (*path, flags, mode*)   [C Function]

> Similar to **open** but return a file descriptor instead of a port.

close *fd_or_port*   [Scheme Procedure]
scm_close (*fd_or_port*)   [C Function]

> Similar to **close-port** (see Section 6.14.4 [Closing], page 321), but also works on file descriptors. A side effect of closing a file descriptor is that any ports using that file descriptor are moved to a different file descriptor and have their revealed counts set to zero.

close-fdes *fd*   [Scheme Procedure]
scm_close_fdes (*fd*)   [C Function]

> A simple wrapper for the **close** system call. Close file descriptor *fd*, which must be an integer. Unlike **close**, the file descriptor will be closed even if a port is using it. The return value is unspecified.

unread-char *char* [*port*]   [Scheme Procedure]
scm_unread_char (*char, port*)   [C Function]

> Place *char* in *port* so that it will be read by the next read operation on that port. If called multiple times, the unread characters will be read again in "last-in, first-out" order (i.e. a stack). If *port* is not supplied, the current input port is used.

unread-string *str port*   [Scheme Procedure]

> Place the string *str* in *port* so that its characters will be read in subsequent read operations. If called multiple times, the unread characters will be read again in last-in first-out order. If *port* is not supplied, the current-input-port is used.

pipe   [Scheme Procedure]
scm_pipe ()   [C Function]

> Return a newly created pipe: a pair of ports which are linked together on the local machine. The CAR is the input port and the CDR is the output port. Data written (and flushed) to the output port can be read from the input port. Pipes are commonly used for communication with a newly forked child process. The need to flush the output port can be avoided by making it unbuffered using **setvbuf**.

PIPE_BUF   [Variable]
> A write of up to PIPE_BUF many bytes to a pipe is atomic, meaning when done it goes into the pipe instantaneously and as a contiguous block (see Section "Atomicity of Pipe I/O" in *The GNU C Library Reference Manual*).

Note that the output port is likely to block if too much data has been written but not yet read from the input port. Typically the capacity is PIPE_BUF bytes.

The next group of procedures perform a dup2 system call, if *newfd* (an integer) is supplied, otherwise a dup. The file descriptor to be duplicated can be supplied as an integer or contained in a port. The type of value returned varies depending on which procedure is used.

All procedures also have the side effect when performing dup2 that any ports using *newfd* are moved to a different file descriptor and have their revealed counts set to zero.

dup->fdes *fd_or_port* [*fd*]   [Scheme Procedure]
scm_dup_to_fdes (*fd_or_port*, *fd*)   [C Function]
> Return a new integer file descriptor referring to the open file designated by *fd_or_port*, which must be either an open file port or a file descriptor.

dup->inport *port/fd* [*newfd*]   [Scheme Procedure]
> Returns a new input port using the new file descriptor.

dup->outport *port/fd* [*newfd*]   [Scheme Procedure]
> Returns a new output port using the new file descriptor.

dup *port/fd* [*newfd*]   [Scheme Procedure]
> Returns a new port if *port/fd* is a port, with the same mode as the supplied port, otherwise returns an integer file descriptor.

dup->port *port/fd* *mode* [*newfd*]   [Scheme Procedure]
> Returns a new port using the new file descriptor. *mode* supplies a mode string for the port (see Section 6.14.9.1 [File Ports], page 326).

duplicate-port *port* *modes*   [Scheme Procedure]
> Returns a new port which is opened on a duplicate of the file descriptor underlying *port*, with mode string *modes* as for Section 6.14.9.1 [File Ports], page 326. The two ports will share a file position and file status flags.
>
> Unexpected behaviour can result if both ports are subsequently used and the original and/or duplicate ports are buffered. The mode string can include 0 to obtain an unbuffered duplicate port.
>
> This procedure is equivalent to (dup->port *port* *modes*).

redirect-port *old_port* *new_port*   [Scheme Procedure]
scm_redirect_port (*old_port*, *new_port*)   [C Function]
> This procedure takes two ports and duplicates the underlying file descriptor from *old_port* into *new_port*. The current file descriptor in *new_port* will be closed. After the redirection the two ports will share a file position and file status flags.
>
> The return value is unspecified.

Unexpected behaviour can result if both ports are subsequently used and the original and/or duplicate ports are buffered.

This procedure does not have any side effects on other ports or revealed counts.

dup2 *oldfd newfd*   [Scheme Procedure]
scm_dup2 (*oldfd, newfd*)   [C Function]
> A simple wrapper for the **dup2** system call. Copies the file descriptor *oldfd* to descriptor number *newfd*, replacing the previous meaning of *newfd*. Both *oldfd* and *newfd* must be integers. Unlike for **dup->fdes** or **primitive-move->fdes**, no attempt is made to move away ports which are using *newfd*. The return value is unspecified.

port-mode *port*   [Scheme Procedure]
> Return the port modes associated with the open port *port*. These will not necessarily be identical to the modes used when the port was opened, since modes such as "append" which are used only during port creation are not retained.

port-for-each *proc*   [Scheme Procedure]
scm_port_for_each (*SCM proc*)   [C Function]
scm_c_port_for_each (*void (*proc)(void *, SCM), void *data*)   [C Function]
> Apply *proc* to each port in the Guile port table (FIXME: what is the Guile port table?) in turn. The return value is unspecified. More specifically, *proc* is applied exactly once to every port that exists in the system at the time **port-for-each** is invoked. Changes to the port table while **port-for-each** is running have no effect as far as **port-for-each** is concerned.
>
> The C function **scm_port_for_each** takes a Scheme procedure encoded as a **SCM** value, while **scm_c_port_for_each** takes a pointer to a C function and passes along a arbitrary *data* cookie.

setvbuf *port mode* [*size*]   [Scheme Procedure]
scm_setvbuf (*port, mode, size*)   [C Function]
> Set the buffering mode for *port*. *mode* can be:

> > **_IONBF**   [Variable]
> > > non-buffered

> > **_IOLBF**   [Variable]
> > > line buffered

> > **_IOFBF**   [Variable]
> > > block buffered, using a newly allocated buffer of *size* bytes. If *size* is omitted, a default size will be used.

> Only certain types of ports are supported, most importantly file ports.

fcntl *port/fd cmd* [*value*]   [Scheme Procedure]
scm_fcntl (*object, cmd, value*)   [C Function]
> Apply *cmd* on *port/fd*, either a port or file descriptor. The *value* argument is used by the **SET** commands described below, it's an integer value.
>
> Values for *cmd* are:

F_DUPFD   [Variable]
> Duplicate the file descriptor, the same as **dup->fdes** above does.

F_GETFD   [Variable]
F_SETFD   [Variable]
> Get or set flags associated with the file descriptor. The only flag is the following,

> FD_CLOEXEC   [Variable]
>> "Close on exec", meaning the file descriptor will be closed on an **exec** call (a successful such call). For example to set that flag,

>> ```
>> (fcntl port F_SETFD FD_CLOEXEC)
>> ```

>> Or better, set it but leave any other possible future flags unchanged,

>> ```
>> (fcntl port F_SETFD (logior FD_CLOEXEC
>>                             (fcntl port F_GETFD)))
>> ```

F_GETFL   [Variable]
F_SETFL   [Variable]
> Get or set flags associated with the open file. These flags are **O_RDONLY** etc described under **open** above.

> A common use is to set **O_NONBLOCK** on a network socket. The following sets that flag, and leaves other flags unchanged.

> ```
> (fcntl sock F_SETFL (logior O_NONBLOCK
>                             (fcntl sock F_GETFL)))
> ```

F_GETOWN   [Variable]
F_SETOWN   [Variable]
> Get or set the process ID of a socket's owner, for **SIGIO** signals.

flock *file operation*   [Scheme Procedure]
scm_flock (*file, operation*)   [C Function]
> Apply or remove an advisory lock on an open file. *operation* specifies the action to be done:

LOCK_SH   [Variable]
> Shared lock. More than one process may hold a shared lock for a given file at a given time.

LOCK_EX   [Variable]
> Exclusive lock. Only one process may hold an exclusive lock for a given file at a given time.

LOCK_UN   [Variable]
> Unlock the file.

LOCK_NB   [Variable]
> Don't block when locking. This is combined with one of the other operations using **logior** (see Section 6.6.2.13 [Bitwise Operations], page 125). If **flock** would block an **EWOULDBLOCK** error is thrown (see Section 7.2.1 [Conventions], page 468).

The return value is not specified. *file* may be an open file descriptor or an open file descriptor port.

Note that `flock` does not lock files across NFS.

select *reads writes excepts* [*secs* [*usecs*]]   [Scheme Procedure]
scm_select (*reads, writes, excepts, secs, usecs*)   [C Function]
> This procedure has a variety of uses: waiting for the ability to provide input, accept output, or the existence of exceptional conditions on a collection of ports or file descriptors, or waiting for a timeout to occur. It also returns if interrupted by a signal.
>
> *reads*, *writes* and *excepts* can be lists or vectors, with each member a port or a file descriptor. The value returned is a list of three corresponding lists or vectors containing only the members which meet the specified requirement. The ability of port buffers to provide input or accept output is taken into account. Ordering of the input lists or vectors is not preserved.
>
> The optional arguments *secs* and *usecs* specify the timeout. Either *secs* can be specified alone, as either an integer or a real number, or both *secs* and *usecs* can be specified as integers, in which case *usecs* is an additional timeout expressed in microseconds. If *secs* is omitted or is `#f` then select will wait for as long as it takes for one of the other conditions to be satisfied.
>
> The scsh version of `select` differs as follows: Only vectors are accepted for the first three arguments. The *usecs* argument is not supported. Multiple values are returned instead of a list. Duplicates in the input vectors appear only once in output. An additional `select!` interface is provided.

7.2.3 File System

These procedures allow querying and setting file system attributes (such as owner, permissions, sizes and types of files); deleting, copying, renaming and linking files; creating and removing directories and querying their contents; syncing the file system and creating special files.

access? *path how*   [Scheme Procedure]
scm_access (*path, how*)   [C Function]
> Test accessibility of a file under the real UID and GID of the calling process. The return is `#t` if *path* exists and the permissions requested by *how* are all allowed, or `#f` if not.
>
> *how* is an integer which is one of the following values, or a bitwise-OR (`logior`) of multiple values.

> **R_OK**   [Variable]
> > Test for read permission.

> **W_OK**   [Variable]
> > Test for write permission.

> **X_OK**   [Variable]
> > Test for execute permission.

F_OK   [Variable]
>   Test for existence of the file. This is implied by each of the other tests, so
>   there's no need to combine it with them.

It's important to note that access? does not simply indicate what will happen on
attempting to read or write a file. In normal circumstances it does, but in a set-UID
or set-GID program it doesn't because access? tests the real ID, whereas an open or
execute attempt uses the effective ID.

A program which will never run set-UID/GID can ignore the difference between real
and effective IDs, but for maximum generality, especially in library functions, it's
best not to use access? to predict the result of an open or execute, instead simply
attempt that and catch any exception.

The main use for access? is to let a set-UID/GID program determine what the
invoking user would have been allowed to do, without the greater (or perhaps lesser)
privileges afforded by the effective ID. For more on this, see Section "Testing File
Access" in The GNU C Library Reference Manual.

stat object   [Scheme Procedure]
scm_stat (object)   [C Function]
>   Return an object containing various information about the file determined by object.
>   object can be a string containing a file name or a port or integer file descriptor which
>   is open on a file (in which case fstat is used as the underlying system call).

>   The object returned by stat can be passed as a single parameter to the following
>   procedures, all of which return integers:

>   stat:dev st   [Scheme Procedure]
>   >   The device number containing the file.

>   stat:ino st   [Scheme Procedure]
>   >   The file serial number, which distinguishes this file from all other files on the
>   >   same device.

>   stat:mode st   [Scheme Procedure]
>   >   The mode of the file. This is an integer which incorporates file type information
>   >   and file permission bits. See also stat:type and stat:perms below.

>   stat:nlink st   [Scheme Procedure]
>   >   The number of hard links to the file.

>   stat:uid st   [Scheme Procedure]
>   >   The user ID of the file's owner.

>   stat:gid st   [Scheme Procedure]
>   >   The group ID of the file.

>   stat:rdev st   [Scheme Procedure]
>   >   Device ID; this entry is defined only for character or block special files. On
>   >   some systems this field is not available at all, in which case stat:rdev returns
>   >   #f.

stat:size *st*   [Scheme Procedure]
>   The size of a regular file in bytes.

stat:atime *st*   [Scheme Procedure]
>   The last access time for the file, in seconds.

stat:mtime *st*   [Scheme Procedure]
>   The last modification time for the file, in seconds.

stat:ctime *st*   [Scheme Procedure]
>   The last modification time for the attributes of the file, in seconds.

stat:atimensec *st*   [Scheme Procedure]
stat:mtimensec *st*   [Scheme Procedure]
stat:ctimensec *st*   [Scheme Procedure]
>   The fractional part of a file's access, modification, or attribute modification
>   time, in nanoseconds. Nanosecond timestamps are only available on some op-
>   erating systems and file systems. If Guile cannot retrieve nanosecond-level
>   timestamps for a file, these fields will be set to 0.

stat:blksize *st*   [Scheme Procedure]
>   The optimal block size for reading or writing the file, in bytes. On some sys-
>   tems this field is not available, in which case stat:blksize returns a sensible
>   suggested block size.

stat:blocks *st*   [Scheme Procedure]
>   The amount of disk space that the file occupies measured in units of 512 byte
>   blocks. On some systems this field is not available, in which case stat:blocks
>   returns #f.

In addition, the following procedures return the information from stat:mode in a
more convenient form:

stat:type *st*   [Scheme Procedure]
>   A symbol representing the type of file. Possible values are 'regular',
>   'directory', 'symlink', 'block-special', 'char-special', 'fifo', 'socket',
>   and 'unknown'.

stat:perms *st*   [Scheme Procedure]
>   An integer representing the access permission bits.

lstat *path*   [Scheme Procedure]
scm_lstat (*path*)   [C Function]
>   Similar to stat, but does not follow symbolic links, i.e., it will return information
>   about a symbolic link itself, not the file it points to. *path* must be a string.

readlink *path*   [Scheme Procedure]
scm_readlink (*path*)   [C Function]
>   Return the value of the symbolic link named by *path* (a string), i.e., the file that the
>   link points to.

chown *object owner group*   [Scheme Procedure]
scm_chown (*object, owner, group*)   [C Function]

> Change the ownership and group of the file referred to by *object* to the integer values *owner* and *group*. *object* can be a string containing a file name or, if the platform supports **fchown** (see Section "File Owner" in *The GNU C Library Reference Manual*), a port or integer file descriptor which is open on the file. The return value is unspecified.
>
> If *object* is a symbolic link, either the ownership of the link or the ownership of the referenced file will be changed depending on the operating system (lchown is unsupported at present). If *owner* or *group* is specified as -1, then that ID is not changed.

chmod *object mode*   [Scheme Procedure]
scm_chmod (*object, mode*)   [C Function]

> Changes the permissions of the file referred to by *object*. *object* can be a string containing a file name or a port or integer file descriptor which is open on a file (in which case **fchmod** is used as the underlying system call). *mode* specifies the new permissions as a decimal number, e.g., (**chmod "foo" #o755**). The return value is unspecified.

utime *pathname* [*actime* [*modtime* [*actimens* [*modtimens*   [Scheme Procedure]
     [*flags*]]]]]
scm_utime (*pathname, actime, modtime, actimens, modtimens, flags*)   [C Function]

> **utime** sets the access and modification times for the file named by *pathname*. If *actime* or *modtime* is not supplied, then the current time is used. *actime* and *modtime* must be integer time values as returned by the **current-time** procedure.
>
> The optional *actimens* and *modtimens* are nanoseconds to add *actime* and *modtime*. Nanosecond precision is only supported on some combinations of file systems and operating systems.
>
>   (utime "foo" (- (current-time) 3600))
>
> will set the access time to one hour in the past and the modification time to the current time.

delete-file *str*   [Scheme Procedure]
scm_delete_file (*str*)   [C Function]

> Deletes (or "unlinks") the file whose path is specified by *str*.

copy-file *oldfile newfile*   [Scheme Procedure]
scm_copy_file (*oldfile, newfile*)   [C Function]

> Copy the file specified by *oldfile* to *newfile*. The return value is unspecified.

sendfile *out in count* [*offset*]   [Scheme Procedure]
scm_sendfile (*out, in, count, offset*)   [C Function]

> Send *count* bytes from *in* to *out*, both of which must be either open file ports or file descriptors. When *offset* is omitted, start reading from *in*'s current position; otherwise, start reading at *offset*. Return the number of bytes actually sent.
>
> When *in* is a port, it is often preferable to specify *offset*, because *in*'s offset as a port may be different from the offset of its underlying file descriptor.

On systems that support it, such as GNU/Linux, this procedure uses the `sendfile` libc function, which usually corresponds to a system call. This is faster than doing a series of `read` and `write` system calls. A typical application is to send a file over a socket.

In some cases, the `sendfile` libc function may return `EINVAL` or `ENOSYS`. In that case, Guile's `sendfile` procedure automatically falls back to doing a series of `read` and `write` calls.

In other cases, the libc function may send fewer bytes than *count*—for instance because *out* is a slow or limited device, such as a pipe. When that happens, Guile's `sendfile` automatically retries until exactly *count* bytes were sent or an error occurs.

rename-file *oldname newname*   [Scheme Procedure]
scm_rename (*oldname, newname*)   [C Function]
    Renames the file specified by *oldname* to *newname*. The return value is unspecified.

link *oldpath newpath*   [Scheme Procedure]
scm_link (*oldpath, newpath*)   [C Function]
    Creates a new name *newpath* in the file system for the file named by *oldpath*. If *oldpath* is a symbolic link, the link may or may not be followed depending on the system.

symlink *oldpath newpath*   [Scheme Procedure]
scm_symlink (*oldpath, newpath*)   [C Function]
    Create a symbolic link named *newpath* with the value (i.e., pointing to) *oldpath*. The return value is unspecified.

mkdir *path* [*mode*]   [Scheme Procedure]
scm_mkdir (*path, mode*)   [C Function]
    Create a new directory named by *path*. If *mode* is omitted then the permissions of the directory file are set using the current umask (see Section 7.2.7 [Processes], page 490). Otherwise they are set to the decimal value specified with *mode*. The return value is unspecified.

rmdir *path*   [Scheme Procedure]
scm_rmdir (*path*)   [C Function]
    Remove the existing directory named by *path*. The directory must be empty for this to succeed. The return value is unspecified.

opendir *dirname*   [Scheme Procedure]
scm_opendir (*dirname*)   [C Function]
    Open the directory specified by *dirname* and return a directory stream.

    Before using this and the procedures below, make sure to see the higher-level procedures for directory traversal that are available (see Section 7.11 [File Tree Walk], page 676).

directory-stream? *object*   [Scheme Procedure]
scm_directory_stream_p (*object*)   [C Function]
    Return a boolean indicating whether *object* is a directory stream as returned by `opendir`.

readdir *stream* [Scheme Procedure]

scm_readdir (*stream*) [C Function]

> Return (as a string) the next directory entry from the directory stream *stream*. If there is no remaining entry to be read then the end of file object is returned.

rewinddir *stream* [Scheme Procedure]

scm_rewinddir (*stream*) [C Function]

> Reset the directory port *stream* so that the next call to readdir will return the first directory entry.

closedir *stream* [Scheme Procedure]

scm_closedir (*stream*) [C Function]

> Close the directory stream *stream*. The return value is unspecified.

Here is an example showing how to display all the entries in a directory:

```
(define dir (opendir "/usr/lib"))
(do ((entry (readdir dir) (readdir dir)))
    ((eof-object? entry))
  (display entry)(newline))
(closedir dir)
```

sync [Scheme Procedure]

scm_sync () [C Function]

> Flush the operating system disk buffers. The return value is unspecified.

mknod *path type perms dev* [Scheme Procedure]

scm_mknod (*path, type, perms, dev*) [C Function]

> Creates a new special file, such as a file corresponding to a device. *path* specifies the name of the file. *type* should be one of the following symbols: 'regular', 'directory', 'symlink', 'block-special', 'char-special', 'fifo', or 'socket'. *perms* (an integer) specifies the file permissions. *dev* (an integer) specifies which device the special file refers to. Its exact interpretation depends on the kind of special file being created.

> E.g.,

> (mknod "/dev/fd0" 'block-special #o660 (+ (* 2 256) 2))

> The return value is unspecified.

tmpnam [Scheme Procedure]

scm_tmpnam () [C Function]

> Return an auto-generated name of a temporary file, a file which doesn't already exist. The name includes a path, it's usually in /tmp but that's system dependent.

> Care must be taken when using tmpnam. In between choosing the name and creating the file another program might use that name, or an attacker might even make it a symlink pointing at something important and causing you to overwrite that.

> The safe way is to create the file using open with O_EXCL to avoid any overwriting. A loop can try again with another name if the file exists (error EEXIST). mkstemp! below does that.

`mkstemp!` *tmpl*   [Scheme Procedure]

`scm_mkstemp` (*tmpl*)   [C Function]

> Create a new unique file in the file system and return a new buffered port open for reading and writing to the file.
>
> *tmpl* is a string specifying where the file should be created: it must end with 'XXXXXX' and those 'X's will be changed in the string to return the name of the file. (`port-filename` on the port also gives the name.)
>
> POSIX doesn't specify the permissions mode of the file, on GNU and most systems it's #o600. An application can use `chmod` to relax that if desired. For example #o666 less `umask`, which is usual for ordinary file creation,
>
> ```
> (let ((port (mkstemp! (string-copy "/tmp/myfile-XXXXXX"))))
>   (chmod port (logand #o666 (lognot (umask))))
>   ...)
> ```

`tmpfile`   [Scheme Procedure]

`scm_tmpfile` ()   [C Function]

> Return an input/output port to a unique temporary file named using the path prefix `P_tmpdir` defined in `stdio.h`. The file is automatically deleted when the port is closed or the program terminates.

`dirname` *filename*   [Scheme Procedure]

`scm_dirname` (*filename*)   [C Function]

> Return the directory name component of the file name *filename*. If *filename* does not contain a directory component, . is returned.

`basename` *filename* [*suffix*]   [Scheme Procedure]

`scm_basename` (*filename*, *suffix*)   [C Function]

> Return the base name of the file name *filename*. The base name is the file name without any directory components. If *suffix* is provided, and is equal to the end of *basename*, it is removed also.
>
> ```
> (basename "/tmp/test.xml" ".xml")
> ⇒ "test"
> ```

`file-exists?` *filename*   [Scheme Procedure]

> Return #t if the file named *filename* exists, #f if not.

Many operating systems, such as GNU, use / (forward slash) to separate the components of a file name; any file name starting with / is considered an *absolute file name*. These conventions are specified by the POSIX Base Definitions, which refer to conforming file names as "pathnames". Some operating systems use a different convention; in particular, Windows uses \ (backslash) as the file name separator, and also has the notion of *volume names* like C:\ for absolute file names. The following procedures and variables provide support for portable file name manipulations.

`system-file-name-convention`   [Scheme Procedure]

> Return either `posix` or `windows`, depending on what kind of system this Guile is running on.

`file-name-separator?` *c*   [Scheme Procedure]
> Return true if character *c* is a file name separator on the host platform.

`absolute-file-name?` *file-name*   [Scheme Procedure]
> Return true if *file-name* denotes an absolute file name on the host platform.

`file-name-separator-string`   [Scheme Variable]
> The preferred file name separator.
>
> Note that on MinGW builds for Windows, both / and \ are valid separators. Thus, programs should not assume that `file-name-separator-string` is the *only* file name separator—e.g., when extracting the components of a file name.

7.2.4 User Information

The facilities in this section provide an interface to the user and group database. They should be used with care since they are not reentrant.

The following functions accept an object representing user information and return a selected component:

`passwd:name` *pw*   [Scheme Procedure]
> The name of the userid.

`passwd:passwd` *pw*   [Scheme Procedure]
> The encrypted passwd.

`passwd:uid` *pw*   [Scheme Procedure]
> The user id number.

`passwd:gid` *pw*   [Scheme Procedure]
> The group id number.

`passwd:gecos` *pw*   [Scheme Procedure]
> The full name.

`passwd:dir` *pw*   [Scheme Procedure]
> The home directory.

`passwd:shell` *pw*   [Scheme Procedure]
> The login shell.

`getpwuid` *uid*   [Scheme Procedure]
> Look up an integer userid in the user database.

`getpwnam` *name*   [Scheme Procedure]
> Look up a user name string in the user database.

`setpwent`   [Scheme Procedure]
> Initializes a stream used by `getpwent` to read from the user database. The next use of `getpwent` will return the first entry. The return value is unspecified.

getpwent   [Scheme Procedure]

Read the next entry in the user database stream. The return is a passwd user object as above, or #f when no more entries.

endpwent   [Scheme Procedure]

Closes the stream used by getpwent. The return value is unspecified.

setpw [*arg*]   [Scheme Procedure]
scm_setpwent (*arg*)   [C Function]

If called with a true argument, initialize or reset the password data stream. Otherwise, close the stream. The setpwent and endpwent procedures are implemented on top of this.

getpw [*user*]   [Scheme Procedure]
scm_getpwuid (*user*)   [C Function]

Look up an entry in the user database. *user* can be an integer, a string, or omitted, giving the behaviour of getpwuid, getpwnam or getpwent respectively.

The following functions accept an object representing group information and return a selected component:

group:name *gr*   [Scheme Procedure]

The group name.

group:passwd *gr*   [Scheme Procedure]

The encrypted group password.

group:gid *gr*   [Scheme Procedure]

The group id number.

group:mem *gr*   [Scheme Procedure]

A list of userids which have this group as a supplementary group.

getgrgid *gid*   [Scheme Procedure]

Look up an integer group id in the group database.

getgrnam *name*   [Scheme Procedure]

Look up a group name in the group database.

setgrent   [Scheme Procedure]

Initializes a stream used by getgrent to read from the group database. The next use of getgrent will return the first entry. The return value is unspecified.

getgrent   [Scheme Procedure]

Return the next entry in the group database, using the stream set by setgrent.

endgrent   [Scheme Procedure]

Closes the stream used by getgrent. The return value is unspecified.

setgr [*arg*]   [Scheme Procedure]

scm_setgrent (*arg*)   [C Function]

>   If called with a true argument, initialize or reset the group data stream. Otherwise, close the stream. The **setgrent** and **endgrent** procedures are implemented on top of this.

getgr [*group*]   [Scheme Procedure]

scm_getgrgid (*group*)   [C Function]

>   Look up an entry in the group database. *group* can be an integer, a string, or omitted, giving the behaviour of getgrgid, getgrnam or getgrent respectively.

In addition to the accessor procedures for the user database, the following shortcut procedure is also available.

getlogin   [Scheme Procedure]

scm_getlogin ()   [C Function]

>   Return a string containing the name of the user logged in on the controlling terminal of the process, or **#f** if this information cannot be obtained.

7.2.5 Time

current-time   [Scheme Procedure]

scm_current_time ()   [C Function]

>   Return the number of seconds since 1970-01-01 00:00:00 UTC, excluding leap seconds.

gettimeofday   [Scheme Procedure]

scm_gettimeofday ()   [C Function]

>   Return a pair containing the number of seconds and microseconds since 1970-01-01 00:00:00 UTC, excluding leap seconds. Note: whether true microsecond resolution is available depends on the operating system.

The following procedures either accept an object representing a broken down time and return a selected component, or accept an object representing a broken down time and a value and set the component to the value. The numbers in parentheses give the usual range.

tm:sec *tm*   [Scheme Procedure]

set-tm:sec *tm val*   [Scheme Procedure]

>   Seconds (0-59).

tm:min *tm*   [Scheme Procedure]

set-tm:min *tm val*   [Scheme Procedure]

>   Minutes (0-59).

tm:hour *tm*   [Scheme Procedure]

set-tm:hour *tm val*   [Scheme Procedure]

>   Hours (0-23).

tm:mday *tm*   [Scheme Procedure]

set-tm:mday *tm val*   [Scheme Procedure]

>   Day of the month (1-31).

tm:mon *tm*   [Scheme Procedure]
set-tm:mon *tm* *val*   [Scheme Procedure]
    Month (0-11).

tm:year *tm*   [Scheme Procedure]
set-tm:year *tm* *val*   [Scheme Procedure]
    Year (70-), the year minus 1900.

tm:wday *tm*   [Scheme Procedure]
set-tm:wday *tm* *val*   [Scheme Procedure]
    Day of the week (0-6) with Sunday represented as 0.

tm:yday *tm*   [Scheme Procedure]
set-tm:yday *tm* *val*   [Scheme Procedure]
    Day of the year (0-364, 365 in leap years).

tm:isdst *tm*   [Scheme Procedure]
set-tm:isdst *tm* *val*   [Scheme Procedure]
    Daylight saving indicator (0 for "no", greater than 0 for "yes", less than 0 for "unknown").

tm:gmtoff *tm*   [Scheme Procedure]
set-tm:gmtoff *tm* *val*   [Scheme Procedure]
    Time zone offset in seconds west of UTC (-46800 to 43200). For example on East coast USA (zone 'EST+5') this would be 18000 (ie. $5 \times 60 \times 60$) in winter, or 14400 (ie. $4 \times 60 \times 60$) during daylight savings.

    Note **tm:gmtoff** is not the same as **tm_gmtoff** in the C **tm** structure. **tm_gmtoff** is seconds east and hence the negative of the value here.

tm:zone *tm*   [Scheme Procedure]
set-tm:zone *tm* *val*   [Scheme Procedure]
    Time zone label (a string), not necessarily unique.

localtime *time* [*zone*]   [Scheme Procedure]
scm_localtime (*time*, *zone*)   [C Function]
    Return an object representing the broken down components of *time*, an integer like the one returned by **current-time**. The time zone for the calculation is optionally specified by *zone* (a string), otherwise the **TZ** environment variable or the system default is used.

gmtime *time*   [Scheme Procedure]
scm_gmtime (*time*)   [C Function]
    Return an object representing the broken down components of *time*, an integer like the one returned by **current-time**. The values are calculated for UTC.

mktime *sbd-time* [*zone*]   [Scheme Procedure]
scm_mktime (*sbd_time*, *zone*)   [C Function]
    For a broken down time object *sbd-time*, return a pair the **car** of which is an integer time like **current-time**, and the **cdr** of which is a new broken down time with normalized fields.

zone is a timezone string, or the default is the **TZ** environment variable or the system default (see Section "Specifying the Time Zone with TZ" in *GNU C Library Reference Manual*). *sbd-time* is taken to be in that *zone*.

The following fields of *sbd-time* are used: **tm:year**, **tm:mon**, **tm:mday**, **tm:hour**, **tm:min**, **tm:sec**, **tm:isdst**. The values can be outside their usual ranges. For example **tm:hour** normally goes up to 23, but a value say 33 would mean 9 the following day.

tm:isdst in *sbd-time* says whether the time given is with daylight savings or not. This is ignored if *zone* doesn't have any daylight savings adjustment amount.

The broken down time in the return normalizes the values of *sbd-time* by bringing them into their usual ranges, and using the actual daylight savings rule for that time in *zone* (which may differ from what *sbd-time* had). The easiest way to think of this is that *sbd-time* plus *zone* converts to the integer UTC time, then a **localtime** is applied to get the normal presentation of that time, in *zone*.

tzset   [Scheme Procedure]
scm_tzset ()   [C Function]
> Initialize the timezone from the **TZ** environment variable or the system default. It's not usually necessary to call this procedure since it's done automatically by other procedures that depend on the timezone.

strftime *format tm*   [Scheme Procedure]
scm_strftime (*format, tm*)   [C Function]
> Return a string which is broken-down time structure *tm* formatted according to the given *format* string.
>
> *format* contains field specifications introduced by a '%' character. See Section "Formatting Calendar Time" in *The GNU C Library Reference Manual*, or 'man 3 strftime', for the available formatting.
>
>   (strftime "%c" (localtime (current-time)))
>   ⇒ "Mon Mar 11 20:17:43 2002"
>
> If **setlocale** has been called (see Section 7.2.13 [Locales], page 518), month and day names are from the current locale and in the locale character set.

strptime *format string*   [Scheme Procedure]
scm_strptime (*format, string*)   [C Function]
> Performs the reverse action to **strftime**, parsing *string* according to the specification supplied in *format*. The interpretation of month and day names is dependent on the current locale. The value returned is a pair. The CAR has an object with time components in the form returned by **localtime** or **gmtime**, but the time zone components are not usefully set. The CDR reports the number of characters from *string* which were used for the conversion.

internal-time-units-per-second   [Variable]
> The value of this variable is the number of time units per second reported by the following procedures.

`times`   [Scheme Procedure]
`scm_times ()`   [C Function]
>   Return an object with information about real and processor time. The following
>   procedures accept such an object as an argument and return a selected component:

>   `tms:clock` *tms*   [Scheme Procedure]
>   >   The current real time, expressed as time units relative to an arbitrary base.

>   `tms:utime` *tms*   [Scheme Procedure]
>   >   The CPU time units used by the calling process.

>   `tms:stime` *tms*   [Scheme Procedure]
>   >   The CPU time units used by the system on behalf of the calling process.

>   `tms:cutime` *tms*   [Scheme Procedure]
>   >   The CPU time units used by terminated child processes of the calling process,
>   >   whose status has been collected (e.g., using `waitpid`).

>   `tms:cstime` *tms*   [Scheme Procedure]
>   >   Similarly, the CPU times units used by the system on behalf of terminated child
>   >   processes.

`get-internal-real-time`   [Scheme Procedure]
`scm_get_internal_real_time ()`   [C Function]
>   Return the number of time units since the interpreter was started.

`get-internal-run-time`   [Scheme Procedure]
`scm_get_internal_run_time ()`   [C Function]
>   Return the number of time units of processor time used by the interpreter. Both
>   *system* and *user* time are included but subprocesses are not.

7.2.6 Runtime Environment

`program-arguments`   [Scheme Procedure]
`command-line`   [Scheme Procedure]
`set-program-arguments`   [Scheme Procedure]
`scm_program_arguments ()`   [C Function]
`scm_set_program_arguments_scm (`*lst*`)`   [C Function]
>   Get the command line arguments passed to Guile, or set new arguments.

>   The arguments are a list of strings, the first of which is the invoked program name.
>   This is just `"guile"` (or the executable path) when run interactively, or it's the script
>   name when running a script with `-s` (see Section 4.2 [Invoking Guile], page 35).

```
guile -L /my/extra/dir -s foo.scm abc def
```

>   (program-arguments) ⇒ ("foo.scm" "abc" "def")

>   `set-program-arguments` allows a library module or similar to modify the arguments,
>   for example to strip options it recognises, leaving the rest for the mainline.

>   The argument list is held in a fluid, which means it's separate for each thread. Neither
>   the list nor the strings within it are copied at any point and normally should not be
>   mutated.

The two names `program-arguments` and `command-line` are an historical accident, they both do exactly the same thing. The name `scm_set_program_arguments_scm` has an extra `_scm` on the end to avoid clashing with the C function below.

void scm_set_program_arguments (*int argc, char **argv, char *first*)   [C Function]
Set the list of command line arguments for `program-arguments` and `command-line` above.

argv is an array of null-terminated strings, as in a C `main` function. *argc* is the number of strings in *argv*, or if it's negative then a `NULL` in *argv* marks its end.

first is an extra string put at the start of the arguments, or `NULL` for no such extra. This is a convenient way to pass the program name after advancing *argv* to strip option arguments. Eg.

```
{
  char *progname = argv[0];
  for (argv++; argv[0] != NULL && argv[0][0] == '-'; argv++)
    {
      /* munch option ... */
    }
  /* remaining args for scheme level use */
  scm_set_program_arguments (-1, argv, progname);
}
```

This sort of thing is often done at startup under `scm_boot_guile` with options handled at the C level removed. The given strings are all copied, so the C data is not accessed again once `scm_set_program_arguments` returns.

getenv *name*   [Scheme Procedure]
scm_getenv (*name*)   [C Function]
Looks up the string *name* in the current environment. The return value is `#f` unless a string of the form `NAME=VALUE` is found, in which case the string `VALUE` is returned.

setenv *name value*   [Scheme Procedure]
Modifies the environment of the current process, which is also the default environment inherited by child processes.

If *value* is `#f`, then *name* is removed from the environment. Otherwise, the string *name=value* is added to the environment, replacing any existing string with name matching *name*.

The return value is unspecified.

unsetenv *name*   [Scheme Procedure]
Remove variable *name* from the environment. The name can not contain a '=' character.

environ [*env*]   [Scheme Procedure]
scm_environ (*env*)   [C Function]
If *env* is omitted, return the current environment (in the Unix sense) as a list of strings. Otherwise set the current environment, which is also the default environment for child processes, to the supplied list of strings. Each member of *env* should be of

the form *name=value* and values of *name* should not be duplicated. If *env* is supplied then the return value is unspecified.

putenv *str*   [Scheme Procedure]
scm_putenv (*str*)   [C Function]
> Modifies the environment of the current process, which is also the default environment inherited by child processes.
>
> If *str* is of the form `NAME=VALUE` then it will be written directly into the environment, replacing any existing environment string with name matching `NAME`. If *str* does not contain an equal sign, then any existing string with name matching *str* will be removed.
>
> The return value is unspecified.

7.2.7 Processes

chdir *str*   [Scheme Procedure]
scm_chdir (*str*)   [C Function]
> Change the current working directory to *str*. The return value is unspecified.

getcwd   [Scheme Procedure]
scm_getcwd ()   [C Function]
> Return the name of the current working directory.

umask [*mode*]   [Scheme Procedure]
scm_umask (*mode*)   [C Function]
> If *mode* is omitted, returns a decimal number representing the current file creation mask. Otherwise the file creation mask is set to *mode* and the previous value is returned. See Section "Assigning File Permissions" in *The GNU C Library Reference Manual*, for more on how to use umasks.
>
> E.g., (umask #o022) sets the mask to octal 22/decimal 18.

chroot *path*   [Scheme Procedure]
scm_chroot (*path*)   [C Function]
> Change the root directory to that specified in *path*. This directory will be used for path names beginning with /. The root directory is inherited by all children of the current process. Only the superuser may change the root directory.

getpid   [Scheme Procedure]
scm_getpid ()   [C Function]
> Return an integer representing the current process ID.

getgroups   [Scheme Procedure]
scm_getgroups ()   [C Function]
> Return a vector of integers representing the current supplementary group IDs.

getppid   [Scheme Procedure]
scm_getppid ()   [C Function]
> Return an integer representing the process ID of the parent process.

getuid   [Scheme Procedure]
scm_getuid ()   [C Function]
> Return an integer representing the current real user ID.

getgid   [Scheme Procedure]
scm_getgid ()   [C Function]
> Return an integer representing the current real group ID.

geteuid   [Scheme Procedure]
scm_geteuid ()   [C Function]
> Return an integer representing the current effective user ID. If the system does not
> support effective IDs, then the real ID is returned. (provided? 'EIDs) reports
> whether the system supports effective IDs.

getegid   [Scheme Procedure]
scm_getegid ()   [C Function]
> Return an integer representing the current effective group ID. If the system does
> not support effective IDs, then the real ID is returned. (provided? 'EIDs) reports
> whether the system supports effective IDs.

setgroups vec   [Scheme Procedure]
scm_setgroups (vec)   [C Function]
> Set the current set of supplementary group IDs to the integers in the given vector
> vec. The return value is unspecified.
>
> Generally only the superuser can set the process group IDs (see Section "Setting
> Groups" in The GNU C Library Reference Manual).

setuid id   [Scheme Procedure]
scm_setuid (id)   [C Function]
> Sets both the real and effective user IDs to the integer id, provided the process has
> appropriate privileges. The return value is unspecified.

setgid id   [Scheme Procedure]
scm_setgid (id)   [C Function]
> Sets both the real and effective group IDs to the integer id, provided the process has
> appropriate privileges. The return value is unspecified.

seteuid id   [Scheme Procedure]
scm_seteuid (id)   [C Function]
> Sets the effective user ID to the integer id, provided the process has appropriate
> privileges. If effective IDs are not supported, the real ID is set instead—(provided?
> 'EIDs) reports whether the system supports effective IDs. The return value is un-
> specified.

setegid id   [Scheme Procedure]
scm_setegid (id)   [C Function]
> Sets the effective group ID to the integer id, provided the process has appropriate
> privileges. If effective IDs are not supported, the real ID is set instead—(provided?
> 'EIDs) reports whether the system supports effective IDs. The return value is un-
> specified.

getpgrp   [Scheme Procedure]
scm_getpgrp ()   [C Function]
> Return an integer representing the current process group ID. This is the POSIX defi-
> nition, not BSD.

setpgid *pid pgid*   [Scheme Procedure]
scm_setpgid (*pid, pgid*)   [C Function]
> Move the process *pid* into the process group *pgid*. *pid* or *pgid* must be integers: they
> can be zero to indicate the ID of the current process. Fails on systems that do not
> support job control. The return value is unspecified.

setsid   [Scheme Procedure]
scm_setsid ()   [C Function]
> Creates a new session. The current process becomes the session leader and is put in
> a new process group. The process will be detached from its controlling terminal if it
> has one. The return value is an integer representing the new process group ID.

getsid *pid*   [Scheme Procedure]
scm_getsid (*pid*)   [C Function]
> Returns the session ID of process *pid*. (The session ID of a process is the process
> group ID of its session leader.)

waitpid *pid* [*options*]   [Scheme Procedure]
scm_waitpid (*pid, options*)   [C Function]
> This procedure collects status information from a child process which has terminated
> or (optionally) stopped. Normally it will suspend the calling process until this can
> be done. If more than one child process is eligible then one will be chosen by the
> operating system.
>
> The value of *pid* determines the behaviour:
>
> *pid* greater than 0
>> Request status information from the specified child process.
>
> *pid* equal to -1 or WAIT_ANY
>> Request status information for any child process.
>
> *pid* equal to 0 or WAIT_MYPGRP
>> Request status information for any child process in the current process
>> group.
>
> *pid* less than -1
>> Request status information for any child process whose process group ID
>> is −*pid*.
>
> The *options* argument, if supplied, should be the bitwise OR of the values of zero or
> more of the following variables:

WNOHANG   [Variable]
> Return immediately even if there are no child processes to be collected.

WUNTRACED   [Variable]
> Report status information for stopped processes as well as terminated processes.

The return value is a pair containing:

1. The process ID of the child process, or 0 if `WNOHANG` was specified and no process was collected.
2. The integer status value.

The following three functions can be used to decode the process status code returned by `waitpid`.

`status:exit-val` *status*   [Scheme Procedure]
`scm_status_exit_val` (*status*)   [C Function]
> Return the exit status value, as would be set if a process ended normally through a call to `exit` or `_exit`, if any, otherwise `#f`.

`status:term-sig` *status*   [Scheme Procedure]
`scm_status_term_sig` (*status*)   [C Function]
> Return the signal number which terminated the process, if any, otherwise `#f`.

`status:stop-sig` *status*   [Scheme Procedure]
`scm_status_stop_sig` (*status*)   [C Function]
> Return the signal number which stopped the process, if any, otherwise `#f`.

`system` [*cmd*]   [Scheme Procedure]
`scm_system` (*cmd*)   [C Function]
> Execute *cmd* using the operating system's "command processor". Under Unix this is usually the default shell `sh`. The value returned is *cmd*'s exit status as returned by `waitpid`, which can be interpreted using the functions above.
>
> If `system` is called without arguments, return a boolean indicating whether the command processor is available.

`system*` *arg1 arg2 ...*   [Scheme Procedure]
`scm_system_star` (*args*)   [C Function]
> Execute the command indicated by *arg1 arg2 ....* The first element must be a string indicating the command to be executed, and the remaining items must be strings representing each of the arguments to that command.
>
> This function returns the exit status of the command as provided by `waitpid`. This value can be handled with `status:exit-val` and the related functions.
>
> `system*` is similar to `system`, but accepts only one string per-argument, and performs no shell interpretation. The command is executed using fork and execlp. Accordingly this function may be safer than `system` in situations where shell interpretation is not required.
>
> Example: (system* "echo" "foo" "bar")

`quit` [*status*]   [Scheme Procedure]
`exit` [*status*]   [Scheme Procedure]
> Terminate the current process with proper unwinding of the Scheme stack. The exit status zero if *status* is not supplied. If *status* is supplied, and it is an integer, that integer is used as the exit status. If *status* is `#t` or `#f`, the exit status is 0 or 1, respectively.
>
> The procedure `exit` is an alias of `quit`. They have the same functionality.

`primitive-exit` [*status*]   [Scheme Procedure]
`primitive-_exit` [*status*]   [Scheme Procedure]
`scm_primitive_exit` (*status*)   [C Function]
`scm_primitive__exit` (*status*)   [C Function]

> Terminate the current process without unwinding the Scheme stack. The exit status is *status* if supplied, otherwise zero.
>
> `primitive-exit` uses the C `exit` function and hence runs usual C level cleanups (flush output streams, call `atexit` functions, etc, see Section "Normal Termination" in *The GNU C Library Reference Manual*)).
>
> `primitive-_exit` is the `_exit` system call (see Section "Termination Internals" in *The GNU C Library Reference Manual*). This terminates the program immediately, with neither Scheme-level nor C-level cleanups.
>
> The typical use for `primitive-_exit` is from a child process created with `primitive-fork`. For example in a Gdk program the child process inherits the X server connection and a C-level `atexit` cleanup which will close that connection. But closing in the child would upset the protocol in the parent, so `primitive-_exit` should be used to exit without that.

`execl` *filename arg* ...   [Scheme Procedure]
`scm_execl` (*filename, args*)   [C Function]

> Executes the file named by *filename* as a new process image. The remaining arguments are supplied to the process; from a C program they are accessible as the `argv` argument to `main`. Conventionally the first *arg* is the same as *filename*. All arguments must be strings.
>
> If *arg* is missing, *filename* is executed with a null argument list, which may have system-dependent side-effects.
>
> This procedure is currently implemented using the `execv` system call, but we call it `execl` because of its Scheme calling interface.

`execlp` *filename arg* ...   [Scheme Procedure]
`scm_execlp` (*filename, args*)   [C Function]

> Similar to `execl`, however if *filename* does not contain a slash then the file to execute will be located by searching the directories listed in the `PATH` environment variable.
>
> This procedure is currently implemented using the `execvp` system call, but we call it `execlp` because of its Scheme calling interface.

`execle` *filename env arg* ...   [Scheme Procedure]
`scm_execle` (*filename, env, args*)   [C Function]

> Similar to `execl`, but the environment of the new process is specified by *env*, which must be a list of strings as returned by the `environ` procedure.
>
> This procedure is currently implemented using the `execve` system call, but we call it `execle` because of its Scheme calling interface.

`primitive-fork`   [Scheme Procedure]
`scm_fork` ()   [C Function]

> Creates a new "child" process by duplicating the current "parent" process. In the child the return value is 0. In the parent the return value is the integer process ID of the child.

Note that it is unsafe to fork a process that has multiple threads running, as only the thread that calls `primitive-fork` will persist in the child. Any resources that other threads held, such as locked mutexes or open file descriptors, are lost. Indeed, POSIX specifies that only async-signal-safe procedures are safe to call after a multithreaded fork, which is a very limited set. Guile issues a warning if it detects a fork from a multi-threaded program.

If you are going to `exec` soon after forking, the procedures in `(ice-9 popen)` may be useful to you, as they fork and exec within an async-signal-safe function carefully written to ensure robust program behavior, even in the presence of threads. See Section 7.2.10 [Pipes], page 500, for more.

This procedure has been renamed from `fork` to avoid a naming conflict with the scsh fork.

`nice` *incr*   [Scheme Procedure]
`scm_nice` (*incr*)   [C Function]

> Increment the priority of the current process by *incr*. A higher priority value means that the process runs less often. The return value is unspecified.

`setpriority` *which who prio*   [Scheme Procedure]
`scm_setpriority` (*which, who, prio*)   [C Function]

> Set the scheduling priority of the process, process group or user, as indicated by *which* and *who*. *which* is one of the variables `PRIO_PROCESS`, `PRIO_PGRP` or `PRIO_USER`, and *who* is interpreted relative to *which* (a process identifier for `PRIO_PROCESS`, process group identifier for `PRIO_PGRP`, and a user identifier for `PRIO_USER`. A zero value of *who* denotes the current process, process group, or user. *prio* is a value in the range [−20,20]. The default priority is 0; lower priorities (in numerical terms) cause more favorable scheduling. Sets the priority of all of the specified processes. Only the super-user may lower priorities. The return value is not specified.

`getpriority` *which who*   [Scheme Procedure]
`scm_getpriority` (*which, who*)   [C Function]

> Return the scheduling priority of the process, process group or user, as indicated by *which* and *who*. *which* is one of the variables `PRIO_PROCESS`, `PRIO_PGRP` or `PRIO_USER`, and *who* should be interpreted depending on *which* (a process identifier for `PRIO_PROCESS`, process group identifier for `PRIO_PGRP`, and a user identifier for `PRIO_USER`). A zero value of *who* denotes the current process, process group, or user. Return the highest priority (lowest numerical value) of any of the specified processes.

`getaffinity` *pid*   [Scheme Procedure]
`scm_getaffinity` (*pid*)   [C Function]

> Return a bitvector representing the CPU affinity mask for process *pid*. Each CPU the process has affinity with has its corresponding bit set in the returned bitvector. The number of bits set is a good estimate of how many CPUs Guile can use without stepping on other processes' toes.

> Currently this procedure is only defined on GNU variants (see Section "CPU Affinity" in *The GNU C Library Reference Manual*).

`setaffinity` *pid mask*   [Scheme Procedure]
`scm_setaffinity` (*pid*, *mask*)   [C Function]
> Install the CPU affinity mask *mask*, a bitvector, for the process or thread with ID *pid*. The return value is unspecified.
>
> Currently this procedure is only defined on GNU variants (see Section "CPU Affinity" in *The GNU C Library Reference Manual*).

`total-processor-count`   [Scheme Procedure]
`scm_total_processor_count` ()   [C Function]
> Return the total number of processors of the machine, which is guaranteed to be at least 1. A "processor" here is a thread execution unit, which can be either:
>
> - an execution core in a (possibly multi-core) chip, in a (possibly multi- chip) module, in a single computer, or
>
> - a thread execution unit inside a core in the case of *hyper-threaded* CPUs.
>
> Which of the two definitions is used, is unspecified.

`current-processor-count`   [Scheme Procedure]
`scm_current_processor_count` ()   [C Function]
> Like `total-processor-count`, but return the number of processors available to the current process. See `setaffinity` and `getaffinity` for more information.

7.2.8 Signals

The following procedures raise, handle and wait for signals.

Scheme code signal handlers are run via a system async (see Section 6.21.2.1 [System asyncs], page 411), so they're called in the handler's thread at the next safe opportunity. Generally this is after any currently executing primitive procedure finishes (which could be a long time for primitives that wait for an external event).

`kill` *pid sig*   [Scheme Procedure]
`scm_kill` (*pid*, *sig*)   [C Function]
> Sends a signal to the specified process or group of processes.
>
> *pid* specifies the processes to which the signal is sent:
>
> *pid* greater than 0
> > The process whose identifier is *pid*.
>
> *pid* equal to 0
> > All processes in the current process group.
>
> *pid* less than -1
> > The process group whose identifier is -*pid*
>
> *pid* equal to -1
> > If the process is privileged, all processes except for some special system processes. Otherwise, all processes with the current effective user ID.
>
> *sig* should be specified using a variable corresponding to the Unix symbolic name, e.g.,

`SIGHUP`   [Variable]

> Hang-up signal.

`SIGINT`   [Variable]

> Interrupt signal.

A full list of signals on the GNU system may be found in Section "Standard Signals" in *The GNU C Library Reference Manual*.

`raise` *sig*   [Scheme Procedure]
`scm_raise` (*sig*)   [C Function]

> Sends a specified signal *sig* to the current process, where *sig* is as described for the `kill` procedure.

`sigaction` *signum* [*handler* [*flags* [*thread*]]]   [Scheme Procedure]
`scm_sigaction` (*signum*, *handler*, *flags*)   [C Function]
`scm_sigaction_for_thread` (*signum*, *handler*, *flags*, *thread*)   [C Function]

> Install or report the signal handler for a specified signal.
>
> *signum* is the signal number, which can be specified using the value of variables such as `SIGINT`.
>
> If *handler* is omitted, `sigaction` returns a pair: the CAR is the current signal hander, which will be either an integer with the value `SIG_DFL` (default action) or `SIG_IGN` (ignore), or the Scheme procedure which handles the signal, or `#f` if a non-Scheme procedure handles the signal. The CDR contains the current `sigaction` flags for the handler.
>
> If *handler* is provided, it is installed as the new handler for *signum*. *handler* can be a Scheme procedure taking one argument, or the value of `SIG_DFL` (default action) or `SIG_IGN` (ignore), or `#f` to restore whatever signal handler was installed before `sigaction` was first used. When a scheme procedure has been specified, that procedure will run in the given *thread*. When no thread has been given, the thread that made this call to `sigaction` is used.
>
> *flags* is a `logior` (see Section 6.6.2.13 [Bitwise Operations], page 125) of the following (where provided by the system), or 0 for none.

`SA_NOCLDSTOP`   [Variable]

> By default, `SIGCHLD` is signalled when a child process stops (ie. receives `SIGSTOP`), and when a child process terminates. With the `SA_NOCLDSTOP` flag, `SIGCHLD` is only signalled for termination, not stopping.
>
> `SA_NOCLDSTOP` has no effect on signals other than `SIGCHLD`.

`SA_RESTART`   [Variable]

> If a signal occurs while in a system call, deliver the signal then restart the system call (as opposed to returning an `EINTR` error from that call).

The return value is a pair with information about the old handler as described above.

This interface does not provide access to the "signal blocking" facility. Maybe this is not needed, since the thread support may provide solutions to the problem of consistent access to data structures.

restore-signals   [Scheme Procedure]
scm_restore_signals ()   [C Function]
    Return all signal handlers to the values they had before any call to sigaction was
    made. The return value is unspecified.

alarm *i*   [Scheme Procedure]
scm_alarm (*i*)   [C Function]
    Set a timer to raise a SIGALRM signal after the specified number of seconds (an integer).
    It's advisable to install a signal handler for SIGALRM beforehand, since the default
    action is to terminate the process.

    The return value indicates the time remaining for the previous alarm, if any. The
    new value replaces the previous alarm. If there was no previous alarm, the return
    value is zero.

pause   [Scheme Procedure]
scm_pause ()   [C Function]
    Pause the current process (thread?) until a signal arrives whose action is to either
    terminate the current process or invoke a handler procedure. The return value is
    unspecified.

sleep *secs*   [Scheme Procedure]
usleep *usecs*   [Scheme Procedure]
scm_sleep (*secs*)   [C Function]
scm_usleep (*usecs*)   [C Function]
    Wait the given period *secs* seconds or *usecs* microseconds (both integers). If a signal
    arrives the wait stops and the return value is the time remaining, in seconds or
    microseconds respectively. If the period elapses with no signal the return is zero.

    On most systems the process scheduler is not microsecond accurate and the actual
    period slept by usleep might be rounded to a system clock tick boundary, which
    might be 10 milliseconds for instance.

    See scm_std_sleep and scm_std_usleep for equivalents at the C level (see
    Section 6.21.5 [Blocking], page 418).

getitimer *which_timer*   [Scheme Procedure]
setitimer *which_timer interval_seconds interval_microseconds*   [Scheme Procedure]
        periodic_seconds periodic_microseconds
scm_getitimer (*which_timer*)   [C Function]
scm_setitimer (*which_timer, interval_seconds, interval_microseconds,*   [C Function]
        periodic_seconds, periodic_microseconds)
    Get or set the periods programmed in certain system timers. These timers have
    a current interval value which counts down and on reaching zero raises a signal.
    An optional periodic value can be set to restart from there each time, for periodic
    operation. *which_timer* is one of the following values

    ITIMER_REAL   [Variable]
        A real-time timer, counting down elapsed real time. At zero it raises SIGALRM.
        This is like alarm above, but with a higher resolution period.

ITIMER_VIRTUAL   [Variable]

> A virtual-time timer, counting down while the current process is actually using CPU. At zero it raises SIGVTALRM.

ITIMER_PROF   [Variable]

> A profiling timer, counting down while the process is running (like ITIMER_VIRTUAL) and also while system calls are running on the process's behalf. At zero it raises a SIGPROF.
>
> This timer is intended for profiling where a program is spending its time (by looking where it is when the timer goes off).

getitimer returns the current timer value and its programmed restart value, as a list containing two pairs. Each pair is a time in seconds and microseconds: ((*interval_secs . interval_usecs*) (*periodic_secs . periodic_usecs*)).

setitimer sets the timer values similarly, in seconds and microseconds (which must be integers). The periodic value can be zero to have the timer run down just once. The return value is the timer's previous setting, in the same form as getitimer returns.

```
(setitimer ITIMER_REAL
           5 500000    ;; first SIGALRM in 5.5 seconds time
           2 0)        ;; then repeat every 2 seconds
```

Although the timers are programmed in microseconds, the actual accuracy might not be that high.

7.2.9 Terminals and Ptys

isatty? *port*   [Scheme Procedure]
scm_isatty_p (*port*)   [C Function]

> Return #t if *port* is using a serial non–file device, otherwise #f.

ttyname *port*   [Scheme Procedure]
scm_ttyname (*port*)   [C Function]

> Return a string with the name of the serial terminal device underlying *port*.

ctermid   [Scheme Procedure]
scm_ctermid ()   [C Function]

> Return a string containing the file name of the controlling terminal for the current process.

tcgetpgrp *port*   [Scheme Procedure]
scm_tcgetpgrp (*port*)   [C Function]

> Return the process group ID of the foreground process group associated with the terminal open on the file descriptor underlying *port*.
>
> If there is no foreground process group, the return value is a number greater than 1 that does not match the process group ID of any existing process group. This can happen if all of the processes in the job that was formerly the foreground job have terminated, and no other job has yet been moved into the foreground.

`tcsetpgrp` *port pgid*   [Scheme Procedure]

`scm_tcsetpgrp` (*port, pgid*)   [C Function]

> Set the foreground process group ID for the terminal used by the file descriptor underlying *port* to the integer *pgid*. The calling process must be a member of the same session as *pgid* and must have the same controlling terminal. The return value is unspecified.

7.2.10 Pipes

The following procedures are similar to the `popen` and `pclose` system routines. The code is in a separate "popen" module[1]:

```
(use-modules (ice-9 popen))
```

`open-pipe` *command mode*   [Scheme Procedure]

`open-pipe*` *mode prog* [*args...*]   [Scheme Procedure]

> Execute a command in a subprocess, with a pipe to it or from it, or with pipes in both directions.
>
> `open-pipe` runs the shell *command* using '/bin/sh -c'. `open-pipe*` executes *prog* directly, with the optional *args* arguments (all strings).
>
> *mode* should be one of the following values. `OPEN_READ` is an input pipe, ie. to read from the subprocess. `OPEN_WRITE` is an output pipe, ie. to write to it.

> `OPEN_READ`   [Variable]
> `OPEN_WRITE`   [Variable]
> `OPEN_BOTH`   [Variable]
>
> For an input pipe, the child's standard output is the pipe and standard input is inherited from `current-input-port`. For an output pipe, the child's standard input is the pipe and standard output is inherited from `current-output-port`. In all cases cases the child's standard error is inherited from `current-error-port` (see Section 6.14.8 [Default Ports], page 325).
>
> If those `current-X-ports` are not files of some kind, and hence don't have file descriptors for the child, then /dev/null is used instead.
>
> Care should be taken with `OPEN_BOTH`, a deadlock will occur if both parent and child are writing, and waiting until the write completes before doing any reading. Each direction has `PIPE_BUF` bytes of buffering (see Section 7.2.2 [Ports and File Descriptors], page 469), which will be enough for small writes, but not for say putting a big file through a filter.

`open-input-pipe` *command*   [Scheme Procedure]

> Equivalent to `open-pipe` with mode `OPEN_READ`.
>
> ```
>       (let* ((port (open-input-pipe "date --utc"))
>              (str  (read-line port)))
>         (close-pipe port)
>         str)
>       ⇒ "Mon Mar 11 20:10:44 UTC 2002"
> ```

---

[1] This module is only available on systems where the `fork` feature is provided (see Section 6.22.2.2 [Common Feature Symbols], page 429).

open-output-pipe *command*   [Scheme Procedure]
>   Equivalent to open-pipe with mode OPEN_WRITE.

```
(let ((port (open-output-pipe "lpr")))
  (display "Something for the line printer.\n" port)
  (if (not (eqv? 0 (status:exit-val (close-pipe port))))
      (error "Cannot print")))
```

open-input-output-pipe *command*   [Scheme Procedure]
>   Equivalent to open-pipe with mode OPEN_BOTH.

close-pipe *port*   [Scheme Procedure]
>   Close a pipe created by open-pipe, wait for the process to terminate, and return the
>   wait status code. The status is as per waitpid and can be decoded with status:exit-
>   val etc (see Section 7.2.7 [Processes], page 490)

waitpid WAIT_ANY should not be used when pipes are open, since it can reap a pipe's child process, causing an error from a subsequent close-pipe.

close-port (see Section 6.14.4 [Closing], page 321) can close a pipe, but it doesn't reap the child process.

The garbage collector will close a pipe no longer in use, and reap the child process with waitpid. If the child hasn't yet terminated the garbage collector doesn't block, but instead checks again in the next GC.

Many systems have per-user and system-wide limits on the number of processes, and a system-wide limit on the number of pipes, so pipes should be closed explicitly when no longer needed, rather than letting the garbage collector pick them up at some later time.

7.2.11 Networking

7.2.11.1 Network Address Conversion

This section describes procedures which convert internet addresses between numeric and string formats.

IPv4 Address Conversion

An IPv4 Internet address is a 4-byte value, represented in Guile as an integer in host byte order, so that say "0.0.0.1" is 1, or "1.0.0.0" is 16777216.

Some underlying C functions use network byte order for addresses, Guile converts as necessary so that at the Scheme level its host byte order everywhere.

INADDR_ANY   [Variable]
>   For a server, this can be used with bind (see Section 7.2.11.4 [Network Sockets and
>   Communication], page 511) to allow connections from any interface on the machine.

INADDR_BROADCAST   [Variable]
>   The broadcast address on the local network.

INADDR_LOOPBACK   [Variable]
>   The address of the local host using the loopback device, ie. '127.0.0.1'.

`inet-aton` *address*   [Scheme Procedure]
`scm_inet_aton` (*address*)   [C Function]

>   This function is deprecated in favor of `inet-pton`.
>
>   Convert an IPv4 Internet address from printable string (dotted decimal notation) to
>   an integer. E.g.,
>
> >   `(inet-aton "127.0.0.1")` $\Rightarrow$ 2130706433

`inet-ntoa` *inetid*   [Scheme Procedure]
`scm_inet_ntoa` (*inetid*)   [C Function]

>   This function is deprecated in favor of `inet-ntop`.
>
>   Convert an IPv4 Internet address to a printable (dotted decimal notation) string.
>   E.g.,
>
> >   `(inet-ntoa 2130706433)` $\Rightarrow$ `"127.0.0.1"`

`inet-netof` *address*   [Scheme Procedure]
`scm_inet_netof` (*address*)   [C Function]

>   Return the network number part of the given IPv4 Internet address. E.g.,
>
> >   `(inet-netof 2130706433)` $\Rightarrow$ 127

`inet-lnaof` *address*   [Scheme Procedure]
`scm_lnaof` (*address*)   [C Function]

>   Return the local-address-with-network part of the given IPv4 Internet address, using
>   the obsolete class A/B/C system. E.g.,
>
> >   `(inet-lnaof 2130706433)` $\Rightarrow$ 1

`inet-makeaddr` *net lna*   [Scheme Procedure]
`scm_inet_makeaddr` (*net, lna*)   [C Function]

>   Make an IPv4 Internet address by combining the network number *net* with the local-
>   address-within-network number *lna*. E.g.,
>
> >   `(inet-makeaddr 127 1)` $\Rightarrow$ 2130706433

IPv6 Address Conversion

An IPv6 Internet address is a 16-byte value, represented in Guile as an integer in host byte
order, so that say "::1" is 1.

`inet-ntop` *family address*   [Scheme Procedure]
`scm_inet_ntop` (*family, address*)   [C Function]

>   Convert a network address from an integer to a printable string. *family* can be `AF_`
>   `INET` or `AF_INET6`. E.g.,
>
> >   `(inet-ntop AF_INET 2130706433)` $\Rightarrow$ `"127.0.0.1"`
> >   `(inet-ntop AF_INET6 (- (expt 2 128) 1))`
> > $\Rightarrow$ `"ffff:ffff:ffff:ffff:ffff:ffff:ffff:ffff"`

`inet-pton` *family address*   [Scheme Procedure]
`scm_inet_pton` (*family, address*)   [C Function]

>   Convert a string containing a printable network address to an integer address. *family*
>   can be `AF_INET` or `AF_INET6`. E.g.,

```
(inet-pton AF_INET "127.0.0.1") ⇒ 2130706433
(inet-pton AF_INET6 "::1") ⇒ 1
```

7.2.11.2 Network Databases

This section describes procedures which query various network databases. Care should be taken when using the database routines since they are not reentrant.

getaddrinfo

The getaddrinfo procedure maps host and service names to socket addresses and associated information in a protocol-independent way.

getaddrinfo *name service* [*hint_flags* [*hint_family* [*hint_socktype*   [Scheme Procedure]
        [*hint_protocol*]]]]
scm_getaddrinfo (*name, service, hint_flags, hint_family, hint_socktype,*   [C Function]
        hint_protocol)

> Return a list of addrinfo structures containing a socket address and associated information for host *name* and/or *service* to be used in creating a socket with which to address the specified service.
>
> ```
> (let* ((ai (car (getaddrinfo "www.gnu.org" "http")))
>        (s  (socket (addrinfo:fam ai) (addrinfo:socktype ai)
>                    (addrinfo:protocol ai))))
>   (connect s (addrinfo:addr ai))
>   s)
> ```
>
> When *service* is omitted or is #f, return network-level addresses for *name*. When *name* is #f *service* must be provided and service locations local to the caller are returned.
>
> Additional hints can be provided. When specified, *hint_flags* should be a bitwise-or of zero or more constants among the following:

AI_PASSIVE
> Socket address is intended for bind.

AI_CANONNAME
> Request for canonical host name, available via addrinfo:canonname. This makes sense mainly when DNS lookups are involved.

AI_NUMERICHOST
> Specifies that *name* is a numeric host address string (e.g., "127.0.0.1"), meaning that name resolution will not be used.

AI_NUMERICSERV
> Likewise, specifies that *service* is a numeric port string (e.g., "80").

AI_ADDRCONFIG
> Return only addresses configured on the local system It is highly recommended to provide this flag when the returned socket addresses are to be used to make connections; otherwise, some of the returned addresses could be unreachable or use a protocol that is not supported.

AI_V4MAPPED
> When looking up IPv6 addresses, return mapped IPv4 addresses if there is no IPv6 address available at all.

AI_ALL
> If this flag is set along with AI_V4MAPPED when looking up IPv6 addresses, return all IPv6 addresses as well as all IPv4 addresses, the latter mapped to IPv6 format.

When given, *hint_family* should specify the requested address family, e.g., AF_INET6. Similarly, *hint_socktype* should specify the requested socket type (e.g., SOCK_DGRAM), and *hint_protocol* should specify the requested protocol (its value is interpreted as in calls to socket).

On error, an exception with key getaddrinfo-error is thrown, with an error code (an integer) as its argument:

```
(catch 'getaddrinfo-error
  (lambda ()
    (getaddrinfo "www.gnu.org" "gopher"))
  (lambda (key errcode)
    (cond ((= errcode EAI_SERVICE)
    (display "doesn't know about Gopher!\n"))
    ((= errcode EAI_NONAME)
    (display "www.gnu.org not found\\n"))
    (else
    (format #t "something wrong: ~a\n"
    (gai-strerror errcode)))))))
```

Error codes are:

EAI_AGAIN
> The name or service could not be resolved at this time. Future attempts may succeed.

EAI_BADFLAGS
> *hint_flags* contains an invalid value.

EAI_FAIL A non-recoverable error occurred when attempting to resolve the name.

EAI_FAMILY
> *hint_family* was not recognized.

EAI_NONAME
> Either *name* does not resolve for the supplied parameters, or neither *name* nor *service* were supplied.

EAI_NODATA
> This non-POSIX error code can be returned on some systems (GNU and Darwin, at least), for example when *name* is known but requests that were made turned out no data. Error handling code should be prepared to handle it when it is defined.

EAI_SERVICE
> *service* was not recognized for the specified socket type.

EAI_SOCKTYPE

> *hint_socktype* was not recognized.

EAI_SYSTEM

> A system error occurred. In C, the error code can be found in **errno**; this value is not accessible from Scheme, but in practice it provides little information about the actual error cause.

Users are encouraged to read the "POSIX specification for more details.

The following procedures take an **addrinfo** object as returned by **getaddrinfo**:

addrinfo:flags *ai*   [Scheme Procedure]
> Return flags for *ai* as a bitwise or of **AI_** values (see above).

addrinfo:fam *ai*   [Scheme Procedure]
> Return the address family of *ai* (a **AF_** value).

addrinfo:socktype *ai*   [Scheme Procedure]
> Return the socket type for *ai* (a **SOCK_** value).

addrinfo:protocol *ai*   [Scheme Procedure]
> Return the protocol of *ai*.

addrinfo:addr *ai*   [Scheme Procedure]
> Return the socket address associated with *ai* as a **sockaddr** object (see Section 7.2.11.3 [Network Socket Address], page 509).

addrinfo:canonname *ai*   [Scheme Procedure]
> Return a string for the canonical name associated with *ai* if the **AI_CANONNAME** flag was supplied.

The Host Database

A *host object* is a structure that represents what is known about a network host, and is the usual way of representing a system's network identity inside software.

The following functions accept a host object and return a selected component:

hostent:name *host*   [Scheme Procedure]
> The "official" hostname for *host*.

hostent:aliases *host*   [Scheme Procedure]
> A list of aliases for *host*.

hostent:addrtype *host*   [Scheme Procedure]
> The host address type, one of the **AF** constants, such as **AF_INET** or **AF_INET6**.

hostent:length *host*   [Scheme Procedure]
> The length of each address for *host*, in bytes.

hostent:addr-list *host*   [Scheme Procedure]
> The list of network addresses associated with *host*. For **AF_INET** these are integer IPv4 address (see Section 7.2.11.1 [Network Address Conversion], page 501).

The following procedures can be used to search the host database. However, `getaddrinfo` should be preferred over them since it's more generic and thread-safe.

`gethost` [*host*]   [Scheme Procedure]
`gethostbyname` *hostname*   [Scheme Procedure]
`gethostbyaddr` *address*   [Scheme Procedure]
`scm_gethost` (*host*)   [C Function]

    Look up a host by name or address, returning a host object. The `gethost` procedure will accept either a string name or an integer address; if given no arguments, it behaves like `gethostent` (see below). If a name or address is supplied but the address can not be found, an error will be thrown to one of the keys: `host-not-found`, `try-again`, `no-recovery` or `no-data`, corresponding to the equivalent `h_error` values. Unusual conditions may result in errors thrown to the `system-error` or `misc_error` keys.

```
(gethost "www.gnu.org")
⇒ #("www.gnu.org" () 2 4 (3353880842))

(gethostbyname "www.emacs.org")
⇒ #("emacs.org" ("www.emacs.org") 2 4 (1073448978))
```

The following procedures may be used to step through the host database from beginning to end.

`sethostent` [*stayopen*]   [Scheme Procedure]

    Initialize an internal stream from which host objects may be read. This procedure must be called before any calls to `gethostent`, and may also be called afterward to reset the host entry stream. If *stayopen* is supplied and is not `#f`, the database is not closed by subsequent `gethostbyname` or `gethostbyaddr` calls, possibly giving an efficiency gain.

`gethostent`   [Scheme Procedure]

    Return the next host object from the host database, or `#f` if there are no more hosts to be found (or an error has been encountered). This procedure may not be used before `sethostent` has been called.

`endhostent`   [Scheme Procedure]

    Close the stream used by `gethostent`. The return value is unspecified.

`sethost` [*stayopen*]   [Scheme Procedure]
`scm_sethost` (*stayopen*)   [C Function]

    If *stayopen* is omitted, this is equivalent to `endhostent`. Otherwise it is equivalent to `sethostent stayopen`.

The Network Database

The following functions accept an object representing a network and return a selected component:

`netent:name` *net*   [Scheme Procedure]

    The "official" network name.

`netent:aliases` *net*   [Scheme Procedure]
> A list of aliases for the network.

`netent:addrtype` *net*   [Scheme Procedure]
> The type of the network number. Currently, this returns only `AF_INET`.

`netent:net` *net*   [Scheme Procedure]
> The network number.

The following procedures are used to search the network database:

`getnet` [*net*]   [Scheme Procedure]
`getnetbyname` *net-name*   [Scheme Procedure]
`getnetbyaddr` *net-number*   [Scheme Procedure]
`scm_getnet` (*net*)   [C Function]
> Look up a network by name or net number in the network database. The *net-name*
> argument must be a string, and the *net-number* argument must be an integer. `getnet`
> will accept either type of argument, behaving like `getnetent` (see below) if no argu-
> ments are given.

The following procedures may be used to step through the network database from beginning to end.

`setnetent` [*stayopen*]   [Scheme Procedure]
> Initialize an internal stream from which network objects may be read. This procedure
> must be called before any calls to `getnetent`, and may also be called afterward to
> reset the net entry stream. If *stayopen* is supplied and is not `#f`, the database is
> not closed by subsequent `getnetbyname` or `getnetbyaddr` calls, possibly giving an
> efficiency gain.

`getnetent`   [Scheme Procedure]
> Return the next entry from the network database.

`endnetent`   [Scheme Procedure]
> Close the stream used by `getnetent`. The return value is unspecified.

`setnet` [*stayopen*]   [Scheme Procedure]
`scm_setnet` (*stayopen*)   [C Function]
> If *stayopen* is omitted, this is equivalent to `endnetent`. Otherwise it is equivalent to
> `setnetent stayopen`.

The Protocol Database

The following functions accept an object representing a protocol and return a selected
component:

`protoent:name` *protocol*   [Scheme Procedure]
> The "official" protocol name.

`protoent:aliases` *protocol*   [Scheme Procedure]
> A list of aliases for the protocol.

`protoent:proto` *protocol*   [Scheme Procedure]
> The protocol number.

The following procedures are used to search the protocol database:

`getproto` [*protocol*]   [Scheme Procedure]
`getprotobyname` *name*   [Scheme Procedure]
`getprotobynumber` *number*   [Scheme Procedure]
`scm_getproto` (*protocol*)   [C Function]
> Look up a network protocol by name or by number. `getprotobyname` takes a string
> argument, and `getprotobynumber` takes an integer argument. `getproto` will accept
> either type, behaving like `getprotoent` (see below) if no arguments are supplied.

The following procedures may be used to step through the protocol database from beginning to end.

`setprotoent` [*stayopen*]   [Scheme Procedure]
> Initialize an internal stream from which protocol objects may be read. This procedure
> must be called before any calls to `getprotoent`, and may also be called afterward to
> reset the protocol entry stream. If *stayopen* is supplied and is not `#f`, the database
> is not closed by subsequent `getprotobyname` or `getprotobynumber` calls, possibly
> giving an efficiency gain.

`getprotoent`   [Scheme Procedure]
> Return the next entry from the protocol database.

`endprotoent`   [Scheme Procedure]
> Close the stream used by `getprotoent`. The return value is unspecified.

`setproto` [*stayopen*]   [Scheme Procedure]
`scm_setproto` (*stayopen*)   [C Function]
> If *stayopen* is omitted, this is equivalent to `endprotoent`. Otherwise it is equivalent
> to `setprotoent stayopen`.

The Service Database

The following functions accept an object representing a service and return a selected component:

`servent:name` *serv*   [Scheme Procedure]
> The "official" name of the network service.

`servent:aliases` *serv*   [Scheme Procedure]
> A list of aliases for the network service.

`servent:port` *serv*   [Scheme Procedure]
> The Internet port used by the service.

`servent:proto` *serv*   [Scheme Procedure]
> The protocol used by the service. A service may be listed many times in the database
> under different protocol names.

The following procedures are used to search the service database:

getserv [*name* [*protocol*]]   [Scheme Procedure]
getservbyname *name protocol*   [Scheme Procedure]
getservbyport *port protocol*   [Scheme Procedure]
scm_getserv (*name, protocol*)   [C Function]
> Look up a network service by name or by service number, and return a network
> service object. The *protocol* argument specifies the name of the desired protocol;
> if the protocol found in the network service database does not match this name, a
> system error is signalled.
>
> The getserv procedure will take either a service name or number as its first argument;
> if given no arguments, it behaves like getservent (see below).

```
(getserv "imap" "tcp")
⇒ #("imap2" ("imap") 143 "tcp")


(getservbyport 88 "udp")
⇒ #("kerberos" ("kerberos5" "krb5") 88 "udp")
```

The following procedures may be used to step through the service database from beginning to end.

setservent [*stayopen*]   [Scheme Procedure]
> Initialize an internal stream from which service objects may be read. This procedure
> must be called before any calls to getservent, and may also be called afterward to
> reset the service entry stream. If *stayopen* is supplied and is not #f, the database is
> not closed by subsequent getservbyname or getservbyport calls, possibly giving an
> efficiency gain.

getservent   [Scheme Procedure]
> Return the next entry from the services database.

endservent   [Scheme Procedure]
> Close the stream used by getservent. The return value is unspecified.

setserv [*stayopen*]   [Scheme Procedure]
scm_setserv (*stayopen*)   [C Function]
> If *stayopen* is omitted, this is equivalent to endservent. Otherwise it is equivalent
> to setservent stayopen.

7.2.11.3 Network Socket Address

A *socket address* object identifies a socket endpoint for communication. In the case of
AF_INET for instance, the socket address object comprises the host address (or interface on
the host) and a port number which specifies a particular open socket in a running client or
server process. A socket address object can be created with,

make-socket-address *AF_INET ipv4addr port*   [Scheme Procedure]
make-socket-address *AF_INET6 ipv6addr port* [*flowinfo*   [Scheme Procedure]
          [*scopeid*]]
make-socket-address *AF_UNIX path*   [Scheme Procedure]

`scm_make_socket_address` (*family, address, arglist*)   [C Function]
>   Return a new socket address object. The first argument is the address family, one of
>   the `AF` constants, then the arguments vary according to the family.
>
>   For `AF_INET` the arguments are an IPv4 network address number (see Section 7.2.11.1
>   [Network Address Conversion], page 501), and a port number.
>
>   For `AF_INET6` the arguments are an IPv6 network address number and a port number.
>   Optional *flowinfo* and *scopeid* arguments may be given (both integers, default 0).
>
>   For `AF_UNIX` the argument is a filename (a string).
>
>   The C function `scm_make_socket_address` takes the *family* and *address* arguments
>   directly, then *arglist* is a list of further arguments, being the port for IPv4, port and
>   optional flowinfo and scopeid for IPv6, or the empty list `SCM_EOL` for Unix domain.

The following functions access the fields of a socket address object,

`sockaddr:fam` *sa*   [Scheme Procedure]
>   Return the address family from socket address object *sa*. This is one of the `AF`
>   constants (e.g. `AF_INET`).

`sockaddr:path` *sa*   [Scheme Procedure]
>   For an `AF_UNIX` socket address object *sa*, return the filename.

`sockaddr:addr` *sa*   [Scheme Procedure]
>   For an `AF_INET` or `AF_INET6` socket address object *sa*, return the network address
>   number.

`sockaddr:port` *sa*   [Scheme Procedure]
>   For an `AF_INET` or `AF_INET6` socket address object *sa*, return the port number.

`sockaddr:flowinfo` *sa*   [Scheme Procedure]
>   For an `AF_INET6` socket address object *sa*, return the flowinfo value.

`sockaddr:scopeid` *sa*   [Scheme Procedure]
>   For an `AF_INET6` socket address object *sa*, return the scope ID value.

The functions below convert to and from the C `struct sockaddr` (see Section "Address
Formats" in *The GNU C Library Reference Manual*). That structure is a generic type,
an application can cast to or from `struct sockaddr_in`, `struct sockaddr_in6` or `struct
sockaddr_un` according to the address family.

In a `struct sockaddr` taken or returned, the byte ordering in the fields follows the
C conventions (see Section "Byte Order Conversion" in *The GNU C Library Reference
Manual*). This means network byte order for `AF_INET` host address (`sin_addr.s_addr`) and
port number (`sin_port`), and `AF_INET6` port number (`sin6_port`). But at the Scheme level
these values are taken or returned in host byte order, so the port is an ordinary integer, and
the host address likewise is an ordinary integer (as described in Section 7.2.11.1 [Network
Address Conversion], page 501).

`struct sockaddr * scm_c_make_socket_address` (*SCM family,*   [C Function]
>   *SCM address, SCM args, size_t *outsize*)
>   Return a newly-malloced `struct sockaddr` created from arguments like those taken
>   by `scm_make_socket_address` above.

The size (in bytes) of the **struct sockaddr** return is stored into *outsize*. An application must call **free** to release the returned structure when no longer required.

SCM **scm_from_sockaddr** (*const struct sockaddr *address, unsigned*   [C Function]
    address_size)

> Return a Scheme socket address object from the C *address* structure. *address_size* is the size in bytes of *address*.

struct sockaddr * **scm_to_sockaddr** (*SCM address, size_t*   [C Function]
    **address_size*)

> Return a newly-malloced **struct sockaddr** from a Scheme level socket address object.

> The size (in bytes) of the **struct sockaddr** return is stored into *outsize*. An application must call **free** to release the returned structure when no longer required.

7.2.11.4 Network Sockets and Communication

Socket ports can be created using **socket** and **socketpair**. The ports are initially unbuffered, to make reading and writing to the same port more reliable. A buffer can be added to the port using **setvbuf**; see Section 7.2.2 [Ports and File Descriptors], page 469.

Most systems have limits on how many files and sockets can be open, so it's strongly recommended that socket ports be closed explicitly when no longer required (see Section 6.14.1 [Ports], page 316).

Some of the underlying C functions take values in network byte order, but the convention in Guile is that at the Scheme level everything is ordinary host byte order and conversions are made automatically where necessary.

socket *family style proto*   [Scheme Procedure]
scm_socket (*family, style, proto*)   [C Function]

> Return a new socket port of the type specified by *family*, *style* and *proto*. All three parameters are integers. The possible values for *family* are as follows, where supported by the system,

> PF_UNIX   [Variable]
> PF_INET   [Variable]
> PF_INET6   [Variable]

> The possible values for *style* are as follows, again where supported by the system,

> SOCK_STREAM   [Variable]
> SOCK_DGRAM   [Variable]
> SOCK_RAW   [Variable]
> SOCK_RDM   [Variable]
> SOCK_SEQPACKET   [Variable]

> *proto* can be obtained from a protocol name using **getprotobyname** (see Section 7.2.11.2 [Network Databases], page 503). A value of zero means the default protocol, which is usually right.

> A socket cannot by used for communication until it has been connected somewhere, usually with either **connect** or **accept** below.

socketpair *family style proto*   [Scheme Procedure]
scm_socketpair (*family, style, proto*)   [C Function]
> Return a pair, the `car` and `cdr` of which are two unnamed socket ports connected
> to each other. The connection is full-duplex, so data can be transferred in either
> direction between the two.
>
> *family*, *style* and *proto* are as per `socket` above. But many systems only support
> socket pairs in the `PF_UNIX` family. Zero is likely to be the only meaningful value for
> *proto*.

getsockopt *sock level optname*   [Scheme Procedure]
setsockopt *sock level optname value*   [Scheme Procedure]
scm_getsockopt (*sock, level, optname*)   [C Function]
scm_setsockopt (*sock, level, optname, value*)   [C Function]
> Get or set an option on socket port *sock*. `getsockopt` returns the current value.
> `setsockopt` sets a value and the return is unspecified.
>
> *level* is an integer specifying a protocol layer, either `SOL_SOCKET` for socket level
> options, or a protocol number from the `IPPROTO` constants or `getprotoent` (see
> Section 7.2.11.2 [Network Databases], page 503).

SOL_SOCKET   [Variable]
IPPROTO_IP   [Variable]
IPPROTO_TCP   [Variable]
IPPROTO_UDP   [Variable]
> *optname* is an integer specifying an option within the protocol layer.
>
> For `SOL_SOCKET` level the following *optnames* are defined (when provided by the
> system). For their meaning see Section "Socket-Level Options" in *The GNU C Library
> Reference Manual*, or `man 7 socket`.

SO_DEBUG   [Variable]
SO_REUSEADDR   [Variable]
SO_STYLE   [Variable]
SO_TYPE   [Variable]
SO_ERROR   [Variable]
SO_DONTROUTE   [Variable]
SO_BROADCAST   [Variable]
SO_SNDBUF   [Variable]
SO_RCVBUF   [Variable]
SO_KEEPALIVE   [Variable]
SO_OOBINLINE   [Variable]
SO_NO_CHECK   [Variable]
SO_PRIORITY   [Variable]
SO_REUSEPORT   [Variable]
> The *value* taken or returned is an integer.

SO_LINGER   [Variable]
> The *value* taken or returned is a pair of integers (*ENABLE . TIMEOUT*). On old
> systems without timeout support (ie. without `struct linger`), only *ENABLE*
> has an effect but the value in Guile is always a pair.

For IP level (`IPPROTO_IP`) the following *optname*s are defined (when provided by the system). See `man ip` for what they mean.

IP_MULTICAST_IF   [Variable]
> This sets the source interface used by multicast traffic.

IP_MULTICAST_TTL   [Variable]
> This sets the default TTL for multicast traffic. This defaults to 1 and should be increased to allow traffic to pass beyond the local network.

IP_ADD_MEMBERSHIP   [Variable]
IP_DROP_MEMBERSHIP   [Variable]
> These can be used only with `setsockopt`, not `getsockopt`. *value* is a pair (*MULTIADDR . INTERFACEADDR*) of integer IPv4 addresses (see Section 7.2.11.1 [Network Address Conversion], page 501). *MULTIADDR* is a multicast address to be added to or dropped from the interface *INTERFACEADDR*. *INTERFACEADDR* can be `INADDR_ANY` to have the system select the interface. *INTERFACEADDR* can also be an interface index number, on systems supporting that.

shutdown *sock how*   [Scheme Procedure]
scm_shutdown (*sock, how*)   [C Function]
> Sockets can be closed simply by using `close-port`. The `shutdown` procedure allows reception or transmission on a connection to be shut down individually, according to the parameter *how*:

0
> Stop receiving data for this socket. If further data arrives, reject it.

1
> Stop trying to transmit data from this socket. Discard any data waiting to be sent. Stop looking for acknowledgement of data already sent; don't retransmit it if it is lost.

2
> Stop both reception and transmission.

> The return value is unspecified.

connect *sock sockaddr*   [Scheme Procedure]
connect *sock AF_INET ipv4addr port*   [Scheme Procedure]
connect *sock AF_INET6 ipv6addr port* [*flowinfo* [*scopeid*]]   [Scheme Procedure]
connect *sock AF_UNIX path*   [Scheme Procedure]
scm_connect (*sock, fam, address, args*)   [C Function]
> Initiate a connection on socket port *sock* to a given address. The destination is either a socket address object, or arguments the same as `make-socket-address` would take to make such an object (see Section 7.2.11.3 [Network Socket Address], page 509). The return value is unspecified.

```
(connect sock AF_INET INADDR_LOOPBACK 23)
(connect sock (make-socket-address AF_INET INADDR_LOOPBACK 23))
```

bind *sock sockaddr*   [Scheme Procedure]
bind *sock AF_INET ipv4addr port*   [Scheme Procedure]
bind *sock AF_INET6 ipv6addr port* [*flowinfo* [*scopeid*]]   [Scheme Procedure]

`bind` *sock AF_UNIX path*   [Scheme Procedure]
`scm_bind` (*sock, fam, address, args*)   [C Function]

> Bind socket port *sock* to the given address. The address is either a socket address object, or arguments the same as `make-socket-address` would take to make such an object (see Section 7.2.11.3 [Network Socket Address], page 509). The return value is unspecified.

> Generally a socket is only explicitly bound to a particular address when making a server, i.e. to listen on a particular port. For an outgoing connection the system will assign a local address automatically, if not already bound.

> ```
> (bind sock AF_INET INADDR_ANY 12345)
> (bind sock (make-socket-address AF_INET INADDR_ANY 12345))
> ```

`listen` *sock backlog*   [Scheme Procedure]
`scm_listen` (*sock, backlog*)   [C Function]

> Enable *sock* to accept connection requests. *backlog* is an integer specifying the maximum length of the queue for pending connections. If the queue fills, new clients will fail to connect until the server calls `accept` to accept a connection from the queue.

> The return value is unspecified.

`accept` *sock*   [Scheme Procedure]
`scm_accept` (*sock*)   [C Function]

> Accept a connection from socket port *sock* which has been enabled for listening with `listen` above. If there are no incoming connections in the queue, wait until one is available (unless `O_NONBLOCK` has been set on the socket, see Section 7.2.2 [Ports and File Descriptors], page 469).

> The return value is a pair. The `car` is a new socket port, connected and ready to communicate. The `cdr` is a socket address object (see Section 7.2.11.3 [Network Socket Address], page 509) which is where the remote connection is from (like `getpeername` below).

> All communication takes place using the new socket returned. The given *sock* remains bound and listening, and `accept` may be called on it again to get another incoming connection when desired.

`getsockname` *sock*   [Scheme Procedure]
`scm_getsockname` (*sock*)   [C Function]

> Return a socket address object which is the where *sock* is bound locally. *sock* may have obtained its local address from `bind` (above), or if a `connect` is done with an otherwise unbound socket (which is usual) then the system will have assigned an address.

> Note that on many systems the address of a socket in the `AF_UNIX` namespace cannot be read.

`getpeername` *sock*   [Scheme Procedure]
`scm_getpeername` (*sock*)   [C Function]

> Return a socket address object which is where *sock* is connected to, i.e. the remote endpoint.

> Note that on many systems the address of a socket in the `AF_UNIX` namespace cannot be read.

`recv!` *sock buf* [*flags*]   [Scheme Procedure]

`scm_recv` (*sock, buf, flags*)   [C Function]

> Receive data from a socket port. *sock* must already be bound to the address from which data is to be received. *buf* is a bytevector into which the data will be written. The size of *buf* limits the amount of data which can be received: in the case of packet protocols, if a packet larger than this limit is encountered then some data will be irrevocably lost.
>
> The optional *flags* argument is a value or bitwise OR of `MSG_OOB`, `MSG_PEEK`, `MSG_DONTROUTE` etc.
>
> The value returned is the number of bytes read from the socket.
>
> Note that the data is read directly from the socket file descriptor: any unread buffered port data is ignored.

`send` *sock message* [*flags*]   [Scheme Procedure]

`scm_send` (*sock, message, flags*)   [C Function]

> Transmit bytevector *message* on socket port *sock*. *sock* must already be bound to a destination address. The value returned is the number of bytes transmitted—it's possible for this to be less than the length of *message* if the socket is set to be non-blocking. The optional *flags* argument is a value or bitwise OR of `MSG_OOB`, `MSG_PEEK`, `MSG_DONTROUTE` etc.
>
> Note that the data is written directly to the socket file descriptor: any unflushed buffered port data is ignored.

`recvfrom!` *sock buf* [*flags* [*start* [*end*]]]   [Scheme Procedure]

`scm_recvfrom` (*sock, buf, flags, start, end*)   [C Function]

> Receive data from socket port *sock*, returning the originating address as well as the data. This function is usually for datagram sockets, but can be used on stream-oriented sockets too.
>
> The data received is stored in bytevector *buf*, using either the whole bytevector or just the region between the optional *start* and *end* positions. The size of *buf* limits the amount of data that can be received. For datagram protocols if a packet larger than this is received then excess bytes are irrevocably lost.
>
> The return value is a pair. The `car` is the number of bytes read. The `cdr` is a socket address object (see Section 7.2.11.3 [Network Socket Address], page 509) which is where the data came from, or `#f` if the origin is unknown.
>
> The optional *flags* argument is a or bitwise-OR (`logior`) of `MSG_OOB`, `MSG_PEEK`, `MSG_DONTROUTE` etc.
>
> Data is read directly from the socket file descriptor, any buffered port data is ignored.
>
> On a GNU/Linux system `recvfrom!` is not multi-threading, all threads stop while a `recvfrom!` call is in progress. An application may need to use `select`, `O_NONBLOCK` or `MSG_DONTWAIT` to avoid this.

`sendto` *sock message sockaddr* [*flags*]   [Scheme Procedure]

`sendto` *sock message AF_INET ipv4addr port* [*flags*]   [Scheme Procedure]

`sendto` *sock message AF_INET6 ipv6addr port* [*flowinfo* [*scopeid*   [Scheme Procedure]
   [*flags*]]]

sendto *sock message AF_UNIX path* [*flags*]   [Scheme Procedure]
scm_sendto (*sock, message, fam, address, args_and_flags*)   [C Function]
> Transmit bytevector *message* as a datagram socket port *sock*. The destination is specified either as a socket address object, or as arguments the same as would be taken by **make-socket-address** to create such an object (see Section 7.2.11.3 [Network Socket Address], page 509).
>
> The destination address may be followed by an optional *flags* argument which is a **logior** (see Section 6.6.2.13 [Bitwise Operations], page 125) of MSG_OOB, MSG_PEEK, MSG_DONTROUTE etc.
>
> The value returned is the number of bytes transmitted – it's possible for this to be less than the length of *message* if the socket is set to be non-blocking. Note that the data is written directly to the socket file descriptor: any unflushed buffered port data is ignored.

7.2.11.5 Network Socket Examples

The following give examples of how to use network sockets.

Internet Socket Client Example

The following example demonstrates an Internet socket client. It connects to the HTTP daemon running on the local machine and returns the contents of the root index URL.

```
(let ((s (socket PF_INET SOCK_STREAM 0)))
  (connect s AF_INET (inet-pton AF_INET "127.0.0.1") 80)
  (display "GET / HTTP/1.0\r\n\r\n" s)

  (do ((line (read-line s) (read-line s)))
      ((eof-object? line))
    (display line)
    (newline)))
```

Internet Socket Server Example

The following example shows a simple Internet server which listens on port 2904 for incoming connections and sends a greeting back to the client.

```
(let ((s (socket PF_INET SOCK_STREAM 0)))
  (setsockopt s SOL_SOCKET SO_REUSEADDR 1)
  ;; Specific address?
  ;; (bind s AF_INET (inet-pton AF_INET "127.0.0.1") 2904)
  (bind s AF_INET INADDR_ANY 2904)
  (listen s 5)

  (simple-format #t "Listening for clients in pid: ~S" (getpid))
  (newline)

  (while #t
    (let* ((client-connection (accept s))
           (client-details (cdr client-connection))
           (client (car client-connection)))
```

```
(simple-format #t "Got new client connection: ~S"
               client-details)
(newline)
(simple-format #t "Client address: ~S"
               (gethostbyaddr
                (sockaddr:addr client-details)))
(newline)
;; Send back the greeting to the client port
(display "Hello client\r\n" client)
(close client))))
```

7.2.12 System Identification

This section lists the various procedures Guile provides for accessing information about the system it runs on.

uname   [Scheme Procedure]
scm_uname ()   [C Function]
> Return an object with some information about the computer system the program is running on.

> The following procedures accept an object as returned by uname and return a selected component (all of which are strings).

> utsname:sysname *un*   [Scheme Procedure]
> > The name of the operating system.

> utsname:nodename *un*   [Scheme Procedure]
> > The network name of the computer.

> utsname:release *un*   [Scheme Procedure]
> > The current release level of the operating system implementation.

> utsname:version *un*   [Scheme Procedure]
> > The current version level within the release of the operating system.

> utsname:machine *un*   [Scheme Procedure]
> > A description of the hardware.

gethostname   [Scheme Procedure]
scm_gethostname ()   [C Function]
> Return the host name of the current processor.

sethostname *name*   [Scheme Procedure]
scm_sethostname (*name*)   [C Function]
> Set the host name of the current processor to *name*. May only be used by the superuser. The return value is not specified.

7.2.13 Locales

`setlocale` *category* [*locale*]   [Scheme Procedure]
`scm_setlocale` (*category, locale*)   [C Function]

Get or set the current locale, used for various internationalizations. Locales are strings, such as 'sv_SE'.

If *locale* is given then the locale for the given *category* is set and the new value returned. If *locale* is not given then the current value is returned. *category* should be one of the following values (see Section "Locale Categories" in *The GNU C Library Reference Manual*):

`LC_ALL`	[Variable]
`LC_COLLATE`	[Variable]
`LC_CTYPE`	[Variable]
`LC_MESSAGES`	[Variable]
`LC_MONETARY`	[Variable]
`LC_NUMERIC`	[Variable]
`LC_TIME`	[Variable]

A common usage is '(setlocale LC_ALL "")', which initializes all categories based on standard environment variables (`LANG` etc). For full details on categories and locale names see Section "Locales and Internationalization" in *The GNU C Library Reference Manual*.

Note that `setlocale` affects locale settings for the whole process. See Section 6.24.1 [i18n Introduction], page 436, for a thread-safe alternative.

7.2.14 Encryption

Please note that the procedures in this section are not suited for strong encryption, they are only interfaces to the well-known and common system library functions of the same name. They are just as good (or bad) as the underlying functions, so you should refer to your system documentation before using them (see Section "Encrypting Passwords" in *The GNU C Library Reference Manual*).

`crypt` *key salt*   [Scheme Procedure]
`scm_crypt` (*key, salt*)   [C Function]

Encrypt *key*, with the addition of *salt* (both strings), using the `crypt` C library call.

Although `getpass` is not an encryption procedure per se, it appears here because it is often used in combination with `crypt`:

`getpass` *prompt*   [Scheme Procedure]
`scm_getpass` (*prompt*)   [C Function]

Display *prompt* to the standard error output and read a password from `/dev/tty`. If this file is not accessible, it reads from standard input. The password may be up to 127 characters in length. Additional characters and the terminating newline character are discarded. While reading the password, echoing and the generation of signals by special characters is disabled.

7.3 HTTP, the Web, and All That

It has always been possible to connect computers together and share information between them, but the rise of the World Wide Web over the last couple of decades has made it much easier to do so. The result is a richly connected network of computation, in which Guile forms a part.

By "the web", we mean the HTTP protocol[2] as handled by servers, clients, proxies, caches, and the various kinds of messages and message components that can be sent and received by that protocol, notably HTML.

On one level, the web is text in motion: the protocols themselves are textual (though the payload may be binary), and it's possible to create a socket and speak text to the web. But such an approach is obviously primitive. This section details the higher-level data types and operations provided by Guile: URIs, HTTP request and response records, and a conventional web server implementation.

The material in this section is arranged in ascending order, in which later concepts build on previous ones. If you prefer to start with the highest-level perspective, see Section 7.3.10 [Web Examples], page 542, and work your way back.

7.3.1 Types and the Web

It is a truth universally acknowledged, that a program with good use of data types, will be free from many common bugs. Unfortunately, the common practice in web programming seems to ignore this maxim. This subsection makes the case for expressive data types in web programming.

By "expressive data types", we mean that the data types *say* something about how a program solves a problem. For example, if we choose to represent dates using SRFI 19 date records (see Section 7.5.16 [SRFI-19], page 583), this indicates that there is a part of the program that will always have valid dates. Error handling for a number of basic cases, like invalid dates, occurs on the boundary in which we produce a SRFI 19 date record from other types, like strings.

With regards to the web, data types are helpful in the two broad phases of HTTP messages: parsing and generation.

Consider a server, which has to parse a request, and produce a response. Guile will parse the request into an HTTP request object (see Section 7.3.6 [Requests], page 534), with each header parsed into an appropriate Scheme data type. This transition from an incoming stream of characters to typed data is a state change in a program—the strings might parse, or they might not, and something has to happen if they do not. (Guile throws an error in this case.) But after you have the parsed request, "client" code (code built on top of the Guile web framework) will not have to check for syntactic validity. The types already make this information manifest.

This state change on the parsing boundary makes programs more robust, as they themselves are freed from the need to do a number of common error checks, and they can use normal Scheme procedures to handle a request instead of ad-hoc string parsers.

---

[2] Yes, the P is for protocol, but this phrase appears repeatedly in RFC 2616.

The need for types on the response generation side (in a server) is more subtle, though not less important. Consider the example of a POST handler, which prints out the text that a user submits from a form. Such a handler might include a procedure like this:

```
;; First, a helper procedure
(define (para . contents)
  (string-append "<p>" (string-concatenate contents) "</p>"))

;; Now the meat of our simple web application
(define (you-said text)
  (para "You said: " text))

(display (you-said "Hi!"))
⊣ <p>You said: Hi!</p>
```

This is a perfectly valid implementation, provided that the incoming text does not contain the special HTML characters '<', '>', or '&'. But this provision of a restricted character set is not reflected anywhere in the program itself: we must *assume* that the programmer understands this, and performs the check elsewhere.

Unfortunately, the short history of the practice of programming does not bear out this assumption. A *cross-site scripting* (XSS) vulnerability is just such a common error in which unfiltered user input is allowed into the output. A user could submit a crafted comment to your web site which results in visitors running malicious Javascript, within the security context of your domain:

```
(display (you-said "<script src=\"http://bad.com/nasty.js\" />"))
⊣ <p>You said: <script src="http://bad.com/nasty.js" /></p>
```

The fundamental problem here is that both user data and the program template are represented using strings. This identity means that types can't help the programmer to make a distinction between these two, so they get confused.

There are a number of possible solutions, but perhaps the best is to treat HTML not as strings, but as native s-expressions: as SXML. The basic idea is that HTML is either text, represented by a string, or an element, represented as a tagged list. So 'foo' becomes '"foo"', and 'foo' becomes '(b "foo")'. Attributes, if present, go in a tagged list headed by '@', like '(img (@ (src "http://example.com/foo.png")))'. See Section 7.22 [SXML], page 697, for more information.

The good thing about SXML is that HTML elements cannot be confused with text. Let's make a new definition of para:

```
(define (para . contents)
  '(p ,@contents))

(use-modules (sxml simple))
(sxml->xml (you-said "Hi!"))
⊣ <p>You said: Hi!</p>

(sxml->xml (you-said "<i>Rats, foiled again!</i>"))
⊣ <p>You said: &lt;i&gt;Rats, foiled again!&lt;/i&gt;</p>
```

So we see in the second example that HTML elements cannot be unwittingly introduced into the output. However it is now perfectly acceptable to pass SXML to `you-said`; in fact, that is the big advantage of SXML over everything-as-a-string.

```
(sxml->xml (you-said (you-said "<Hi!>")))
⊣ <p>You said: <p>You said: &lt;Hi!&gt;</p></p>
```

The SXML types allow procedures to *compose*. The types make manifest which parts are HTML elements, and which are text. So you needn't worry about escaping user input; the type transition back to a string handles that for you. XSS vulnerabilities are a thing of the past.

Well. That's all very nice and opinionated and such, but how do I use the thing? Read on!

7.3.2 Universal Resource Identifiers

Guile provides a standard data type for Universal Resource Identifiers (URIs), as defined in RFC 3986.

The generic URI syntax is as follows:

```
URI := scheme ":" ["//" [userinfo "@"] host [":" port]] path \
       [ "?" query ] [ "#" fragment ]
```

For example, in the URI, 'http://www.gnu.org/help/', the scheme is `http`, the host is `www.gnu.org`, the path is `/help/`, and there is no userinfo, port, query, or fragment. All URIs have a scheme and a path (though the path might be empty). Some URIs have a host, and some of those have ports and userinfo. Any URI might have a query part or a fragment.

Userinfo is something of an abstraction, as some legacy URI schemes allowed userinfo of the form *username:passwd*. But since passwords do not belong in URIs, the RFC does not want to condone this practice, so it calls anything before the @ sign *userinfo*.

Properly speaking, a fragment is not part of a URI. For example, when a web browser follows a link to 'http://example.com/#foo', it sends a request for 'http://example.com/', then looks in the resulting page for the fragment identified `foo` reference. A fragment identifies a part of a resource, not the resource itself. But it is useful to have a fragment field in the URI record itself, so we hope you will forgive the inconsistency.

```
(use-modules (web uri))
```

The following procedures can be found in the (`web uri`) module. Load it into your Guile, using a form like the above, to have access to them.

`build-uri` *scheme* [*#:userinfo=#f*] [*#:host=#f*] [*#:port=#f*]   [Scheme Procedure]
      [*#:path=""*] [*#:query=#f*] [*#:fragment=#f*] [*#:validate?=#t*]
      Construct a URI object. *scheme* should be a symbol, *port* either a positive, exact integer or #f, and the rest of the fields are either strings or #f. If *validate?* is true, also run some consistency checks to make sure that the constructed URI is valid.

`uri?` *obj*   [Scheme Procedure]
`uri-scheme` *uri*   [Scheme Procedure]
`uri-userinfo` *uri*   [Scheme Procedure]
`uri-host` *uri*   [Scheme Procedure]

`uri-port` *uri*   [Scheme Procedure]

`uri-path` *uri*   [Scheme Procedure]

`uri-query` *uri*   [Scheme Procedure]

`uri-fragment` *uri*   [Scheme Procedure]

> A predicate and field accessors for the URI record type. The URI scheme will be a symbol, the port either a positive, exact integer or `#f`, and the rest either strings or `#f` if not present.

`string->uri` *string*   [Scheme Procedure]

> Parse *string* into a URI object. Return `#f` if the string could not be parsed.

`uri->string` *uri*   [Scheme Procedure]

> Serialize *uri* to a string. If the URI has a port that is the default port for its scheme, the port is not included in the serialization.

`declare-default-port!` *scheme port*   [Scheme Procedure]

> Declare a default port for the given URI scheme.

`uri-decode` *str* [*#:encoding*=`"utf-8"`]   [Scheme Procedure]

> Percent-decode the given *str*, according to *encoding*, which should be the name of a character encoding.

> Note that this function should not generally be applied to a full URI string. For paths, use `split-and-decode-uri-path` instead. For query strings, split the query on `&` and `=` boundaries, and decode the components separately.

> Note also that percent-encoded strings encode *bytes*, not characters. There is no guarantee that a given byte sequence is a valid string encoding. Therefore this routine may signal an error if the decoded bytes are not valid for the given encoding. Pass `#f` for *encoding* if you want decoded bytes as a bytevector directly. See Section 6.14.1 [Ports], page 316, for more information on character encodings.

> Returns a string of the decoded characters, or a bytevector if *encoding* was `#f`.

Fixme: clarify return type. indicate default values. type of unescaped-chars.

`uri-encode` *str* [*#:encoding*=`"utf-8"`] [*#:unescaped-chars*]   [Scheme Procedure]

> Percent-encode any character not in the character set, *unescaped-chars*.

> The default character set includes alphanumerics from ASCII, as well as the special characters '-', '.', '_', and '~'. Any other character will be percent-encoded, by writing out the character to a bytevector within the given *encoding*, then encoding each byte as %*HH*, where *HH* is the hexadecimal representation of the byte.

`split-and-decode-uri-path` *path*   [Scheme Procedure]

> Split *path* into its components, and decode each component, removing empty components.

> For example, `"/foo/bar%20baz/"` decodes to the two-element list, (`"foo"` `"bar baz"`).

`encode-and-join-uri-path` *parts*   [Scheme Procedure]

> URI-encode each element of *parts*, which should be a list of strings, and join the parts together with / as a delimiter.

For example, the list ("scrambled eggs" "biscuits&gravy") encodes as
"scrambled%20eggs/biscuits%26gravy".

7.3.3 The Hyper-Text Transfer Protocol

The initial motivation for including web functionality in Guile, rather than rely on an external package, was to establish a standard base on which people can share code. To that end, we continue the focus on data types by providing a number of low-level parsers and unparsers for elements of the HTTP protocol.

If you are want to skip the low-level details for now and move on to web pages, see Section 7.3.8 [Web Client], page 538, and see Section 7.3.9 [Web Server], page 540. Otherwise, load the HTTP module, and read on.

```
(use-modules (web http))
```

The focus of the (web http) module is to parse and unparse standard HTTP headers, representing them to Guile as native data structures. For example, a Date: header will be represented as a SRFI-19 date record (see Section 7.5.16 [SRFI-19], page 583), rather than as a string.

Guile tries to follow RFCs fairly strictly—the road to perdition being paved with compatibility hacks—though some allowances are made for not-too-divergent texts.

Header names are represented as lower-case symbols.

string->header *name*   [Scheme Procedure]
> Parse *name* to a symbolic header name.

header->string *sym*   [Scheme Procedure]
> Return the string form for the header named *sym*.

> For example:
> ```
> (string->header "Content-Length")
> ⇒ content-length
> (header->string 'content-length)
> ⇒ "Content-Length"
>
> (string->header "FOO")
> ⇒ foo
> (header->string 'foo)
> ⇒ "Foo"
> ```

Guile keeps a registry of known headers, their string names, and some parsing and serialization procedures. If a header is unknown, its string name is simply its symbol name in title-case.

known-header? *sym*   [Scheme Procedure]
> Return #t if *sym* is a known header, with associated parsers and serialization procedures, or #f otherwise.

header-parser *sym*   [Scheme Procedure]
> Return the value parser for headers named *sym*. The result is a procedure that takes one argument, a string, and returns the parsed value. If the header isn't known to Guile, a default parser is returned that passes through the string unchanged.

header-validator *sym*   [Scheme Procedure]

Return a predicate which returns #t if the given value is valid for headers named *sym*.
The default validator for unknown headers is string?.

header-writer *sym*   [Scheme Procedure]

Return a procedure that writes values for headers named *sym* to a port. The resulting
procedure takes two arguments: a value and a port. The default writer is display.

For more on the set of headers that Guile knows about out of the box, see Section 7.3.4
[HTTP Headers], page 525. To add your own, use the declare-header! procedure:

declare-header! *name parser validator writer*   [Scheme Procedure]
    [*#:multiple?=#f*]
Declare a parser, validator, and writer for a given header.

For example, let's say you are running a web server behind some sort of proxy, and your
proxy adds an X-Client-Address header, indicating the IPv4 address of the original client.
You would like for the HTTP request record to parse out this header to a Scheme value,
instead of leaving it as a string. You could register this header with Guile's HTTP stack
like this:

```
(declare-header! "X-Client-Address"
  (lambda (str)
    (inet-aton str))
  (lambda (ip)
    (and (integer? ip) (exact? ip) (<= 0 ip #xffffffff)))
  (lambda (ip port)
    (display (inet-ntoa ip) port)))
```

declare-opaque-header! *name*   [Scheme Procedure]

A specialised version of declare-header! for the case in which you want a header's
value to be returned/written "as-is".

valid-header? *sym val*   [Scheme Procedure]

Return a true value if *val* is a valid Scheme value for the header with name *sym*, or
#f otherwise.

Now that we have a generic interface for reading and writing headers, we do just that.

read-header *port*   [Scheme Procedure]

Read one HTTP header from *port*. Return two values: the header name and the
parsed Scheme value. May raise an exception if the header was known but the value
was invalid.

Returns the end-of-file object for both values if the end of the message body was
reached (i.e., a blank line).

parse-header *name val*   [Scheme Procedure]

Parse *val*, a string, with the parser for the header named *name*. Returns the parsed
value.

write-header *name val port*   [Scheme Procedure]
> Write the given header name and value to *port*, using the writer from **header-writer**.

read-headers *port*   [Scheme Procedure]
> Read the headers of an HTTP message from *port*, returning them as an ordered alist.

write-headers *headers port*   [Scheme Procedure]
> Write the given header alist to *port*. Doesn't write the final '\r\n', as the user might want to add another header.

The (**web http**) module also has some utility procedures to read and write request and response lines.

parse-http-method *str [start] [end]*   [Scheme Procedure]
> Parse an HTTP method from *str*. The result is an upper-case symbol, like **GET**.

parse-http-version *str [start] [end]*   [Scheme Procedure]
> Parse an HTTP version from *str*, returning it as a major–minor pair. For example, **HTTP/1.1** parses as the pair of integers, (1 . 1).

parse-request-uri *str [start] [end]*   [Scheme Procedure]
> Parse a URI from an HTTP request line. Note that URIs in requests do not have to have a scheme or host name. The result is a URI object.

read-request-line *port*   [Scheme Procedure]
> Read the first line of an HTTP request from *port*, returning three values: the method, the URI, and the version.

write-request-line *method uri version port*   [Scheme Procedure]
> Write the first line of an HTTP request to *port*.

read-response-line *port*   [Scheme Procedure]
> Read the first line of an HTTP response from *port*, returning three values: the HTTP version, the response code, and the "reason phrase".

write-response-line *version code reason-phrase port*   [Scheme Procedure]
> Write the first line of an HTTP response to *port*.

7.3.4 HTTP Headers

In addition to defining the infrastructure to parse headers, the (**web http**) module defines specific parsers and unparsers for all headers defined in the HTTP/1.1 standard.

For example, if you receive a header named 'Accept-Language' with a value 'en, es;q=0.8', Guile parses it as a quality list (defined below):

```
(parse-header 'accept-language "en, es;q=0.8")
⇒ ((1000 . "en") (800 . "es"))
```

The format of the value for 'Accept-Language' headers is defined below, along with all other headers defined in the HTTP standard. (If the header were unknown, the value would have been returned as a string.)

For brevity, the header definitions below are given in the form, *Type* **name**, indicating that values for the header **name** will be of the given *Type*. Since Guile internally treats header names in lower case, in this document we give types title-cased names. A short description of the each header's purpose and an example follow.

For full details on the meanings of all of these headers, see the HTTP 1.1 standard, RFC 2616.

7.3.4.1 HTTP Header Types

Here we define the types that are used below, when defining headers.

Date   [HTTP Header Type]
> A SRFI-19 date.

KVList   [HTTP Header Type]
> A list whose elements are keys or key-value pairs. Keys are parsed to symbols. Values are strings by default. Non-string values are the exception, and are mentioned explicitly below, as appropriate.

SList   [HTTP Header Type]
> A list of strings.

Quality   [HTTP Header Type]
> An exact integer between 0 and 1000. Qualities are used to express preference, given multiple options. An option with a quality of 870, for example, is preferred over an option with quality 500.
>
> (Qualities are written out over the wire as numbers between 0.0 and 1.0, but since the standard only allows three digits after the decimal, it's equivalent to integers between 0 and 1000, so that's what Guile uses.)

QList   [HTTP Header Type]
> A quality list: a list of pairs, the car of which is a quality, and the cdr a string. Used to express a list of options, along with their qualities.

ETag   [HTTP Header Type]
> An entity tag, represented as a pair. The car of the pair is an opaque string, and the cdr is #t if the entity tag is a "strong" entity tag, and #f otherwise.

7.3.4.2 General Headers

General HTTP headers may be present in any HTTP message.

KVList cache-control   [HTTP Header]
> A key-value list of cache-control directives. See RFC 2616, for more details.
>
> If present, parameters to max-age, max-stale, min-fresh, and s-maxage are all parsed as non-negative integers.
>
> If present, parameters to private and no-cache are parsed as lists of header names, as symbols.
>
> ```
> (parse-header 'cache-control "no-cache,no-store"
> ⇒ (no-cache no-store)
> (parse-header 'cache-control "no-cache=\"Authorization,Date\",no-store"
> ⇒ ((no-cache . (authorization date)) no-store)
> (parse-header 'cache-control "no-cache=\"Authorization,Date\",max-age=10"
> ⇒ ((no-cache . (authorization date)) (max-age . 10))
> ```

List connection   [HTTP Header]

> A list of header names that apply only to this HTTP connection, as symbols. Additionally, the symbol 'close' may be present, to indicate that the server should close the connection after responding to the request.
>
> ```
> (parse-header 'connection "close")
> ⇒ (close)
> ```

Date date   [HTTP Header]

> The date that a given HTTP message was originated.
>
> ```
> (parse-header 'date "Tue, 15 Nov 1994 08:12:31 GMT")
> ⇒ #<date ...>
> ```

KVList pragma   [HTTP Header]

> A key-value list of implementation-specific directives.
>
> ```
> (parse-header 'pragma "no-cache, broccoli=tasty")
> ⇒ (no-cache (broccoli . "tasty"))
> ```

List trailer   [HTTP Header]

> A list of header names which will appear after the message body, instead of with the message headers.
>
> ```
> (parse-header 'trailer "ETag")
> ⇒ (etag)
> ```

List transfer-encoding   [HTTP Header]

> A list of transfer codings, expressed as key-value lists. The only transfer coding defined by the specification is chunked.
>
> ```
> (parse-header 'transfer-encoding "chunked")
> ⇒ ((chunked))
> ```

List upgrade   [HTTP Header]

> A list of strings, indicating additional protocols that a server could use in response to a request.
>
> ```
> (parse-header 'upgrade "WebSocket")
> ⇒ ("WebSocket")
> ```

FIXME: parse out more fully?

List via   [HTTP Header]

> A list of strings, indicating the protocol versions and hosts of intermediate servers and proxies. There may be multiple via headers in one message.
>
> ```
> (parse-header 'via "1.0 venus, 1.1 mars")
> ⇒ ("1.0 venus" "1.1 mars")
> ```

List warning   [HTTP Header]

> A list of warnings given by a server or intermediate proxy. Each warning is a itself a list of four elements: a code, as an exact integer between 0 and 1000, a host as a string, the warning text as a string, and either #f or a SRFI-19 date.
>
> There may be multiple warning headers in one message.

```
(parse-header 'warning "123 foo \"core breach imminent\"")
⇒ ((123 "foo" "core-breach imminent" #f))
```

7.3.4.3 Entity Headers

Entity headers may be present in any HTTP message, and refer to the resource referenced
in the HTTP request or response.

List allow   [HTTP Header]
> A list of allowed methods on a given resource, as symbols.
>
> ```
> (parse-header 'allow "GET, HEAD")
> ⇒ (GET HEAD)
> ```

List content-encoding   [HTTP Header]
> A list of content codings, as symbols.
>
> ```
> (parse-header 'content-encoding "gzip")
> ⇒ (gzip)
> ```

List content-language   [HTTP Header]
> The languages that a resource is in, as strings.
>
> ```
> (parse-header 'content-language "en")
> ⇒ ("en")
> ```

UInt content-length   [HTTP Header]
> The number of bytes in a resource, as an exact, non-negative integer.
>
> ```
> (parse-header 'content-length "300")
> ⇒ 300
> ```

URI content-location   [HTTP Header]
> The canonical URI for a resource, in the case that it is also accessible from a different
> URI.
>
> ```
> (parse-header 'content-location "http://example.com/foo")
> ⇒ #<<uri> ...>
> ```

String content-md5   [HTTP Header]
> The MD5 digest of a resource.
>
> ```
> (parse-header 'content-md5 "ffaea1a79810785575e29e2bd45e2fa5")
> ⇒ "ffaea1a79810785575e29e2bd45e2fa5"
> ```

List content-range   [HTTP Header]
> A range specification, as a list of three elements: the symbol bytes, either the symbol
> * or a pair of integers, indicating the byte rage, and either * or an integer, for the
> instance length. Used to indicate that a response only includes part of a resource.
>
> ```
> (parse-header 'content-range "bytes 10-20/*")
> ⇒ (bytes (10 . 20) *)
> ```

List content-type   [HTTP Header]
> The MIME type of a resource, as a symbol, along with any parameters.

```
(parse-header 'content-length "text/plain")
⇒ (text/plain)
(parse-header 'content-length "text/plain;charset=utf-8")
⇒ (text/plain (charset . "utf-8"))
```

Note that the **charset** parameter is something is a misnomer, and the HTTP specification admits this. It specifies the *encoding* of the characters, not the character set.

Date expires   [HTTP Header]

The date/time after which the resource given in a response is considered stale.

```
(parse-header 'expires "Tue, 15 Nov 1994 08:12:31 GMT")
⇒ #<date ...>
```

Date last-modified   [HTTP Header]

The date/time on which the resource given in a response was last modified.

```
(parse-header 'expires "Tue, 15 Nov 1994 08:12:31 GMT")
⇒ #<date ...>
```

7.3.4.4 Request Headers

Request headers may only appear in an HTTP request, not in a response.

List accept   [HTTP Header]

A list of preferred media types for a response. Each element of the list is itself a list, in the same format as **content-type**.

```
(parse-header 'accept "text/html,text/plain;charset=utf-8")
⇒ ((text/html) (text/plain (charset . "utf-8")))
```

Preference is expressed with quality values:

```
(parse-header 'accept "text/html;q=0.8,text/plain;q=0.6")
⇒ ((text/html (q . 800)) (text/plain (q . 600)))
```

QList accept-charset   [HTTP Header]

A quality list of acceptable charsets. Note again that what HTTP calls a "charset" is what Guile calls a "character encoding".

```
(parse-header 'accept-charset "iso-8859-5, unicode-1-1;q=0.8")
⇒ ((1000 . "iso-8859-5") (800 . "unicode-1-1"))
```

QList accept-encoding   [HTTP Header]

A quality list of acceptable content codings.

```
(parse-header 'accept-encoding "gzip,identity=0.8")
⇒ ((1000 . "gzip") (800 . "identity"))
```

QList accept-language   [HTTP Header]

A quality list of acceptable languages.

```
(parse-header 'accept-language "cn,en=0.75")
⇒ ((1000 . "cn") (750 . "en"))
```

Pair authorization   [HTTP Header]

> Authorization credentials. The car of the pair indicates the authentication scheme, like `basic`. For basic authentication, the cdr of the pair will be the base64-encoded '*user*:*pass*' string. For other authentication schemes, like `digest`, the cdr will be a key-value list of credentials.
>
> ```
> (parse-header 'authorization "Basic QWxhZGRpbjpvcGVuIHNlc2FtZQ=="
> ⇒ (basic . "QWxhZGRpbjpvcGVuIHNlc2FtZQ==")
> ```

List expect   [HTTP Header]

> A list of expectations that a client has of a server. The expectations are key-value lists.
>
> ```
> (parse-header 'expect "100-continue")
> ⇒ ((100-continue))
> ```

String from   [HTTP Header]

> The email address of a user making an HTTP request.
>
> ```
> (parse-header 'from "bob@example.com")
> ⇒ "bob@example.com"
> ```

Pair host   [HTTP Header]

> The host for the resource being requested, as a hostname-port pair. If no port is given, the port is `#f`.
>
> ```
> (parse-header 'host "gnu.org:80")
> ⇒ ("gnu.org" . 80)
> (parse-header 'host "gnu.org")
> ⇒ ("gnu.org" . #f)
> ```

*|List if-match   [HTTP Header]

> A set of etags, indicating that the request should proceed if and only if the etag of the resource is in that set. Either the symbol *, indicating any etag, or a list of entity tags.
>
> ```
> (parse-header 'if-match "*")
> ⇒ *
> (parse-header 'if-match "asdfadf")
> ⇒ (("asdfadf" . #t))
> (parse-header 'if-match W/"asdfadf")
> ⇒ (("asdfadf" . #f))
> ```

Date if-modified-since   [HTTP Header]

> Indicates that a response should proceed if and only if the resource has been modified since the given date.
>
> ```
> (parse-header 'if-modified-since "Tue, 15 Nov 1994 08:12:31 GMT")
> ⇒ #<date ...>
> ```

*|List if-none-match   [HTTP Header]

> A set of etags, indicating that the request should proceed if and only if the etag of the resource is not in the set. Either the symbol *, indicating any etag, or a list of entity tags.

```
(parse-header 'if-none-match "*")
⇒ *
```

ETag|Date if-range   [HTTP Header]

Indicates that the range request should proceed if and only if the resource matches a modification date or an etag. Either an entity tag, or a SRFI-19 date.

```
(parse-header 'if-range "\"original-etag\"")
⇒ ("original-etag" . #t)
```

Date if-unmodified-since   [HTTP Header]

Indicates that a response should proceed if and only if the resource has not been modified since the given date.

```
(parse-header 'if-not-modified-since "Tue, 15 Nov 1994 08:12:31 GMT")
⇒ #<date ...>
```

UInt max-forwards   [HTTP Header]

The maximum number of proxy or gateway hops that a request should be subject to.

```
(parse-header 'max-forwards "10")
⇒ 10
```

Pair proxy-authorization   [HTTP Header]

Authorization credentials for a proxy connection. See the documentation for authorization above for more information on the format.

```
(parse-header 'proxy-authorization "Digest foo=bar,baz=qux"
⇒ (digest (foo . "bar") (baz . "qux"))
```

Pair range   [HTTP Header]

A range request, indicating that the client wants only part of a resource. The car of the pair is the symbol bytes, and the cdr is a list of pairs. Each element of the cdr indicates a range; the car is the first byte position and the cdr is the last byte position, as integers, or #f if not given.

```
(parse-header 'range "bytes=10-30,50-")
⇒ (bytes (10 . 30) (50 . #f))
```

URI referer   [HTTP Header]

The URI of the resource that referred the user to this resource. The name of the header is a misspelling, but we are stuck with it.

```
(parse-header 'referer "http://www.gnu.org/")
⇒ #<uri ...>
```

List te   [HTTP Header]

A list of transfer codings, expressed as key-value lists. A common transfer coding is trailers.

```
(parse-header 'te "trailers")
⇒ ((trailers))
```

String user-agent   [HTTP Header]

> A string indicating the user agent making the request. The specification defines a structured format for this header, but it is widely disregarded, so Guile does not attempt to parse strictly.
>
> ```
> (parse-header 'user-agent "Mozilla/5.0")
> ⇒ "Mozilla/5.0"
> ```

7.3.4.5 Response Headers

List accept-ranges   [HTTP Header]

> A list of range units that the server supports, as symbols.
>
> ```
> (parse-header 'accept-ranges "bytes")
> ⇒ (bytes)
> ```

UInt age   [HTTP Header]

> The age of a cached response, in seconds.
>
> ```
> (parse-header 'age "3600")
> ⇒ 3600
> ```

ETag etag   [HTTP Header]

> The entity-tag of the resource.
>
> ```
> (parse-header 'etag "\"foo\"")
> ⇒ ("foo" . #t)
> ```

URI location   [HTTP Header]

> A URI on which a request may be completed. Used in combination with a redirecting status code to perform client-side redirection.
>
> ```
> (parse-header 'location "http://example.com/other")
> ⇒ #<uri ...>
> ```

List proxy-authenticate   [HTTP Header]

> A list of challenges to a proxy, indicating the need for authentication.
>
> ```
> (parse-header 'proxy-authenticate "Basic realm=\"foo\"")
> ⇒ ((basic (realm . "foo")))
> ```

UInt|Date retry-after   [HTTP Header]

> Used in combination with a server-busy status code, like 503, to indicate that a client should retry later. Either a number of seconds, or a date.
>
> ```
> (parse-header 'retry-after "60")
> ⇒ 60
> ```

String server   [HTTP Header]

> A string identifying the server.
>
> ```
> (parse-header 'server "My first web server")
> ⇒ "My first web server"
> ```

*|List vary												[HTTP Header]
>	A set of request headers that were used in computing this response. Used to indicate
>	that server-side content negotiation was performed, for example in response to the
>	accept-language header. Can also be the symbol *, indicating that all headers were
>	considered.
>
>	```
>	(parse-header 'vary "Accept-Language, Accept")
>	⇒ (accept-language accept)
>	```

List www-authenticate											[HTTP Header]
>	A list of challenges to a user, indicating the need for authentication.
>
>	```
>	(parse-header 'www-authenticate "Basic realm=\"foo\"")
>	⇒ ((basic (realm . "foo")))
>	```

7.3.5 Transfer Codings

HTTP 1.1 allows for various transfer codings to be applied to message bodies. These
include various types of compression, and HTTP chunked encoding. Currently, only chunked
encoding is supported by guile.

Chunked coding is an optional coding that may be applied to message bodies, to allow
messages whose length is not known beforehand to be returned. Such messages can be split
into chunks, terminated by a final zero length chunk.

In order to make dealing with encodings more simple, guile provides procedures to create
ports that "wrap" existing ports, applying transformations transparently under the hood.

These procedures are in the (web http) module.

```
(use-modules (web http))
```

make-chunked-input-port *port* [#:keep-alive?=#f]					[Scheme Procedure]
>	Returns a new port, that transparently reads and decodes chunk-encoded data from
>	*port*. If no more chunk-encoded data is available, it returns the end-of-file object.
>	When the port is closed, *port* will also be closed, unless *keep-alive?* is true.
>
>	```
>	(use-modules (ice-9 rdelim))
>
>	(define s "5\r\nFirst\r\nA\r\n line\n Sec\r\n8\r\nond line\r\n0\r\n")
>	(define p (make-chunked-input-port (open-input-string s)))
>	(read-line s)
>	⇒ "First line"
>	(read-line s)
>	⇒ "Second line"
>	```

make-chunked-output-port *port* [#:keep-alive?=#f]					[Scheme Procedure]
>	Returns a new port, which transparently encodes data as chunk-encoded before writ-
>	ing it to *port*. Whenever a write occurs on this port, it buffers it, until the port is
>	flushed, at which point it writes a chunk containing all the data written so far. When
>	the port is closed, the data remaining is written to *port*, as is the terminating zero
>	chunk. It also causes *port* to be closed, unless *keep-alive?* is true.
>
>	Note. Forcing a chunked output port when there is no data is buffered does not write
>	a zero chunk, as this would cause the data to be interpreted incorrectly by the client.

```
(call-with-output-string
  (lambda (out)
    (define out* (make-chunked-output-port out #:keep-alive? #t))
    (display "first chunk" out*)
    (force-output out*)
    (force-output out*) ; note this does not write a zero chunk
    (display "second chunk" out*)
    (close-port out*)))
⇒ "b\r\nfirst chunk\r\nc\r\nsecond chunk\r\n0\r\n"
```

7.3.6 HTTP Requests

```
(use-modules (web request))
```

The request module contains a data type for HTTP requests.

7.3.6.1 An Important Note on Character Sets

HTTP requests consist of two parts: the request proper, consisting of a request line and a set of headers, and (optionally) a body. The body might have a binary content-type, and even in the textual case its length is specified in bytes, not characters.

Therefore, HTTP is a fundamentally binary protocol. However the request line and headers are specified to be in a subset of ASCII, so they can be treated as text, provided that the port's encoding is set to an ASCII-compatible one-byte-per-character encoding. ISO-8859-1 (latin-1) is just such an encoding, and happens to be very efficient for Guile.

So what Guile does when reading requests from the wire, or writing them out, is to set the port's encoding to latin-1, and treating the request headers as text.

The request body is another issue. For binary data, the data is probably in a bytevector, so we use the R6RS binary output procedures to write out the binary payload. Textual data usually has to be written out to some character encoding, usually UTF-8, and then the resulting bytevector is written out to the port.

In summary, Guile reads and writes HTTP over latin-1 sockets, without any loss of generality.

7.3.6.2 Request API

request? *obj*   [Scheme Procedure]
request-method *request*   [Scheme Procedure]
request-uri *request*   [Scheme Procedure]
request-version *request*   [Scheme Procedure]
request-headers *request*   [Scheme Procedure]
request-meta *request*   [Scheme Procedure]
request-port *request*   [Scheme Procedure]

A predicate and field accessors for the request type. The fields are as follows:

method   The HTTP method, for example, GET.

uri   The URI as a URI record.

version   The HTTP version pair, like (1 . 1).

headers   The request headers, as an alist of parsed values.

meta   An arbitrary alist of other data, for example information returned in
           the sockaddr from accept (see Section 7.2.11.4 [Network Sockets and
           Communication], page 511).

port   The port on which to read or write a request body, if any.

read-request *port* [*meta=’()*]   [Scheme Procedure]
    Read an HTTP request from *port*, optionally attaching the given metadata, *meta*.

    As a side effect, sets the encoding on *port* to ISO-8859-1 (latin-1), so that reading
    one character reads one byte. See the discussion of character sets above, for more
    information.

    Note that the body is not part of the request. Once you have read a request, you
    may read the body separately, and likewise for writing requests.

build-request *uri* [*#:method=’GET*] [*#:version=’(1 . 1)*]   [Scheme Procedure]
        [*#:headers=’()*] [*#:port=#f*] [*#:meta=’()*] [*#:validate-headers?=#t*]
    Construct an HTTP request object. If *validate-headers?* is true, the headers are each
    run through their respective validators.

write-request *r port*   [Scheme Procedure]
    Write the given HTTP request to *port*.

    Return a new request, whose request-port will continue writing on *port*, perhaps
    using some transfer encoding.

read-request-body *r*   [Scheme Procedure]
    Reads the request body from *r*, as a bytevector. Return #f if there was no request
    body.

write-request-body *r bv*   [Scheme Procedure]
    Write *bv*, a bytevector, to the port corresponding to the HTTP request *r*.

    The various headers that are typically associated with HTTP requests may be accessed
with these dedicated accessors. See Section 7.3.4 [HTTP Headers], page 525, for more
information on the format of parsed headers.

request-accept *request* [*default=’()*]   [Scheme Procedure]
request-accept-charset *request* [*default=’()*]   [Scheme Procedure]
request-accept-encoding *request* [*default=’()*]   [Scheme Procedure]
request-accept-language *request* [*default=’()*]   [Scheme Procedure]
request-allow *request* [*default=’()*]   [Scheme Procedure]
request-authorization *request* [*default=#f*]   [Scheme Procedure]
request-cache-control *request* [*default=’()*]   [Scheme Procedure]
request-connection *request* [*default=’()*]   [Scheme Procedure]
request-content-encoding *request* [*default=’()*]   [Scheme Procedure]
request-content-language *request* [*default=’()*]   [Scheme Procedure]
request-content-length *request* [*default=#f*]   [Scheme Procedure]
request-content-location *request* [*default=#f*]   [Scheme Procedure]
request-content-md5 *request* [*default=#f*]   [Scheme Procedure]

request-content-range *request* [*default=#f*]   [Scheme Procedure]
request-content-type *request* [*default=#f*]   [Scheme Procedure]
request-date *request* [*default=#f*]   [Scheme Procedure]
request-expect *request* [*default='()*]   [Scheme Procedure]
request-expires *request* [*default=#f*]   [Scheme Procedure]
request-from *request* [*default=#f*]   [Scheme Procedure]
request-host *request* [*default=#f*]   [Scheme Procedure]
request-if-match *request* [*default=#f*]   [Scheme Procedure]
request-if-modified-since *request* [*default=#f*]   [Scheme Procedure]
request-if-none-match *request* [*default=#f*]   [Scheme Procedure]
request-if-range *request* [*default=#f*]   [Scheme Procedure]
request-if-unmodified-since *request* [*default=#f*]   [Scheme Procedure]
request-last-modified *request* [*default=#f*]   [Scheme Procedure]
request-max-forwards *request* [*default=#f*]   [Scheme Procedure]
request-pragma *request* [*default='()*]   [Scheme Procedure]
request-proxy-authorization *request* [*default=#f*]   [Scheme Procedure]
request-range *request* [*default=#f*]   [Scheme Procedure]
request-referer *request* [*default=#f*]   [Scheme Procedure]
request-te *request* [*default=#f*]   [Scheme Procedure]
request-trailer *request* [*default='()*]   [Scheme Procedure]
request-transfer-encoding *request* [*default='()*]   [Scheme Procedure]
request-upgrade *request* [*default='()*]   [Scheme Procedure]
request-user-agent *request* [*default=#f*]   [Scheme Procedure]
request-via *request* [*default='()*]   [Scheme Procedure]
request-warning *request* [*default='()*]   [Scheme Procedure]
> Return the given request header, or *default* if none was present.

request-absolute-uri *r* [*default-host=#f*] [*default-port=#f*]   [Scheme Procedure]
> A helper routine to determine the absolute URI of a request, using the `host` header
> and the default host and port.

7.3.7 HTTP Responses

`(use-modules (web response))`

As with requests (see Section 7.3.6 [Requests], page 534), Guile offers a data type for
HTTP responses. Again, the body is represented separately from the request.

response? *obj*   [Scheme Procedure]
response-version *response*   [Scheme Procedure]
response-code *response*   [Scheme Procedure]
response-reason-phrase *response*   [Scheme Procedure]
response-headers *response*   [Scheme Procedure]
response-port *response*   [Scheme Procedure]
> A predicate and field accessors for the response type. The fields are as follows:

version   The HTTP version pair, like `(1 . 1)`.

code   The HTTP response code, like 200.

reason-phrase
> The reason phrase, or the standard reason phrase for the response's code.

        `headers`   The response headers, as an alist of parsed values.

        `port`   The port on which to read or write a response body, if any.

`read-response` *port*   [Scheme Procedure]
> Read an HTTP response from *port*.
>
> As a side effect, sets the encoding on *port* to ISO-8859-1 (latin-1), so that reading one character reads one byte. See the discussion of character sets in Section 7.3.7 [Responses], page 536, for more information.

`build-response` [*#:version='(1 . 1)*] [*#:code=200*]   [Scheme Procedure]
       [*#:reason-phrase=#f*] [*#:headers='()*] [*#:port=#f*] [*#:validate-headers?=#t*]
> Construct an HTTP response object. If *validate-headers?* is true, the headers are each run through their respective validators.

`adapt-response-version` *response version*   [Scheme Procedure]
> Adapt the given response to a different HTTP version. Return a new HTTP response.
>
> The idea is that many applications might just build a response for the default HTTP version, and this method could handle a number of programmatic transformations to respond to older HTTP versions (0.9 and 1.0). But currently this function is a bit heavy-handed, just updating the version field.

`write-response` *r port*   [Scheme Procedure]
> Write the given HTTP response to *port*.
>
> Return a new response, whose `response-port` will continue writing on *port*, perhaps using some transfer encoding.

`response-must-not-include-body?` *r*   [Scheme Procedure]
> Some responses, like those with status code 304, are specified as never having bodies. This predicate returns `#t` for those responses.
>
> Note also, though, that responses to `HEAD` requests must also not have a body.

`response-body-port` *r* [*#:decode?=#t*] [*#:keep-alive?=#t*]   [Scheme Procedure]
> Return an input port from which the body of *r* can be read. The encoding of the returned port is set according to *r*'s `content-type` header, when it's textual, except if *decode?* is `#f`. Return `#f` when no body is available.
>
> When *keep-alive?* is `#f`, closing the returned port also closes *r*'s response port.

`read-response-body` *r*   [Scheme Procedure]
> Read the response body from *r*, as a bytevector. Returns `#f` if there was no response body.

`write-response-body` *r bv*   [Scheme Procedure]
> Write *bv*, a bytevector, to the port corresponding to the HTTP response *r*.

As with requests, the various headers that are typically associated with HTTP responses may be accessed with these dedicated accessors. See Section 7.3.4 [HTTP Headers], page 525, for more information on the format of parsed headers.

response-accept-ranges *response* [*default=#f*]   [Scheme Procedure]
response-age *response* [*default='()*]   [Scheme Procedure]
response-allow *response* [*default='()*]   [Scheme Procedure]
response-cache-control *response* [*default='()*]   [Scheme Procedure]
response-connection *response* [*default='()*]   [Scheme Procedure]
response-content-encoding *response* [*default='()*]   [Scheme Procedure]
response-content-language *response* [*default='()*]   [Scheme Procedure]
response-content-length *response* [*default=#f*]   [Scheme Procedure]
response-content-location *response* [*default=#f*]   [Scheme Procedure]
response-content-md5 *response* [*default=#f*]   [Scheme Procedure]
response-content-range *response* [*default=#f*]   [Scheme Procedure]
response-content-type *response* [*default=#f*]   [Scheme Procedure]
response-date *response* [*default=#f*]   [Scheme Procedure]
response-etag *response* [*default=#f*]   [Scheme Procedure]
response-expires *response* [*default=#f*]   [Scheme Procedure]
response-last-modified *response* [*default=#f*]   [Scheme Procedure]
response-location *response* [*default=#f*]   [Scheme Procedure]
response-pragma *response* [*default='()*]   [Scheme Procedure]
response-proxy-authenticate *response* [*default=#f*]   [Scheme Procedure]
response-retry-after *response* [*default=#f*]   [Scheme Procedure]
response-server *response* [*default=#f*]   [Scheme Procedure]
response-trailer *response* [*default='()*]   [Scheme Procedure]
response-transfer-encoding *response* [*default='()*]   [Scheme Procedure]
response-upgrade *response* [*default='()*]   [Scheme Procedure]
response-vary *response* [*default='()*]   [Scheme Procedure]
response-via *response* [*default='()*]   [Scheme Procedure]
response-warning *response* [*default='()*]   [Scheme Procedure]
response-www-authenticate *response* [*default=#f*]   [Scheme Procedure]
    Return the given response header, or *default* if none was present.

text-content-type? *type*   [Scheme Procedure]
    Return #t if *type*, a symbol as returned by response-content-type, represents a
    textual type such as text/plain.

7.3.8 Web Client

(web client) provides a simple, synchronous HTTP client, built on the lower-level HTTP,
request, and response modules.

        (use-modules (web client))

open-socket-for-uri *uri*   [Scheme Procedure]
    Return an open input/output port for a connection to URI.

http-get *uri arg...*   [Scheme Procedure]
http-head *uri arg...*   [Scheme Procedure]
http-post *uri arg...*   [Scheme Procedure]
http-put *uri arg...*   [Scheme Procedure]
http-delete *uri arg...*   [Scheme Procedure]
http-trace *uri arg...*   [Scheme Procedure]

`http-options` *uri arg...*   [Scheme Procedure]
>   Connect to the server corresponding to *uri* and make a request over HTTP, using the
>   appropriate method (`GET`, `HEAD`, etc.).
>
>   All of these procedures have the same prototype: a URI followed by an optional
>   sequence of keyword arguments. These keyword arguments allow you to modify the
>   requests in various ways, for example attaching a body to the request, or setting
>   specific headers. The following table lists the keyword arguments and their default
>   values.
>
>   `#:body #f`
>
>   `#:port (open-socket-for-uri uri)]`
>   `#:version '(1 . 1)`
>   `#:keep-alive? #f`
>   `#:headers '()`
>   `#:decode-body? #t`
>   `#:streaming? #f`
>
>   If you already have a port open, pass it as *port*. Otherwise, a connection will be
>   opened to the server corresponding to *uri*. Any extra headers in the alist *headers* will
>   be added to the request.
>
>   If *body* is not `#f`, a message body will also be sent with the HTTP request. If *body* is
>   a string, it is encoded according to the content-type in *headers*, defaulting to UTF-8.
>   Otherwise *body* should be a bytevector, or `#f` for no body. Although a message body
>   may be sent with any request, usually only `POST` and `PUT` requests have bodies.
>
>   If *decode-body?* is true, as is the default, the body of the response will be decoded to
>   string, if it is a textual content-type. Otherwise it will be returned as a bytevector.
>
>   However, if *streaming?* is true, instead of eagerly reading the response body from the
>   server, this function only reads off the headers. The response body will be returned
>   as a port on which the data may be read.
>
>   Unless *keep-alive?* is true, the port will be closed after the full response body has
>   been read.
>
>   Returns two values: the response read from the server, and the response body as a
>   string, bytevector, #f value, or as a port (if *streaming?* is true).

`http-get` is useful for making one-off requests to web sites. If you are writing a web
spider or some other client that needs to handle a number of requests in parallel, it's better
to build an event-driven URL fetcher, similar in structure to the web server (see Section 7.3.9
[Web Server], page 540).

Another option, good but not as performant, would be to use threads, possibly via
par-map or futures.

`current-http-proxy`   [Scheme Parameter]
>   Either `#f` or a non-empty string containing the URL of the HTTP proxy server to be
>   used by the procedures in the (`web client`) module, including `open-socket-for-`
>   `uri`. Its initial value is based on the `http_proxy` environment variable.
>
>   ```
>   (current-http-proxy) ⇒ "http://localhost:8123/"
>   (parameterize ((current-http-proxy #f))
>   ```

```
(http-get "http://example.com/"))  ; temporarily bypass proxy
(current-http-proxy) ⇒ "http://localhost:8123/"
```

7.3.9 Web Server

(web server) is a generic web server interface, along with a main loop implementation for web servers controlled by Guile.

```
(use-modules (web server))
```

The lowest layer is the `<server-impl>` object, which defines a set of hooks to open a server, read a request from a client, write a response to a client, and close a server. These hooks – `open`, `read`, `write`, and `close`, respectively – are bound together in a `<server-impl>` object. Procedures in this module take a `<server-impl>` object, if needed.

A `<server-impl>` may also be looked up by name. If you pass the `http` symbol to `run-server`, Guile looks for a variable named `http` in the (web server http) module, which should be bound to a `<server-impl>` object. Such a binding is made by instantiation of the `define-server-impl` syntax. In this way the run-server loop can automatically load other backends if available.

The life cycle of a server goes as follows:

1. The `open` hook is called, to open the server. `open` takes zero or more arguments, depending on the backend, and returns an opaque server socket object, or signals an error.

2. The `read` hook is called, to read a request from a new client. The `read` hook takes one argument, the server socket. It should return three values: an opaque client socket, the request, and the request body. The request should be a `<request>` object, from (web request). The body should be a string or a bytevector, or #f if there is no body.

   If the read failed, the `read` hook may return #f for the client socket, request, and body.

3. A user-provided handler procedure is called, with the request and body as its arguments. The handler should return two values: the response, as a `<response>` record from (web response), and the response body as bytevector, or #f if not present.

   The respose and response body are run through `sanitize-response`, documented below. This allows the handler writer to take some convenient shortcuts: for example, instead of a `<response>`, the handler can simply return an alist of headers, in which case a default response object is constructed with those headers. Instead of a bytevector for the body, the handler can return a string, which will be serialized into an appropriate encoding; or it can return a procedure, which will be called on a port to write out the data. See the `sanitize-response` documentation, for more.

4. The `write` hook is called with three arguments: the client socket, the response, and the body. The `write` hook returns no values.

5. At this point the request handling is complete. For a loop, we loop back and try to read a new request.

6. If the user interrupts the loop, the `close` hook is called on the server socket.

A user may define a server implementation with the following form:

define-server-impl *name open read write close*   [Scheme Syntax]

Make a `<server-impl>` object with the hooks *open*, *read*, *write*, and *close*, and bind it to the symbol *name* in the current module.

lookup-server-impl *impl*   [Scheme Procedure]
> Look up a server implementation. If *impl* is a server implementation already, it is
> returned directly. If it is a symbol, the binding named *impl* in the (web server *impl*)
> module is looked up. Otherwise an error is signaled.
>
> Currently a server implementation is a somewhat opaque type, useful only for passing
> to other procedures in this module, like `read-client`.

The (web server) module defines a number of routines that use `<server-impl>` objects
to implement parts of a web server. Given that we don't expose the accessors for the various
fields of a `<server-impl>`, indeed these routines are the only procedures with any access
to the impl objects.

open-server *impl open-params*   [Scheme Procedure]
> Open a server for the given implementation. Return one value, the new server object.
> The implementation's `open` procedure is applied to *open-params*, which should be a
> list.

read-client *impl server*   [Scheme Procedure]
> Read a new client from *server*, by applying the implementation's `read` procedure to
> the server. If successful, return three values: an object corresponding to the client, a
> request object, and the request body. If any exception occurs, return `#f` for all three
> values.

handle-request *handler request body state*   [Scheme Procedure]
> Handle a given request, returning the response and body.
>
> The response and response body are produced by calling the given *handler* with
> *request* and *body* as arguments.
>
> The elements of *state* are also passed to *handler* as arguments, and may be returned
> as additional values. The new *state*, collected from the *handler*'s return values, is
> then returned as a list. The idea is that a server loop receives a handler from the
> user, along with whatever state values the user is interested in, allowing the user's
> handler to explicitly manage its state.

sanitize-response *request response body*   [Scheme Procedure]
> "Sanitize" the given response and body, making them appropriate for the given re-
> quest.
>
> As a convenience to web handler authors, *response* may be given as an alist of headers,
> in which case it is used to construct a default response. Ensures that the response
> version corresponds to the request version. If *body* is a string, encodes the string to
> a bytevector, in an encoding appropriate for *response*. Adds a `content-length` and
> `content-type` header, as necessary.
>
> If *body* is a procedure, it is called with a port as an argument, and the output collected
> as a bytevector. In the future we might try to instead use a compressing, chunk-
> encoded port, and call this procedure later, in the write-client procedure. Authors
> are advised not to rely on the procedure being called at any particular time.

write-client *impl server client response body*   [Scheme Procedure]
> Write an HTTP response and body to *client*. If the server and client support persistent connections, it is the implementation's responsibility to keep track of the client thereafter, presumably by attaching it to the *server* argument somehow.

close-server *impl server*   [Scheme Procedure]
> Release resources allocated by a previous invocation of **open-server**.

Given the procedures above, it is a small matter to make a web server:

serve-one-client *handler impl server state*   [Scheme Procedure]
> Read one request from *server*, call *handler* on the request and body, and write the response to the client. Return the new state produced by the handler procedure.

run-server *handler* [*impl='http*] [*open-params='()*] *arg . . .*   [Scheme Procedure]
> Run Guile's built-in web server.
>
> *handler* should be a procedure that takes two or more arguments, the HTTP request and request body, and returns two or more values, the response and response body.
>
> For examples, skip ahead to the next section, Section 7.3.10 [Web Examples], page 542.
>
> The response and body will be run through **sanitize-response** before sending back to the client.
>
> Additional arguments to *handler* are taken from *arg . . . .* These arguments comprise a *state*. Additional return values are accumulated into a new state, which will be used for subsequent requests. In this way a handler can explicitly manage its state.

The default web server implementation is **http**, which binds to a socket, listening for request on that port.

http [*#:host=#f*] [*#:family=AF_INET*]   [HTTP Implementation]
>   [*#:addr=INADDR_LOOPBACK*] [*#:port 8080*] [*#:socket*]
> The default HTTP implementation. We document it as a function with keyword arguments, because that is precisely the way that it is – all of the *open-params* to **run-server** get passed to the implementation's open function.

```
;; The defaults: localhost:8080
(run-server handler)
;; Same thing
(run-server handler 'http '())
;; On a different port
(run-server handler 'http '(#:port 8081))
;; IPv6
(run-server handler 'http '(#:family AF_INET6 #:port 8081))
;; Custom socket
(run-server handler 'http `(#:socket ,(sudo-make-me-a-socket)))
```

7.3.10 Web Examples

Well, enough about the tedious internals. Let's make a web application!

7.3.10.1 Hello, World!

The first program we have to write, of course, is "Hello, World!". This means that we have to implement a web handler that does what we want.

Now we define a handler, a function of two arguments and two return values:

```
(define (handler request request-body)
  (values response response-body))
```

In this first example, we take advantage of a short-cut, returning an alist of headers instead of a proper response object. The response body is our payload:

```
(define (hello-world-handler request request-body)
  (values '((content-type . (text/plain)))
          "Hello World!"))
```

Now let's test it, by running a server with this handler. Load up the web server module if you haven't yet done so, and run a server with this handler:

```
(use-modules (web server))
(run-server hello-world-handler)
```

By default, the web server listens for requests on `localhost:8080`. Visit that address in your web browser to test. If you see the string, `Hello World!`, sweet!

7.3.10.2 Inspecting the Request

The Hello World program above is a general greeter, responding to all URIs. To make a more exclusive greeter, we need to inspect the request object, and conditionally produce different results. So let's load up the request, response, and URI modules, and do just that.

```
(use-modules (web server)) ; you probably did this already
(use-modules (web request)
             (web response)
             (web uri))


(define (request-path-components request)
  (split-and-decode-uri-path (uri-path (request-uri request))))


(define (hello-hacker-handler request body)
  (if (equal? (request-path-components request)
              '("hacker"))
      (values '((content-type . (text/plain)))
              "Hello hacker!")
      (not-found request)))


(run-server hello-hacker-handler)
```

Here we see that we have defined a helper to return the components of the URI path as a list of strings, and used that to check for a request to /hacker/. Then the success case is just as before – visit `http://localhost:8080/hacker/` in your browser to check.

You should always match against URI path components as decoded by **split-and-decode-uri-path**. The above example will work for /hacker/, //hacker///, and /h%61ck%65r.

But we forgot to define `not-found`! If you are pasting these examples into a REPL, accessing any other URI in your web browser will drop your Guile console into the debugger:

```
<unnamed port>:38:7: In procedure module-lookup:
<unnamed port>:38:7: Unbound variable: not-found

Entering a new prompt. Type ',bt' for a backtrace or ',q' to continue.
scheme@(guile-user) [1]>
```

So let's define the function, right there in the debugger. As you probably know, we'll want to return a 404 response.

```
;; Paste this in your REPL
(define (not-found request)
  (values (build-response #:code 404)
          (string-append "Resource not found: "
                              (uri->string (request-uri request)))))

;; Now paste this to let the web server keep going:
,continue
```

Now if you access `http://localhost/foo/`, you get this error message. (Note that some popular web browsers won't show server-generated 404 messages, showing their own instead, unless the 404 message body is long enough.)

7.3.10.3 Higher-Level Interfaces

The web handler interface is a common baseline that all kinds of Guile web applications can use. You will usually want to build something on top of it, however, especially when producing HTML. Here is a simple example that builds up HTML output using SXML (see Section 7.22 [SXML], page 697).

First, load up the modules:

```
(use-modules (web server)
             (web request)
             (web response)
             (sxml simple))
```

Now we define a simple templating function that takes a list of HTML body elements, as SXML, and puts them in our super template:

```
(define (templatize title body)
  `(html (head (title ,title))
         (body ,@body)))
```

For example, the simplest Hello HTML can be produced like this:

```
(sxml->xml (templatize "Hello!" '((b "Hi!"))))
⊣
<html><head><title>Hello!</title></head><body><b>Hi!</b></body></html>
```

Much better to work with Scheme data types than to work with HTML as strings. Now we define a little response helper:

```
(define* (respond #:optional body #:key
                  (status 200)
```

```
                        (title "Hello hello!")
                        (doctype "<!DOCTYPE html>\n")
                        (content-type-params '((charset . "utf-8")))
                        (content-type 'text/html)
                        (extra-headers '())
                        (sxml (and body (templatize title body))))
       (values (build-response
                #:code status
                #:headers '((content-type
                             . (,content-type ,@content-type-params))
                            ,@extra-headers))
               (lambda (port)
                 (if sxml
                     (begin
                       (if doctype (display doctype port))
                       (sxml->xml sxml port))))))))
```

Here we see the power of keyword arguments with default initializers. By the time the arguments are fully parsed, the sxml local variable will hold the templated SXML, ready for sending out to the client.

Also, instead of returning the body as a string, respond gives a procedure, which will be called by the web server to write out the response to the client.

Now, a simple example using this responder, which lays out the incoming headers in an HTML table.

```
    (define (debug-page request body)
      (respond
       '((h1 "hello world!")
         (table
          (tr (th "header") (th "value"))
          ,@(map (lambda (pair)
                   '(tr (td (tt ,(with-output-to-string
                                  (lambda () (display (car pair))))))
                        (td (tt ,(with-output-to-string
                                  (lambda ()
                                    (write (cdr pair))))))))
                 (request-headers request))))))

    (run-server debug-page)
```

Now if you visit any local address in your web browser, we actually see some HTML, finally.

7.3.10.4 Conclusion

Well, this is about as far as Guile's built-in web support goes, for now. There are many ways to make a web application, but hopefully by standardizing the most fundamental data types, users will be able to choose the approach that suits them best, while also being able to switch between implementations of the server. This is a relatively new part of Guile, so if you have feedback, let us know, and we can take it into account. Happy hacking on the web!

7.4 The (ice-9 getopt-long) Module

The (ice-9 getopt-long) module exports two procedures: getopt-long and option-ref.

- getopt-long takes a list of strings — the command line arguments — an *option specification*, and some optional keyword parameters. It parses the command line arguments according to the option specification and keyword parameters, and returns a data structure that encapsulates the results of the parsing.

- option-ref then takes the parsed data structure and a specific option's name, and returns information about that option in particular.

To make these procedures available to your Guile script, include the expression (use-modules (ice-9 getopt-long)) somewhere near the top, before the first usage of getopt-long or option-ref.

7.4.1 A Short getopt-long Example

This section illustrates how getopt-long is used by presenting and dissecting a simple example. The first thing that we need is an *option specification* that tells getopt-long how to parse the command line. This specification is an association list with the long option name as the key. Here is how such a specification might look:

```
(define option-spec
  '((version (single-char #\v) (value #f))
    (help    (single-char #\h) (value #f))))
```

This alist tells getopt-long that it should accept two long options, called *version* and *help*, and that these options can also be selected by the single-letter abbreviations *v* and *h*, respectively. The (value #f) clauses indicate that neither of the options accepts a value.

With this specification we can use getopt-long to parse a given command line:

```
(define options (getopt-long (command-line) option-spec))
```

After this call, options contains the parsed command line and is ready to be examined by option-ref. option-ref is called like this:

```
(option-ref options 'help #f)
```

It expects the parsed command line, a symbol indicating the option to examine, and a default value. The default value is returned if the option was not present in the command line, or if the option was present but without a value; otherwise the value from the command line is returned. Usually option-ref is called once for each possible option that a script supports.

The following example shows a main program which puts all this together to parse its command line and figure out what the user wanted.

```
(define (main args)
  (let* ((option-spec '((version (single-char #\v) (value #f))
                        (help    (single-char #\h) (value #f))))
         (options (getopt-long args option-spec))
         (help-wanted (option-ref options 'help #f))
```

```
              (version-wanted (option-ref options 'version #f)))
      (if (or version-wanted help-wanted)
          (begin
            (if version-wanted
                (display "getopt-long-example version 0.3\n"))
            (if help-wanted
                (display "\
getopt-long-example [options]
  -v, --version    Display version
  -h, --help       Display this help
")))
          (begin
            (display "Hello, World!") (newline)))))
```

7.4.2 How to Write an Option Specification

An option specification is an association list (see Section 6.7.12 [Association Lists], page 228) with one list element for each supported option. The key of each list element is a symbol that names the option, while the value is a list of option properties:

```
OPTION-SPEC ::=  '( (OPT-NAME1 (PROP-NAME PROP-VALUE) ...)
                    (OPT-NAME2 (PROP-NAME PROP-VALUE) ...)
                    (OPT-NAME3 (PROP-NAME PROP-VALUE) ...)

                    ...
                  )
```

Each *opt-name* specifies the long option name for that option. For example, a list element with *opt-name* background specifies an option that can be specified on the command line using the long option --background. Further information about the option — whether it takes a value, whether it is required to be present in the command line, and so on — is specified by the option properties.

In the example of the preceding section, we already saw that a long option name can have a equivalent *short option* character. The equivalent short option character can be set for an option by specifying a single-char property in that option's property list. For example, a list element like '(output (single-char #\o) ...) specifies an option with long name --output that can also be specified by the equivalent short name -o.

The value property specifies whether an option requires or accepts a value. If the value property is set to #t, the option requires a value: getopt-long will signal an error if the option name is present without a corresponding value. If set to #f, the option does not take a value; in this case, a non-option word that follows the option name in the command line will be treated as a non-option argument. If set to the symbol optional, the option accepts a value but does not require one: a non-option word that follows the option name in the command line will be interpreted as that option's value. If the option name for an option with '(value optional) is immediately followed in the command line by *another* option name, the value for the first option is implicitly #t.

The required? property indicates whether an option is required to be present in the command line. If the required? property is set to #t, getopt-long will signal an error if the option is not specified.

Finally, the `predicate` property can be used to constrain the possible values of an option. If used, the `predicate` property should be set to a procedure that takes one argument — the proposed option value as a string — and returns either `#t` or `#f` according as the proposed value is or is not acceptable. If the predicate procedure returns `#f`, `getopt-long` will signal an error.

By default, options do not have single-character equivalents, are not required, and do not take values. Where the list element for an option includes a `value` property but no `predicate` property, the option values are unconstrained.

7.4.3 Expected Command Line Format

In order for `getopt-long` to correctly parse a command line, that command line must conform to a standard set of rules for how command line options are specified. This section explains what those rules are.

`getopt-long` splits a given command line into several pieces. All elements of the argument list are classified to be either options or normal arguments. Options consist of two dashes and an option name (so-called *long* options), or of one dash followed by a single letter (*short* options).

Options can behave as switches, when they are given without a value, or they can be used to pass a value to the program. The value for an option may be specified using an equals sign, or else is simply the next word in the command line, so the following two invocations are equivalent:

```
$ ./foo.scm --output=bar.txt
$ ./foo.scm --output bar.txt
```

Short options can be used instead of their long equivalents and can be grouped together after a single dash. For example, the following commands are equivalent.

```
$ ./foo.scm --version --help
$ ./foo.scm -v --help
$ ./foo.scm -vh
```

If an option requires a value, it can only be grouped together with other short options if it is the last option in the group; the value is the next argument. So, for example, with the following option specification —

```
((apples    (single-char #\a))
 (blimps    (single-char #\b) (value #t))
 (catalexis (single-char #\c) (value #t)))
```

— the following command lines would all be acceptable:

```
$ ./foo.scm -a -b bang -c couth
$ ./foo.scm -ab bang -c couth
$ ./foo.scm -ac couth -b bang
```

But the next command line is an error, because `-b` is not the last option in its combination, and because a group of short options cannot include two options that both require values:

```
$ ./foo.scm -abc couth bang
```

If an option's value is optional, `getopt-long` decides whether the option has a value by looking at what follows it in the argument list. If the next element is a string, and it does not appear to be an option itself, then that string is the option's value.

If the option -- appears in the argument list, argument parsing stops there and subsequent arguments are returned as ordinary arguments, even if they resemble options. So, with the command line

```
$ ./foo.scm --apples "Granny Smith" -- --blimp Goodyear
```

getopt-long will recognize the --apples option as having the value "Granny Smith", but will not treat --blimp as an option. The strings --blimp and Goodyear will be returned as ordinary argument strings.

7.4.4 Reference Documentation for getopt-long

getopt-long *args grammar* [*#:stop-at-first-non-option #t*]   [Scheme Procedure]
> Parse the command line given in *args* (which must be a list of strings) according to the option specification *grammar*.
>
> The *grammar* argument is expected to be a list of this form:
>
> `((option (property value) ...) ...)`
>
> where each *option* is a symbol denoting the long option, but without the two leading dashes (e.g. version if the option is called --version).
>
> For each option, there may be list of arbitrarily many property/value pairs. The order of the pairs is not important, but every property may only appear once in the property list. The following table lists the possible properties:
>
> (single-char *char*)
> > Accept -*char* as a single-character equivalent to --*option*. This is how to specify traditional Unix-style flags.
>
> (required? *bool*)
> > If *bool* is true, the option is required. getopt-long will raise an error if it is not found in *args*.
>
> (value *bool*)
> > If *bool* is #t, the option accepts a value; if it is #f, it does not; and if it is the symbol optional, the option may appear in *args* with or without a value.
>
> (predicate *func*)
> > If the option accepts a value (i.e. you specified (value #t) for this option), then getopt-long will apply *func* to the value, and throw an exception if it returns #f. *func* should be a procedure which accepts a string and returns a boolean value; you may need to use quasiquotes to get it into *grammar*.
>
> The #:stop-at-first-non-option keyword, if specified with any true value, tells getopt-long to stop when it gets to the first non-option in the command line. That is, at the first word which is neither an option itself, nor the value of an option. Everything in the command line from that word onwards will be returned as non-option arguments.

getopt-long's *args* parameter is expected to be a list of strings like the one returned by command-line, with the first element being the name of the command. Therefore getopt-

`long` ignores the first element in *args* and starts argument interpretation with the second element.

> `getopt-long` signals an error if any of the following conditions hold.

- The option grammar has an invalid syntax.
- One of the options in the argument list was not specified by the grammar.
- A required option is omitted.
- An option which requires an argument did not get one.
- An option that doesn't accept an argument does get one (this can only happen using the long option `--opt=value` syntax).
- An option predicate fails.

> `#:stop-at-first-non-option` is useful for command line invocations like `guild [--help | --version] [script [script-options]]` and `cvs [general-options] command [command-options]`, where there are options at two levels: some generic and understood by the outer command, and some that are specific to the particular script or command being invoked. To use `getopt-long` in such cases, you would call it twice: firstly with `#:stop-at-first-non-option #t`, so as to parse any generic options and identify the wanted script or sub-command; secondly, and after trimming off the initial generic command words, with a script- or sub-command-specific option grammar, so as to process those specific options.

7.4.5 Reference Documentation for `option-ref`

`option-ref` *options key default*   [Scheme Procedure]
> Search *options* for a command line option named *key* and return its value, if found. If the option has no value, but was given, return `#t`. If the option was not given, return *default*. *options* must be the result of a call to `getopt-long`.

> `option-ref` always succeeds, either by returning the requested option value from the command line, or the default value.

> The special key `'()` can be used to get a list of all non-option arguments.

7.5 SRFI Support Modules

SRFI is an acronym for Scheme Request For Implementation. The SRFI documents define a lot of syntactic and procedure extensions to standard Scheme as defined in R5RS.

Guile has support for a number of SRFIs. This chapter gives an overview over the available SRFIs and some usage hints. For complete documentation, design rationales and further examples, we advise you to get the relevant SRFI documents from the SRFI home page `http://srfi.schemers.org/`.

7.5.1 About SRFI Usage

SRFI support in Guile is currently implemented partly in the core library, and partly as add-on modules. That means that some SRFIs are automatically available when the interpreter is started, whereas the other SRFIs require you to use the appropriate support module explicitly.

There are several reasons for this inconsistency. First, the feature checking syntactic form **cond-expand** (see Section 7.5.2 [SRFI-0], page 551) must be available immediately, because it must be there when the user wants to check for the Scheme implementation, that is, before she can know that it is safe to use `use-modules` to load SRFI support modules. The second reason is that some features defined in SRFIs had been implemented in Guile before the developers started to add SRFI implementations as modules (for example SRFI-13 (see Section 7.5.11 [SRFI-13], page 578)). In the future, it is possible that SRFIs in the core library might be factored out into separate modules, requiring explicit module loading when they are needed. So you should be prepared to have to use `use-modules` someday in the future to access SRFI-13 bindings. If you want, you can do that already. We have included the module `(srfi srfi-13)` in the distribution, which currently does nothing, but ensures that you can write future-safe code.

Generally, support for a specific SRFI is made available by using modules named `(srfi srfi-number)`, where *number* is the number of the SRFI needed. Another possibility is to use the command line option `--use-srfi`, which will load the necessary modules automatically (see Section 4.2 [Invoking Guile], page 35).

7.5.2 SRFI-0 - cond-expand

This SRFI lets a portable Scheme program test for the presence of certain features, and adapt itself by using different blocks of code, or fail if the necessary features are not available. There's no module to load, this is in the Guile core.

A program designed only for Guile will generally not need this mechanism, such a program can of course directly use the various documented parts of Guile.

`cond-expand` (*feature body...*) ...   [syntax]

Expand to the *body* of the first clause whose *feature* specification is satisfied. It is an error if no *feature* is satisfied.

Features are symbols such as `srfi-1`, and a feature specification can use **and**, **or** and **not** forms to test combinations. The last clause can be an **else**, to be used if no other passes.

For example, define a private version of `alist-cons` if SRFI-1 is not available.

```
(cond-expand (srfi-1
              )
             (else
              (define (alist-cons key val alist)
                (cons (cons key val) alist))))
```

Or demand a certain set of SRFIs (list operations, string ports, **receive** and string operations), failing if they're not available.

```
(cond-expand ((and srfi-1 srfi-6 srfi-8 srfi-13)
              ))
```

The Guile core has the following features,

```
guile
guile-2  ;; starting from Guile 2.x
r5rs
srfi-0
srfi-4
srfi-13
```

```
srfi-14
srfi-16
srfi-23
srfi-30
srfi-39
srfi-46
srfi-55
srfi-61
srfi-62
srfi-87
srfi-105
```

Other SRFI feature symbols are defined once their code has been loaded with use-modules, since only then are their bindings available.

The '--use-srfi' command line option (see Section 4.2 [Invoking Guile], page 35) is a good way to load SRFIs to satisfy cond-expand when running a portable program.

Testing the guile feature allows a program to adapt itself to the Guile module system, but still run on other Scheme systems. For example the following demands SRFI-8 (receive), but also knows how to load it with the Guile mechanism.

```
(cond-expand (srfi-8
              )
             (guile
              (use-modules (srfi srfi-8))))
```

Likewise, testing the guile-2 feature allows code to be portable between Guile 2.0 and previous versions of Guile. For instance, it makes it possible to write code that accounts for Guile 2.0's compiler, yet be correctly interpreted on 1.8 and earlier versions:

```
(cond-expand (guile-2 (eval-when (compile)
                        ;; This must be evaluated at compile time.
                        (fluid-set! current-reader my-reader)))
             (guile
                        ;; Earlier versions of Guile do not have a
                        ;; separate compilation phase.
                        (fluid-set! current-reader my-reader)))
```

It should be noted that cond-expand is separate from the *features* mechanism (see Section 6.22.2 [Feature Tracking], page 429), feature symbols in one are unrelated to those in the other.

7.5.3 SRFI-1 - List library

The list library defined in SRFI-1 contains a lot of useful list processing procedures for construction, examining, destructuring and manipulating lists and pairs.

Since SRFI-1 also defines some procedures which are already contained in R5RS and thus are supported by the Guile core library, some list and pair procedures which appear in the SRFI-1 document may not appear in this section. So when looking for a particular list/pair processing procedure, you should also have a look at the sections Section 6.7.2 [Lists], page 188 and Section 6.7.1 [Pairs], page 185.

7.5.3.1 Constructors

New lists can be constructed by calling one of the following procedures.

xcons *d a*   [Scheme Procedure]

> Like `cons`, but with interchanged arguments. Useful mostly when passed to higher-order procedures.

list-tabulate *n init-proc*   [Scheme Procedure]

> Return an *n*-element list, where each list element is produced by applying the procedure *init-proc* to the corresponding list index. The order in which *init-proc* is applied to the indices is not specified.

list-copy *lst*   [Scheme Procedure]

> Return a new list containing the elements of the list *lst*.
>
> This function differs from the core `list-copy` (see Section 6.7.2.3 [List Constructors], page 189) in accepting improper lists too. And if *lst* is not a pair at all then it's treated as the final tail of an improper list and simply returned.

circular-list *elt1 elt2 ...*   [Scheme Procedure]

> Return a circular list containing the given arguments *elt1 elt2 ...*.

iota *count* [*start step*]   [Scheme Procedure]

> Return a list containing *count* numbers, starting from *start* and adding *step* each time. The default *start* is 0, the default *step* is 1. For example,
>
> ```
> (iota 6)        ⇒ (0 1 2 3 4 5)
> (iota 4 2.5 -2) ⇒ (2.5 0.5 -1.5 -3.5)
> ```
>
> This function takes its name from the corresponding primitive in the APL language.

7.5.3.2 Predicates

The procedures in this section test specific properties of lists.

proper-list? *obj*   [Scheme Procedure]

> Return #t if *obj* is a proper list, or #f otherwise. This is the same as the core `list?` (see Section 6.7.2.2 [List Predicates], page 188).
>
> A proper list is a list which ends with the empty list () in the usual way. The empty list () itself is a proper list too.
>
> ```
> (proper-list? '(1 2 3))  ⇒ #t
> (proper-list? '())       ⇒ #t
> ```

circular-list? *obj*   [Scheme Procedure]

> Return #t if *obj* is a circular list, or #f otherwise.
>
> A circular list is a list where at some point the `cdr` refers back to a previous pair in the list (either the start or some later point), so that following the `cdr`s takes you around in a circle, with no end.
>
> ```
> (define x (list 1 2 3 4))
> (set-cdr! (last-pair x) (cddr x))
> x ⇒ (1 2 3 4 3 4 3 4 ...)
> (circular-list? x)  ⇒ #t
> ```

`dotted-list?` *obj*   [Scheme Procedure]

> Return #t if *obj* is a dotted list, or #f otherwise.
>
> A dotted list is a list where the `cdr` of the last pair is not the empty list (). Any non-pair *obj* is also considered a dotted list, with length zero.
>
> ```
> (dotted-list? '(1 2 . 3))  ⇒ #t
> (dotted-list? 99)          ⇒ #t
> ```

It will be noted that any Scheme object passes exactly one of the above three tests `proper-list?`, `circular-list?` and `dotted-list?`. Non-lists are `dotted-list?`, finite lists are either `proper-list?` or `dotted-list?`, and infinite lists are `circular-list?`.

`null-list?` *lst*   [Scheme Procedure]

> Return #t if *lst* is the empty list (), #f otherwise. If something else than a proper or circular list is passed as *lst*, an error is signalled. This procedure is recommended for checking for the end of a list in contexts where dotted lists are not allowed.

`not-pair?` *obj*   [Scheme Procedure]

> Return #t is *obj* is not a pair, #f otherwise. This is shorthand notation (`not (pair? obj)`) and is supposed to be used for end-of-list checking in contexts where dotted lists are allowed.

`list=` *elt= list1* ...   [Scheme Procedure]

> Return #t if all argument lists are equal, #f otherwise. List equality is determined by testing whether all lists have the same length and the corresponding elements are equal in the sense of the equality predicate *elt=*. If no or only one list is given, #t is returned.

7.5.3.3 Selectors

`first` *pair*   [Scheme Procedure]
`second` *pair*   [Scheme Procedure]
`third` *pair*   [Scheme Procedure]
`fourth` *pair*   [Scheme Procedure]
`fifth` *pair*   [Scheme Procedure]
`sixth` *pair*   [Scheme Procedure]
`seventh` *pair*   [Scheme Procedure]
`eighth` *pair*   [Scheme Procedure]
`ninth` *pair*   [Scheme Procedure]
`tenth` *pair*   [Scheme Procedure]

> These are synonyms for `car`, `cadr`, `caddr`, ...

`car+cdr` *pair*   [Scheme Procedure]

> Return two values, the CAR and the CDR of *pair*.

`take` *lst i*   [Scheme Procedure]
`take!` *lst i*   [Scheme Procedure]

> Return a list containing the first *i* elements of *lst*.
>
> `take!` may modify the structure of the argument list *lst* in order to produce the result.

`drop` *lst i*   [Scheme Procedure]
>   Return a list containing all but the first *i* elements of *lst*.

`take-right` *lst i*   [Scheme Procedure]
>   Return a list containing the *i* last elements of *lst*. The return shares a common tail
>   with *lst*.

`drop-right` *lst i*   [Scheme Procedure]
`drop-right!` *lst i*   [Scheme Procedure]
>   Return a list containing all but the *i* last elements of *lst*.
>
>   `drop-right` always returns a new list, even when *i* is zero. `drop-right!` may modify
>   the structure of the argument list *lst* in order to produce the result.

`split-at` *lst i*   [Scheme Procedure]
`split-at!` *lst i*   [Scheme Procedure]
>   Return two values, a list containing the first *i* elements of the list *lst* and a list
>   containing the remaining elements.
>
>   `split-at!` may modify the structure of the argument list *lst* in order to produce the
>   result.

`last` *lst*   [Scheme Procedure]
>   Return the last element of the non-empty, finite list *lst*.

7.5.3.4 Length, Append, Concatenate, etc.

`length+` *lst*   [Scheme Procedure]
>   Return the length of the argument list *lst*. When *lst* is a circular list, `#f` is returned.

`concatenate` *list-of-lists*   [Scheme Procedure]
`concatenate!` *list-of-lists*   [Scheme Procedure]
>   Construct a list by appending all lists in *list-of-lists*.
>
>   `concatenate!` may modify the structure of the given lists in order to produce the
>   result.
>
>   `concatenate` is the same as (`apply append` *list-of-lists*). It exists because some
>   Scheme implementations have a limit on the number of arguments a function takes,
>   which the `apply` might exceed. In Guile there is no such limit.

`append-reverse` *rev-head tail*   [Scheme Procedure]
`append-reverse!` *rev-head tail*   [Scheme Procedure]
>   Reverse *rev-head*, append *tail* to it, and return the result. This is equivalent to
>   (`append` (`reverse` *rev-head*) *tail*), but its implementation is more efficient.
>
>   (append-reverse '(1 2 3) '(4 5 6)) ⇒ (3 2 1 4 5 6)
>
>   `append-reverse!` may modify *rev-head* in order to produce the result.

`zip` *lst1 lst2 ...*   [Scheme Procedure]
>   Return a list as long as the shortest of the argument lists, where each element is a
>   list. The first list contains the first elements of the argument lists, the second list
>   contains the second elements, and so on.

`unzip1` *lst*   [Scheme Procedure]
`unzip2` *lst*   [Scheme Procedure]
`unzip3` *lst*   [Scheme Procedure]
`unzip4` *lst*   [Scheme Procedure]
`unzip5` *lst*   [Scheme Procedure]

> `unzip1` takes a list of lists, and returns a list containing the first elements of each list, `unzip2` returns two lists, the first containing the first elements of each lists and the second containing the second elements of each lists, and so on.

`count` *pred lst1 lst2 ...*   [Scheme Procedure]

> Return a count of the number of times *pred* returns true when called on elements from the given lists.
>
> *pred* is called with *N* parameters (`pred elem1 ... elemN`), each element being from the corresponding list. The first call is with the first element of each list, the second with the second element from each, and so on.
>
> Counting stops when the end of the shortest list is reached. At least one list must be non-circular.

7.5.3.5 Fold, Unfold & Map

`fold` *proc init lst1 lst2 ...*   [Scheme Procedure]
`fold-right` *proc init lst1 lst2 ...*   [Scheme Procedure]

> Apply *proc* to the elements of *lst1 lst2 ...* to build a result, and return that result.
>
> Each *proc* call is (`proc elem1 elem2 ... previous`), where *elem1* is from *lst1*, *elem2* is from *lst2*, and so on. *previous* is the return from the previous call to *proc*, or the given *init* for the first call. If any list is empty, just *init* is returned.
>
> `fold` works through the list elements from first to last. The following shows a list reversal and the calls it makes,

```
(fold cons '() '(1 2 3))


(cons 1 '())
(cons 2 '(1))
(cons 3 '(2 1))
⇒ (3 2 1)
```

> `fold-right` works through the list elements from last to first, ie. from the right. So for example the following finds the longest string, and the last among equal longest,

```
(fold-right (lambda (str prev)
              (if (> (string-length str) (string-length prev))
                  str
                  prev))
            ""
            '("x" "abc" "xyz" "jk"))
⇒ "xyz"
```

> If *lst1 lst2 ...* have different lengths, `fold` stops when the end of the shortest is reached; `fold-right` commences at the last element of the shortest. Ie. elements

past the length of the shortest are ignored in the other *lsts*. At least one *lst* must be non-circular.

`fold` should be preferred over `fold-right` if the order of processing doesn't matter, or can be arranged either way, since `fold` is a little more efficient.

The way `fold` builds a result from iterating is quite general, it can do more than other iterations like say `map` or `filter`. The following for example removes adjacent duplicate elements from a list,

```
(define (delete-adjacent-duplicates lst)
  (fold-right (lambda (elem ret)
                (if (equal? elem (first ret))
                    ret
                    (cons elem ret)))
              (list (last lst))
              lst))
(delete-adjacent-duplicates '(1 2 3 3 4 4 4 5))
⇒ (1 2 3 4 5)
```

Clearly the same sort of thing can be done with a `for-each` and a variable in which to build the result, but a self-contained *proc* can be re-used in multiple contexts, where a `for-each` would have to be written out each time.

pair-fold *proc init lst1 lst2 …*   [Scheme Procedure]
pair-fold-right *proc init lst1 lst2 …*   [Scheme Procedure]
> The same as `fold` and `fold-right`, but apply *proc* to the pairs of the lists instead of the list elements.

reduce *proc default lst*   [Scheme Procedure]
reduce-right *proc default lst*   [Scheme Procedure]
> `reduce` is a variant of `fold`, where the first call to *proc* is on two elements from *lst*, rather than one element and a given initial value.
>
> If *lst* is empty, `reduce` returns *default* (this is the only use for *default*). If *lst* has just one element then that's the return value. Otherwise *proc* is called on the elements of *lst*.
>
> Each *proc* call is (**proc** **elem** **previous**), where *elem* is from *lst* (the second and subsequent elements of *lst*), and *previous* is the return from the previous call to *proc*. The first element of *lst* is the *previous* for the first call to *proc*.
>
> For example, the following adds a list of numbers, the calls made to + are shown. (Of course + accepts multiple arguments and can add a list directly, with `apply`.)
>
> ```
> (reduce + 0 '(5 6 7))  ⇒ 18
>
> (+ 6 5)   ⇒ 11
> (+ 7 11)  ⇒ 18
> ```
>
> `reduce` can be used instead of `fold` where the *init* value is an "identity", meaning a value which under *proc* doesn't change the result, in this case 0 is an identity since (+ 5 0) is just 5. `reduce` avoids that unnecessary call.

reduce-right is a similar variation on fold-right, working from the end (ie. the right) of *lst*. The last element of *lst* is the *previous* for the first call to *proc*, and the *elem* values go from the second last.

reduce should be preferred over reduce-right if the order of processing doesn't matter, or can be arranged either way, since reduce is a little more efficient.

unfold *p f g seed* [*tail-gen*]   [Scheme Procedure]
unfold is defined as follows:

```
(unfold p f g seed) =
  (if (p seed) (tail-gen seed)
    (cons (f seed)
          (unfold p f g (g seed)))))
```

p   Determines when to stop unfolding.

f   Maps each seed value to the corresponding list element.

g   Maps each seed value to next seed value.

seed   The state value for the unfold.

tail-gen   Creates the tail of the list; defaults to (lambda (x) '()).

g produces a series of seed values, which are mapped to list elements by *f*. These elements are put into a list in left-to-right order, and *p* tells when to stop unfolding.

unfold-right *p f g seed* [*tail*]   [Scheme Procedure]
Construct a list with the following loop.

```
(let lp ((seed seed) (lis tail))
  (if (p seed) lis
    (lp (g seed)
        (cons (f seed) lis))))
```

p   Determines when to stop unfolding.

f   Maps each seed value to the corresponding list element.

g   Maps each seed value to next seed value.

seed   The state value for the unfold.

tail   The tail of the list; defaults to '().

map *f lst1 lst2 ...*   [Scheme Procedure]
Map the procedure over the list(s) *lst1*, *lst2*, ... and return a list containing the results of the procedure applications. This procedure is extended with respect to R5RS, because the argument lists may have different lengths. The result list will have the same length as the shortest argument lists. The order in which *f* will be applied to the list element(s) is not specified.

for-each *f lst1 lst2 ...*   [Scheme Procedure]
Apply the procedure *f* to each pair of corresponding elements of the list(s) *lst1*, *lst2*, ... The return value is not specified. This procedure is extended with respect to R5RS, because the argument lists may have different lengths. The shortest argument list determines the number of times *f* is called. *f* will be applied to the list elements in left-to-right order.

`append-map` *f lst1 lst2 ...*   [Scheme Procedure]
`append-map!` *f lst1 lst2 ...*   [Scheme Procedure]
> Equivalent to
>
>> `(apply append (map f clist1 clist2 ...))`
>
> and
>
>> `(apply append! (map f clist1 clist2 ...))`
>
> Map *f* over the elements of the lists, just as in the `map` function. However, the results of the applications are appended together to make the final result. `append-map` uses `append` to append the results together; `append-map!` uses `append!`.
>
> The dynamic order in which the various applications of *f* are made is not specified.

`map!` *f lst1 lst2 ...*   [Scheme Procedure]
> Linear-update variant of `map` – `map!` is allowed, but not required, to alter the cons cells of *lst1* to construct the result list.
>
> The dynamic order in which the various applications of *f* are made is not specified. In the n-ary case, *lst2*, *lst3*, ... must have at least as many elements as *lst1*.

`pair-for-each` *f lst1 lst2 ...*   [Scheme Procedure]
> Like `for-each`, but applies the procedure *f* to the pairs from which the argument lists are constructed, instead of the list elements. The return value is not specified.

`filter-map` *f lst1 lst2 ...*   [Scheme Procedure]
> Like `map`, but only results from the applications of *f* which are true are saved in the result list.

7.5.3.6 Filtering and Partitioning

Filtering means to collect all elements from a list which satisfy a specific condition. Partitioning a list means to make two groups of list elements, one which contains the elements satisfying a condition, and the other for the elements which don't.

The `filter` and `filter!` functions are implemented in the Guile core, See Section 6.7.2.6 [List Modification], page 191.

`partition` *pred lst*   [Scheme Procedure]
`partition!` *pred lst*   [Scheme Procedure]
> Split *lst* into those elements which do and don't satisfy the predicate *pred*.
>
> The return is two values (see Section 6.13.7 [Multiple Values], page 301), the first being a list of all elements from *lst* which satisfy *pred*, the second a list of those which do not.
>
> The elements in the result lists are in the same order as in *lst* but the order in which the calls (`pred` elem) are made on the list elements is unspecified.
>
> `partition` does not change *lst*, but one of the returned lists may share a tail with it. `partition!` may modify *lst* to construct its return.

`remove` *pred lst*   [Scheme Procedure]
`remove!` *pred lst*   [Scheme Procedure]
> Return a list containing all elements from *lst* which do not satisfy the predicate *pred*. The elements in the result list have the same order as in *lst*. The order in which *pred* is applied to the list elements is not specified.

`remove!` is allowed, but not required to modify the structure of the input list.

7.5.3.7 Searching

The procedures for searching elements in lists either accept a predicate or a comparison object for determining which elements are to be searched.

`find` *pred lst*   [Scheme Procedure]
> Return the first element of *lst* which satisfies the predicate *pred* and `#f` if no such element is found.

`find-tail` *pred lst*   [Scheme Procedure]
> Return the first pair of *lst* whose CAR satisfies the predicate *pred* and `#f` if no such element is found.

`take-while` *pred lst*   [Scheme Procedure]
`take-while!` *pred lst*   [Scheme Procedure]
> Return the longest initial prefix of *lst* whose elements all satisfy the predicate *pred*.
>
> `take-while!` is allowed, but not required to modify the input list while producing the result.

`drop-while` *pred lst*   [Scheme Procedure]
> Drop the longest initial prefix of *lst* whose elements all satisfy the predicate *pred*.

`span` *pred lst*   [Scheme Procedure]
`span!` *pred lst*   [Scheme Procedure]
`break` *pred lst*   [Scheme Procedure]
`break!` *pred lst*   [Scheme Procedure]
> `span` splits the list *lst* into the longest initial prefix whose elements all satisfy the predicate *pred*, and the remaining tail. `break` inverts the sense of the predicate.
>
> `span!` and `break!` are allowed, but not required to modify the structure of the input list *lst* in order to produce the result.
>
> Note that the name `break` conflicts with the `break` binding established by `while` (see Section 6.13.4 [while do], page 294). Applications wanting to use `break` from within a `while` loop will need to make a new define under a different name.

`any` *pred lst1 lst2 ...*   [Scheme Procedure]
> Test whether any set of elements from *lst1 lst2 ...* satisfies *pred*. If so, the return value is the return value from the successful *pred* call, or if not, the return value is `#f`.
>
> If there are n list arguments, then *pred* must be a predicate taking n arguments. Each *pred* call is (`pred elem1 elem2 ...`) taking an element from each *lst*. The calls are made successively for the first, second, etc. elements of the lists, stopping when *pred* returns non-`#f`, or when the end of the shortest list is reached.
>
> The *pred* call on the last set of elements (i.e., when the end of the shortest list has been reached), if that point is reached, is a tail call.

every *pred lst1 lst2 ...*   [Scheme Procedure]

> Test whether every set of elements from *lst1 lst2 ...* satisfies *pred*. If so, the return value is the return from the final *pred* call, or if not, the return value is `#f`.
>
> If there are n list arguments, then *pred* must be a predicate taking n arguments. Each *pred* call is (`pred elem1 elem2 ...`) taking an element from each *lst*. The calls are made successively for the first, second, etc. elements of the lists, stopping if *pred* returns `#f`, or when the end of any of the lists is reached.
>
> The *pred* call on the last set of elements (i.e., when the end of the shortest list has been reached) is a tail call.
>
> If one of *lst1 lst2 ...* is empty then no calls to *pred* are made, and the return value is `#t`.

list-index *pred lst1 lst2 ...*   [Scheme Procedure]

> Return the index of the first set of elements, one from each of *lst1 lst2 ...*, which satisfies *pred*.
>
> *pred* is called as (`elem1 elem2 ...`). Searching stops when the end of the shortest *lst* is reached. The return index starts from 0 for the first set of elements. If no set of elements pass, then the return value is `#f`.
>
> ```
> (list-index odd? '(2 4 6 9))      ⇒ 3
> (list-index = '(1 2 3) '(3 1 2))  ⇒ #f
> ```

member *x lst* [=]   [Scheme Procedure]

> Return the first sublist of *lst* whose CAR is equal to *x*. If *x* does not appear in *lst*, return `#f`.
>
> Equality is determined by `equal?`, or by the equality predicate = if given. = is called (`= x elem`), ie. with the given *x* first, so for example to find the first element greater than 5,
>
> ```
> (member 5 '(3 5 1 7 2 9) <) ⇒ (7 2 9)
> ```
>
> This version of `member` extends the core `member` (see Section 6.7.2.7 [List Searching], page 192) by accepting an equality predicate.

7.5.3.8 Deleting

delete *x lst* [=]   [Scheme Procedure]
delete! *x lst* [=]   [Scheme Procedure]

> Return a list containing the elements of *lst* but with those equal to *x* deleted. The returned elements will be in the same order as they were in *lst*.
>
> Equality is determined by the = predicate, or `equal?` if not given. An equality call is made just once for each element, but the order in which the calls are made on the elements is unspecified.
>
> The equality calls are always (`= x elem`), ie. the given *x* is first. This means for instance elements greater than 5 can be deleted with (`delete 5 lst <`).
>
> `delete` does not modify *lst*, but the return might share a common tail with *lst*. `delete!` may modify the structure of *lst* to construct its return.
>
> These functions extend the core `delete` and `delete!` (see Section 6.7.2.6 [List Modification], page 191) in accepting an equality predicate. See also `lset-difference` (see

Section 7.5.3.10 [SRFI-1 Set Operations], page 563) for deleting multiple elements from a list.

delete-duplicates *lst* [=]   [Scheme Procedure]
delete-duplicates! *lst* [=]   [Scheme Procedure]
Return a list containing the elements of *lst* but without duplicates.

When elements are equal, only the first in *lst* is retained. Equal elements can be anywhere in *lst*, they don't have to be adjacent. The returned list will have the retained elements in the same order as they were in *lst*.

Equality is determined by the = predicate, or **equal?** if not given. Calls (= x y) are made with element *x* being before *y* in *lst*. A call is made at most once for each combination, but the sequence of the calls across the elements is unspecified.

delete-duplicates does not modify *lst*, but the return might share a common tail with *lst*. **delete-duplicates!** may modify the structure of *lst* to construct its return.

In the worst case, this is an $O(N^2)$ algorithm because it must check each element against all those preceding it. For long lists it is more efficient to sort and then compare only adjacent elements.

7.5.3.9 Association Lists

Association lists are described in detail in section Section 6.7.12 [Association Lists], page 228. The present section only documents the additional procedures for dealing with association lists defined by SRFI-1.

assoc *key alist* [=]   [Scheme Procedure]
Return the pair from *alist* which matches *key*. This extends the core **assoc** (see Section 6.7.12.3 [Retrieving Alist Entries], page 230) by taking an optional = comparison procedure.

The default comparison is **equal?**. If an = parameter is given it's called (= *key alistcar*), i.e. the given target *key* is the first argument, and a **car** from *alist* is second.

For example a case-insensitive string lookup,

```
(assoc "yy" '(("XX" . 1) ("YY" . 2)) string-ci=?)
⇒ ("YY" . 2)
```

alist-cons *key datum alist*   [Scheme Procedure]
Cons a new association *key* and *datum* onto *alist* and return the result. This is equivalent to

```
(cons (cons key datum) alist)
```

acons (see Section 6.7.12.2 [Adding or Setting Alist Entries], page 228) in the Guile core does the same thing.

alist-copy *alist*   [Scheme Procedure]
Return a newly allocated copy of *alist*, that means that the spine of the list as well as the pairs are copied.

alist-delete *key alist* [=] [Scheme Procedure]
alist-delete! *key alist* [=] [Scheme Procedure]

> Return a list containing the elements of *alist* but with those elements whose keys are equal to *key* deleted. The returned elements will be in the same order as they were in *alist*.
>
> Equality is determined by the = predicate, or `equal?` if not given. The order in which elements are tested is unspecified, but each equality call is made (= `key alistkey`), i.e. the given *key* parameter is first and the key from *alist* second. This means for instance all associations with a key greater than 5 can be removed with (`alist-delete 5 alist <`).
>
> `alist-delete` does not modify *alist*, but the return might share a common tail with *alist*. `alist-delete!` may modify the list structure of *alist* to construct its return.

7.5.3.10 Set Operations on Lists

Lists can be used to represent sets of objects. The procedures in this section operate on such lists as sets.

Note that lists are not an efficient way to implement large sets. The procedures here typically take time $m \times n$ when operating on m and n element lists. Other data structures like trees, bitsets (see Section 6.7.4 [Bit Vectors], page 198) or hash tables (see Section 6.7.14 [Hash Tables], page 236) are faster.

All these procedures take an equality predicate as the first argument. This predicate is used for testing the objects in the list sets for sameness. This predicate must be consistent with `eq?` (see Section 6.11.1 [Equality], page 276) in the sense that if two list elements are `eq?` then they must also be equal under the predicate. This simply means a given object must be equal to itself.

lset<= *= list* ... [Scheme Procedure]

> Return #t if each list is a subset of the one following it. I.e., *list1* is a subset of *list2*, *list2* is a subset of *list3*, etc., for as many lists as given. If only one list or no lists are given, the return value is #t.
>
> A list x is a subset of y if each element of x is equal to some element in y. Elements are compared using the given = procedure, called as (= `xelem yelem`).
>
> ```
> (lset<= eq?)                  ⇒ #t
> (lset<= eqv? '(1 2 3) '(1))   ⇒ #f
> (lset<= eqv? '(1 3 2) '(4 3 1 2)) ⇒ #t
> ```

lset= *= list* ... [Scheme Procedure]

> Return #t if all argument lists are set-equal. *list1* is compared to *list2*, *list2* to *list3*, etc., for as many lists as given. If only one list or no lists are given, the return value is #t.
>
> Two lists x and y are set-equal if each element of x is equal to some element of y and conversely each element of y is equal to some element of x. The order of the elements in the lists doesn't matter. Element equality is determined with the given = procedure, called as (= `xelem yelem`), but exactly which calls are made is unspecified.
>
> ```
> (lset= eq?)                  ⇒ #t
> (lset= eqv? '(1 2 3) '(3 2 1)) ⇒ #t
> ```

```
(lset= string-ci=? '("a" "A" "b") '("B" "b" "a")) ⇒ #t
```

lset-adjoin = *list elem* ...   [Scheme Procedure]

Add to *list* any of the given *elems* not already in the list. *elems* are `cons`ed onto the start of *list* (so the return value shares a common tail with *list*), but the order that the *elems* are added is unspecified.

The given = procedure is used for comparing elements, called as (= `listelem elem`), i.e., the second argument is one of the given *elem* parameters.

```
(lset-adjoin eqv? '(1 2 3) 4 1 5) ⇒ (5 4 1 2 3)
```

lset-union = *list* ...   [Scheme Procedure]
lset-union! = *list* ...   [Scheme Procedure]

Return the union of the argument list sets. The result is built by taking the union of *list1* and *list2*, then the union of that with *list3*, etc., for as many lists as given. For one list argument that list itself is the result, for no list arguments the result is the empty list.

The union of two lists *x* and *y* is formed as follows. If *x* is empty then the result is *y*. Otherwise start with *x* as the result and consider each *y* element (from first to last). A *y* element not equal to something already in the result is `cons`ed onto the result.

The given = procedure is used for comparing elements, called as (= `relem yelem`). The first argument is from the result accumulated so far, and the second is from the list being union-ed in. But exactly which calls are made is otherwise unspecified.

Notice that duplicate elements in *list1* (or the first non-empty list) are preserved, but that repeated elements in subsequent lists are only added once.

```
(lset-union eqv?)                         ⇒ ()
(lset-union eqv? '(1 2 3))                ⇒ (1 2 3)
(lset-union eqv? '(1 2 1 3) '(2 4 5) '(5)) ⇒ (5 4 1 2 1 3)
```

`lset-union` doesn't change the given lists but the result may share a tail with the first non-empty list. `lset-union!` can modify all of the given lists to form the result.

lset-intersection = *list1 list2* ...   [Scheme Procedure]
lset-intersection! = *list1 list2* ...   [Scheme Procedure]

Return the intersection of *list1* with the other argument lists, meaning those elements of *list1* which are also in all of *list2* etc. For one list argument, just that list is returned.

The test for an element of *list1* to be in the return is simply that it's equal to some element in each of *list2* etc. Notice this means an element appearing twice in *list1* but only once in each of *list2* etc will go into the return twice. The return has its elements in the same order as they were in *list1*.

The given = procedure is used for comparing elements, called as (= `elem1 elemN`). The first argument is from *list1* and the second is from one of the subsequent lists. But exactly which calls are made and in what order is unspecified.

```
(lset-intersection eqv? '(x y))                    ⇒ (x y)
(lset-intersection eqv? '(1 2 3) '(4 3 2))         ⇒ (2 3)
(lset-intersection eqv? '(1 1 2 2) '(1 2) '(2 1) '(2)) ⇒ (2 2)
```

The return from `lset-intersection` may share a tail with *list1*. `lset-intersection!` may modify *list1* to form its result.

`lset-difference` = *list1 list2 ...*   [Scheme Procedure]
`lset-difference!` = *list1 list2 ...*   [Scheme Procedure]

Return *list1* with any elements in *list2*, *list3* etc removed (ie. subtracted). For one list argument, just that list is returned.

The given = procedure is used for comparing elements, called as (= `elem1` `elemN`). The first argument is from *list1* and the second from one of the subsequent lists. But exactly which calls are made and in what order is unspecified.

```
(lset-difference eqv? '(x y))              ⇒ (x y)
(lset-difference eqv? '(1 2 3) '(3 1))     ⇒ (2)
(lset-difference eqv? '(1 2 3) '(3) '(2))  ⇒ (1)
```

The return from `lset-difference` may share a tail with *list1*. `lset-difference!` may modify *list1* to form its result.

`lset-diff+intersection` = *list1 list2 ...*   [Scheme Procedure]
`lset-diff+intersection!` = *list1 list2 ...*   [Scheme Procedure]

Return two values (see Section 6.13.7 [Multiple Values], page 301), the difference and intersection of the argument lists as per `lset-difference` and `lset-intersection` above.

For two list arguments this partitions *list1* into those elements of *list1* which are in *list2* and not in *list2*. (But for more than two arguments there can be elements of *list1* which are neither part of the difference nor the intersection.)

One of the return values from `lset-diff+intersection` may share a tail with *list1*. `lset-diff+intersection!` may modify *list1* to form its results.

`lset-xor` = *list ...*   [Scheme Procedure]
`lset-xor!` = *list ...*   [Scheme Procedure]

Return an XOR of the argument lists. For two lists this means those elements which are in exactly one of the lists. For more than two lists it means those elements which appear in an odd number of the lists.

To be precise, the XOR of two lists x and y is formed by taking those elements of x not equal to any element of y, plus those elements of y not equal to any element of x. Equality is determined with the given = procedure, called as (= `e1` `e2`). One argument is from x and the other from y, but which way around is unspecified. Exactly which calls are made is also unspecified, as is the order of the elements in the result.

```
(lset-xor eqv? '(x y))              ⇒ (x y)
(lset-xor eqv? '(1 2 3) '(4 3 2))   ⇒ (4 1)
```

The return from `lset-xor` may share a tail with one of the list arguments. `lset-xor!` may modify *list1* to form its result.

7.5.4 SRFI-2 - and-let*

The following syntax can be obtained with

```
(use-modules (srfi srfi-2))
```

or alternatively

```
(use-modules (ice-9 and-let-star))
```

and-let* (*clause* ...) *body* ...   [library syntax]
> A combination of **and** and **let***.

> Each *clause* is evaluated in turn, and if **#f** is obtained then evaluation stops and **#f** is returned. If all are non-**#f** then *body* is evaluated and the last form gives the return value, or if *body* is empty then the result is **#t**. Each *clause* should be one of the following,

> (symbol expr)
>> Evaluate *expr*, check for **#f**, and bind it to *symbol*. Like **let***, that binding is available to subsequent clauses.

> (expr)   Evaluate *expr* and check for **#f**.

> symbol   Get the value bound to *symbol* and check for **#f**.

> Notice that **(expr)** has an "extra" pair of parentheses, for instance **((eq? x y))**. One way to remember this is to imagine the **symbol** in **(symbol expr)** is omitted.

> **and-let*** is good for calculations where a **#f** value means termination, but where a non-**#f** value is going to be needed in subsequent expressions.

> The following illustrates this, it returns text between brackets '[...]' in a string, or **#f** if there are no such brackets (ie. either **string-index** gives **#f**).

```
(define (extract-brackets str)
  (and-let* ((start (string-index str #\[))
             (end   (string-index str #\] start)))
    (substring str (1+ start) end)))
```

> The following shows plain variables and expressions tested too. **diagnostic-levels** is taken to be an alist associating a diagnostic type with a level. **str** is printed only if the type is known and its level is high enough.

```
(define (show-diagnostic type str)
  (and-let* (want-diagnostics
             (level (assq-ref diagnostic-levels type))
             ((>= level current-diagnostic-level)))
    (display str)))
```

> The advantage of **and-let*** is that an extended sequence of expressions and tests doesn't require lots of nesting as would arise from separate **and** and **let***, or from **cond** with **=>**.

7.5.5 SRFI-4 - Homogeneous numeric vector datatypes

SRFI-4 provides an interface to uniform numeric vectors: vectors whose elements are all of a single numeric type. Guile offers uniform numeric vectors for signed and unsigned 8-bit, 16-bit, 32-bit, and 64-bit integers, two sizes of floating point values, and, as an extension to SRFI-4, complex floating-point numbers of these two sizes.

The standard SRFI-4 procedures and data types may be included via loading the appropriate module:

```
(use-modules (srfi srfi-4))
```

This module is currently a part of the default Guile environment, but it is a good practice to explicitly import the module. In the future, using SRFI-4 procedures without importing the SRFI-4 module will cause a deprecation message to be printed. (Of course, one may call the C functions at any time. Would that C had modules!)

7.5.5.1 SRFI-4 - Overview

Uniform numeric vectors can be useful since they consume less memory than the non-uniform, general vectors. Also, since the types they can store correspond directly to C types, it is easier to work with them efficiently on a low level. Consider image processing as an example, where you want to apply a filter to some image. While you could store the pixels of an image in a general vector and write a general convolution function, things are much more efficient with uniform vectors: the convolution function knows that all pixels are unsigned 8-bit values (say), and can use a very tight inner loop.

This is implemented in Scheme by having the compiler notice calls to the SRFI-4 accessors, and inline them to appropriate compiled code. From C you have access to the raw array; functions for efficiently working with uniform numeric vectors from C are listed at the end of this section.

Uniform numeric vectors are the special case of one dimensional uniform numeric arrays.

There are 12 standard kinds of uniform numeric vectors, and they all have their own complement of constructors, accessors, and so on. Procedures that operate on a specific kind of uniform numeric vector have a "tag" in their name, indicating the element type.

u8   unsigned 8-bit integers

s8   signed 8-bit integers

u16   unsigned 16-bit integers

s16   signed 16-bit integers

u32   unsigned 32-bit integers

s32   signed 32-bit integers

u64   unsigned 64-bit integers

s64   signed 64-bit integers

f32   the C type `float`

f64   the C type `double`

In addition, Guile supports uniform arrays of complex numbers, with the nonstandard tags:

c32   complex numbers in rectangular form with the real and imaginary part being a `float`

c64   complex numbers in rectangular form with the real and imaginary part being a `double`

The external representation (ie. read syntax) for these vectors is similar to normal Scheme vectors, but with an additional tag from the tables above indicating the vector's type. For example,

```
#u16(1 2 3)
#f64(3.1415 2.71)
```

Note that the read syntax for floating-point here conflicts with #f for false. In Standard Scheme one can write (1 #f3) for a three element list (1 #f 3), but for Guile (1 #f3) is invalid. (1 #f 3) is almost certainly what one should write anyway to make the intention clear, so this is rarely a problem.

7.5.5.2 SRFI-4 - API

Note that the c32 and c64 functions are only available from (srfi srfi-4 gnu).

u8vector? *obj*	[Scheme Procedure]
s8vector? *obj*	[Scheme Procedure]
u16vector? *obj*	[Scheme Procedure]
s16vector? *obj*	[Scheme Procedure]
u32vector? *obj*	[Scheme Procedure]
s32vector? *obj*	[Scheme Procedure]
u64vector? *obj*	[Scheme Procedure]
s64vector? *obj*	[Scheme Procedure]
f32vector? *obj*	[Scheme Procedure]
f64vector? *obj*	[Scheme Procedure]
c32vector? *obj*	[Scheme Procedure]
c64vector? *obj*	[Scheme Procedure]
scm_u8vector_p (*obj*)	[C Function]
scm_s8vector_p (*obj*)	[C Function]
scm_u16vector_p (*obj*)	[C Function]
scm_s16vector_p (*obj*)	[C Function]
scm_u32vector_p (*obj*)	[C Function]
scm_s32vector_p (*obj*)	[C Function]
scm_u64vector_p (*obj*)	[C Function]
scm_s64vector_p (*obj*)	[C Function]
scm_f32vector_p (*obj*)	[C Function]
scm_f64vector_p (*obj*)	[C Function]
scm_c32vector_p (*obj*)	[C Function]
scm_c64vector_p (*obj*)	[C Function]

Return #t if *obj* is a homogeneous numeric vector of the indicated type.

make-u8vector *n* [*value*]	[Scheme Procedure]
make-s8vector *n* [*value*]	[Scheme Procedure]
make-u16vector *n* [*value*]	[Scheme Procedure]
make-s16vector *n* [*value*]	[Scheme Procedure]
make-u32vector *n* [*value*]	[Scheme Procedure]
make-s32vector *n* [*value*]	[Scheme Procedure]
make-u64vector *n* [*value*]	[Scheme Procedure]
make-s64vector *n* [*value*]	[Scheme Procedure]
make-f32vector *n* [*value*]	[Scheme Procedure]
make-f64vector *n* [*value*]	[Scheme Procedure]
make-c32vector *n* [*value*]	[Scheme Procedure]

make-c64vector *n* [*value*]   [Scheme Procedure]
scm_make_u8vector (*n, value*)   [C Function]
scm_make_s8vector (*n, value*)   [C Function]
scm_make_u16vector (*n, value*)   [C Function]
scm_make_s16vector (*n, value*)   [C Function]
scm_make_u32vector (*n, value*)   [C Function]
scm_make_s32vector (*n, value*)   [C Function]
scm_make_u64vector (*n, value*)   [C Function]
scm_make_s64vector (*n, value*)   [C Function]
scm_make_f32vector (*n, value*)   [C Function]
scm_make_f64vector (*n, value*)   [C Function]
scm_make_c32vector (*n, value*)   [C Function]
scm_make_c64vector (*n, value*)   [C Function]

> Return a newly allocated homogeneous numeric vector holding *n* elements of the indicated type. If *value* is given, the vector is initialized with that value, otherwise the contents are unspecified.

u8vector *value* ...   [Scheme Procedure]
s8vector *value* ...   [Scheme Procedure]
u16vector *value* ...   [Scheme Procedure]
s16vector *value* ...   [Scheme Procedure]
u32vector *value* ...   [Scheme Procedure]
s32vector *value* ...   [Scheme Procedure]
u64vector *value* ...   [Scheme Procedure]
s64vector *value* ...   [Scheme Procedure]
f32vector *value* ...   [Scheme Procedure]
f64vector *value* ...   [Scheme Procedure]
c32vector *value* ...   [Scheme Procedure]
c64vector *value* ...   [Scheme Procedure]
scm_u8vector (*values*)   [C Function]
scm_s8vector (*values*)   [C Function]
scm_u16vector (*values*)   [C Function]
scm_s16vector (*values*)   [C Function]
scm_u32vector (*values*)   [C Function]
scm_s32vector (*values*)   [C Function]
scm_u64vector (*values*)   [C Function]
scm_s64vector (*values*)   [C Function]
scm_f32vector (*values*)   [C Function]
scm_f64vector (*values*)   [C Function]
scm_c32vector (*values*)   [C Function]
scm_c64vector (*values*)   [C Function]

> Return a newly allocated homogeneous numeric vector of the indicated type, holding the given parameter *values*. The vector length is the number of parameters given.

u8vector-length *vec*   [Scheme Procedure]
s8vector-length *vec*   [Scheme Procedure]
u16vector-length *vec*   [Scheme Procedure]
s16vector-length *vec*   [Scheme Procedure]

u32vector-length *vec*   [Scheme Procedure]
s32vector-length *vec*   [Scheme Procedure]
u64vector-length *vec*   [Scheme Procedure]
s64vector-length *vec*   [Scheme Procedure]
f32vector-length *vec*   [Scheme Procedure]
f64vector-length *vec*   [Scheme Procedure]
c32vector-length *vec*   [Scheme Procedure]
c64vector-length *vec*   [Scheme Procedure]
scm_u8vector_length (*vec*)   [C Function]
scm_s8vector_length (*vec*)   [C Function]
scm_u16vector_length (*vec*)   [C Function]
scm_s16vector_length (*vec*)   [C Function]
scm_u32vector_length (*vec*)   [C Function]
scm_s32vector_length (*vec*)   [C Function]
scm_u64vector_length (*vec*)   [C Function]
scm_s64vector_length (*vec*)   [C Function]
scm_f32vector_length (*vec*)   [C Function]
scm_f64vector_length (*vec*)   [C Function]
scm_c32vector_length (*vec*)   [C Function]
scm_c64vector_length (*vec*)   [C Function]
     Return the number of elements in *vec*.

u8vector-ref *vec i*   [Scheme Procedure]
s8vector-ref *vec i*   [Scheme Procedure]
u16vector-ref *vec i*   [Scheme Procedure]
s16vector-ref *vec i*   [Scheme Procedure]
u32vector-ref *vec i*   [Scheme Procedure]
s32vector-ref *vec i*   [Scheme Procedure]
u64vector-ref *vec i*   [Scheme Procedure]
s64vector-ref *vec i*   [Scheme Procedure]
f32vector-ref *vec i*   [Scheme Procedure]
f64vector-ref *vec i*   [Scheme Procedure]
c32vector-ref *vec i*   [Scheme Procedure]
c64vector-ref *vec i*   [Scheme Procedure]
scm_u8vector_ref (*vec, i*)   [C Function]
scm_s8vector_ref (*vec, i*)   [C Function]
scm_u16vector_ref (*vec, i*)   [C Function]
scm_s16vector_ref (*vec, i*)   [C Function]
scm_u32vector_ref (*vec, i*)   [C Function]
scm_s32vector_ref (*vec, i*)   [C Function]
scm_u64vector_ref (*vec, i*)   [C Function]
scm_s64vector_ref (*vec, i*)   [C Function]
scm_f32vector_ref (*vec, i*)   [C Function]
scm_f64vector_ref (*vec, i*)   [C Function]
scm_c32vector_ref (*vec, i*)   [C Function]
scm_c64vector_ref (*vec, i*)   [C Function]
     Return the element at index *i* in *vec*. The first element in *vec* is index 0.

`u8vector-set!` *vec i value*	[Scheme Procedure]
`s8vector-set!` *vec i value*	[Scheme Procedure]
`u16vector-set!` *vec i value*	[Scheme Procedure]
`s16vector-set!` *vec i value*	[Scheme Procedure]
`u32vector-set!` *vec i value*	[Scheme Procedure]
`s32vector-set!` *vec i value*	[Scheme Procedure]
`u64vector-set!` *vec i value*	[Scheme Procedure]
`s64vector-set!` *vec i value*	[Scheme Procedure]
`f32vector-set!` *vec i value*	[Scheme Procedure]
`f64vector-set!` *vec i value*	[Scheme Procedure]
`c32vector-set!` *vec i value*	[Scheme Procedure]
`c64vector-set!` *vec i value*	[Scheme Procedure]
`scm_u8vector_set_x` (*vec, i, value*)	[C Function]
`scm_s8vector_set_x` (*vec, i, value*)	[C Function]
`scm_u16vector_set_x` (*vec, i, value*)	[C Function]
`scm_s16vector_set_x` (*vec, i, value*)	[C Function]
`scm_u32vector_set_x` (*vec, i, value*)	[C Function]
`scm_s32vector_set_x` (*vec, i, value*)	[C Function]
`scm_u64vector_set_x` (*vec, i, value*)	[C Function]
`scm_s64vector_set_x` (*vec, i, value*)	[C Function]
`scm_f32vector_set_x` (*vec, i, value*)	[C Function]
`scm_f64vector_set_x` (*vec, i, value*)	[C Function]
`scm_c32vector_set_x` (*vec, i, value*)	[C Function]
`scm_c64vector_set_x` (*vec, i, value*)	[C Function]

Set the element at index *i* in *vec* to *value*. The first element in *vec* is index 0. The return value is unspecified.

`u8vector->list` *vec*	[Scheme Procedure]
`s8vector->list` *vec*	[Scheme Procedure]
`u16vector->list` *vec*	[Scheme Procedure]
`s16vector->list` *vec*	[Scheme Procedure]
`u32vector->list` *vec*	[Scheme Procedure]
`s32vector->list` *vec*	[Scheme Procedure]
`u64vector->list` *vec*	[Scheme Procedure]
`s64vector->list` *vec*	[Scheme Procedure]
`f32vector->list` *vec*	[Scheme Procedure]
`f64vector->list` *vec*	[Scheme Procedure]
`c32vector->list` *vec*	[Scheme Procedure]
`c64vector->list` *vec*	[Scheme Procedure]
`scm_u8vector_to_list` (*vec*)	[C Function]
`scm_s8vector_to_list` (*vec*)	[C Function]
`scm_u16vector_to_list` (*vec*)	[C Function]
`scm_s16vector_to_list` (*vec*)	[C Function]
`scm_u32vector_to_list` (*vec*)	[C Function]
`scm_s32vector_to_list` (*vec*)	[C Function]
`scm_u64vector_to_list` (*vec*)	[C Function]
`scm_s64vector_to_list` (*vec*)	[C Function]

scm_f32vector_to_list (*vec*)   [C Function]
scm_f64vector_to_list (*vec*)   [C Function]
scm_c32vector_to_list (*vec*)   [C Function]
scm_c64vector_to_list (*vec*)   [C Function]
> Return a newly allocated list holding all elements of *vec*.

list->u8vector *lst*   [Scheme Procedure]
list->s8vector *lst*   [Scheme Procedure]
list->u16vector *lst*   [Scheme Procedure]
list->s16vector *lst*   [Scheme Procedure]
list->u32vector *lst*   [Scheme Procedure]
list->s32vector *lst*   [Scheme Procedure]
list->u64vector *lst*   [Scheme Procedure]
list->s64vector *lst*   [Scheme Procedure]
list->f32vector *lst*   [Scheme Procedure]
list->f64vector *lst*   [Scheme Procedure]
list->c32vector *lst*   [Scheme Procedure]
list->c64vector *lst*   [Scheme Procedure]
scm_list_to_u8vector (*lst*)   [C Function]
scm_list_to_s8vector (*lst*)   [C Function]
scm_list_to_u16vector (*lst*)   [C Function]
scm_list_to_s16vector (*lst*)   [C Function]
scm_list_to_u32vector (*lst*)   [C Function]
scm_list_to_s32vector (*lst*)   [C Function]
scm_list_to_u64vector (*lst*)   [C Function]
scm_list_to_s64vector (*lst*)   [C Function]
scm_list_to_f32vector (*lst*)   [C Function]
scm_list_to_f64vector (*lst*)   [C Function]
scm_list_to_c32vector (*lst*)   [C Function]
scm_list_to_c64vector (*lst*)   [C Function]
> Return a newly allocated homogeneous numeric vector of the indicated type, initialized with the elements of the list *lst*.

SCM scm_take_u8vector (*const scm_t_uint8 *data, size_t len*)   [C Function]
SCM scm_take_s8vector (*const scm_t_int8 *data, size_t len*)   [C Function]
SCM scm_take_u16vector (*const scm_t_uint16 *data, size_t len*)   [C Function]
SCM scm_take_s16vector (*const scm_t_int16 *data, size_t len*)   [C Function]
SCM scm_take_u32vector (*const scm_t_uint32 *data, size_t len*)   [C Function]
SCM scm_take_s32vector (*const scm_t_int32 *data, size_t len*)   [C Function]
SCM scm_take_u64vector (*const scm_t_uint64 *data, size_t len*)   [C Function]
SCM scm_take_s64vector (*const scm_t_int64 *data, size_t len*)   [C Function]
SCM scm_take_f32vector (*const float *data, size_t len*)   [C Function]
SCM scm_take_f64vector (*const double *data, size_t len*)   [C Function]
SCM scm_take_c32vector (*const float *data, size_t len*)   [C Function]
SCM scm_take_c64vector (*const double *data, size_t len*)   [C Function]
> Return a new uniform numeric vector of the indicated type and length that uses the memory pointed to by *data* to store its elements. This memory will eventually be

freed with `free`. The argument *len* specifies the number of elements in *data*, not its size in bytes.

The `c32` and `c64` variants take a pointer to a C array of `float`s or `double`s. The real parts of the complex numbers are at even indices in that array, the corresponding imaginary parts are at the following odd index.

const scm_t_uint8 * scm_u8vector_elements (*SCM vec*,   [C Function]
        *scm_t_array_handle *handle, size_t *lenp, ssize_t *incp*)
const scm_t_int8 * scm_s8vector_elements (*SCM vec*,   [C Function]
        *scm_t_array_handle *handle, size_t *lenp, ssize_t *incp*)
const scm_t_uint16 * scm_u16vector_elements (*SCM vec*,   [C Function]
        *scm_t_array_handle *handle, size_t *lenp, ssize_t *incp*)
const scm_t_int16 * scm_s16vector_elements (*SCM vec*,   [C Function]
        *scm_t_array_handle *handle, size_t *lenp, ssize_t *incp*)
const scm_t_uint32 * scm_u32vector_elements (*SCM vec*,   [C Function]
        *scm_t_array_handle *handle, size_t *lenp, ssize_t *incp*)
const scm_t_int32 * scm_s32vector_elements (*SCM vec*,   [C Function]
        *scm_t_array_handle *handle, size_t *lenp, ssize_t *incp*)
const scm_t_uint64 * scm_u64vector_elements (*SCM vec*,   [C Function]
        *scm_t_array_handle *handle, size_t *lenp, ssize_t *incp*)
const scm_t_int64 * scm_s64vector_elements (*SCM vec*,   [C Function]
        *scm_t_array_handle *handle, size_t *lenp, ssize_t *incp*)
const float * scm_f32vector_elements (*SCM vec*,   [C Function]
        *scm_t_array_handle *handle, size_t *lenp, ssize_t *incp*)
const double * scm_f64vector_elements (*SCM vec*,   [C Function]
        *scm_t_array_handle *handle, size_t *lenp, ssize_t *incp*)
const float * scm_c32vector_elements (*SCM vec*,   [C Function]
        *scm_t_array_handle *handle, size_t *lenp, ssize_t *incp*)
const double * scm_c64vector_elements (*SCM vec*,   [C Function]
        *scm_t_array_handle *handle, size_t *lenp, ssize_t *incp*)
        Like `scm_vector_elements` (see Section 6.7.3.4 [Vector Accessing from C], page 196), but returns a pointer to the elements of a uniform numeric vector of the indicated kind.

scm_t_uint8 * scm_u8vector_writable_elements (*SCM vec*,   [C Function]
        *scm_t_array_handle *handle, size_t *lenp, ssize_t *incp*)
scm_t_int8 * scm_s8vector_writable_elements (*SCM vec*,   [C Function]
        *scm_t_array_handle *handle, size_t *lenp, ssize_t *incp*)
scm_t_uint16 * scm_u16vector_writable_elements (*SCM vec*,   [C Function]
        *scm_t_array_handle *handle, size_t *lenp, ssize_t *incp*)
scm_t_int16 * scm_s16vector_writable_elements (*SCM vec*,   [C Function]
        *scm_t_array_handle *handle, size_t *lenp, ssize_t *incp*)
scm_t_uint32 * scm_u32vector_writable_elements (*SCM vec*,   [C Function]
        *scm_t_array_handle *handle, size_t *lenp, ssize_t *incp*)
scm_t_int32 * scm_s32vector_writable_elements (*SCM vec*,   [C Function]
        *scm_t_array_handle *handle, size_t *lenp, ssize_t *incp*)

```
scm_t_uint64 * scm_u64vector_writable_elements (SCM vec,              [C Function]
        scm_t_array_handle *handle, size_t *lenp, ssize_t *incp)
scm_t_int64 * scm_s64vector_writable_elements (SCM vec,               [C Function]
        scm_t_array_handle *handle, size_t *lenp, ssize_t *incp)
float * scm_f32vector_writable_elements (SCM vec,                     [C Function]
        scm_t_array_handle *handle, size_t *lenp, ssize_t *incp)
double * scm_f64vector_writable_elements (SCM vec,                    [C Function]
        scm_t_array_handle *handle, size_t *lenp, ssize_t *incp)
float * scm_c32vector_writable_elements (SCM vec,                     [C Function]
        scm_t_array_handle *handle, size_t *lenp, ssize_t *incp)
double * scm_c64vector_writable_elements (SCM vec,                    [C Function]
        scm_t_array_handle *handle, size_t *lenp, ssize_t *incp)
```

> Like `scm_vector_writable_elements` (see Section 6.7.3.4 [Vector Accessing from C], page 196), but returns a pointer to the elements of a uniform numeric vector of the indicated kind.

7.5.5.3 SRFI-4 - Relation to bytevectors

Guile implements SRFI-4 vectors using bytevectors (see Section 6.6.6 [Bytevectors], page 163). Often when you have a numeric vector, you end up wanting to write its bytes somewhere, or have access to the underlying bytes, or read in bytes from somewhere else. Bytevectors are very good at this sort of thing. But the SRFI-4 APIs are nicer to use when doing number-crunching, because they are addressed by element and not by byte.

So as a compromise, Guile allows all bytevector functions to operate on numeric vectors. They address the underlying bytes in the native endianness, as one would expect.

Following the same reasoning, that it's just bytes underneath, Guile also allows uniform vectors of a given type to be accessed as if they were of any type. One can fill a u32vector, and access its elements with u8vector-ref. One can use f64vector-ref on bytevectors. It's all the same to Guile.

In this way, uniform numeric vectors may be written to and read from input/output ports using the procedures that operate on bytevectors.

See Section 6.6.6 [Bytevectors], page 163, for more information.

7.5.5.4 SRFI-4 - Guile extensions

Guile defines some useful extensions to SRFI-4, which are not available in the default Guile environment. They may be imported by loading the extensions module:

```
(use-modules (srfi srfi-4 gnu))
```

any->u8vector *obj*	[Scheme Procedure]
any->s8vector *obj*	[Scheme Procedure]
any->u16vector *obj*	[Scheme Procedure]
any->s16vector *obj*	[Scheme Procedure]
any->u32vector *obj*	[Scheme Procedure]
any->s32vector *obj*	[Scheme Procedure]
any->u64vector *obj*	[Scheme Procedure]
any->s64vector *obj*	[Scheme Procedure]
any->f32vector *obj*	[Scheme Procedure]

`any->f64vector` *obj*	[Scheme Procedure]
`any->c32vector` *obj*	[Scheme Procedure]
`any->c64vector` *obj*	[Scheme Procedure]
`scm_any_to_u8vector` (*obj*)	[C Function]
`scm_any_to_s8vector` (*obj*)	[C Function]
`scm_any_to_u16vector` (*obj*)	[C Function]
`scm_any_to_s16vector` (*obj*)	[C Function]
`scm_any_to_u32vector` (*obj*)	[C Function]
`scm_any_to_s32vector` (*obj*)	[C Function]
`scm_any_to_u64vector` (*obj*)	[C Function]
`scm_any_to_s64vector` (*obj*)	[C Function]
`scm_any_to_f32vector` (*obj*)	[C Function]
`scm_any_to_f64vector` (*obj*)	[C Function]
`scm_any_to_c32vector` (*obj*)	[C Function]
`scm_any_to_c64vector` (*obj*)	[C Function]

Return a (maybe newly allocated) uniform numeric vector of the indicated type, initialized with the elements of *obj*, which must be a list, a vector, or a uniform vector. When *obj* is already a suitable uniform numeric vector, it is returned unchanged.

7.5.6 SRFI-6 - Basic String Ports

SRFI-6 defines the procedures `open-input-string`, `open-output-string` and `get-output-string`.

Note that although versions of these procedures are included in the Guile core, the core versions are not fully conformant with SRFI-6: attempts to read or write characters that are not supported by the current `%default-port-encoding` will fail.

We therefore recommend that you import this module, which supports all characters:

```
(use-modules (srfi srfi-6))
```

7.5.7 SRFI-8 - receive

`receive` is a syntax for making the handling of multiple-value procedures easier. It is documented in See Section 6.13.7 [Multiple Values], page 301.

7.5.8 SRFI-9 - define-record-type

This SRFI is a syntax for defining new record types and creating predicate, constructor, and field getter and setter functions. It is documented in the "Compound Data Types" section of the manual (see Section 6.7.8 [SRFI-9 Records], page 216).

7.5.9 SRFI-10 - Hash-Comma Reader Extension

This SRFI implements a reader extension `#,()` called hash-comma. It allows the reader to give new kinds of objects, for use both in data and as constants or literals in source code. This feature is available with

```
(use-modules (srfi srfi-10))
```

The new read syntax is of the form

```
#,(tag arg...)
```

where *tag* is a symbol and the *args* are objects taken as parameters. *tags* are registered with the following procedure.

define-reader-ctor *tag proc*   [Scheme Procedure]

>   Register *proc* as the constructor for a hash-comma read syntax starting with symbol *tag*, i.e. #,(*tag arg*...). *proc* is called with the given arguments (*proc arg*...) and the object it returns is the result of the read.

For example, a syntax giving a list of *N* copies of an object.

```
(define-reader-ctor 'repeat
  (lambda (obj reps)
    (make-list reps obj)))

(display '#,(repeat 99 3))
⊣ (99 99 99)
```

Notice the quote ' when the #,( ) is used. The **repeat** handler returns a list and the program must quote to use it literally, the same as any other list. Ie.

```
(display '#,(repeat 99 3))
⇒
(display '(99 99 99))
```

When a handler returns an object which is self-evaluating, like a number or a string, then there's no need for quoting, just as there's no need when giving those directly as literals. For example an addition,

```
(define-reader-ctor 'sum
  (lambda (x y)
    (+ x y)))
(display #,(sum 123 456)) ⊣ 579
```

A typical use for #,( ) is to get a read syntax for objects which don't otherwise have one. For example, the following allows a hash table to be given literally, with tags and values, ready for fast lookup.

```
(define-reader-ctor 'hash
  (lambda elems
    (let ((table (make-hash-table)))
      (for-each (lambda (elem)
                  (apply hash-set! table elem))
                elems)
      table)))

(define (animal->family animal)
  (hash-ref '#,(hash ("tiger" "cat")
                     ("lion"  "cat")
                     ("wolf"  "dog"))
            animal))

(animal->family "lion") ⇒ "cat"
```

Or for example the following is a syntax for a compiled regular expression (see Section 6.15 [Regular Expressions], page 349).

```
(use-modules (ice-9 regex))

(define-reader-ctor 'regexp make-regexp)

(define (extract-angs str)
  (let ((match (regexp-exec '#,(regexp "<([A-Z0-9]+)>") str)))
    (and match
         (match:substring match 1))))

(extract-angs "foo <BAR> quux")  ⇒  "BAR"
```

#,() is somewhat similar to **define-macro** (see Section 6.10 [Macros], page 257) in that handler code is run to produce a result, but #,() operates at the read stage, so it can appear in data for **read** (see Section 6.17.2 [Scheme Read], page 360), not just in code to be executed.

Because #,() is handled at read-time it has no direct access to variables etc. A symbol in the arguments is just a symbol, not a variable reference. The arguments are essentially constants, though the handler procedure can use them in any complicated way it might want.

Once (srfi srfi-10) has loaded, #,() is available globally, there's no need to use (srfi srfi-10) in later modules. Similarly the tags registered are global and can be used anywhere once registered.

There's no attempt to record what previous #,() forms have been seen, if two identical forms occur then two calls are made to the handler procedure. The handler might like to maintain a cache or similar to avoid making copies of large objects, depending on expected usage.

In code the best uses of #,() are generally when there's a lot of objects of a particular kind as literals or constants. If there's just a few then some local variables and initializers are fine, but that becomes tedious and error prone when there's a lot, and the anonymous and compact syntax of #,() is much better.

7.5.10 SRFI-11 - let-values

This module implements the binding forms for multiple values **let-values** and **let*-values**. These forms are similar to **let** and **let*** (see Section 6.12.2 [Local Bindings], page 287), but they support binding of the values returned by multiple-valued expressions.

Write (use-modules (srfi srfi-11)) to make the bindings available.

```
(let-values (((x y) (values 1 2))
             ((z f) (values 3 4)))
  (+ x y z f))
⇒
10
```

let-values performs all bindings simultaneously, which means that no expression in the binding clauses may refer to variables bound in the same clause list. **let*-values**, on the other hand, performs the bindings sequentially, just like `let*` does for single-valued expressions.

7.5.11 SRFI-13 - String Library

The SRFI-13 procedures are always available, See Section 6.6.5 [Strings], page 141.

7.5.12 SRFI-14 - Character-set Library

The SRFI-14 data type and procedures are always available, See Section 6.6.4 [Character Sets], page 133.

7.5.13 SRFI-16 - case-lambda

SRFI-16 defines a variable-arity `lambda` form, `case-lambda`. This form is available in the default Guile environment. See Section 6.9.5 [Case-lambda], page 251, for more information.

7.5.14 SRFI-17 - Generalized set!

This SRFI implements a generalized `set!`, allowing some "referencing" functions to be used as the target location of a `set!`. This feature is available from

```
(use-modules (srfi srfi-17))
```

For example `vector-ref` is extended so that

```
(set! (vector-ref vec idx) new-value)
```

is equivalent to

```
(vector-set! vec idx new-value)
```

The idea is that a `vector-ref` expression identifies a location, which may be either fetched or stored. The same form is used for the location in both cases, encouraging visual clarity. This is similar to the idea of an "lvalue" in C.

The mechanism for this kind of `set!` is in the Guile core (see Section 6.9.8 [Procedures with Setters], page 255). This module adds definitions of the following functions as procedures with setters, allowing them to be targets of a `set!`,

> `car`, `cdr`, `caar`, `cadr`, `cdar`, `cddr`, `caaar`, `caadr`, `cadar`, `caddr`, `cdaar`, `cdadr`, `cddar`, `cdddr`, `caaaar`, `caaadr`, `caadar`, `caaddr`, `cadaar`, `cadadr`, `caddar`, `cadddr`, `cdaaar`, `cdaadr`, `cdadar`, `cdaddr`, `cddaar`, `cddadr`, `cdddar`, `cddddr`
>
> `string-ref`, `vector-ref`

The SRFI specifies `setter` (see Section 6.9.8 [Procedures with Setters], page 255) as a procedure with setter, allowing the setter for a procedure to be changed, eg. `(set! (setter foo) my-new-setter-handler)`. Currently Guile does not implement this, a setter can only be specified on creation (`getter-with-setter` below).

`getter-with-setter`   [Function]
> The same as the Guile core `make-procedure-with-setter` (see Section 6.9.8 [Procedures with Setters], page 255).

7.5.15 SRFI-18 - Multithreading support

This is an implementation of the SRFI-18 threading and synchronization library. The functions and variables described here are provided by

```
(use-modules (srfi srfi-18))
```

As a general rule, the data types and functions in this SRFI-18 implementation are compatible with the types and functions in Guile's core threading code. For example, mutexes created with the SRFI-18 `make-mutex` function can be passed to the built-in Guile function `lock-mutex` (see Section 6.21.4 [Mutexes and Condition Variables], page 415), and mutexes created with the built-in Guile function `make-mutex` can be passed to the SRFI-18 function `mutex-lock!`. Cases in which this does not hold true are noted in the following sections.

7.5.15.1 SRFI-18 Threads

Threads created by SRFI-18 differ in two ways from threads created by Guile's built-in thread functions. First, a thread created by SRFI-18 `make-thread` begins in a blocked state and will not start execution until `thread-start!` is called on it. Second, SRFI-18 threads are constructed with a top-level exception handler that captures any exceptions that are thrown on thread exit. In all other regards, SRFI-18 threads are identical to normal Guile threads.

current-thread   [Function]
> Returns the thread that called this function. This is the same procedure as the same-named built-in procedure `current-thread` (see Section 6.21.3 [Threads], page 413).

thread? *obj*   [Function]
> Returns `#t` if *obj* is a thread, `#f` otherwise. This is the same procedure as the same-named built-in procedure `thread?` (see Section 6.21.3 [Threads], page 413).

make-thread *thunk* [*name*]   [Function]
> Call `thunk` in a new thread and with a new dynamic state, returning the new thread and optionally assigning it the object name *name*, which may be any Scheme object.
>
> Note that the name `make-thread` conflicts with the (`ice-9 threads`) function `make-thread`. Applications wanting to use both of these functions will need to refer to them by different names.

thread-name *thread*   [Function]
> Returns the name assigned to *thread* at the time of its creation, or `#f` if it was not given a name.

thread-specific *thread*   [Function]
thread-specific-set! *thread obj*   [Function]
> Get or set the "object-specific" property of *thread*. In Guile's implementation of SRFI-18, this value is stored as an object property, and will be `#f` if not set.

thread-start! *thread*   [Function]
> Unblocks *thread* and allows it to begin execution if it has not done so already.

thread-yield!   [Function]
> If one or more threads are waiting to execute, calling `thread-yield!` forces an immediate context switch to one of them. Otherwise, `thread-yield!` has no effect. `thread-yield!` behaves identically to the Guile built-in function `yield`.

thread-sleep! *timeout*   [Function]
> The current thread waits until the point specified by the time object *timeout* is reached (see Section 7.5.15.4 [SRFI-18 Time], page 582). This blocks the thread only if *timeout* represents a point in the future. it is an error for *timeout* to be #f.

thread-terminate! *thread*   [Function]
> Causes an abnormal termination of *thread*. If *thread* is not already terminated, all mutexes owned by *thread* become unlocked/abandoned. If *thread* is the current thread, thread-terminate! does not return. Otherwise thread-terminate! returns an unspecified value; the termination of *thread* will occur before thread-terminate! returns. Subsequent attempts to join on *thread* will cause a "terminated thread exception" to be raised.
>
> thread-terminate! is compatible with the thread cancellation procedures in the core threads API (see Section 6.21.3 [Threads], page 413) in that if a cleanup handler has been installed for the target thread, it will be called before the thread exits and its return value (or exception, if any) will be stored for later retrieval via a call to thread-join!.

thread-join! *thread* [*timeout* [*timeout-val*]]   [Function]
> Wait for *thread* to terminate and return its exit value. When a time value *timeout* is given, it specifies a point in time where the waiting should be aborted. When the waiting is aborted, *timeout-val* is returned if it is specified; otherwise, a join-timeout-exception exception is raised (see Section 7.5.15.5 [SRFI-18 Exceptions], page 582). Exceptions may also be raised if the thread was terminated by a call to thread-terminate! (terminated-thread-exception will be raised) or if the thread exited by raising an exception that was handled by the top-level exception handler (uncaught-exception will be raised; the original exception can be retrieved using uncaught-exception-reason).

7.5.15.2 SRFI-18 Mutexes

The behavior of Guile's built-in mutexes is parameterized via a set of flags passed to the make-mutex procedure in the core (see Section 6.21.4 [Mutexes and Condition Variables], page 415). To satisfy the requirements for mutexes specified by SRFI-18, the make-mutex procedure described below sets the following flags:

- recursive: the mutex can be locked recursively

- unchecked-unlock: attempts to unlock a mutex that is already unlocked will not raise an exception

- allow-external-unlock: the mutex can be unlocked by any thread, not just the thread that locked it originally

make-mutex [*name*]   [Function]
> Returns a new mutex, optionally assigning it the object name *name*, which may be any Scheme object. The returned mutex will be created with the configuration described above. Note that the name make-mutex conflicts with Guile core function make-mutex. Applications wanting to use both of these functions will need to refer to them by different names.

mutex-name *mutex*   [Function]

> Returns the name assigned to *mutex* at the time of its creation, or #f if it was not given a name.

mutex-specific *mutex*   [Function]
mutex-specific-set! *mutex obj*   [Function]

> Get or set the "object-specific" property of *mutex*. In Guile's implementation of SRFI-18, this value is stored as an object property, and will be #f if not set.

mutex-state *mutex*   [Function]

> Returns information about the state of *mutex*. Possible values are:
>
> - thread T: the mutex is in the locked/owned state and thread T is the owner of the mutex
> - symbol not-owned: the mutex is in the locked/not-owned state
> - symbol abandoned: the mutex is in the unlocked/abandoned state
> - symbol not-abandoned: the mutex is in the unlocked/not-abandoned state

mutex-lock! *mutex* [*timeout* [*thread*]]   [Function]

> Lock *mutex*, optionally specifying a time object *timeout* after which to abort the lock attempt and a thread *thread* giving a new owner for *mutex* different than the current thread. This procedure has the same behavior as the lock-mutex procedure in the core library.

mutex-unlock! *mutex* [*condition-variable* [*timeout*]]   [Function]

> Unlock *mutex*, optionally specifying a condition variable *condition-variable* on which to wait, either indefinitely or, optionally, until the time object *timeout* has passed, to be signalled. This procedure has the same behavior as the unlock-mutex procedure in the core library.

7.5.15.3 SRFI-18 Condition variables

SRFI-18 does not specify a "wait" function for condition variables. Waiting on a condition variable can be simulated using the SRFI-18 mutex-unlock! function described in the previous section, or Guile's built-in wait-condition-variable procedure can be used.

condition-variable? *obj*   [Function]

> Returns #t if *obj* is a condition variable, #f otherwise. This is the same procedure as the same-named built-in procedure (see Section 6.21.4 [Mutexes and Condition Variables], page 415).

make-condition-variable [*name*]   [Function]

> Returns a new condition variable, optionally assigning it the object name *name*, which may be any Scheme object. This procedure replaces a procedure of the same name in the core library.

condition-variable-name *condition-variable*   [Function]

> Returns the name assigned to *condition-variable* at the time of its creation, or #f if it was not given a name.

`condition-variable-specific` *condition-variable*   [Function]
`condition-variable-specific-set!` *condition-variable obj*   [Function]

> Get or set the "object-specific" property of *condition-variable*. In Guile's implementation of SRFI-18, this value is stored as an object property, and will be `#f` if not set.

`condition-variable-signal!` *condition-variable*   [Function]
`condition-variable-broadcast!` *condition-variable*   [Function]

> Wake up one thread that is waiting for *condition-variable*, in the case of `condition-variable-signal!`, or all threads waiting for it, in the case of `condition-variable-broadcast!`. The behavior of these procedures is equivalent to that of the procedures `signal-condition-variable` and `broadcast-condition-variable` in the core library.

7.5.15.4 SRFI-18 Time

The SRFI-18 time functions manipulate time in two formats: a "time object" type that represents an absolute point in time in some implementation-specific way; and the number of seconds since some unspecified "epoch". In Guile's implementation, the epoch is the Unix epoch, 00:00:00 UTC, January 1, 1970.

`current-time`   [Function]

> Return the current time as a time object. This procedure replaces the procedure of the same name in the core library, which returns the current time in seconds since the epoch.

`time?` *obj*   [Function]

> Returns `#t` if *obj* is a time object, `#f` otherwise.

`time->seconds` *time*   [Function]
`seconds->time` *seconds*   [Function]

> Convert between time objects and numerical values representing the number of seconds since the epoch. When converting from a time object to seconds, the return value is the number of seconds between *time* and the epoch. When converting from seconds to a time object, the return value is a time object that represents a time *seconds* seconds after the epoch.

7.5.15.5 SRFI-18 Exceptions

SRFI-18 exceptions are identical to the exceptions provided by Guile's implementation of SRFI-34. The behavior of exception handlers invoked to handle exceptions thrown from SRFI-18 functions, however, differs from the conventional behavior of SRFI-34 in that the continuation of the handler is the same as that of the call to the function. Handlers are called in a tail-recursive manner; the exceptions do not "bubble up".

`current-exception-handler`   [Function]

> Returns the current exception handler.

`with-exception-handler` *handler thunk*   [Function]

> Installs *handler* as the current exception handler and calls the procedure *thunk* with no arguments, returning its value as the value of the exception. *handler* must be a

procedure that accepts a single argument. The current exception handler at the time
this procedure is called will be restored after the call returns.

`raise` *obj*   [Function]

> Raise *obj* as an exception. This is the same procedure as the same-named procedure
> defined in SRFI 34.

`join-timeout-exception?` *obj*   [Function]

> Returns `#t` if *obj* is an exception raised as the result of performing a timed join on a
> thread that does not exit within the specified timeout, `#f` otherwise.

`abandoned-mutex-exception?` *obj*   [Function]

> Returns `#t` if *obj* is an exception raised as the result of attempting to lock a mutex
> that has been abandoned by its owner thread, `#f` otherwise.

`terminated-thread-exception?` *obj*   [Function]

> Returns `#t` if *obj* is an exception raised as the result of joining on a thread that exited
> as the result of a call to `thread-terminate!`.

`uncaught-exception?` *obj*   [Function]
`uncaught-exception-reason` *exc*   [Function]

> `uncaught-exception?` returns `#t` if *obj* is an exception thrown as the result of joining
> a thread that exited by raising an exception that was handled by the top-level ex-
> ception handler installed by `make-thread`. When this occurs, the original exception
> is preserved as part of the exception thrown by `thread-join!` and can be accessed
> by calling `uncaught-exception-reason` on that exception. Note that because this
> exception-preservation mechanism is a side-effect of `make-thread`, joining on threads
> that exited as described above but were created by other means will not raise this
> `uncaught-exception` error.

7.5.16 SRFI-19 - Time/Date Library

This is an implementation of the SRFI-19 time/date library. The functions and variables
described here are provided by

```
(use-modules (srfi srfi-19))
```

Caution: The current code in this module incorrectly extends the Gregorian calendar
leap year rule back prior to the introduction of those reforms in 1582 (or the appropriate
year in various countries). The Julian calendar was used prior to 1582, and there were 10
days skipped for the reform, but the code doesn't implement that.

This will be fixed some time. Until then calculations for 1583 onwards are correct, but
prior to that any day/month/year and day of the week calculations are wrong.

7.5.16.1 SRFI-19 Introduction

This module implements time and date representations and calculations, in various time
systems, including universal time (UTC) and atomic time (TAI).

For those not familiar with these time systems, TAI is based on a fixed length second
derived from oscillations of certain atoms. UTC differs from TAI by an integral number
of seconds, which is increased or decreased at announced times to keep UTC aligned to a
mean solar day (the orbit and rotation of the earth are not quite constant).

So far, only increases in the TAI ↔ UTC difference have been needed. Such an increase is a "leap second", an extra second of TAI introduced at the end of a UTC day. When working entirely within UTC this is never seen, every day simply has 86400 seconds. But when converting from TAI to a UTC date, an extra 23:59:60 is present, where normally a day would end at 23:59:59. Effectively the UTC second from 23:59:59 to 00:00:00 has taken two TAI seconds.

In the current implementation, the system clock is assumed to be UTC, and a table of leap seconds in the code converts to TAI. See comments in `srfi-19.scm` for how to update this table.

Also, for those not familiar with the terminology, a *Julian Day* is a real number which is a count of days and fraction of a day, in UTC, starting from -4713-01-01T12:00:00Z, ie. midday Monday 1 Jan 4713 B.C. A *Modified Julian Day* is the same, but starting from 1858-11-17T00:00:00Z, ie. midnight 17 November 1858 UTC. That time is julian day 2400000.5.

7.5.16.2 SRFI-19 Time

A *time* object has type, seconds and nanoseconds fields representing a point in time starting from some epoch. This is an arbitrary point in time, not just a time of day. Although times are represented in nanoseconds, the actual resolution may be lower.

The following variables hold the possible time types. For instance (`current-time time-process`) would give the current CPU process time.

`time-utc`   [Variable]
    Universal Coordinated Time (UTC).

`time-tai`   [Variable]
    International Atomic Time (TAI).

`time-monotonic`   [Variable]
    Monotonic time, meaning a monotonically increasing time starting from an unspecified epoch.

    Note that in the current implementation `time-monotonic` is the same as `time-tai`, and unfortunately is therefore affected by adjustments to the system clock. Perhaps this will change in the future.

`time-duration`   [Variable]
    A duration, meaning simply a difference between two times.

`time-process`   [Variable]
    CPU time spent in the current process, starting from when the process began.

`time-thread`   [Variable]
    CPU time spent in the current thread. Not currently implemented.

`time?` *obj*   [Function]
    Return `#t` if *obj* is a time object, or `#f` if not.

make-time *type nanoseconds seconds*   [Function]
>   Create a time object with the given *type*, *seconds* and *nanoseconds*.

time-type *time*   [Function]
time-nanosecond *time*   [Function]
time-second *time*   [Function]
set-time-type! *time type*   [Function]
set-time-nanosecond! *time nsec*   [Function]
set-time-second! *time sec*   [Function]
>   Get or set the type, seconds or nanoseconds fields of a time object.
>
>   set-time-type! merely changes the field, it doesn't convert the time value. For
>   conversions, see Section 7.5.16.4 [SRFI-19 Time/Date conversions], page 587.

copy-time *time*   [Function]
>   Return a new time object, which is a copy of the given *time*.

current-time [*type*]   [Function]
>   Return the current time of the given *type*. The default *type* is time-utc.
>
>   Note that the name current-time conflicts with the Guile core current-time func-
>   tion (see Section 7.2.5 [Time], page 485) as well as the SRFI-18 current-time function
>   (see Section 7.5.15.4 [SRFI-18 Time], page 582). Applications wanting to use more
>   than one of these functions will need to refer to them by different names.

time-resolution [*type*]   [Function]
>   Return the resolution, in nanoseconds, of the given time *type*. The default *type* is
>   time-utc.

time<=? *t1 t2*   [Function]
time<? *t1 t2*   [Function]
time=? *t1 t2*   [Function]
time>=? *t1 t2*   [Function]
time>? *t1 t2*   [Function]
>   Return #t or #f according to the respective relation between time objects *t1* and *t2*.
>   *t1* and *t2* must be the same time type.

time-difference *t1 t2*   [Function]
time-difference! *t1 t2*   [Function]
>   Return a time object of type time-duration representing the period between *t1* and
>   *t2*. *t1* and *t2* must be the same time type.
>
>   time-difference returns a new time object, time-difference! may modify *t1* to
>   form its return.

add-duration *time duration*   [Function]
add-duration! *time duration*   [Function]
subtract-duration *time duration*   [Function]
subtract-duration! *time duration*   [Function]
>   Return a time object which is *time* with the given *duration* added or subtracted.
>   *duration* must be a time object of type time-duration.
>
>   add-duration and subtract-duration return a new time object. add-duration!
>   and subtract-duration! may modify the given *time* to form their return.

7.5.16.3 SRFI-19 Date

A *date* object represents a date in the Gregorian calendar and a time of day on that date in some timezone.

The fields are year, month, day, hour, minute, second, nanoseconds and timezone. A date object is immutable, its fields can be read but they cannot be modified once the object is created.

date? *obj*   [Function]
> Return #t if *obj* is a date object, or #f if not.

make-date *nsecs seconds minutes hours date month year zone-offset*   [Function]
> Create a new date object.

date-nanosecond *date*   [Function]
> Nanoseconds, 0 to 999999999.

date-second *date*   [Function]
> Seconds, 0 to 59, or 60 for a leap second. 60 is never seen when working entirely within UTC, it's only when converting to or from TAI.

date-minute *date*   [Function]
> Minutes, 0 to 59.

date-hour *date*   [Function]
> Hour, 0 to 23.

date-day *date*   [Function]
> Day of the month, 1 to 31 (or less, according to the month).

date-month *date*   [Function]
> Month, 1 to 12.

date-year *date*   [Function]
> Year, eg. 2003. Dates B.C. are negative, eg. −46 is 46 B.C. There is no year 0, year −1 is followed by year 1.

date-zone-offset *date*   [Function]
> Time zone, an integer number of seconds east of Greenwich.

date-year-day *date*   [Function]
> Day of the year, starting from 1 for 1st January.

date-week-day *date*   [Function]
> Day of the week, starting from 0 for Sunday.

date-week-number *date dstartw*   [Function]
> Week of the year, ignoring a first partial week. *dstartw* is the day of the week which is taken to start a week, 0 for Sunday, 1 for Monday, etc.

current-date [*tz-offset*]   [Function]
> Return a date object representing the current date/time, in UTC offset by *tz-offset*. *tz-offset* is seconds east of Greenwich and defaults to the local timezone.

`current-julian-day`   [Function]
> Return the current Julian Day.

`current-modified-julian-day`   [Function]
> Return the current Modified Julian Day.

7.5.16.4 SRFI-19 Time/Date conversions

`date->julian-day` *date*   [Function]
`date->modified-julian-day` *date*   [Function]
`date->time-monotonic` *date*   [Function]
`date->time-tai` *date*   [Function]
`date->time-utc` *date*   [Function]

`julian-day->date` *jdn* [*tz-offset*]   [Function]
`julian-day->time-monotonic` *jdn*   [Function]
`julian-day->time-tai` *jdn*   [Function]
`julian-day->time-utc` *jdn*   [Function]

`modified-julian-day->date` *jdn* [*tz-offset*]   [Function]
`modified-julian-day->time-monotonic` *jdn*   [Function]
`modified-julian-day->time-tai` *jdn*   [Function]
`modified-julian-day->time-utc` *jdn*   [Function]

`time-monotonic->date` *time* [*tz-offset*]   [Function]
`time-monotonic->time-tai` *time*   [Function]
`time-monotonic->time-tai!` *time*   [Function]
`time-monotonic->time-utc` *time*   [Function]
`time-monotonic->time-utc!` *time*   [Function]

`time-tai->date` *time* [*tz-offset*]   [Function]
`time-tai->julian-day` *time*   [Function]
`time-tai->modified-julian-day` *time*   [Function]
`time-tai->time-monotonic` *time*   [Function]
`time-tai->time-monotonic!` *time*   [Function]
`time-tai->time-utc` *time*   [Function]
`time-tai->time-utc!` *time*   [Function]

`time-utc->date` *time* [*tz-offset*]   [Function]
`time-utc->julian-day` *time*   [Function]
`time-utc->modified-julian-day` *time*   [Function]
`time-utc->time-monotonic` *time*   [Function]
`time-utc->time-monotonic!` *time*   [Function]
`time-utc->time-tai` *time*   [Function]
`time-utc->time-tai!` *time*   [Function]

> Convert between dates, times and days of the respective types. For instance `time-tai->time-utc` accepts a *time* object of type `time-tai` and returns an object of type `time-utc`.
>
> The ! variants may modify their *time* argument to form their return. The plain functions create a new object.

For conversions to dates, *tz-offset* is seconds east of Greenwich. The default is the local timezone, at the given time, as provided by the system, using `localtime` (see Section 7.2.5 [Time], page 485).

On 32-bit systems, `localtime` is limited to a 32-bit `time_t`, so a default *tz-offset* is only available for times between Dec 1901 and Jan 2038. For prior dates an application might like to use the value in 1902, though some locations have zone changes prior to that. For future dates an application might like to assume today's rules extend indefinitely. But for correct daylight savings transitions it will be necessary to take an offset for the same day and time but a year in range and which has the same starting weekday and same leap/non-leap (to support rules like last Sunday in October).

7.5.16.5 SRFI-19 Date to string

date->string *date [format]*   [Function]
Convert a date to a string under the control of a format. *format* should be a string containing '~' escapes, which will be expanded as per the following conversion table. The default *format* is '~c', a locale-dependent date and time.

Many of these conversion characters are the same as POSIX `strftime` (see Section 7.2.5 [Time], page 485), but there are some extras and some variations.

~~	literal ~
~a	locale abbreviated weekday, eg. 'Sun'
~A	locale full weekday, eg. 'Sunday'
~b	locale abbreviated month, eg. 'Jan'
~B	locale full month, eg. 'January'
~c	locale date and time, eg. 'Fri Jul 14 20:28:42-0400 2000'
~d	day of month, zero padded, '01' to '31'
~e	day of month, blank padded, ' 1' to '31'
~f	seconds and fractional seconds, with locale decimal point, eg. '5.2'
~h	same as ~b
~H	hour, 24-hour clock, zero padded, '00' to '23'
~I	hour, 12-hour clock, zero padded, '01' to '12'
~j	day of year, zero padded, '001' to '366'
~k	hour, 24-hour clock, blank padded, ' 0' to '23'
~l	hour, 12-hour clock, blank padded, ' 1' to '12'
~m	month, zero padded, '01' to '12'
~M	minute, zero padded, '00' to '59'
~n	newline
~N	nanosecond, zero padded, '000000000' to '999999999'
~p	locale AM or PM
~r	time, 12 hour clock, '~I:~M:~S ~p'
~s	number of full seconds since "the epoch" in UTC
~S	second, zero padded '00' to '60' (usual limit is 59, 60 is a leap second)
~t	horizontal tab character

~T	time, 24 hour clock, '~H:~M:~S'
~U	week of year, Sunday first day of week, '00' to '52'
~V	week of year, Monday first day of week, '01' to '53'
~w	day of week, 0 for Sunday, '0' to '6'
~W	week of year, Monday first day of week, '00' to '52'
~y	year, two digits, '00' to '99'
~Y	year, full, eg. '2003'
~z	time zone, RFC-822 style
~Z	time zone symbol (not currently implemented)
~1	ISO-8601 date, '~Y-~m-~d'
~2	ISO-8601 time+zone, '~H:~M:~S~z'
~3	ISO-8601 time, '~H:~M:~S'
~4	ISO-8601 date/time+zone, '~Y-~m-~dT~H:~M:~S~z'
~5	ISO-8601 date/time, '~Y-~m-~dT~H:~M:~S'

Conversions '~D', '~x' and '~X' are not currently described here, since the specification and reference implementation differ.

Conversion is locale-dependent on systems that support it (see Section 6.24.5 [Accessing Locale Information], page 439). See Section 7.2.13 [Locales], page 518, for information on how to change the current locale.

7.5.16.6 SRFI-19 String to date

string->date *input template*   [Function]

Convert an *input* string to a date under the control of a *template* string. Return a newly created date object.

Literal characters in *template* must match characters in *input* and '~' escapes must match the input forms described in the table below. "Skip to" means characters up to one of the given type are ignored, or "no skip" for no skipping. "Read" is what's then read, and "Set" is the field affected in the date object.

For example '~Y' skips input characters until a digit is reached, at which point it expects a year and stores that to the year field of the date.

	Skip to	Read	Set
~~	no skip	literal ~	nothing
~a	char-alphabetic?	locale abbreviated weekday name	nothing
~A	char-alphabetic?	locale full weekday name	nothing
~b	char-alphabetic?	locale abbreviated month name	date-month
~B	char-alphabetic?	locale full month name	date-month
~d	char-numeric?	day of month	date-day

~e	no skip	day of month, blank padded	date-d
~h	same as '~b'		
~H	char-numeric?	hour	date-h
~k	no skip	hour, blank padded	date-h
~m	char-numeric?	month	date-m
~M	char-numeric?	minute	date-m
~S	char-numeric?	second	date-s
~y	no skip	2-digit year	date-y 50 year
~Y	char-numeric?	year	date-y
~z	no skip	time zone	date-zo

Notice that the weekday matching forms don't affect the date object returned, instead the weekday will be derived from the day, month and year.

Conversion is locale-dependent on systems that support it (see Section 6.24.5 [Accessing Locale Information], page 439). See Section 7.2.13 [Locales], page 518, for information on how to change the current locale.

7.5.17 SRFI-23 - Error Reporting

The SRFI-23 `error` procedure is always available.

7.5.18 SRFI-26 - specializing parameters

This SRFI provides a syntax for conveniently specializing selected parameters of a function. It can be used with,

```
(use-modules (srfi srfi-26))
```

cut *slot1 slot2 ...*   [library syntax]
cute *slot1 slot2 ...*   [library syntax]

    Return a new procedure which will make a call (*slot1 slot2 ...*) but with selected parameters specialized to given expressions.

    An example will illustrate the idea. The following is a specialization of `write`, sending output to `my-output-port`,

```
(cut write <> my-output-port)
⇒
(lambda (obj) (write obj my-output-port))
```

    The special symbol `<>` indicates a slot to be filled by an argument to the new procedure. `my-output-port` on the other hand is an expression to be evaluated and passed, ie. it specializes the behaviour of `write`.

<>   A slot to be filled by an argument from the created procedure. Arguments
                are assigned to <> slots in the order they appear in the cut form, there's
                no way to re-arrange arguments.

                The first argument to cut is usually a procedure (or expression giving a
                procedure), but <> is allowed there too. For example,

```
(cut <> 1 2 3)
⇒
(lambda (proc) (proc 1 2 3))
```

<...>   A slot to be filled by all remaining arguments from the new procedure.
                This can only occur at the end of a cut form.

                For example, a procedure taking a variable number of arguments like max
                but in addition enforcing a lower bound,

```
(define my-lower-bound 123)

(cut max my-lower-bound <...>)
⇒
(lambda arglist (apply max my-lower-bound arglist))
```

For cut the specializing expressions are evaluated each time the new procedure is
called. For cute they're evaluated just once, when the new procedure is created. The
name cute stands for "cut with evaluated arguments". In all cases the evaluations
take place in an unspecified order.

The following illustrates the difference between cut and cute,

```
(cut format <> "the time is ~s" (current-time))
⇒
(lambda (port) (format port "the time is ~s" (current-time)))

(cute format <> "the time is ~s" (current-time))
⇒
(let ((val (current-time)))
  (lambda (port) (format port "the time is ~s" val))
```

(There's no provision for a mixture of cut and cute where some expressions would
be evaluated every time but others evaluated only once.)

cut is really just a shorthand for the sort of lambda forms shown in the above examples. But notice cut avoids the need to name unspecialized parameters, and is more
compact. Use in functional programming style or just with map, for-each or similar
is typical.

```
(map (cut * 2 <>) '(1 2 3 4))

(for-each (cut write <> my-port) my-list)
```

7.5.19 SRFI-27 - Sources of Random Bits

This subsection is based on the specification of SRFI-27 written by Sebastian Egner.

This SRFI provides access to a (pseudo) random number generator; for Guile's built-
in random number facilities, which SRFI-27 is implemented upon, See Section 6.6.2.14

[Random], page 127. With SRFI-27, random numbers are obtained from a *random source*, which encapsulates a random number generation algorithm and its state.

7.5.19.1 The Default Random Source

random-integer *n*   [Function]

> Return a random number between zero (inclusive) and *n* (exclusive), using the default random source. The numbers returned have a uniform distribution.

random-real   [Function]

> Return a random number in (0,1), using the default random source. The numbers returned have a uniform distribution.

default-random-source   [Function]

> A random source from which **random-integer** and **random-real** have been derived using **random-source-make-integers** and **random-source-make-reals** (see Section 7.5.19.3 [SRFI-27 Random Number Generators], page 593 for those procedures). Note that an assignment to **default-random-source** does not change **random-integer** or **random-real**; it is also strongly recommended not to assign a new value.

7.5.19.2 Random Sources

make-random-source   [Function]

> Create a new random source. The stream of random numbers obtained from each random source created by this procedure will be identical, unless its state is changed by one of the procedures below.

random-source? *object*   [Function]

> Tests whether *object* is a random source. Random sources are a disjoint type.

random-source-randomize! *source*   [Function]

> Attempt to set the state of the random source to a truly random value. The current implementation uses a seed based on the current system time.

random-source-pseudo-randomize! *source i j*   [Function]

> Changes the state of the random source s into the initial state of the (*i*, *j*)-th independent random source, where *i* and *j* are non-negative integers. This procedure provides a mechanism to obtain a large number of independent random sources (usually all derived from the same backbone generator), indexed by two integers. In contrast to **random-source-randomize!**, this procedure is entirely deterministic.

The state associated with a random state can be obtained an reinstated with the following procedures:

random-source-state-ref *source*   [Function]
random-source-state-set! *source state*   [Function]

> Get and set the state of a random source. No assumptions should be made about the nature of the state object, besides it having an external representation (i.e. it can be passed to **write** and subsequently **read** back).

7.5.19.3 Obtaining random number generator procedures

`random-source-make-integers` *source*   [Function]

Obtains a procedure to generate random integers using the random source *source*. The returned procedure takes a single argument *n*, which must be a positive integer, and returns the next uniformly distributed random integer from the interval {0, ..., *n*-1} by advancing the state of *source*.

If an application obtains and uses several generators for the same random source *source*, a call to any of these generators advances the state of *source*. Hence, the generators do not produce the same sequence of random integers each but rather share a state. This also holds for all other types of generators derived from a fixed random sources.

While the SRFI text specifies that "Implementations that support concurrency make sure that the state of a generator is properly advanced", this is currently not the case in Guile's implementation of SRFI-27, as it would cause a severe performance penalty. So in multi-threaded programs, you either must perform locking on random sources shared between threads yourself, or use different random sources for multiple threads.

`random-source-make-reals` *source*   [Function]
`random-source-make-reals` *source unit*   [Function]

Obtains a procedure to generate random real numbers $0 < x < 1$ using the random source *source*. The procedure rand is called without arguments.

The optional parameter *unit* determines the type of numbers being produced by the returned procedure and the quantization of the output. *unit* must be a number such that $0 < unit < 1$. The numbers created by the returned procedure are of the same numerical type as *unit* and the potential output values are spaced by at most *unit*. One can imagine rand to create numbers as $x * unit$ where x is a random integer in {1, ..., floor(1/unit)-1}. Note, however, that this need not be the way the values are actually created and that the actual resolution of rand can be much higher than *unit*. In case *unit* is absent it defaults to a reasonably small value (related to the width of the mantissa of an efficient number format).

7.5.20 SRFI-30 - Nested Multi-line Comments

Starting from version 2.0, Guile's `read` supports SRFI-30/R6RS nested multi-line comments by default, Section 6.17.1.3 [Block Comments], page 359.

7.5.21 SRFI-31 - A special form 'rec' for recursive evaluation

SRFI-31 defines a special form that can be used to create self-referential expressions more conveniently. The syntax is as follows:

```
<rec expression> --> (rec <variable> <expression>)
<rec expression> --> (rec (<variable>+) <body>)
```

The first syntax can be used to create self-referential expressions, for example:

```
guile> (define tmp (rec ones (cons 1 (delay ones))))
```

The second syntax can be used to create anonymous recursive functions:

```
guile> (define tmp (rec (display-n item n)
                        (if (positive? n)
                            (begin (display n) (display-n (- n 1)))))))
guile> (tmp 42 3)
424242
guile>
```

7.5.22 SRFI-34 - Exception handling for programs

Guile provides an implementation of SRFI-34's exception handling mechanisms as an alternative to its own built-in mechanisms (see Section 6.13.8 [Exceptions], page 303). It can be made available as follows:

```
(use-modules (srfi srfi-34))
```

7.5.23 SRFI-35 - Conditions

SRFI-35 implements *conditions*, a data structure akin to records designed to convey information about exceptional conditions between parts of a program. It is normally used in conjunction with SRFI-34's `raise`:

```
(raise (condition (&message
                    (message "An error occurred"))))
```

Users can define *condition types* containing arbitrary information. Condition types may inherit from one another. This allows the part of the program that handles (or "catches") conditions to get accurate information about the exceptional condition that arose.

SRFI-35 conditions are made available using:

```
(use-modules (srfi srfi-35))
```

The procedures available to manipulate condition types are the following:

make-condition-type *id parent field-names*   [Scheme Procedure]
Return a new condition type named *id*, inheriting from *parent*, and with the fields whose names are listed in *field-names*. *field-names* must be a list of symbols and must not contain names already used by *parent* or one of its supertypes.

condition-type? *obj*   [Scheme Procedure]
Return true if *obj* is a condition type.

Conditions can be created and accessed with the following procedures:

make-condition *type . field+value*   [Scheme Procedure]
Return a new condition of type *type* with fields initialized as specified by *field+value*, a sequence of field names (symbols) and values as in the following example:

```
(let ((&ct (make-condition-type 'foo &condition '(a b c))))
  (make-condition &ct 'a 1 'b 2 'c 3))
```

Note that all fields of *type* and its supertypes must be specified.

make-compound-condition *condition1 condition2 ...*   [Scheme Procedure]
Return a new compound condition composed of *condition1 condition2 ....* The returned condition has the type of each condition of condition1 condition2 ... (per `condition-has-type?`).

`condition-has-type?` *c type*   [Scheme Procedure]
>   Return true if condition *c* has type *type*.

`condition-ref` *c field-name*   [Scheme Procedure]
>   Return the value of the field named *field-name* from condition *c*.
>
>   If *c* is a compound condition and several underlying condition types contain a field named *field-name*, then the value of the first such field is returned, using the order in which conditions were passed to `make-compound-condition`.

`extract-condition` *c type*   [Scheme Procedure]
>   Return a condition of condition type *type* with the field values specified by *c*.
>
>   If *c* is a compound condition, extract the field values from the subcondition belonging to *type* that appeared first in the call to `make-compound-condition` that created the condition.

Convenience macros are also available to create condition types and conditions.

`define-condition-type` *type supertype predicate field-spec...*   [library syntax]
>   Define a new condition type named *type* that inherits from *supertype*. In addition, bind *predicate* to a type predicate that returns true when passed a condition of type *type* or any of its subtypes. *field-spec* must have the form (`field accessor`) where *field* is the name of field of *type* and *accessor* is the name of a procedure to access field *field* in conditions of type *type*.
>
>   The example below defines condition type `&foo`, inheriting from `&condition` with fields `a`, `b` and `c`:
>
> ```
> (define-condition-type &foo &condition
>   foo-condition?
>   (a  foo-a)
>   (b  foo-b)
>   (c  foo-c))
> ```

`condition` *type-field-binding1 type-field-binding2 ...*   [library syntax]
>   Return a new condition or compound condition, initialized according to *type-field-binding1 type-field-binding2 ....* Each *type-field-binding* must have the form (`type field-specs...`), where *type* is the name of a variable bound to a condition type; each *field-spec* must have the form (`field-name value`) where *field-name* is a symbol denoting the field being initialized to *value*. As for `make-condition`, all fields must be specified.
>
>   The following example returns a simple condition:
>
> ```
> (condition (&message (message "An error occurred")))
> ```
>
>   The one below returns a compound condition:
>
> ```
> (condition (&message (message "An error occurred"))
>            (&serious))
> ```

Finally, SRFI-35 defines a several standard condition types.

`&condition`   [Variable]
>   This condition type is the root of all condition types. It has no fields.

&message   [Variable]

> A condition type that carries a message describing the nature of the condition to humans.

message-condition? *c*   [Scheme Procedure]

> Return true if *c* is of type **&message** or one of its subtypes.

condition-message *c*   [Scheme Procedure]

> Return the message associated with message condition *c*.

&serious   [Variable]

> This type describes conditions serious enough that they cannot safely be ignored. It has no fields.

serious-condition? *c*   [Scheme Procedure]

> Return true if *c* is of type **&serious** or one of its subtypes.

&error   [Variable]

> This condition describes errors, typically caused by something that has gone wrong in the interaction of the program with the external world or the user.

error? *c*   [Scheme Procedure]

> Return true if *c* is of type **&error** or one of its subtypes.

7.5.24 SRFI-37 - args-fold

This is a processor for GNU `getopt_long`-style program arguments. It provides an alternative, less declarative interface than `getopt-long` in `(ice-9 getopt-long)` (see Section 7.4 [The (ice-9 getopt-long) Module], page 546). Unlike `getopt-long`, it supports repeated options and any number of short and long names per option. Access it with:

```
(use-modules (srfi srfi-37))
```

SRFI-37 principally provides an `option` type and the `args-fold` function. To use the library, create a set of options with `option` and use it as a specification for invoking `args-fold`.

Here is an example of a simple argument processor for the typical '`--version`' and '`--help`' options, which returns a backwards list of files given on the command line:

```
(args-fold (cdr (program-arguments))
           (let ((display-and-exit-proc
                  (lambda (msg)
                    (lambda (opt name arg loads)
                      (display msg) (quit)))))
             (list (option '(#\v "version") #f #f
                           (display-and-exit-proc "Foo version 42.0\n"))
                   (option '(#\h "help") #f #f
                           (display-and-exit-proc
                            "Usage: foo scheme-file ..."))))
           (lambda (opt name arg loads)
             (error "Unrecognized option '~A'" name))
           (lambda (op loads) (cons op loads))
           '())
```

option *names required-arg? optional-arg? processor*   [Scheme Procedure]

> Return an object that specifies a single kind of program option.
>
> *names* is a list of command-line option names, and should consist of characters for traditional `getopt` short options and strings for `getopt_long`-style long options.
>
> *required-arg?* and *optional-arg?* are mutually exclusive; one or both must be #f. If *required-arg?*, the option must be followed by an argument on the command line, such as '`--opt=value`' for long options, or an error will be signalled. If *optional-arg?*, an argument will be taken if available.
>
> *processor* is a procedure that takes at least 3 arguments, called when `args-fold` encounters the option: the containing option object, the name used on the command line, and the argument given for the option (or #f if none). The rest of the arguments are `args-fold` "seeds", and the *processor* should return seeds as well.

option-names *opt*   [Scheme Procedure]
option-required-arg? *opt*   [Scheme Procedure]
option-optional-arg? *opt*   [Scheme Procedure]
option-processor *opt*   [Scheme Procedure]

> Return the specified field of *opt*, an option object, as described above for `option`.

args-fold *args options unrecognized-option-proc operand-proc*   [Scheme Procedure]
> *seed* . . .
>
> Process *args*, a list of program arguments such as that returned by (`cdr` (`program-arguments`)), in order against *options*, a list of option objects as described above. All functions called take the "seeds", or the last multiple-values as multiple arguments, starting with *seed* . . ., and must return the new seeds. Return the final seeds.
>
> Call `unrecognized-option-proc`, which is like an option object's processor, for any options not found in *options*.
>
> Call `operand-proc` with any items on the command line that are not named options. This includes arguments after '`--`'. It is called with the argument in question, as well as the seeds.

7.5.25 SRFI-38 - External Representation for Data With Shared Structure

This subsection is based on the specification of SRFI-38 written by Ray Dillinger.

This SRFI creates an alternative external representation for data written and read using `write-with-shared-structure` and `read-with-shared-structure`. It is identical to the grammar for external representation for data written and read with `write` and `read` given in section 7 of R5RS, except that the single production

```
<datum> --> <simple datum> | <compound datum>
```

is replaced by the following five productions:

```
<datum> --> <defining datum> | <nondefining datum> | <defined datum>
<defining datum> -->  #<indexnum>=<nondefining datum>
<defined datum> --> #<indexnum>#
<nondefining datum> --> <simple datum> | <compound datum>
<indexnum> --> <digit 10>+
```

write-with-shared-structure *obj*   [Scheme procedure]
write-with-shared-structure *obj port*   [Scheme procedure]
write-with-shared-structure *obj port optarg*   [Scheme procedure]

> Writes an external representation of *obj* to the given port. Strings that appear in the written representation are enclosed in doublequotes, and within those strings backslash and doublequote characters are escaped by backslashes. Character objects are written using the #\ notation.
>
> Objects which denote locations rather than values (cons cells, vectors, and non-zero-length strings in R5RS scheme; also Guile's structs, bytevectors and ports and hash-tables), if they appear at more than one point in the data being written, are preceded by '#*N*=' the first time they are written and replaced by '#*N*#' all subsequent times they are written, where N is a natural number used to identify that particular object. If objects which denote locations occur only once in the structure, then **write-with-shared-structure** must produce the same external representation for those objects as **write**.
>
> **write-with-shared-structure** terminates in finite time and produces a finite representation when writing finite data.
>
> **write-with-shared-structure** returns an unspecified value. The *port* argument may be omitted, in which case it defaults to the value returned by (**current-output-port**). The *optarg* argument may also be omitted. If present, its effects on the output and return value are unspecified but **write-with-shared-structure** must still write a representation that can be read by **read-with-shared-structure**. Some implementations may wish to use *optarg* to specify formatting conventions, numeric radixes, or return values. Guile's implementation ignores *optarg*.
>
> For example, the code
>
> ```
> (begin (define a (cons 'val1 'val2))
>        (set-cdr! a a)
>        (write-with-shared-structure a))
> ```
>
> should produce the output #1=(val1 . #1#). This shows a cons cell whose **cdr** contains itself.

read-with-shared-structure   [Scheme procedure]
read-with-shared-structure *port*   [Scheme procedure]

> **read-with-shared-structure** converts the external representations of Scheme objects produced by **write-with-shared-structure** into Scheme objects. That is, it is a parser for the nonterminal '<datum>' in the augmented external representation grammar defined above. **read-with-shared-structure** returns the next object parsable from the given input port, updating *port* to point to the first character past the end of the external representation of the object.
>
> If an end-of-file is encountered in the input before any characters are found that can begin an object, then an end-of-file object is returned. The port remains open, and further attempts to read it (by **read-with-shared-structure** or **read** will also return an end-of-file object. If an end of file is encountered after the beginning of an object's external representation, but the external representation is incomplete and therefore not parsable, an error is signalled.

The *port* argument may be omitted, in which case it defaults to the value returned by (current-input-port). It is an error to read from a closed port.

7.5.26 SRFI-39 - Parameters

This SRFI adds support for dynamically-scoped parameters. SRFI 39 is implemented in the Guile core; there's no module needed to get SRFI-39 itself. Parameters are documented in Section 6.21.8 [Parameters], page 422.

This module does export one extra function: with-parameters*. This is a Guile-specific addition to the SRFI, similar to the core with-fluids* (see Section 6.21.7 [Fluids and Dynamic States], page 419).

with-parameters* *param-list value-list thunk*   [Function]
> Establish a new dynamic scope, as per parameterize above, taking parameters from *param-list* and corresponding values from *value-list*. A call (thunk) is made in the new scope and the result from that *thunk* is the return from with-parameters*.

7.5.27 SRFI-41 - Streams

This subsection is based on the specification of SRFI-41 by Philip L. Bewig.

This SRFI implements streams, sometimes called lazy lists, a sequential data structure containing elements computed only on demand. A stream is either null or is a pair with a stream in its cdr. Since elements of a stream are computed only when accessed, streams can be infinite. Once computed, the value of a stream element is cached in case it is needed again. SRFI-41 can be made available with:

```
(use-modules (srfi srfi-41))
```

7.5.27.1 SRFI-41 Stream Fundamentals

SRFI-41 Streams are based on two mutually-recursive abstract data types: An object of the stream abstract data type is a promise that, when forced, is either stream-null or is an object of type stream-pair. An object of the stream-pair abstract data type contains a stream-car and a stream-cdr, which must be a stream. The essential feature of streams is the systematic suspensions of the recursive promises between the two data types.

The object stored in the stream-car of a stream-pair is a promise that is forced the first time the stream-car is accessed; its value is cached in case it is needed again. The object may have any type, and different stream elements may have different types. If the stream-car is never accessed, the object stored there is never evaluated. Likewise, the stream-cdr is a promise to return a stream, and is only forced on demand.

7.5.27.2 SRFI-41 Stream Primitives

This library provides eight operators: constructors for stream-null and stream-pairs, type predicates for streams and the two kinds of streams, accessors for both fields of a stream-pair, and a lambda that creates procedures that return streams.

stream-null   [Scheme Variable]
> A promise that, when forced, is a single object, distinguishable from all other objects, that represents the null stream. stream-null is immutable and unique.

stream-cons *object-expr stream-expr*   [Scheme Syntax]

Creates a newly-allocated stream containing a promise that, when forced, is a **stream-pair** with *object-expr* in its **stream-car** and *stream-expr* in its **stream-cdr**. Neither *object-expr* nor *stream-expr* is evaluated when **stream-cons** is called.

Once created, a **stream-pair** is immutable; there is no **stream-set-car!** or **stream-set-cdr!** that modifies an existing stream-pair. There is no dotted-pair or improper stream as with lists.

stream? *object*   [Scheme Procedure]

Returns true if *object* is a stream, otherwise returns false. If *object* is a stream, its promise will not be forced. If (**stream?** obj) returns true, then one of (**stream-null?** obj) or (**stream-pair?** obj) will return true and the other will return false.

stream-null? *object*   [Scheme Procedure]

Returns true if *object* is the distinguished null stream, otherwise returns false. If *object* is a stream, its promise will be forced.

stream-pair? *object*   [Scheme Procedure]

Returns true if *object* is a **stream-pair** constructed by **stream-cons**, otherwise returns false. If *object* is a stream, its promise will be forced.

stream-car *stream*   [Scheme Procedure]

Returns the object stored in the **stream-car** of *stream*. An error is signalled if the argument is not a **stream-pair**. This causes the *object-expr* passed to **stream-cons** to be evaluated if it had not yet been; the value is cached in case it is needed again.

stream-cdr *stream*   [Scheme Procedure]

Returns the stream stored in the **stream-cdr** of *stream*. An error is signalled if the argument is not a **stream-pair**.

stream-lambda *formals body* ...   [Scheme Syntax]

Creates a procedure that returns a promise to evaluate the *body* of the procedure. The last *body* expression to be evaluated must yield a stream. As with normal **lambda**, *formals* may be a single variable name, in which case all the formal arguments are collected into a single list, or a list of variable names, which may be null if there are no arguments, proper if there are an exact number of arguments, or dotted if a fixed number of arguments is to be followed by zero or more arguments collected into a list. *Body* must contain at least one expression, and may contain internal definitions preceding any expressions to be evaluated.

```
(define strm123
  (stream-cons 1
    (stream-cons 2
      (stream-cons 3
        stream-null))))

(stream-car strm123)  ⇒  1
(stream-car (stream-cdr strm123)  ⇒  2
```

```
(stream-pair?
  (stream-cdr
    (stream-cons (/ 1 0) stream-null))) ⇒ #f

(stream? (list 1 2 3)) ⇒ #f

(define iter
  (stream-lambda (f x)
    (stream-cons x (iter f (f x)))))

(define nats (iter (lambda (x) (+ x 1)) 0))

(stream-car (stream-cdr nats)) ⇒ 1

(define stream-add
  (stream-lambda (s1 s2)
    (stream-cons
      (+ (stream-car s1) (stream-car s2))
      (stream-add (stream-cdr s1)
                  (stream-cdr s2)))))

(define evens (stream-add nats nats))

(stream-car evens) ⇒ 0
(stream-car (stream-cdr evens)) ⇒ 2
(stream-car (stream-cdr (stream-cdr evens))) ⇒ 4
```

7.5.27.3 SRFI-41 Stream Library

define-stream (*name args* . . .) *body* . . .   [Scheme Syntax]

    Creates a procedure that returns a stream, and may appear anywhere a normal define may appear, including as an internal definition. It may contain internal definitions of its own. The defined procedure takes arguments in the same way as stream-lambda. define-stream is syntactic sugar on stream-lambda; see also stream-let, which is also a sugaring of stream-lambda.

    A simple version of stream-map that takes only a single input stream calls itself recursively:

```
(define-stream (stream-map proc strm)
  (if (stream-null? strm)
      stream-null
      (stream-cons
        (proc (stream-car strm))
        (stream-map proc (stream-cdr strm)))))
```

list->stream *list*   [Scheme Procedure]

    Returns a newly-allocated stream containing the elements from *list*.

`port->stream` [*port*]   [Scheme Procedure]

Returns a newly-allocated stream containing in its elements the characters on the port. If *port* is not given it defaults to the current input port. The returned stream has finite length and is terminated by `stream-null`.

It looks like one use of `port->stream` would be this:

```
(define s ;wrong!
  (with-input-from-file filename
    (lambda () (port->stream))))
```

But that fails, because `with-input-from-file` is eager, and closes the input port prematurely, before the first character is read. To read a file into a stream, say:

```
(define-stream (file->stream filename)
  (let ((p (open-input-file filename)))
    (stream-let loop ((c (read-char p)))
      (if (eof-object? c)
          (begin (close-input-port p)
                 stream-null)
          (stream-cons c
            (loop (read-char p)))))))
```

`stream` *object-expr* ...   [Scheme Syntax]

Creates a newly-allocated stream containing in its elements the objects, in order. The *object-exprs* are evaluated when they are accessed, not when the stream is created. If no objects are given, as in (stream), the null stream is returned. See also `list->stream`.

```
(define strm123 (stream 1 2 3))


; (/ 1 0) not evaluated when stream is created
(define s (stream 1 (/ 1 0) -1))
```

`stream->list` [*n*] *stream*   [Scheme Procedure]

Returns a newly-allocated list containing in its elements the first *n* items in *stream*. If *stream* has less than *n* items, all the items in the stream will be included in the returned list. If *n* is not given it defaults to infinity, which means that unless *stream* is finite `stream->list` will never return.

```
(stream->list 10
  (stream-map (lambda (x) (* x x))
    (stream-from 0)))
  ⇒ (0 1 4 9 16 25 36 49 64 81)
```

`stream-append` *stream* ...   [Scheme Procedure]

Returns a newly-allocated stream containing in its elements those elements contained in its input *streams*, in order of input. If any of the input streams is infinite, no elements of any of the succeeding input streams will appear in the output stream. See also `stream-concat`.

`stream-concat` *stream*   [Scheme Procedure]

Takes a *stream* consisting of one or more streams and returns a newly-allocated stream containing all the elements of the input streams. If any of the streams in the input *stream* is infinite, any remaining streams in the input stream will never appear in the output stream. See also `stream-append`.

`stream-constant` *object* ...   [Scheme Procedure]

 Returns a newly-allocated stream containing in its elements the *objects*, repeating in succession forever.

```
(stream-constant 1) ⇒ 1 1 1 ...
(stream-constant #t #f) ⇒ #t #f #t #f #t #f ...
```

`stream-drop` *n stream*   [Scheme Procedure]

 Returns the suffix of the input *stream* that starts at the next element after the first *n* elements. The output stream shares structure with the input *stream*; thus, promises forced in one instance of the stream are also forced in the other instance of the stream. If the input *stream* has less than *n* elements, `stream-drop` returns the null stream. See also `stream-take`.

`stream-drop-while` *pred stream*   [Scheme Procedure]

 Returns the suffix of the input *stream* that starts at the first element *x* for which (`pred x`) returns false. The output stream shares structure with the input *stream*. See also `stream-take-while`.

`stream-filter` *pred stream*   [Scheme Procedure]

 Returns a newly-allocated stream that contains only those elements *x* of the input *stream* which satisfy the predicate `pred`.

```
(stream-filter odd? (stream-from 0))
   ⇒ 1 3 5 7 9 ...
```

`stream-fold` *proc base stream*   [Scheme Procedure]

 Applies a binary procedure *proc* to *base* and the first element of *stream* to compute a new *base*, then applies the procedure to the new *base* and the next element of *stream* to compute a succeeding *base*, and so on, accumulating a value that is finally returned as the value of `stream-fold` when the end of the stream is reached. *stream* must be finite, or `stream-fold` will enter an infinite loop. See also `stream-scan`, which is similar to `stream-fold`, but useful for infinite streams. For readers familiar with other functional languages, this is a left-fold; there is no corresponding right-fold, since right-fold relies on finite streams that are fully-evaluated, in which case they may as well be converted to a list.

`stream-for-each` *proc stream* ...   [Scheme Procedure]

 Applies *proc* element-wise to corresponding elements of the input *streams* for side-effects; it returns nothing. `stream-for-each` stops as soon as any of its input streams is exhausted.

`stream-from` *first* [*step*]   [Scheme Procedure]

 Creates a newly-allocated stream that contains *first* as its first element and increments each succeeding element by *step*. If *step* is not given it defaults to 1. *first* and *step* may be of any numeric type. `stream-from` is frequently useful as a generator in `stream-of` expressions. See also `stream-range` for a similar procedure that creates finite streams.

stream-iterate *proc base*   [Scheme Procedure]
> Creates a newly-allocated stream containing *base* in its first element and applies *proc*
> to each element in turn to determine the succeeding element. See also `stream-unfold`
> and `stream-unfolds`.

stream-length *stream*   [Scheme Procedure]
> Returns the number of elements in the *stream*; it does not evaluate its elements.
> `stream-length` may only be used on finite streams; it enters an infinite loop with
> infinite streams.

stream-let *tag* ((*var expr*) ...) *body* ...   [Scheme Syntax]
> Creates a local scope that binds each variable to the value of its corresponding ex-
> pression. It additionally binds *tag* to a procedure which takes the bound variables
> as arguments and *body* as its defining expressions, binding the *tag* with `stream-`
> `lambda`. *tag* is in scope within body, and may be called recursively. When the
> expanded expression defined by the `stream-let` is evaluated, `stream-let` evaluates
> the expressions in its *body* in an environment containing the newly-bound variables,
> returning the value of the last expression evaluated, which must yield a stream.
>
> `stream-let` provides syntactic sugar on `stream-lambda`, in the same manner as nor-
> mal `let` provides syntactic sugar on normal `lambda`. However, unlike normal `let`,
> the *tag* is required, not optional, because unnamed `stream-let` is meaningless.
>
> For example, `stream-member` returns the first `stream-pair` of the input *strm* with
> a `stream-car` x that satisfies (`eql? obj x`), or the null stream if x is not present in
> *strm*.

```
(define-stream (stream-member eql? obj strm)
  (stream-let loop ((strm strm))
    (cond ((stream-null? strm) strm)
          ((eql? obj (stream-car strm)) strm)
          (else (loop (stream-cdr strm))))))
```

stream-map *proc stream* ...   [Scheme Procedure]
> Applies *proc* element-wise to corresponding elements of the input *streams*, returning
> a newly-allocated stream containing elements that are the results of those procedure
> applications. The output stream has as many elements as the minimum-length input
> stream, and may be infinite.

stream-match *stream clause* ...   [Scheme Syntax]
> Provides pattern-matching for streams. The input *stream* is an expression that eval-
> uates to a stream. Clauses are of the form (`pattern [fender] expression`), con-
> sisting of a *pattern* that matches a stream of a particular shape, an optional *fender*
> that must succeed if the pattern is to match, and an *expression* that is evaluated if
> the pattern matches. There are four types of patterns:
>
> - () matches the null stream.
> - (*pat0 pat1* ...) matches a finite stream with length exactly equal to the number
>   of pattern elements.
> - (*pat0 pat1* ... . *pat-rest*) matches an infinite stream, or a finite stream with
>   length at least as great as the number of pattern elements before the literal dot.

- *pat* matches an entire stream. Should always appear last in the list of clauses; it's not an error to appear elsewhere, but subsequent clauses could never match.

Each pattern element may be either:

- An identifier, which matches any stream element. Additionally, the value of the stream element is bound to the variable named by the identifier, which is in scope in the *fender* and *expression* of the corresponding *clause*. Each identifier in a single pattern must be unique.

- A literal underscore (_), which matches any stream element but creates no bindings.

The *patterns* are tested in order, left-to-right, until a matching pattern is found; if *fender* is present, it must evaluate to a true value for the match to be successful. Pattern variables are bound in the corresponding *fender* and *expression*. Once the matching *pattern* is found, the corresponding *expression* is evaluated and returned as the result of the match. An error is signaled if no pattern matches the input *stream*.

`stream-match` is often used to distinguish null streams from non-null streams, binding *head* and *tail*:

```
(define (len strm)
  (stream-match strm
    (() 0)
    ((head . tail) (+ 1 (len tail)))))
```

Fenders can test the common case where two stream elements must be identical; the `else` pattern is an identifier bound to the entire stream, not a keyword as in `cond`.

```
(stream-match strm
  ((x y . _) (equal? x y) 'ok)
  (else 'error))
```

A more complex example uses two nested matchers to match two different stream arguments; `(stream-merge lt? . strms)` stably merges two or more streams ordered by the `lt?` predicate:

```
(define-stream (stream-merge lt? . strms)
  (define-stream (merge xx yy)
    (stream-match xx (() yy) ((x . xs)
      (stream-match yy (() xx) ((y . ys)
        (if (lt? y x)
            (stream-cons y (merge xx ys))
            (stream-cons x (merge xs yy))))))))
  (stream-let loop ((strms strms))
    (cond ((null? strms) stream-null)
          ((null? (cdr strms)) (car strms))
          (else (merge (car strms)
                       (apply stream-merge lt?
                         (cdr strms)))))))
```

stream-of *expr clause ...*   [Scheme Syntax]

Provides the syntax of stream comprehensions, which generate streams by means of looping expressions. The result is a stream of objects of the type returned by *expr*. There are four types of clauses:

- (*var* **in** *stream-expr*) loops over the elements of *stream-expr*, in order from the start of the stream, binding each element of the stream in turn to *var*. **stream-from** and **stream-range** are frequently useful as generators for *stream-expr*.

- (*var* **is** *expr*) binds *var* to the value obtained by evaluating *expr*.

- (*pred* *expr*) includes in the output stream only those elements *x* which satisfy the predicate *pred*.

The scope of variables bound in the stream comprehension is the clauses to the right of the binding clause (but not the binding clause itself) plus the result expression.

When two or more generators are present, the loops are processed as if they are nested from left to right; that is, the rightmost generator varies fastest. A consequence of this is that only the first generator may be infinite and all subsequent generators must be finite. If no generators are present, the result of a stream comprehension is a stream containing the result expression; thus, '(stream-of 1)' produces a finite stream containing only the element 1.

```
(stream-of (* x x)
  (x in (stream-range 0 10))
  (even? x))
  ⇒ 0 4 16 36 64

(stream-of (list a b)
  (a in (stream-range 1 4))
  (b in (stream-range 1 3)))
  ⇒ (1 1) (1 2) (2 1) (2 2) (3 1) (3 2)

(stream-of (list i j)
  (i in (stream-range 1 5))
  (j in (stream-range (+ i 1) 5)))
  ⇒ (1 2) (1 3) (1 4) (2 3) (2 4) (3 4)
```

stream-range *first past* [*step*]   [Scheme Procedure]

Creates a newly-allocated stream that contains *first* as its first element and increments each succeeding element by *step*. The stream is finite and ends before *past*, which is not an element of the stream. If *step* is not given it defaults to 1 if *first* is less than past and -1 otherwise. *first*, *past* and *step* may be of any real numeric type. **stream-range** is frequently useful as a generator in **stream-of** expressions. See also **stream-from** for a similar procedure that creates infinite streams.

```
(stream-range 0 10) ⇒ 0 1 2 3 4 5 6 7 8 9
(stream-range 0 10 2) ⇒ 0 2 4 6 8
```

Successive elements of the stream are calculated by adding *step* to *first*, so if any of *first*, *past* or *step* are inexact, the length of the output stream may differ from (ceiling (- (/ (- past first) step) 1).

stream-ref *stream n*   [Scheme Procedure]

 Returns the *n*th element of stream, counting from zero. An error is signaled if *n* is
 greater than or equal to the length of stream.

```
(define (fact n)
  (stream-ref
    (stream-scan * 1 (stream-from 1))
    n))
```

stream-reverse *stream*   [Scheme Procedure]

 Returns a newly-allocated stream containing the elements of the input *stream* but in
 reverse order. stream-reverse may only be used with finite streams; it enters an
 infinite loop with infinite streams. stream-reverse does not force evaluation of the
 elements of the stream.

stream-scan *proc base stream*   [Scheme Procedure]

 Accumulates the partial folds of an input *stream* into a newly-allocated output stream.
 The output stream is the *base* followed by (stream-fold proc base (stream-take
 i stream)) for each of the first *i* elements of *stream*.

```
(stream-scan + 0 (stream-from 1))
  ⇒ (stream 0 1 3 6 10 15 ...)
```

```
(stream-scan * 1 (stream-from 1))
  ⇒ (stream 1 1 2 6 24 120 ...)
```

stream-take *n stream*   [Scheme Procedure]

 Returns a newly-allocated stream containing the first *n* elements of the input *stream*.
 If the input *stream* has less than *n* elements, so does the output stream. See also
 stream-drop.

stream-take-while *pred stream*   [Scheme Procedure]

 Takes a predicate and a stream and returns a newly-allocated stream containing those
 elements x that form the maximal prefix of the input stream which satisfy *pred*. See
 also stream-drop-while.

stream-unfold *map pred gen base*   [Scheme Procedure]

 The fundamental recursive stream constructor. It constructs a stream by repeatedly
 applying *gen* to successive values of *base*, in the manner of stream-iterate, then
 applying *map* to each of the values so generated, appending each of the mapped
 values to the output stream as long as (pred? base) returns a true value. See also
 stream-iterate and stream-unfolds.

 The expression below creates the finite stream '0 1 4 9 16 25 36 49 64 81'. Initially
 the *base* is 0, which is less than 10, so *map* squares the *base* and the mapped value
 becomes the first element of the output stream. Then *gen* increments the *base* by 1,
 so it becomes 1; this is less than 10, so *map* squares the new *base* and 1 becomes the
 second element of the output stream. And so on, until the base becomes 10, when
 pred stops the recursion and stream-null ends the output stream.

```
(stream-unfold
  (lambda (x) (expt x 2)) ; map
```

```
(lambda (x) (< x 10))    ; pred?
(lambda (x) (+ x 1))     ; gen
0)                       ; base
```

stream-unfolds *proc seed*   [Scheme Procedure]

Returns *n* newly-allocated streams containing those elements produced by successive calls to the generator *proc*, which takes the current *seed* as its argument and returns *n*+1 values

(*proc seed*) $\Rightarrow$ *seed result_0 ... result_n-1*

where the returned *seed* is the input *seed* to the next call to the generator and *result_i* indicates how to produce the next element of the *i*th result stream:

- (*value*): *value* is the next car of the result stream.

- #f: no value produced by this iteration of the generator *proc* for the result stream.

- (): the end of the result stream.

It may require multiple calls of *proc* to produce the next element of any particular result stream. See also stream-iterate and stream-unfold.

```
(define (stream-partition pred? strm)
  (stream-unfolds
    (lambda (s)
      (if (stream-null? s)
          (values s '() '())
          (let ((a (stream-car s))
                (d (stream-cdr s)))
            (if (pred? a)
                (values d (list a) #f)
                (values d #f (list a))))))
    strm))

(call-with-values
  (lambda ()
    (stream-partition odd?
      (stream-range 1 6)))
  (lambda (odds evens)
    (list (stream->list odds)
          (stream->list evens))))
⇒ ((1 3 5) (2 4))
```

stream-zip *stream ...*   [Scheme Procedure]

Returns a newly-allocated stream in which each element is a list (not a stream) of the corresponding elements of the input *streams*. The output stream is as long as the shortest input *stream*, if any of the input *streams* is finite, or is infinite if all the input *streams* are infinite.

7.5.28 SRFI-42 - Eager Comprehensions

See the specification of SRFI-42.

7.5.29 SRFI-43 - Vector Library

This subsection is based on the specification of SRFI-43 by Taylor Campbell.

SRFI-43 implements a comprehensive library of vector operations. It can be made available with:

```
(use-modules (srfi srfi-43))
```

7.5.29.1 SRFI-43 Constructors

make-vector *size* [*fill*]   [Scheme Procedure]

> Create and return a vector of size *size*, optionally filling it with *fill*. The default value of *fill* is unspecified.
>
> ```
> (make-vector 5 3) ⇒ #(3 3 3 3 3)
> ```

vector *x* ...   [Scheme Procedure]

> Create and return a vector whose elements are *x* ....
>
> ```
> (vector 0 1 2 3 4) ⇒ #(0 1 2 3 4)
> ```

vector-unfold *f length initial-seed* ...   [Scheme Procedure]

> The fundamental vector constructor. Create a vector whose length is *length* and iterates across each index k from 0 up to *length* - 1, applying *f* at each iteration to the current index and current seeds, in that order, to receive n + 1 values: first, the element to put in the kth slot of the new vector and n new seeds for the next iteration. It is an error for the number of seeds to vary between iterations.
>
> ```
> (vector-unfold (lambda (i x) (values x (- x 1)))
>                10 0)
> ⇒ #(0 -1 -2 -3 -4 -5 -6 -7 -8 -9)
>
> (vector-unfold values 10)
> ⇒ #(0 1 2 3 4 5 6 7 8 9)
> ```

vector-unfold-right *f length initial-seed* ...   [Scheme Procedure]

> Like **vector-unfold**, but it uses *f* to generate elements from right-to-left, rather than left-to-right.
>
> ```
> (vector-unfold-right (lambda (i x) (values x (+ x 1)))
>                      10 0)
> ⇒ #(9 8 7 6 5 4 3 2 1 0)
> ```

vector-copy *vec* [*start* [*end* [*fill*]]]   [Scheme Procedure]

> Allocate a new vector whose length is *end* - *start* and fills it with elements from *vec*, taking elements from *vec* starting at index *start* and stopping at index *end*. *start* defaults to 0 and *end* defaults to the value of (**vector-length** *vec*). If *end* extends beyond the length of *vec*, the slots in the new vector that obviously cannot be filled by elements from *vec* are filled with *fill*, whose default value is unspecified.
>
> ```
> (vector-copy '#(a b c d e f g h i))
> ⇒ #(a b c d e f g h i)
>
> (vector-copy '#(a b c d e f g h i) 6)
> ```

```
⇒ #(g h i)

(vector-copy '#(a b c d e f g h i) 3 6)
⇒ #(d e f)

(vector-copy '#(a b c d e f g h i) 6 12 'x)
⇒ #(g h i x x x)
```

vector-reverse-copy *vec* [*start* [*end*]]   [Scheme Procedure]
    Like `vector-copy`, but it copies the elements in the reverse order from *vec*.

```
(vector-reverse-copy '#(5 4 3 2 1 0) 1 5)
⇒ #(1 2 3 4)
```

vector-append *vec* ...   [Scheme Procedure]
    Return a newly allocated vector that contains all elements in order from the subsequent locations in *vec* ....

```
(vector-append '#(a) '#(b c d))
⇒ #(a b c d)
```

vector-concatenate *list-of-vectors*   [Scheme Procedure]
    Append each vector in *list-of-vectors*. Equivalent to (`apply vector-append list-of-vectors`).

```
(vector-concatenate '(#(a b) #(c d)))
⇒ #(a b c d)
```

7.5.29.2 SRFI-43 Predicates

vector? *obj*   [Scheme Procedure]
    Return true if *obj* is a vector, else return false.

vector-empty? *vec*   [Scheme Procedure]
    Return true if *vec* is empty, i.e. its length is 0, else return false.

vector= *elt=?* *vec* ...   [Scheme Procedure]
    Return true if the vectors *vec* ... have equal lengths and equal elements according to *elt=?*. *elt=?* is always applied to two arguments. Element comparison must be consistent with `eq?` in the following sense: if (`eq? a b`) returns true, then (`elt=? a b`) must also return true. The order in which comparisons are performed is unspecified.

7.5.29.3 SRFI-43 Selectors

vector-ref *vec i*   [Scheme Procedure]
    Return the element at index *i* in *vec*. Indexing is based on zero.

vector-length *vec*   [Scheme Procedure]
    Return the length of *vec*.

7.5.29.4 SRFI-43 Iteration

`vector-fold` *kons knil vec1 vec2* ...   [Scheme Procedure]

The fundamental vector iterator. *kons* is iterated over each index in all of the vectors, stopping at the end of the shortest; *kons* is applied as

```
(kons i state (vector-ref vec1 i) (vector-ref vec2 i) ...)
```

where *state* is the current state value, and *i* is the current index. The current state value begins with *knil*, and becomes whatever *kons* returned at the respective iteration. The iteration is strictly left-to-right.

`vector-fold-right` *kons knil vec1 vec2* ...   [Scheme Procedure]

Similar to `vector-fold`, but it iterates right-to-left instead of left-to-right.

`vector-map` *f vec1 vec2* ...   [Scheme Procedure]

Return a new vector of the shortest size of the vector arguments. Each element at index i of the new vector is mapped from the old vectors by

```
(f i (vector-ref vec1 i) (vector-ref vec2 i) ...)
```

The dynamic order of application of *f* is unspecified.

`vector-map!` *f vec1 vec2* ...   [Scheme Procedure]

Similar to `vector-map`, but rather than mapping the new elements into a new vector, the new mapped elements are destructively inserted into *vec1*. The dynamic order of application of *f* is unspecified.

`vector-for-each` *f vec1 vec2* ...   [Scheme Procedure]

Call `(f i (vector-ref vec1 i) (vector-ref vec2 i) ...)` for each index i less than the length of the shortest vector passed. The iteration is strictly left-to-right.

`vector-count` *pred? vec1 vec2* ...   [Scheme Procedure]

Count the number of parallel elements in the vectors that satisfy *pred?*, which is applied, for each index i less than the length of the smallest vector, to i and each parallel element in the vectors at that index, in order.

```
(vector-count (lambda (i elt) (even? elt))
              '#(3 1 4 1 5 9 2 5 6))
⇒ 3
(vector-count (lambda (i x y) (< x y))
              '#(1 3 6 9) '#(2 4 6 8 10 12))
⇒ 2
```

7.5.29.5 SRFI-43 Searching

`vector-index` *pred? vec1 vec2* ...   [Scheme Procedure]

Find and return the index of the first elements in *vec1 vec2* ... that satisfy *pred?*. If no matching element is found by the end of the shortest vector, return `#f`.

```
(vector-index even? '#(3 1 4 1 5 9))
⇒ 2
(vector-index < '#(3 1 4 1 5 9 2 5 6) '#(2 7 1 8 2))
⇒ 1
(vector-index = '#(3 1 4 1 5 9 2 5 6) '#(2 7 1 8 2))
⇒ #f
```

vector-index-right *pred? vec1 vec2 . . .*   [Scheme Procedure]

 Like `vector-index`, but it searches right-to-left, rather than left-to-right. Note that the SRFI 43 specification requires that all the vectors must have the same length, but both the SRFI 43 reference implementation and Guile's implementation allow vectors with unequal lengths, and start searching from the last index of the shortest vector.

vector-skip *pred? vec1 vec2 . . .*   [Scheme Procedure]

 Find and return the index of the first elements in *vec1 vec2 . . .* that do not satisfy *pred?*. If no matching element is found by the end of the shortest vector, return `#f`. Equivalent to `vector-index` but with the predicate inverted.

```
(vector-skip number? '#(1 2 a b 3 4 c d)) ⇒ 2
```

vector-skip-right *pred? vec1 vec2 . . .*   [Scheme Procedure]

 Like `vector-skip`, but it searches for a non-matching element right-to-left, rather than left-to-right. Note that the SRFI 43 specification requires that all the vectors must have the same length, but both the SRFI 43 reference implementation and Guile's implementation allow vectors with unequal lengths, and start searching from the last index of the shortest vector.

vector-binary-search *vec value cmp [start [end]]*   [Scheme Procedure]

 Find and return an index of *vec* between *start* and *end* whose value is *value* using a binary search. If no matching element is found, return `#f`. The default *start* is 0 and the default *end* is the length of *vec*.

 cmp must be a procedure of two arguments such that (`cmp a b`) returns a negative integer if $a < b$, a positive integer if $a > b$, or zero if $a = b$. The elements of *vec* must be sorted in non-decreasing order according to *cmp*.

 Note that SRFI 43 does not document the *start* and *end* arguments, but both its reference implementation and Guile's implementation support them.

```
(define (char-cmp c1 c2)
  (cond ((char<? c1 c2) -1)
        ((char>? c1 c2) 1)
        (else 0)))

(vector-binary-search '#(#\a #\b #\c #\d #\e #\f #\g #\h)
                      #\g
                      char-cmp)
  ⇒ 6
```

vector-any *pred? vec1 vec2 . . .*   [Scheme Procedure]

 Find the first parallel set of elements from *vec1 vec2 . . .* for which *pred?* returns a true value. If such a parallel set of elements exists, `vector-any` returns the value that *pred?* returned for that set of elements. The iteration is strictly left-to-right.

vector-every *pred? vec1 vec2 . . .*   [Scheme Procedure]

 If, for every index i between 0 and the length of the shortest vector argument, the set of elements (`vector-ref vec1 i`) (`vector-ref vec2 i`) . . . satisfies *pred?*, `vector-every` returns the value that *pred?* returned for the last set of elements, at the last index of the shortest vector. Otherwise it returns `#f`. The iteration is strictly left-to-right.

7.5.29.6 SRFI-43 Mutators

vector-set! *vec i value*   [Scheme Procedure]

>   Assign the contents of the location at *i* in *vec* to *value*.

vector-swap! *vec i j*   [Scheme Procedure]

>   Swap the values of the locations in *vec* at *i* and *j*.

vector-fill! *vec fill* [*start* [*end*]]   [Scheme Procedure]

>   Assign the value of every location in *vec* between *start* and *end* to *fill*. *start* defaults
>   to 0 and *end* defaults to the length of *vec*.

vector-reverse! *vec* [*start* [*end*]]   [Scheme Procedure]

>   Destructively reverse the contents of *vec* between *start* and *end*. *start* defaults to 0
>   and *end* defaults to the length of *vec*.

vector-copy! *target tstart source* [*sstart* [*send*]]   [Scheme Procedure]

>   Copy a block of elements from *source* to *target*, both of which must be vectors,
>   starting in *target* at *tstart* and starting in *source* at *sstart*, ending when (*send* -
>   *sstart*) elements have been copied. It is an error for *target* to have a length less than
>   (*tstart* + *send* - *sstart*). *sstart* defaults to 0 and *send* defaults to the length of *source*.

vector-reverse-copy! *target tstart source* [*sstart* [*send*]]   [Scheme Procedure]

>   Like vector-copy!, but this copies the elements in the reverse order. It is an error
>   if *target* and *source* are identical vectors and the *target* and *source* ranges overlap;
>   however, if *tstart* = *sstart*, vector-reverse-copy! behaves as (vector-reverse!
>   target tstart send) would.

7.5.29.7 SRFI-43 Conversion

vector->list *vec* [*start* [*end*]]   [Scheme Procedure]

>   Return a newly allocated list containing the elements in *vec* between *start* and *end*.
>   *start* defaults to 0 and *end* defaults to the length of *vec*.

reverse-vector->list *vec* [*start* [*end*]]   [Scheme Procedure]

>   Like vector->list, but the resulting list contains the specified range of elements of
>   *vec* in reverse order.

list->vector *proper-list* [*start* [*end*]]   [Scheme Procedure]

>   Return a newly allocated vector of the elements from *proper-list* with indices between
>   *start* and *end*. *start* defaults to 0 and *end* defaults to the length of *proper-list*. Note
>   that SRFI 43 does not document the *start* and *end* arguments, but both its reference
>   implementation and Guile's implementation support them.

reverse-list->vector *proper-list* [*start* [*end*]]   [Scheme Procedure]

>   Like list->vector, but the resulting vector contains the specified range of elements
>   of *proper-list* in reverse order. Note that SRFI 43 does not document the *start* and
>   *end* arguments, but both its reference implementation and Guile's implementation
>   support them.

7.5.30 SRFI-45 - Primitives for Expressing Iterative Lazy Algorithms

This subsection is based on the specification of SRFI-45 written by André van Tonder.

Lazy evaluation is traditionally simulated in Scheme using `delay` and `force`. However, these primitives are not powerful enough to express a large class of lazy algorithms that are iterative. Indeed, it is folklore in the Scheme community that typical iterative lazy algorithms written using delay and force will often require unbounded memory.

This SRFI provides set of three operations: {`lazy`, `delay`, `force`}, which allow the programmer to succinctly express lazy algorithms while retaining bounded space behavior in cases that are properly tail-recursive. A general recipe for using these primitives is provided. An additional procedure `eager` is provided for the construction of eager promises in cases where efficiency is a concern.

Although this SRFI redefines `delay` and `force`, the extension is conservative in the sense that the semantics of the subset {`delay`, `force`} in isolation (i.e., as long as the program does not use `lazy`) agrees with that in R5RS. In other words, no program that uses the R5RS definitions of delay and force will break if those definition are replaced by the SRFI-45 definitions of delay and force.

Guile also adds `promise?` to the list of exports, which is not part of the official SRFI-45.

promise? *obj*   [Scheme Procedure]
> Return true if *obj* is an SRFI-45 promise, otherwise return false.

delay *expression*   [Scheme Syntax]
> Takes an expression of arbitrary type *a* and returns a promise of type (Promise a) which at some point in the future may be asked (by the `force` procedure) to evaluate the expression and deliver the resulting value.

lazy *expression*   [Scheme Syntax]
> Takes an expression of type (Promise a) and returns a promise of type (Promise a) which at some point in the future may be asked (by the `force` procedure) to evaluate the expression and deliver the resulting promise.

force *expression*   [Scheme Procedure]
> Takes an argument of type (Promise a) and returns a value of type *a* as follows: If a value of type *a* has been computed for the promise, this value is returned. Otherwise, the promise is first evaluated, then overwritten by the obtained promise or value, and then force is again applied (iteratively) to the promise.

eager *expression*   [Scheme Procedure]
> Takes an argument of type *a* and returns a value of type (Promise a). As opposed to `delay`, the argument is evaluated eagerly. Semantically, writing (eager expression) is equivalent to writing
>
> ```
> (let ((value expression)) (delay value)).
> ```
>
> However, the former is more efficient since it does not require unnecessary creation and evaluation of thunks. We also have the equivalence
>
> ```
> (delay expression) = (lazy (eager expression))
> ```

The following reduction rules may be helpful for reasoning about these primitives. However, they do not express the memoization and memory usage semantics specified above:

```
(force (delay expression)) -> expression
(force (lazy  expression)) -> (force expression)
(force (eager value))      -> value
```

Correct usage

We now provide a general recipe for using the primitives {lazy, delay, force} to express lazy algorithms in Scheme. The transformation is best described by way of an example: Consider the stream-filter algorithm, expressed in a hypothetical lazy language as

```
(define (stream-filter p? s)
  (if (null? s) '()
      (let ((h (car s))
            (t (cdr s)))
        (if (p? h)
            (cons h (stream-filter p? t))
            (stream-filter p? t)))))
```

This algorithm can be expressed as follows in Scheme:

```
(define (stream-filter p? s)
  (lazy
    (if (null? (force s)) (delay '())
        (let ((h (car (force s)))
              (t (cdr (force s))))
          (if (p? h)
              (delay (cons h (stream-filter p? t)))
              (stream-filter p? t))))))
```

In other words, we

- wrap all constructors (e.g., '(), cons) with delay,

- apply force to arguments of deconstructors (e.g., car, cdr and null?),

- wrap procedure bodies with (lazy ...).

7.5.31 SRFI-46 Basic syntax-rules Extensions

Guile's core syntax-rules supports the extensions specified by SRFI-46/R7RS. Tail patterns have been supported since at least Guile 2.0, and custom ellipsis identifiers have been supported since Guile 2.0.10. See Section 6.10.2 [Syntax Rules], page 258.

7.5.32 SRFI-55 - Requiring Features

SRFI-55 provides require-extension which is a portable mechanism to load selected SRFI modules. This is implemented in the Guile core, there's no module needed to get SRFI-55 itself.

require-extension *clause1 clause2* ...   [library syntax]
> Require the features of *clause1 clause2* ... , throwing an error if any are unavailable.
>
> A *clause* is of the form (*identifier* arg...). The only *identifier* currently supported is srfi and the arguments are SRFI numbers. For example to get SRFI-1 and SRFI-6,

```
(require-extension (srfi 1 6))
```

`require-extension` can only be used at the top-level.

A Guile-specific program can simply `use-modules` to load SRFIs not already in the core, `require-extension` is for programs designed to be portable to other Scheme implementations.

7.5.33 SRFI-60 - Integers as Bits

This SRFI provides various functions for treating integers as bits and for bitwise manipulations. These functions can be obtained with,

```
(use-modules (srfi srfi-60))
```

Integers are treated as infinite precision twos-complement, the same as in the core logical functions (see Section 6.6.2.13 [Bitwise Operations], page 125). And likewise bit indexes start from 0 for the least significant bit. The following functions in this SRFI are already in the Guile core,

logand, logior, logxor, lognot, logtest, logcount, integer-length, logbit?, ash

bitwise-and $n1$ ...   [Function]
bitwise-ior $n1$ ...   [Function]
bitwise-xor $n1$ ...   [Function]
bitwise-not n [Function]
any-bits-set? j k [Function]
bit-set? $index$ n [Function]
arithmetic-shift n $count$ [Function]
bit-field n $start$ end [Function]
bit-count n [Function]

> Aliases for `logand`, `logior`, `logxor`, `lognot`, `logtest`, `logbit?`, `ash`, `bit-extract` and `logcount` respectively.
>
> Note that the name `bit-count` conflicts with `bit-count` in the core (see Section 6.7.4 [Bit Vectors], page 198).

bitwise-if $mask$ $n1$ $n0$ [Function]
bitwise-merge $mask$ $n1$ $n0$ [Function]

> Return an integer with bits selected from $n1$ and $n0$ according to $mask$. Those bits where $mask$ has 1s are taken from $n1$, and those where $mask$ has 0s are taken from $n0$.
>
> ```
> (bitwise-if 3 #b0101 #b1010)  ⇒ 9
> ```

log2-binary-factors n [Function]
first-set-bit n [Function]

> Return a count of how many factors of 2 are present in n. This is also the bit index of the lowest 1 bit in n. If n is 0, the return is -1.
>
> ```
> (log2-binary-factors 6)  ⇒ 1
> (log2-binary-factors -8)  ⇒ 3
> ```

copy-bit *index n newbit*   [Function]

> Return *n* with the bit at *index* set according to *newbit*. *newbit* should be **#t** to set the bit to 1, or **#f** to set it to 0. Bits other than at *index* are unchanged in the return.
>
> > (copy-bit 1 #b0101 #t) ⇒ 7

copy-bit-field *n newbits start end*   [Function]

> Return *n* with the bits from *start* (inclusive) to *end* (exclusive) changed to the value *newbits*.
>
> The least significant bit in *newbits* goes to *start*, the next to *start* + 1, etc. Anything in *newbits* past the *end* given is ignored.
>
> > (copy-bit-field #b10000 #b11 1 3) ⇒ #b10110

rotate-bit-field *n count start end*   [Function]

> Return *n* with the bit field from *start* (inclusive) to *end* (exclusive) rotated upwards by *count* bits.
>
> *count* can be positive or negative, and it can be more than the field width (it'll be reduced modulo the width).
>
> > (rotate-bit-field #b0110 2 1 4) ⇒ #b1010

reverse-bit-field *n start end*   [Function]

> Return *n* with the bits from *start* (inclusive) to *end* (exclusive) reversed.
>
> > (reverse-bit-field #b101001 2 4) ⇒ #b100101

integer->list *n* [*len*]   [Function]

> Return bits from *n* in the form of a list of **#t** for 1 and **#f** for 0. The least significant *len* bits are returned, and the first list element is the most significant of those bits. If *len* is not given, the default is (**integer-length** *n*) (see Section 6.6.2.13 [Bitwise Operations], page 125).
>
> > (integer->list 6)   ⇒ (#t #t #f)
> > (integer->list 1 4) ⇒ (#f #f #f #t)

list->integer *lst*   [Function]
booleans->integer *bool...*   [Function]

> Return an integer formed bitwise from the given *lst* list of booleans, or for **booleans->integer** from the *bool* arguments.
>
> Each boolean is **#t** for a 1 and **#f** for a 0. The first element becomes the most significant bit in the return.
>
> > (list->integer '(#t #f #t #f)) ⇒ 10

7.5.34 SRFI-61 - A more general cond clause

This SRFI extends RnRS **cond** to support test expressions that return multiple values, as well as arbitrary definitions of test success. SRFI 61 is implemented in the Guile core; there's no module needed to get SRFI-61 itself. Extended **cond** is documented in Section 6.13.2 [Simple Conditional Evaluation], page 292.

7.5.35 SRFI-62 - S-expression comments.

Starting from version 2.0, Guile's `read` supports SRFI-62/R7RS S-expression comments by default.

7.5.36 SRFI-64 - A Scheme API for test suites.

See the specification of SRFI-64.

7.5.37 SRFI-67 - Compare procedures

See the specification of SRFI-67.

7.5.38 SRFI-69 - Basic hash tables

This is a portable wrapper around Guile's built-in hash table and weak table support. See Section 6.7.14 [Hash Tables], page 236, for information on that built-in support. Above that, this hash-table interface provides association of equality and hash functions with tables at creation time, so variants of each function are not required, as well as a procedure that takes care of most uses for Guile hash table handles, which this SRFI does not provide as such.

Access it with:

```
(use-modules (srfi srfi-69))
```

7.5.38.1 Creating hash tables

`make-hash-table` [*equal-proc hash-proc #:weak weakness*   [Scheme Procedure]
    start-size]

>   Create and answer a new hash table with *equal-proc* as the equality function and *hash-proc* as the hashing function.
>
>   By default, *equal-proc* is `equal?`. It can be any two-argument procedure, and should answer whether two keys are the same for this table's purposes.
>
>   My default *hash-proc* assumes that `equal-proc` is no coarser than `equal?` unless it is literally `string-ci=?`. If provided, *hash-proc* should be a two-argument procedure that takes a key and the current table size, and answers a reasonably good hash integer between 0 (inclusive) and the size (exclusive).
>
>   *weakness* should be `#f` or a symbol indicating how "weak" the hash table is:
>
>   `#f`   An ordinary non-weak hash table. This is the default.
>
>   `key`   When the key has no more non-weak references at GC, remove that entry.
>
>   `value`   When the value has no more non-weak references at GC, remove that entry.
>
>   `key-or-value`
>   When either has no more non-weak references at GC, remove the association.
>
>   As a legacy of the time when Guile couldn't grow hash tables, *start-size* is an optional integer argument that specifies the approximate starting size for the hash table, which will be rounded to an algorithmically-sounder number.

By *coarser* than `equal?`, we mean that for all *x* and *y* values where (`equal-proc x y`), (`equal? x y`) as well. If that does not hold for your *equal-proc*, you must provide a *hash-proc*.

In the case of weak tables, remember that *references* above always refers to `eq?`-wise references. Just because you have a reference to some string `"foo"` doesn't mean that an association with key `"foo"` in a weak-key table *won't* be collected; it only counts as a reference if the two `"foo"`s are `eq?`, regardless of *equal-proc*. As such, it is usually only sensible to use `eq?` and `hashq` as the equivalence and hash functions for a weak table. See Section 6.18.3 [Weak References], page 378, for more information on Guile's built-in weak table support.

`alist->hash-table` *alist* [*equal-proc hash-proc #:weak*   [Scheme Procedure]
          weakness start-size]

> As with `make-hash-table`, but initialize it with the associations in *alist*. Where keys are repeated in *alist*, the leftmost association takes precedence.

7.5.38.2 Accessing table items

`hash-table-ref` *table key* [*default-thunk*]   [Scheme Procedure]
`hash-table-ref/default` *table key default*   [Scheme Procedure]

> Answer the value associated with *key* in *table*. If *key* is not present, answer the result of invoking the thunk *default-thunk*, which signals an error instead by default.
>
> `hash-table-ref/default` is a variant that requires a third argument, *default*, and answers *default* itself instead of invoking it.

`hash-table-set!` *table key new-value*   [Scheme Procedure]

> Set *key* to *new-value* in *table*.

`hash-table-delete!` *table key*   [Scheme Procedure]

> Remove the association of *key* in *table*, if present. If absent, do nothing.

`hash-table-exists?` *table key*   [Scheme Procedure]

> Answer whether *key* has an association in *table*.

`hash-table-update!` *table key modifier* [*default-thunk*]   [Scheme Procedure]
`hash-table-update!/default` *table key modifier default*   [Scheme Procedure]

> Replace *key*'s associated value in *table* by invoking *modifier* with one argument, the old value.
>
> If *key* is not present, and *default-thunk* is provided, invoke it with no arguments to get the "old value" to be passed to *modifier* as above. If *default-thunk* is not provided in such a case, signal an error.
>
> `hash-table-update!/default` is a variant that requires the fourth argument, which is used directly as the "old value" rather than as a thunk to be invoked to retrieve the "old value".

7.5.38.3 Table properties

`hash-table-size` *table*   [Scheme Procedure]

> Answer the number of associations in *table*. This is guaranteed to run in constant time for non-weak tables.

`hash-table-keys` *table*   [Scheme Procedure]
> Answer an unordered list of the keys in *table*.

`hash-table-values` *table*   [Scheme Procedure]
> Answer an unordered list of the values in *table*.

`hash-table-walk` *table proc*   [Scheme Procedure]
> Invoke *proc* once for each association in *table*, passing the key and value as arguments.

`hash-table-fold` *table proc init*   [Scheme Procedure]
> Invoke (`proc key value previous`) for each *key* and *value* in *table*, where *previous* is the result of the previous invocation, using *init* as the first *previous* value. Answer the final *proc* result.

`hash-table->alist` *table*   [Scheme Procedure]
> Answer an alist where each association in *table* is an association in the result.

7.5.38.4 Hash table algorithms

Each hash table carries an *equivalence function* and a *hash function*, used to implement key lookups. Beginning users should follow the rules for consistency of the default *hash-proc* specified above. Advanced users can use these to implement their own equivalence and hash functions for specialized lookup semantics.

`hash-table-equivalence-function` *hash-table*   [Scheme Procedure]
`hash-table-hash-function` *hash-table*   [Scheme Procedure]
> Answer the equivalence and hash function of *hash-table*, respectively.

`hash` *obj* [*size*]   [Scheme Procedure]
`string-hash` *obj* [*size*]   [Scheme Procedure]
`string-ci-hash` *obj* [*size*]   [Scheme Procedure]
`hash-by-identity` *obj* [*size*]   [Scheme Procedure]
> Answer a hash value appropriate for equality predicate `equal?`, `string=?`, `string-ci=?`, and `eq?`, respectively.

`hash` is a backwards-compatible replacement for Guile's built-in `hash`.

7.5.39 SRFI-87 => in case clauses

Starting from version 2.0.6, Guile's core `case` syntax supports `=>` in clauses, as specified by SRFI-87/R7RS. See Section 6.13.2 [Conditionals], page 292.

7.5.40 SRFI-88 Keyword Objects

SRFI-88 provides *keyword objects*, which are equivalent to Guile's keywords (see Section 6.6.8 [Keywords], page 180). SRFI-88 keywords can be entered using the *postfix keyword syntax*, which consists of an identifier followed by : (see Section 6.17.2 [Scheme Read], page 360). SRFI-88 can be made available with:

```
(use-modules (srfi srfi-88))
```

Doing so installs the right reader option for keyword syntax, using (`read-set! keywords 'postfix`). It also provides the procedures described below.

`keyword?` *obj*   [Scheme Procedure]

> Return #t if *obj* is a keyword. This is the same procedure as the same-named built-in procedure (see Section 6.6.8.4 [Keyword Procedures], page 183).

```
(keyword? foo:)        ⇒ #t
(keyword? 'foo:)       ⇒ #t
(keyword? "foo")       ⇒ #f
```

`keyword->string` *kw*   [Scheme Procedure]

> Return the name of *kw* as a string, i.e., without the trailing colon. The returned string may not be modified, e.g., with `string-set!`.

```
(keyword->string foo:)  ⇒ "foo"
```

`string->keyword` *str*   [Scheme Procedure]

> Return the keyword object whose name is *str*.

```
(keyword->string (string->keyword "a b c"))    ⇒ "a b c"
```

7.5.41 SRFI-98 Accessing environment variables.

This is a portable wrapper around Guile's built-in support for interacting with the current environment, See Section 7.2.6 [Runtime Environment], page 488.

`get-environment-variable` *name*   [Scheme Procedure]

> Returns a string containing the value of the environment variable given by the string `name`, or #f if the named environment variable is not found. This is equivalent to `(getenv name)`.

`get-environment-variables`   [Scheme Procedure]

> Returns the names and values of all the environment variables as an association list in which both the keys and the values are strings.

7.5.42 SRFI-105 Curly-infix expressions.

Guile's built-in reader includes support for SRFI-105 curly-infix expressions. See the specification of SRFI-105. Some examples:

```
{n <= 5}                  ⇒  (<= n 5)
{a + b + c}               ⇒  (+ a b c)
{a * {b + c}}             ⇒  (* a (+ b c))
{(- a) / b}               ⇒  (/ (- a) b)
{-(a) / b}                ⇒  (/ (- a) b) as well
{(f a b) + (g h)}         ⇒  (+ (f a b) (g h))
{f(a b) + g(h)}           ⇒  (+ (f a b) (g h)) as well
{f[a b] + g(h)}           ⇒  (+ ($bracket-apply$ f a b) (g h))
'{a + f(b) + x}           ⇒  '(+ a (f b) x)
{length(x) >= 6}          ⇒  (>= (length x) 6)
{n-1 + n-2}               ⇒  (+ n-1 n-2)
{n * factorial{n - 1}}    ⇒  (* n (factorial (- n 1)))
{{a > 0} and {b >= 1}}    ⇒  (and (> a 0) (>= b 1))
{f{n - 1}(x)}             ⇒  ((f (- n 1)) x)
{a . z}                   ⇒  ($nfx$ a . z)
```

```
{a + b - c}              ⇒   ($nfx$ a + b - c)
```

To enable curly-infix expressions within a file, place the reader directive `#!curly-infix` before the first use of curly-infix notation. To globally enable curly-infix expressions in Guile's reader, set the `curly-infix` read option.

Guile also implements the following non-standard extension to SRFI-105: if `curly-infix` is enabled and there is no other meaning assigned to square brackets (i.e. the `square-brackets` read option is turned off), then lists within square brackets are read as normal lists but with the special symbol `$bracket-list$` added to the front. To enable this combination of read options within a file, use the reader directive `#!curly-infix-and-bracket-lists`. For example:

```
[a b]     ⇒   ($bracket-list$ a b)
[a . b]   ⇒   ($bracket-list$ a . b)
```

For more information on reader options, See Section 6.17.2 [Scheme Read], page 360.

7.5.43 SRFI-111 Boxes.

SRFI-111 provides boxes: objects with a single mutable cell.

box *value*   [Scheme Procedure]
> Return a newly allocated box whose contents is initialized to *value*.

box? *obj*   [Scheme Procedure]
> Return true if *obj* is a box, otherwise return false.

unbox *box*   [Scheme Procedure]
> Return the current contents of *box*.

set-box! *box value*   [Scheme Procedure]
> Set the contents of *box* to *value*.

7.6 R6RS Support

See Section 6.19.6 [R6RS Libraries], page 388, for more information on how to define R6RS libraries, and their integration with Guile modules.

7.6.1 Incompatibilities with the R6RS

There are some incompatibilities between Guile and the R6RS. Some of them are intentional, some of them are bugs, and some are simply unimplemented features. Please let the Guile developers know if you find one that is not on this list.

- The R6RS specifies many situations in which a conforming implementation must signal a specific error. Guile doesn't really care about that too much—if a correct R6RS program would not hit that error, we don't bother checking for it.

- Multiple `library` forms in one file are not yet supported. This is because the expansion of `library` sets the current module, but does not restore it. This is a bug.

- R6RS unicode escapes within strings are disabled by default, because they conflict with Guile's already-existing escapes. The same is the case for R6RS treatment of escaped newlines in strings.

  R6RS behavior can be turned on via a reader option. See Section 6.6.5.1 [String Syntax], page 141, for more information.

- A `set!` to a variable transformer may only expand to an expression, not a definition—even if the original `set!` expression was in definition context.

- Instead of using the algorithm detailed in chapter 10 of the R6RS, expansion of toplevel forms happens sequentially.

  For example, while the expansion of the following set of toplevel definitions does the correct thing:

```
(begin
  (define even?
    (lambda (x)
      (or (= x 0) (odd? (- x 1)))))
  (define-syntax odd?
    (syntax-rules ()
      ((odd? x) (not (even? x)))))
  (even? 10))
⇒ #t
```

  The same definitions outside of the `begin` wrapper do not:

```
(define even?
  (lambda (x)
    (or (= x 0) (odd? (- x 1)))))
(define-syntax odd?
  (syntax-rules ()
    ((odd? x) (not (even? x)))))
(even? 10)
<unnamed port>:4:18: In procedure even?:
<unnamed port>:4:18: Wrong type to apply: #<syntax-transformer odd?>
```

  This is because when expanding the right-hand-side of `even?`, the reference to `odd?` is not yet marked as a syntax transformer, so it is assumed to be a function.

  This bug will only affect top-level programs, not code in `library` forms. Fixing it for toplevel forms seems doable, but tricky to implement in a backward-compatible way. Suggestions and/or patches would be appreciated.

- The (`rnrs io ports`) module is incomplete. Work is ongoing to fix this.

- Guile does not prevent use of textual I/O procedures on binary ports. More generally, it does not make a sharp distinction between binary and textual ports (see Section 6.14.10.6 [R6RS Port Manipulation], page 337).

- Guile's implementation of `equal?` may fail to terminate when applied to arguments containing cycles.

7.6.2 R6RS Standard Libraries

In contrast with earlier versions of the Revised Report, the R6RS organizes the procedures and syntactic forms required of conforming implementations into a set of "standard libraries" which can be imported as necessary by user programs and libraries. Here we briefly list the libraries that have been implemented for Guile.

We do not attempt to document these libraries fully here, as most of their functionality is already available in Guile itself. The expectation is that most Guile users will use the well-known and well-documented Guile modules. These R6RS libraries are mostly useful to users who want to port their code to other R6RS systems.

The documentation in the following sections reproduces some of the content of the library section of the Report, but is mostly intended to provide supplementary information about Guile's implementation of the R6RS standard libraries. For complete documentation, design rationales and further examples, we advise you to consult the "Standard Libraries" section of the Report (see Section "Standard Libraries" in *The Revised^6 Report on the Algorithmic Language Scheme*).

7.6.2.1 Library Usage

Guile implements the R6RS 'library' form as a transformation to a native Guile module definition. As a consequence of this, all of the libraries described in the following subsections, in addition to being available for use by R6RS libraries and top-level programs, can also be imported as if they were normal Guile modules—via a `use-modules` form, say. For example, the R6RS "composite" library can be imported by:

```
(import (rnrs (6)))
(use-modules ((rnrs) :version (6)))
```

For more information on Guile's library implementation, see (see Section 6.19.6 [R6RS Libraries], page 388).

7.6.2.2 rnrs base

The `(rnrs base (6))` library exports the procedures and syntactic forms described in the main section of the Report (see Section "Base library" in *The Revised^6 Report on the Algorithmic Language Scheme*). They are grouped below by the existing manual sections to which they correspond.

`boolean?` *obj*	[Scheme Procedure]
`not` *x*	[Scheme Procedure]

See Section 6.6.1 [Booleans], page 104, for documentation.

`symbol?` *obj*	[Scheme Procedure]
`symbol->string` *sym*	[Scheme Procedure]
`string->symbol` *str*	[Scheme Procedure]

See Section 6.6.7.4 [Symbol Primitives], page 173, for documentation.

`char?` *obj*	[Scheme Procedure]
`char=?`	[Scheme Procedure]
`char<?`	[Scheme Procedure]
`char>?`	[Scheme Procedure]
`char<=?`	[Scheme Procedure]
`char>=?`	[Scheme Procedure]
`integer->char` *n*	[Scheme Procedure]
`char->integer` *chr*	[Scheme Procedure]

See Section 6.6.3 [Characters], page 129, for documentation.

`list?` *x*	[Scheme Procedure]
`null?` *x*	[Scheme Procedure]

See Section 6.7.2.2 [List Predicates], page 188, for documentation.

`pair?` *x*	[Scheme Procedure]
`cons` *x y*	[Scheme Procedure]
`car` *pair*	[Scheme Procedure]
`cdr` *pair*	[Scheme Procedure]
`caar` *pair*	[Scheme Procedure]
`cadr` *pair*	[Scheme Procedure]
`cdar` *pair*	[Scheme Procedure]
`cddr` *pair*	[Scheme Procedure]
`caaar` *pair*	[Scheme Procedure]
`caadr` *pair*	[Scheme Procedure]
`cadar` *pair*	[Scheme Procedure]
`cdaar` *pair*	[Scheme Procedure]
`caddr` *pair*	[Scheme Procedure]
`cdadr` *pair*	[Scheme Procedure]
`cddar` *pair*	[Scheme Procedure]
`cdddr` *pair*	[Scheme Procedure]
`caaaar` *pair*	[Scheme Procedure]
`caaadr` *pair*	[Scheme Procedure]
`caadar` *pair*	[Scheme Procedure]
`cadaar` *pair*	[Scheme Procedure]
`cdaaar` *pair*	[Scheme Procedure]
`cddaar` *pair*	[Scheme Procedure]
`cdadar` *pair*	[Scheme Procedure]
`cdaadr` *pair*	[Scheme Procedure]
`cadadr` *pair*	[Scheme Procedure]
`caaddr` *pair*	[Scheme Procedure]
`caddar` *pair*	[Scheme Procedure]
`cadddr` *pair*	[Scheme Procedure]
`cdaddr` *pair*	[Scheme Procedure]
`cddadr` *pair*	[Scheme Procedure]
`cdddar` *pair*	[Scheme Procedure]
`cddddr` *pair*	[Scheme Procedure]

See Section 6.7.1 [Pairs], page 185, for documentation.

`number?` *obj* [Scheme Procedure]

See Section 6.6.2.1 [Numerical Tower], page 105, for documentation.

`string?` *obj* [Scheme Procedure]

See Section 6.6.5.2 [String Predicates], page 142, for documentation.

`procedure?` *obj* [Scheme Procedure]

See Section 6.9.7 [Procedure Properties], page 254, for documentation.

`define` *name value* [Scheme Syntax]
`set!` *variable-name value* [Scheme Syntax]

See Section 3.1.3 [Definition], page 16, for documentation.

`define-syntax` *keyword expression* [Scheme Syntax]
`let-syntax` *((keyword transformer) ...) exp1 exp2 ...* [Scheme Syntax]

`letrec-syntax ((`*keyword transformer*`) ...) `*exp1 exp2* `...`   [Scheme Syntax]
> See Section 6.10.1 [Defining Macros], page 257, for documentation.

`identifier-syntax` *exp*   [Scheme Syntax]
> See Section 6.10.6 [Identifier Macros], page 271, for documentation.

`syntax-rules` *literals* (*pattern template*) *...*   [Scheme Syntax]
> See Section 6.10.2 [Syntax Rules], page 258, for documentation.

`lambda` *formals body*   [Scheme Syntax]
> See Section 6.9.1 [Lambda], page 244, for documentation.

`let` *bindings body*   [Scheme Syntax]
`let*` *bindings body*   [Scheme Syntax]
`letrec` *bindings body*   [Scheme Syntax]
`letrec*` *bindings body*   [Scheme Syntax]
> See Section 6.12.2 [Local Bindings], page 287, for documentation.

`let-values` *bindings body*   [Scheme Syntax]
`let*-values` *bindings body*   [Scheme Syntax]
> See Section 7.5.10 [SRFI-11], page 577, for documentation.

`begin` *expr1 expr2 ...*   [Scheme Syntax]
> See Section 6.13.1 [begin], page 290, for documentation.

`quote` *expr*   [Scheme Syntax]
`quasiquote` *expr*   [Scheme Syntax]
`unquote` *expr*   [Scheme Syntax]
`unquote-splicing` *expr*   [Scheme Syntax]
> See Section 6.17.1.1 [Expression Syntax], page 357, for documentation.

`if` *test consequence* [*alternate*]   [Scheme Syntax]
`cond` *clause1 clause2 ...*   [Scheme Syntax]
`case` *key clause1 clause2 ...*   [Scheme Syntax]
> See Section 6.13.2 [Conditionals], page 292, for documentation.

`and` *expr ...*   [Scheme Syntax]
`or` *expr ...*   [Scheme Syntax]
> See Section 6.13.3 [and or], page 293, for documentation.

`eq?` *x y*   [Scheme Procedure]
`eqv?` *x y*   [Scheme Procedure]
`equal?` *x y*   [Scheme Procedure]
`symbol=?` *symbol1 symbol2 ...*   [Scheme Procedure]
> See Section 6.11.1 [Equality], page 276, for documentation.

> `symbol=?` is identical to `eq?`.

`complex?` *z*   [Scheme Procedure]
> See Section 6.6.2.4 [Complex Numbers], page 113, for documentation.

`real-part` *z*	[Scheme Procedure]
`imag-part` *z*	[Scheme Procedure]
`make-rectangular` *real_part imaginary_part*	[Scheme Procedure]
`make-polar` *x y*	[Scheme Procedure]
`magnitude` *z*	[Scheme Procedure]
`angle` *z*	[Scheme Procedure]

     See Section 6.6.2.10 [Complex], page 118, for documentation.

`sqrt` *z*	[Scheme Procedure]
`exp` *z*	[Scheme Procedure]
`expt` *z1 z2*	[Scheme Procedure]
`log` *z*	[Scheme Procedure]
`sin` *z*	[Scheme Procedure]
`cos` *z*	[Scheme Procedure]
`tan` *z*	[Scheme Procedure]
`asin` *z*	[Scheme Procedure]
`acos` *z*	[Scheme Procedure]
`atan` *z*	[Scheme Procedure]

     See Section 6.6.2.12 [Scientific], page 123, for documentation.

`real?` *x*	[Scheme Procedure]
`rational?` *x*	[Scheme Procedure]
`numerator` *x*	[Scheme Procedure]
`denominator` *x*	[Scheme Procedure]
`rationalize` *x eps*	[Scheme Procedure]

     See Section 6.6.2.3 [Reals and Rationals], page 110, for documentation.

`exact?` *x*	[Scheme Procedure]
`inexact?` *x*	[Scheme Procedure]
`exact` *z*	[Scheme Procedure]
`inexact` *z*	[Scheme Procedure]

     See Section 6.6.2.5 [Exactness], page 113, for documentation. The `exact` and `inexact` procedures are identical to the `inexact->exact` and `exact->inexact` procedures provided by Guile's code library.

`integer?` *x*	[Scheme Procedure]

     See Section 6.6.2.2 [Integers], page 106, for documentation.

`odd?` *n*	[Scheme Procedure]
`even?` *n*	[Scheme Procedure]
`gcd` *x ...*	[Scheme Procedure]
`lcm` *x ...*	[Scheme Procedure]
`exact-integer-sqrt` *k*	[Scheme Procedure]

     See Section 6.6.2.7 [Integer Operations], page 116, for documentation.

`=`	[Scheme Procedure]
`<`	[Scheme Procedure]
`>`	[Scheme Procedure]
`<=`	[Scheme Procedure]

`>=`   [Scheme Procedure]
`zero?` *x*   [Scheme Procedure]
`positive?` *x*   [Scheme Procedure]
`negative?` *x*   [Scheme Procedure]
      See Section 6.6.2.8 [Comparison], page 117, for documentation.

`for-each` *f lst1 lst2 ...*   [Scheme Procedure]
      See Section 7.5.3.5 [SRFI-1 Fold and Map], page 556, for documentation.

`list` *elem ...*   [Scheme Procedure]
      See Section 6.7.2.3 [List Constructors], page 189, for documentation.

`length` *lst*   [Scheme Procedure]
`list-ref` *lst k*   [Scheme Procedure]
`list-tail` *lst k*   [Scheme Procedure]
      See Section 6.7.2.4 [List Selection], page 190, for documentation.

`append` *lst ... obj*   [Scheme Procedure]
`append`   [Scheme Procedure]
`reverse` *lst*   [Scheme Procedure]
      See Section 6.7.2.5 [Append/Reverse], page 190, for documentation.

`number->string` *n* [*radix*]   [Scheme Procedure]
`string->number` *str* [*radix*]   [Scheme Procedure]
      See Section 6.6.2.9 [Conversion], page 118, for documentation.

`string` *char ...*   [Scheme Procedure]
`make-string` *k* [*chr*]   [Scheme Procedure]
`list->string` *lst*   [Scheme Procedure]
      See Section 6.6.5.3 [String Constructors], page 143, for documentation.

`string->list` *str* [*start* [*end*]]   [Scheme Procedure]
      See Section 6.6.5.4 [List/String Conversion], page 144, for documentation.

`string-length` *str*   [Scheme Procedure]
`string-ref` *str k*   [Scheme Procedure]
`string-copy` *str* [*start* [*end*]]   [Scheme Procedure]
`substring` *str start* [*end*]   [Scheme Procedure]
      See Section 6.6.5.5 [String Selection], page 145, for documentation.

`string=?` *s1 s2 s3 ...*   [Scheme Procedure]
`string<?` *s1 s2 s3 ...*   [Scheme Procedure]
`string>?` *s1 s2 s3 ...*   [Scheme Procedure]
`string<=?` *s1 s2 s3 ...*   [Scheme Procedure]
`string>=?` *s1 s2 s3 ...*   [Scheme Procedure]
      See Section 6.6.5.7 [String Comparison], page 148, for documentation.

`string-append` *arg ...*   [Scheme Procedure]
      See Section 6.6.5.10 [Reversing and Appending Strings], page 155, for documentation.

`string-for-each` *proc s [start [end]]*   [Scheme Procedure]
    See Section 6.6.5.11 [Mapping Folding and Unfolding], page 156, for documentation.

`+` *z1 ...*   [Scheme Procedure]
`-` *z1 z2 ...*   [Scheme Procedure]
`*` *z1 ...*   [Scheme Procedure]
`/` *z1 z2 ...*   [Scheme Procedure]
`max` *x1 x2 ...*   [Scheme Procedure]
`min` *x1 x2 ...*   [Scheme Procedure]
`abs` *x*   [Scheme Procedure]
`truncate` *x*   [Scheme Procedure]
`floor` *x*   [Scheme Procedure]
`ceiling` *x*   [Scheme Procedure]
`round` *x*   [Scheme Procedure]
    See Section 6.6.2.11 [Arithmetic], page 119, for documentation.

`div` *x y*   [Scheme Procedure]
`mod` *x y*   [Scheme Procedure]
`div-and-mod` *x y*   [Scheme Procedure]
    These procedures accept two real numbers x and y, where the divisor y must be non-zero. `div` returns the integer q and `mod` returns the real number r such that $x = q * y + r$ and $0 <= r < abs(y)$. `div-and-mod` returns both q and r, and is more efficient than computing each separately. Note that when $y > 0$, `div` returns $floor(x/y)$, otherwise it returns $ceiling(x/y)$.

```
(div 123 10) ⇒ 12
(mod 123 10) ⇒ 3
(div-and-mod 123 10) ⇒ 12 and 3
(div-and-mod 123 -10) ⇒ -12 and 3
(div-and-mod -123 10) ⇒ -13 and 7
(div-and-mod -123 -10) ⇒ 13 and 7
(div-and-mod -123.2 -63.5) ⇒ 2.0 and 3.8
(div-and-mod 16/3 -10/7) ⇒ -3 and 22/21
```

`div0` *x y*   [Scheme Procedure]
`mod0` *x y*   [Scheme Procedure]
`div0-and-mod0` *x y*   [Scheme Procedure]
    These procedures accept two real numbers x and y, where the divisor y must be non-zero. `div0` returns the integer q and `mod0` returns the real number r such that $x = q * y + r$ and $-abs(y/2) <= r < abs(y/2)$. `div0-and-mod0` returns both q and r, and is more efficient than computing each separately.

    Note that `div0` returns x/y rounded to the nearest integer. When x/y lies exactly half-way between two integers, the tie is broken according to the sign of y. If $y > 0$, ties are rounded toward positive infinity, otherwise they are rounded toward negative infinity. This is a consequence of the requirement that $-abs(y/2) <= r < abs(y/2)$.

```
(div0 123 10) ⇒ 12
(mod0 123 10) ⇒ 3
(div0-and-mod0 123 10) ⇒ 12 and 3
```

```
(div0-and-mod0 123 -10) ⇒ -12 and 3
(div0-and-mod0 -123 10) ⇒ -12 and -3
(div0-and-mod0 -123 -10) ⇒ 12 and -3
(div0-and-mod0 -123.2 -63.5) ⇒ 2.0 and 3.8
(div0-and-mod0 16/3 -10/7) ⇒ -4 and -8/21
```

real-valued? *obj*   [Scheme Procedure]
rational-valued? *obj*   [Scheme Procedure]
integer-valued? *obj*   [Scheme Procedure]
> These procedures return #t if and only if their arguments can, respectively, be coerced to a real, rational, or integer value without a loss of numerical precision.
>
> **real-valued?** will return #t for complex numbers whose imaginary parts are zero.

nan? *x*   [Scheme Procedure]
infinite? *x*   [Scheme Procedure]
finite? *x*   [Scheme Procedure]
> **nan?** returns #t if *x* is a NaN value, #f otherwise. **infinite?** returns #t if *x* is an infinite value, #f otherwise. **finite?** returns #t if *x* is neither infinite nor a NaN value, otherwise it returns #f. Every real number satisfies exactly one of these predicates. An exception is raised if *x* is not real.

assert *expr*   [Scheme Syntax]
> Raises an &assertion condition if *expr* evaluates to #f; otherwise evaluates to the value of *expr*.

error *who message irritant1 ...*   [Scheme Procedure]
assertion-violation *who message irritant1 ...*   [Scheme Procedure]
> These procedures raise compound conditions based on their arguments: If *who* is not #f, the condition will include a &who condition whose who field is set to *who*; a &message condition will be included with a message field equal to *message*; an &irritants condition will be included with its irritants list given by irritant1 . . . .
>
> **error** produces a compound condition with the simple conditions described above, as well as an &error condition; **assertion-violation** produces one that includes an &assertion condition.

vector-map *proc v*   [Scheme Procedure]
vector-for-each *proc v*   [Scheme Procedure]
> These procedures implement the **map** and **for-each** contracts over vectors.

vector *arg ...*   [Scheme Procedure]
vector? *obj*   [Scheme Procedure]
make-vector *len*   [Scheme Procedure]
make-vector *len fill*   [Scheme Procedure]
list->vector *l*   [Scheme Procedure]
vector->list *v*   [Scheme Procedure]
> See Section 6.7.3.2 [Vector Creation], page 194, for documentation.

vector-length *vector*   [Scheme Procedure]
vector-ref *vector k*   [Scheme Procedure]
vector-set! *vector k obj*   [Scheme Procedure]
vector-fill! *v fill*   [Scheme Procedure]
     See Section 6.7.3.3 [Vector Accessors], page 195, for documentation.

call-with-current-continuation *proc*   [Scheme Procedure]
call/cc *proc*   [Scheme Procedure]
     See Section 6.13.6 [Continuations], page 300, for documentation.

values *arg ...*   [Scheme Procedure]
call-with-values *producer consumer*   [Scheme Procedure]
     See Section 6.13.7 [Multiple Values], page 301, for documentation.

dynamic-wind *in_guard thunk out_guard*   [Scheme Procedure]
     See Section 6.13.10 [Dynamic Wind], page 309, for documentation.

apply *proc arg ... arglst*   [Scheme Procedure]
     See Section 6.17.4 [Fly Evaluation], page 362, for documentation.

7.6.2.3 rnrs unicode

The (rnrs unicode (6)) library provides procedures for manipulating Unicode characters and strings.

char-upcase *char*   [Scheme Procedure]
char-downcase *char*   [Scheme Procedure]
char-titlecase *char*   [Scheme Procedure]
char-foldcase *char*   [Scheme Procedure]
     These procedures translate their arguments from one Unicode character set to another. char-upcase, char-downcase, and char-titlecase are identical to their counterparts in the Guile core library; See Section 6.6.3 [Characters], page 129, for documentation.

     char-foldcase returns the result of applying char-upcase to its argument, followed by char-downcase—except in the case of the Turkic characters U+0130 and U+0131, for which the procedure acts as the identity function.

char-ci=? *char1 char2 char3 ...*   [Scheme Procedure]
char-ci<? *char1 char2 char3 ...*   [Scheme Procedure]
char-ci>? *char1 char2 char3 ...*   [Scheme Procedure]
char-ci<=? *char1 char2 char3 ...*   [Scheme Procedure]
char-ci>=? *char1 char2 char3 ...*   [Scheme Procedure]
     These procedures facilitate case-insensitive comparison of Unicode characters. They are identical to the procedures provided by Guile's core library. See Section 6.6.3 [Characters], page 129, for documentation.

char-alphabetic? *char*   [Scheme Procedure]
char-numeric? *char*   [Scheme Procedure]
char-whitespace? *char*   [Scheme Procedure]
char-upper-case? *char*   [Scheme Procedure]

char-lower-case? *char*   [Scheme Procedure]
char-title-case? *char*   [Scheme Procedure]
> These procedures implement various Unicode character set predicates. They are iden-
> tical to the procedures provided by Guile's core library. See Section 6.6.3 [Characters],
> page 129, for documentation.

char-general-category *char*   [Scheme Procedure]
> See Section 6.6.3 [Characters], page 129, for documentation.

string-upcase *string*   [Scheme Procedure]
string-downcase *string*   [Scheme Procedure]
string-titlecase *string*   [Scheme Procedure]
string-foldcase *string*   [Scheme Procedure]
> These procedures perform Unicode case folding operations on their input. See
> Section 6.6.5.9 [Alphabetic Case Mapping], page 154, for documentation.

string-ci=? *string1 string2 string3 ...*   [Scheme Procedure]
string-ci<? *string1 string2 string3 ...*   [Scheme Procedure]
string-ci>? *string1 string2 string3 ...*   [Scheme Procedure]
string-ci<=? *string1 string2 string3 ...*   [Scheme Procedure]
string-ci>=? *string1 string2 string3 ...*   [Scheme Procedure]
> These procedures perform case-insensitive comparison on their input. See
> Section 6.6.5.7 [String Comparison], page 148, for documentation.

string-normalize-nfd *string*   [Scheme Procedure]
string-normalize-nfkd *string*   [Scheme Procedure]
string-normalize-nfc *string*   [Scheme Procedure]
string-normalize-nfkc *string*   [Scheme Procedure]
> These procedures perform Unicode string normalization operations on their input.
> See Section 6.6.5.7 [String Comparison], page 148, for documentation.

7.6.2.4 rnrs bytevectors

The (rnrs bytevectors (6)) library provides procedures for working with blocks of binary
data. This functionality is documented in its own section of the manual; See Section 6.6.6
[Bytevectors], page 163.

7.6.2.5 rnrs lists

The (rnrs lists (6)) library provides procedures additional procedures for working with
lists.

find *proc list*   [Scheme Procedure]
> This procedure is identical to the one defined in Guile's SRFI-1 implementation. See
> Section 7.5.3.7 [SRFI-1 Searching], page 560, for documentation.

for-all *proc list1 list2 ...*   [Scheme Procedure]
exists *proc list1 list2 ...*   [Scheme Procedure]
> The for-all procedure is identical to the every procedure defined by SRFI-1; the
> exists procedure is identical to SRFI-1's any. See Section 7.5.3.7 [SRFI-1 Searching],
> page 560, for documentation.

`filter` *proc list*   [Scheme Procedure]

`partition` *proc list*   [Scheme Procedure]

> These procedures are identical to the ones provided by SRFI-1. See Section 6.7.2.6 [List Modification], page 191, for a description of `filter`; See Section 7.5.3.6 [SRFI-1 Filtering and Partitioning], page 559, for `partition`.

`fold-left` *combine nil list1 list2 ...*   [Scheme Procedure]

`fold-right` *combine nil list1 list2 ...*   [Scheme Procedure]

> These procedures are identical to the `fold` and `fold-right` procedures provided by SRFI-1. See Section 7.5.3.5 [SRFI-1 Fold and Map], page 556, for documentation.

`remp` *proc list*   [Scheme Procedure]

`remove` *obj list*   [Scheme Procedure]

`remv` *obj list*   [Scheme Procedure]

`remq` *obj list*   [Scheme Procedure]

> `remove`, `remv`, and `remq` are identical to the `delete`, `delv`, and `delq` procedures provided by Guile's core library, (see Section 6.7.2.6 [List Modification], page 191). `remp` is identical to the alternate `remove` procedure provided by SRFI-1; See Section 7.5.3.8 [SRFI-1 Deleting], page 561.

`memp` *proc list*   [Scheme Procedure]

`member` *obj list*   [Scheme Procedure]

`memv` *obj list*   [Scheme Procedure]

`memq` *obj list*   [Scheme Procedure]

> `member`, `memv`, and `memq` are identical to the procedures provided by Guile's core library; See Section 6.7.2.7 [List Searching], page 192, for their documentation. `memp` uses the specified predicate function `proc` to test elements of the list *list*—it behaves similarly to `find`, except that it returns the first sublist of *list* whose `car` satisfies *proc*.

`assp` *proc alist*   [Scheme Procedure]

`assoc` *obj alist*   [Scheme Procedure]

`assv` *obj alist*   [Scheme Procedure]

`assq` *obj alist*   [Scheme Procedure]

> `assoc`, `assv`, and `assq` are identical to the procedures provided by Guile's core library; See Section 6.7.12.1 [Alist Key Equality], page 228, for their documentation. `assp` uses the specified predicate function `proc` to test keys in the association list *alist*.

`cons*` *obj1 ... obj*   [Scheme Procedure]

`cons*` *obj*   [Scheme Procedure]

> This procedure is identical to the one exported by Guile's core library. See Section 6.7.2.3 [List Constructors], page 189, for documentation.

7.6.2.6 rnrs sorting

The `(rnrs sorting (6))` library provides procedures for sorting lists and vectors.

`list-sort` *proc list*   [Scheme Procedure]

`vector-sort` *proc vector*   [Scheme Procedure]

> These procedures return their input sorted in ascending order, without modifying the original data. *proc* must be a procedure that takes two elements from the input list

or vector as arguments, and returns a true value if the first is "less" than the second, `#f` otherwise. `list-sort` returns a list; `vector-sort` returns a vector.

Both `list-sort` and `vector-sort` are implemented in terms of the `stable-sort` procedure from Guile's core library. See Section 6.11.3 [Sorting], page 279, for a discussion of the behavior of that procedure.

`vector-sort!` *proc vector*   [Scheme Procedure]

Performs a destructive, "in-place" sort of *vector*, using *proc* as described above to determine an ascending ordering of elements. `vector-sort!` returns an unspecified value.

This procedure is implemented in terms of the `sort!` procedure from Guile's core library. See Section 6.11.3 [Sorting], page 279, for more information.

7.6.2.7 rnrs control

The (`rnrs control (6)`) library provides syntactic forms useful for constructing conditional expressions and controlling the flow of execution.

`when` *test expression1 expression2 ...*   [Scheme Syntax]
`unless` *test expression1 expression2 ...*   [Scheme Syntax]

The `when` form is evaluated by evaluating the specified *test* expression; if the result is a true value, the *expressions* that follow it are evaluated in order, and the value of the final *expression* becomes the value of the entire `when` expression.

The `unless` form behaves similarly, with the exception that the specified *expressions* are only evaluated if the value of *test* is false.

`do` ((*variable init step*) ...) (*test expression ...*) *command ...*   [Scheme Syntax]

This form is identical to the one provided by Guile's core library. See Section 6.13.4 [while do], page 294, for documentation.

`case-lambda` *clause ...*   [Scheme Syntax]

This form is identical to the one provided by Guile's core library. See Section 6.9.5 [Case-lambda], page 251, for documentation.

7.6.2.8 R6RS Records

The manual sections below describe Guile's implementation of R6RS records, which provide support for user-defined data types. The R6RS records API provides a superset of the features provided by Guile's "native" records, as well as those of the SRFI-9 records API; See Section 6.7.9 [Records], page 219, and Section 6.7.8 [SRFI-9 Records], page 216, for a description of those interfaces.

As with SRFI-9 and Guile's native records, R6RS records are constructed using a record-type descriptor that specifies attributes like the record's name, its fields, and the mutability of those fields.

R6RS records extend this framework to support single inheritance via the specification of a "parent" type for a record type at definition time. Accessors and mutator procedures for the fields of a parent type may be applied to records of a subtype of this parent. A record type may be *sealed*, in which case it cannot be used as the parent of another record type.

The inheritance mechanism for record types also informs the process of initializing the fields of a record and its parents. Constructor procedures that generate new instances of a record type are obtained from a record constructor descriptor, which encapsulates the record-type descriptor of the record to be constructed along with a *protocol* procedure that defines how constructors for record subtypes delegate to the constructors of their parent types.

A protocol is a procedure used by the record system at construction time to bind arguments to the fields of the record being constructed. The protocol procedure is passed a procedure n that accepts the arguments required to construct the record's parent type; this procedure, when invoked, will return a procedure p that accepts the arguments required to construct a new instance of the record type itself and returns a new instance of the record type.

The protocol should in turn return a procedure that uses n and p to initialize the fields of the record type and its parent type(s). This procedure will be the constructor returned by

As a trivial example, consider the hypothetical record type `pixel`, which encapsulates an x-y location on a screen, and `voxel`, which has `pixel` as its parent type and stores an additional coordinate. The following protocol produces a constructor procedure that accepts all three coordinates, uses the first two to initialize the fields of `pixel`, and binds the third to the single field of `voxel`.

```
(lambda (n)
  (lambda (x y z)
    (let ((p (n x y)))
      (p z))))
```

It may be helpful to think of protocols as "constructor factories" that produce chains of delegating constructors glued together by the helper procedure n.

An R6RS record type may be declared to be *nongenerative* via the use of a unique generated or user-supplied symbol—or *uid*—such that subsequent record type declarations with the same uid and attributes will return the previously-declared record-type descriptor.

R6RS record types may also be declared to be *opaque*, in which case the various predicates and introspection procedures defined in (`rnrs records introspection`) will behave as if records of this type are not records at all.

Note that while the R6RS records API shares much of its namespace with both the SRFI-9 and native Guile records APIs, it is not currently compatible with either.

7.6.2.9 rnrs records syntactic

The (`rnrs records syntactic (6)`) library exports the syntactic API for working with R6RS records.

define-record-type *name-spec record-clause . . .*   [Scheme Syntax]
> Defines a new record type, introducing bindings for a record-type descriptor, a record constructor descriptor, a constructor procedure, a record predicate, and accessor and mutator procedures for the new record type's fields.
>
> *name-spec* must either be an identifier or must take the form (`record-name constructor-name predicate-name`), where *record-name*, *constructor-name*, and

predicate-name are all identifiers and specify the names to which, respectively, the record-type descriptor, constructor, and predicate procedures will be bound. If *name-spec* is only an identifier, it specifies the name to which the generated record-type descriptor will be bound.

Each *record-clause* must be one of the following:

- (fields field-spec*), where each *field-spec* specifies a field of the new record type and takes one of the following forms:
    - (immutable field-name accessor-name), which specifies an immutable field with the name *field-name* and binds an accessor procedure for it to the name given by *accessor-name*
    - (mutable field-name accessor-name mutator-name), which specifies a mutable field with the name *field-name* and binds accessor and mutator procedures to *accessor-name* and *mutator-name*, respectively
    - (immutable field-name), which specifies an immutable field with the name *field-name*; an accessor procedure for it will be created and named by appending record name and *field-name* with a hyphen separator
    - (mutable field-name), which specifies a mutable field with the name *field-name*; an accessor procedure for it will be created and named as described above; a mutator procedure will also be created and named by appending -set! to the accessor name
    - field-name, which specifies an immutable field with the name *field-name*; an access procedure for it will be created and named as described above
- (parent parent-name), where *parent-name* is a symbol giving the name of the record type to be used as the parent of the new record type
- (protocol expression), where *expression* evaluates to a protocol procedure which behaves as described above, and is used to create a record constructor descriptor for the new record type
- (sealed sealed?), where *sealed?* is a boolean value that specifies whether or not the new record type is sealed
- (opaque opaque?), where *opaque?* is a boolean value that specifies whether or not the new record type is opaque
- (nongenerative [uid]), which specifies that the record type is nongenerative via the optional uid *uid*. If *uid* is not specified, a unique uid will be generated at expansion time
- (parent-rtd parent-rtd parent-cd), a more explicit form of the parent form above; *parent-rtd* and *parent-cd* should evaluate to a record-type descriptor and a record constructor descriptor, respectively

record-type-descriptor *record-name*   [Scheme Syntax]
    Evaluates to the record-type descriptor associated with the type specified by *record-name*.

record-constructor-descriptor *record-name*   [Scheme Syntax]
    Evaluates to the record-constructor descriptor associated with the type specified by *record-name*.

7.6.2.10 rnrs records procedural

The (rnrs records procedural (6)) library exports the procedural API for working with R6RS records.

make-record-type-descriptor *name parent uid sealed?*   [Scheme Procedure]
       opaque? fields

Returns a new record-type descriptor with the specified characteristics: *name* must be a symbol giving the name of the new record type; *parent* must be either #f or a non-sealed record-type descriptor for the returned record type to extend; *uid* must be either #f, indicating that the record type is generative, or a symbol giving the type's nongenerative uid; *sealed?* and *opaque?* must be boolean values that specify the sealedness and opaqueness of the record type; *fields* must be a vector of zero or more field specifiers of the form (mutable name) or (immutable name), where name is a symbol giving a name for the field.

If *uid* is not #f, it must be a symbol

record-type-descriptor? *obj*   [Scheme Procedure]

Returns #t if *obj* is a record-type descriptor, #f otherwise.

make-record-constructor-descriptor *rtd*   [Scheme Procedure]
       parent-constructor-descriptor protocol

Returns a new record constructor descriptor that can be used to produce constructors for the record type specified by the record-type descriptor *rtd* and whose delegation and binding behavior are specified by the protocol procedure *protocol*.

parent-constructor-descriptor specifies a record constructor descriptor for the parent type of *rtd*, if one exists. If *rtd* represents a base type, then *parent-constructor-descriptor* must be #f. If *rtd* is an extension of another type, *parent-constructor-descriptor* may still be #f, but protocol must also be #f in this case.

record-constructor *rcd*   [Scheme Procedure]

Returns a record constructor procedure by invoking the protocol defined by the record-constructor descriptor *rcd*.

record-predicate *rtd*   [Scheme Procedure]

Returns the record predicate procedure for the record-type descriptor *rtd*.

record-accessor *rtd k*   [Scheme Procedure]

Returns the record field accessor procedure for the *k*th field of the record-type descriptor *rtd*.

record-mutator *rtd k*   [Scheme Procedure]

Returns the record field mutator procedure for the *k*th field of the record-type descriptor *rtd*. An &assertion condition will be raised if this field is not mutable.

7.6.2.11 rnrs records inspection

The (rnrs records inspection (6)) library provides procedures useful for accessing metadata about R6RS records.

`record?` *obj*   [Scheme Procedure]
>   Return #t if the specified object is a non-opaque R6RS record, #f otherwise.

`record-rtd` *record*   [Scheme Procedure]
>   Returns the record-type descriptor for *record*. An &assertion is raised if *record* is opaque.

`record-type-name` *rtd*   [Scheme Procedure]
>   Returns the name of the record-type descriptor *rtd*.

`record-type-parent` *rtd*   [Scheme Procedure]
>   Returns the parent of the record-type descriptor *rtd*, or #f if it has none.

`record-type-uid` *rtd*   [Scheme Procedure]
>   Returns the uid of the record-type descriptor *rtd*, or #f if it has none.

`record-type-generative?` *rtd*   [Scheme Procedure]
>   Returns #t if the record-type descriptor *rtd* is generative, #f otherwise.

`record-type-sealed?` *rtd*   [Scheme Procedure]
>   Returns #t if the record-type descriptor *rtd* is sealed, #f otherwise.

`record-type-opaque?` *rtd*   [Scheme Procedure]
>   Returns #t if the record-type descriptor *rtd* is opaque, #f otherwise.

`record-type-field-names` *rtd*   [Scheme Procedure]
>   Returns a vector of symbols giving the names of the fields defined by the record-type descriptor *rtd* (and not any of its sub- or supertypes).

`record-field-mutable?` *rtd k*   [Scheme Procedure]
>   Returns #t if the field at index *k* of the record-type descriptor *rtd* (and not any of its sub- or supertypes) is mutable.

7.6.2.12 rnrs exceptions

The (rnrs exceptions (6)) library provides functionality related to signaling and handling exceptional situations. This functionality is similar to the exception handling systems provided by Guile's core library See Section 6.13.8 [Exceptions], page 303, and by the SRFI-18 and SRFI-34 modules—See Section 7.5.15.5 [SRFI-18 Exceptions], page 582, and Section 7.5.22 [SRFI-34], page 594, respectively—but there are some key differences in concepts and behavior.

A raised exception may be *continuable* or *non-continuable*. When an exception is raised non-continuably, another exception, with the condition type &non-continuable, will be raised when the exception handler returns locally. Raising an exception continuably captures the current continuation and invokes it after a local return from the exception handler.

Like SRFI-18 and SRFI-34, R6RS exceptions are implemented on top of Guile's native throw and catch forms, and use custom "throw keys" to identify their exception types. As a consequence, Guile's catch form can handle exceptions thrown by these APIs, but the reverse is not true: Handlers registered by the with-exception-handler procedure described below will only be called on exceptions thrown by the corresponding raise procedure.

with-exception-handler *handler thunk*   [Scheme Procedure]
> Installs *handler*, which must be a procedure taking one argument, as the current exception handler during the invocation of *thunk*, a procedure taking zero arguments. The handler in place at the time **with-exception-handler** is called is made current again once either *thunk* returns or *handler* is invoked after an exception is thrown from within *thunk*.
>
> This procedure is similar to the **with-throw-handler** procedure provided by Guile's code library; (see Section 6.13.8.3 [Throw Handlers], page 306).

guard (*variable clause1 clause2 ...*) *body*   [Scheme Syntax]
> Evaluates the expression given by *body*, first creating an ad hoc exception handler that binds a raised exception to *variable* and then evaluates the specified *clauses* as if they were part of a **cond** expression, with the value of the first matching clause becoming the value of the **guard** expression (see Section 6.13.2 [Conditionals], page 292). If none of the clause's test expressions evaluates to **#t**, the exception is re-raised, with the exception handler that was current before the evaluation of the **guard** form.
>
> For example, the expression
>
> ```
> (guard (ex ((eq? ex 'foo) 'bar) ((eq? ex 'bar) 'baz))
>   (raise 'bar))
> ```
>
> evaluates to **baz**.

raise *obj*   [Scheme Procedure]
> Raises a non-continuable exception by invoking the currently-installed exception handler on *obj*. If the handler returns, a **&non-continuable** exception will be raised in the dynamic context in which the handler was installed.

raise-continuable *obj*   [Scheme Procedure]
> Raises a continuable exception by invoking currently-installed exception handler on *obj*.

7.6.2.13 rnrs conditions

The (**rnrs condition (6)**) library provides forms and procedures for constructing new condition types, as well as a library of pre-defined condition types that represent a variety of common exceptional situations. Conditions are records of a subtype of the **&condition** record type, which is neither sealed nor opaque. See Section 7.6.2.8 [R6RS Records], page 634.

Conditions may be manipulated singly, as *simple conditions*, or when composed with other conditions to form *compound conditions*. Compound conditions do not "nest"— constructing a new compound condition out of existing compound conditions will "flatten" them into their component simple conditions. For example, making a new condition out of a **&message** condition and a compound condition that contains an **&assertion** condition and another **&message** condition will produce a compound condition that contains two **&message** conditions and one **&assertion** condition.

The record type predicates and field accessors described below can operate on either simple or compound conditions. In the latter case, the predicate returns **#t** if the compound condition contains a component simple condition of the appropriate type; the field accessors return the requisite fields from the first component simple condition found to be of the appropriate type.

This library is quite similar to the SRFI-35 conditions module (see Section 7.5.23 [SRFI-35], page 594). Among other minor differences, the (rnrs conditions) library features slightly different semantics around condition field accessors, and comes with a larger number of pre-defined condition types. The two APIs are not currently compatible, however; the condition? predicate from one API will return #f when applied to a condition object created in the other.

&condition   [Condition Type]
condition? *obj*   [Scheme Procedure]
    The base record type for conditions.

condition *condition1 ...*   [Scheme Procedure]
simple-conditions *condition*   [Scheme Procedure]
    The condition procedure creates a new compound condition out of its condition arguments, flattening any specified compound conditions into their component simple conditions as described above.

    simple-conditions returns a list of the component simple conditions of the compound condition condition, in the order in which they were specified at construction time.

condition-predicate *rtd*   [Scheme Procedure]
condition-accessor *rtd proc*   [Scheme Procedure]
    These procedures return condition predicate and accessor procedures for the specified condition record type *rtd*.

define-condition-type *condition-type supertype constructor*   [Scheme Syntax]
        predicate field-spec ...
    Evaluates to a new record type definition for a condition type with the name *condition-type* that has the condition type *supertype* as its parent. A default constructor, which binds its arguments to the fields of this type and its parent types, will be bound to the identifier *constructor*; a condition predicate will be bound to *predicate*. The fields of the new type, which are immutable, are specified by the *field-spec*s, each of which must be of the form:

        (field accessor)

    where *field* gives the name of the field and *accessor* gives the name for a binding to an accessor procedure created for this field.

&message   [Condition Type]
make-message-condition *message*   [Scheme Procedure]
message-condition? *obj*   [Scheme Procedure]
condition-message *condition*   [Scheme Procedure]
    A type that includes a message describing the condition that occurred.

&warning   [Condition Type]
make-warning   [Scheme Procedure]
warning? *obj*   [Scheme Procedure]
    A base type for representing non-fatal conditions during execution.

`&serious`   [Condition Type]
`make-serious-condition`   [Scheme Procedure]
`serious-condition?` *obj*   [Scheme Procedure]

A base type for conditions representing errors serious enough that cannot be ignored.

`&error`   [Condition Type]
`make-error`   [Scheme Procedure]
`error?` *obj*   [Scheme Procedure]

A base type for conditions representing errors.

`&violation`   [Condition Type]
`make-violation`   [Scheme Procedure]
`violation?`   [Scheme Procedure]

A subtype of `&serious` that can be used to represent violations of a language or library standard.

`&assertion`   [Condition Type]
`make-assertion-violation`   [Scheme Procedure]
`assertion-violation?` *obj*   [Scheme Procedure]

A subtype of `&violation` that indicates an invalid call to a procedure.

`&irritants`   [Condition Type]
`make-irritants-condition` *irritants*   [Scheme Procedure]
`irritants-condition?` *obj*   [Scheme Procedure]
`condition-irritants` *condition*   [Scheme Procedure]

A base type used for storing information about the causes of another condition in a compound condition.

`&who`   [Condition Type]
`make-who-condition` *who*   [Scheme Procedure]
`who-condition?` *obj*   [Scheme Procedure]
`condition-who` *condition*   [Scheme Procedure]

A base type used for storing the identity, a string or symbol, of the entity responsible for another condition in a compound condition.

`&non-continuable`   [Condition Type]
`make-non-continuable-violation`   [Scheme Procedure]
`non-continuable-violation?` *obj*   [Scheme Procedure]

A subtype of `&violation` used to indicate that an exception handler invoked by `raise` has returned locally.

`&implementation-restriction`   [Condition Type]
`make-implementation-restriction-violation`   [Scheme Procedure]
`implementation-restriction-violation?` *obj*   [Scheme Procedure]

A subtype of `&violation` used to indicate a violation of an implementation restriction.

`&lexical`   [Condition Type]
`make-lexical-violation`   [Scheme Procedure]
`lexical-violation?` *obj*   [Scheme Procedure]

A subtype of `&violation` used to indicate a syntax violation at the level of the datum syntax.

&syntax   [Condition Type]
make-syntax-violation *form subform*   [Scheme Procedure]
syntax-violation? *obj*   [Scheme Procedure]
syntax-violation-form *condition*   [Scheme Procedure]
syntax-violation-subform *condition*   [Scheme Procedure]

> A subtype of &violation that indicates a syntax violation. The *form* and *subform*
> fields, which must be datum values, indicate the syntactic form responsible for the
> condition.

&undefined   [Condition Type]
make-undefined-violation   [Scheme Procedure]
undefined-violation? *obj*   [Scheme Procedure]

> A subtype of &violation that indicates a reference to an unbound identifier.

7.6.2.14 I/O Conditions

These condition types are exported by both the (rnrs io ports (6)) and (rnrs io simple
(6)) libraries.

&i/o   [Condition Type]
make-i/o-error   [Scheme Procedure]
i/o-error? *obj*   [Scheme Procedure]

> A condition supertype for more specific I/O errors.

&i/o-read   [Condition Type]
make-i/o-read-error   [Scheme Procedure]
i/o-read-error? *obj*   [Scheme Procedure]

> A subtype of &i/o; represents read-related I/O errors.

&i/o-write   [Condition Type]
make-i/o-write-error   [Scheme Procedure]
i/o-write-error? *obj*   [Scheme Procedure]

> A subtype of &i/o; represents write-related I/O errors.

&i/o-invalid-position   [Condition Type]
make-i/o-invalid-position-error *position*   [Scheme Procedure]
i/o-invalid-position-error? *obj*   [Scheme Procedure]
i/o-error-position *condition*   [Scheme Procedure]

> A subtype of &i/o; represents an error related to an attempt to set the file position
> to an invalid position.

&i/o-filename   [Condition Type]
make-io-filename-error *filename*   [Scheme Procedure]
i/o-filename-error? *obj*   [Scheme Procedure]
i/o-error-filename *condition*   [Scheme Procedure]

> A subtype of &i/o; represents an error related to an operation on a named file.

&i/o-file-protection   [Condition Type]
make-i/o-file-protection-error *filename*   [Scheme Procedure]

`i/o-file-protection-error?` *obj*   [Scheme Procedure]

> A subtype of `&i/o-filename`; represents an error resulting from an attempt to access a named file for which the caller had insufficient permissions.

`&i/o-file-is-read-only`   [Condition Type]
`make-i/o-file-is-read-only-error` *filename*   [Scheme Procedure]
`i/o-file-is-read-only-error?` *obj*   [Scheme Procedure]

> A subtype of `&i/o-file-protection`; represents an error related to an attempt to write to a read-only file.

`&i/o-file-already-exists`   [Condition Type]
`make-i/o-file-already-exists-error` *filename*   [Scheme Procedure]
`i/o-file-already-exists-error?` *obj*   [Scheme Procedure]

> A subtype of `&i/o-filename`; represents an error related to an operation on an existing file that was assumed not to exist.

`&i/o-file-does-not-exist`   [Condition Type]
`make-i/o-file-does-not-exist-error`   [Scheme Procedure]
`i/o-file-does-not-exist-error?` *obj*   [Scheme Procedure]

> A subtype of `&i/o-filename`; represents an error related to an operation on a non-existent file that was assumed to exist.

`&i/o-port`   [Condition Type]
`make-i/o-port-error` *port*   [Scheme Procedure]
`i/o-port-error?` *obj*   [Scheme Procedure]
`i/o-error-port` *condition*   [Scheme Procedure]

> A subtype of `&i/o`; represents an error related to an operation on the port *port*.

7.6.2.15 rnrs io ports

The (`rnrs io ports (6)`) library provides various procedures and syntactic forms for use in writing to and reading from ports. This functionality is documented in its own section of the manual; (see Section 6.14.10 [R6RS I/O Ports], page 332).

7.6.2.16 rnrs io simple

The (`rnrs io simple (6)`) library provides convenience functions for performing textual I/O on ports. This library also exports all of the condition types and associated procedures described in (see Section 7.6.2.14 [I/O Conditions], page 642). In the context of this section, when stating that a procedure behaves "identically" to the corresponding procedure in Guile's core library, this is modulo the behavior wrt. conditions: such procedures raise the appropriate R6RS conditions in case of error, but otherwise behave identically.

> **Note:** There are still known issues regarding condition-correctness; some errors may still be thrown as native Guile exceptions instead of the appropriate R6RS conditions.

`eof-object`   [Scheme Procedure]
`eof-object?` *obj*   [Scheme Procedure]

> These procedures are identical to the ones provided by the (`rnrs io ports (6)`) library. See Section 6.14.10 [R6RS I/O Ports], page 332, for documentation.

input-port? *obj*   [Scheme Procedure]
output-port? *obj*   [Scheme Procedure]
> These procedures are identical to the ones provided by Guile's core library. See
> Section 6.14.1 [Ports], page 316, for documentation.

call-with-input-file *filename proc*   [Scheme Procedure]
call-with-output-file *filename proc*   [Scheme Procedure]
open-input-file *filename*   [Scheme Procedure]
open-output-file *filename*   [Scheme Procedure]
with-input-from-file *filename thunk*   [Scheme Procedure]
with-output-to-file *filename thunk*   [Scheme Procedure]
> These procedures are identical to the ones provided by Guile's core library. See
> Section 6.14.9.1 [File Ports], page 326, for documentation.

close-input-port *input-port*   [Scheme Procedure]
close-output-port *output-port*   [Scheme Procedure]
> These procedures are identical to the ones provided by Guile's core library. See
> Section 6.14.4 [Closing], page 321, for documentation.

peek-char   [Scheme Procedure]
peek-char *textual-input-port*   [Scheme Procedure]
read-char   [Scheme Procedure]
read-char *textual-input-port*   [Scheme Procedure]
> These procedures are identical to the ones provided by Guile's core library. See
> Section 6.14.2 [Reading], page 318, for documentation.

read   [Scheme Procedure]
read *textual-input-port*   [Scheme Procedure]
> This procedure is identical to the one provided by Guile's core library. See
> Section 6.17.2 [Scheme Read], page 360, for documentation.

display *obj*   [Scheme Procedure]
display *obj textual-output-port*   [Scheme Procedure]
newline   [Scheme Procedure]
newline *textual-output-port*   [Scheme Procedure]
write *obj*   [Scheme Procedure]
write *obj textual-output-port*   [Scheme Procedure]
write-char *char*   [Scheme Procedure]
write-char *char textual-output-port*   [Scheme Procedure]
> These procedures are identical to the ones provided by Guile's core library. See
> Section 6.14.3 [Writing], page 320, for documentation.

7.6.2.17 rnrs files

The (rnrs files (6)) library provides the file-exists? and delete-file procedures, which test for the existence of a file and allow the deletion of files from the file system, respectively.

These procedures are identical to the ones provided by Guile's core library. See Section 7.2.3 [File System], page 476, for documentation.

7.6.2.18 rnrs programs

The (rnrs programs (6)) library provides procedures for process management and introspection.

command-line   [Scheme Procedure]
>   This procedure is identical to the one provided by Guile's core library.   See
>   Section 7.2.6 [Runtime Environment], page 488, for documentation.

exit [*status*]   [Scheme Procedure]
>   This procedure is identical to the one provided by Guile's core library.   See
>   Section 7.2.7 [Processes], page 490, for documentation.

7.6.2.19 rnrs arithmetic fixnums

The (rnrs arithmetic fixnums (6)) library provides procedures for performing arithmetic operations on an implementation-dependent range of exact integer values, which
R6RS refers to as *fixnums*. In Guile, the size of a fixnum is determined by the size of the
SCM type; a single SCM struct is guaranteed to be able to hold an entire fixnum, making
fixnum computations particularly efficient—(see Section 6.3 [The SCM Type], page 100).
On 32-bit systems, the most negative and most positive fixnum values are, respectively,
-536870912 and 536870911.

Unless otherwise specified, all of the procedures below take fixnums as arguments,
and will raise an **&assertion** condition if passed a non-fixnum argument or an
&implementation-restriction condition if their result is not itself a fixnum.

fixnum? *obj*   [Scheme Procedure]
>   Returns #t if *obj* is a fixnum, #f otherwise.

fixnum-width   [Scheme Procedure]
least-fixnum   [Scheme Procedure]
greatest-fixnum   [Scheme Procedure]
>   These procedures return, respectively, the maximum number of bits necessary to
>   represent a fixnum value in Guile, the minimum fixnum value, and the maximum
>   fixnum value.

fx=? *fx1 fx2 fx3 ...*   [Scheme Procedure]
fx>? *fx1 fx2 fx3 ...*   [Scheme Procedure]
fx<? *fx1 fx2 fx3 ...*   [Scheme Procedure]
fx>=? *fx1 fx2 fx3 ...*   [Scheme Procedure]
fx<=? *fx1 fx2 fx3 ...*   [Scheme Procedure]
>   These procedures return #t if their fixnum arguments are (respectively): equal,
>   monotonically increasing, monotonically decreasing, monotonically nondecreasing, or
>   monotonically nonincreasing; #f otherwise.

fxzero? *fx*   [Scheme Procedure]
fxpositive? *fx*   [Scheme Procedure]
fxnegative? *fx*   [Scheme Procedure]
fxodd? *fx*   [Scheme Procedure]

fxeven? *fx*   [Scheme Procedure]

These numerical predicates return #t if *fx* is, respectively, zero, greater than zero, less than zero, odd, or even; #f otherwise.

fxmax *fx1 fx2 ...*   [Scheme Procedure]
fxmin *fx1 fx2 ...*   [Scheme Procedure]

These procedures return the maximum or minimum of their arguments.

fx+ *fx1 fx2*   [Scheme Procedure]
fx* *fx1 fx2*   [Scheme Procedure]

These procedures return the sum or product of their arguments.

fx- *fx1 fx2*   [Scheme Procedure]
fx- *fx*   [Scheme Procedure]

Returns the difference of *fx1* and *fx2*, or the negation of *fx*, if called with a single argument.

An &assertion condition is raised if the result is not itself a fixnum.

fxdiv-and-mod *fx1 fx2*   [Scheme Procedure]
fxdiv *fx1 fx2*   [Scheme Procedure]
fxmod *fx1 fx2*   [Scheme Procedure]
fxdiv0-and-mod0 *fx1 fx2*   [Scheme Procedure]
fxdiv0 *fx1 fx2*   [Scheme Procedure]
fxmod0 *fx1 fx2*   [Scheme Procedure]

These procedures implement number-theoretic division on fixnums; See ⟨undefined⟩ [(rnrs base)], page ⟨undefined⟩, for a description of their semantics.

fx+/carry *fx1 fx2 fx3*   [Scheme Procedure]

Returns the two fixnum results of the following computation:

```
(let* ((s (+ fx1 fx2 fx3))
       (s0 (mod0 s (expt 2 (fixnum-width))))
       (s1 (div0 s (expt 2 (fixnum-width)))))
  (values s0 s1))
```

fx-/carry *fx1 fx2 fx3*   [Scheme Procedure]

Returns the two fixnum results of the following computation:

```
(let* ((d (- fx1 fx2 fx3))
       (d0 (mod0 d (expt 2 (fixnum-width))))
       (d1 (div0 d (expt 2 (fixnum-width)))))
  (values d0 d1))
```

fx*/carry *fx1 fx2 fx3*   [Scheme Procedure]

```
Returns the two fixnum results of the following computation:
(let* ((s (+ (* fx1 fx2) fx3))
       (s0 (mod0 s (expt 2 (fixnum-width))))
       (s1 (div0 s (expt 2 (fixnum-width)))))
  (values s0 s1))
```

`fxnot` *fx*   [Scheme Procedure]
`fxand` *fx1 ...*   [Scheme Procedure]
`fxior` *fx1 ...*   [Scheme Procedure]
`fxxor` *fx1 ...*   [Scheme Procedure]

These procedures are identical to the `lognot`, `logand`, `logior`, and `logxor` procedures provided by Guile's core library. See Section 6.6.2.13 [Bitwise Operations], page 125, for documentation.

`fxif` *fx1 fx2 fx3*   [Scheme Procedure]

Returns the bitwise "if" of its fixnum arguments. The bit at position i in the return value will be the `i`th bit from *fx2* if the `i`th bit of *fx1* is 1, the `i`th bit from *fx3*.

`fxbit-count` *fx*   [Scheme Procedure]

Returns the number of 1 bits in the two's complement representation of *fx*.

`fxlength` *fx*   [Scheme Procedure]

Returns the number of bits necessary to represent *fx*.

`fxfirst-bit-set` *fx*   [Scheme Procedure]

Returns the index of the least significant 1 bit in the two's complement representation of *fx*.

`fxbit-set?` *fx1 fx2*   [Scheme Procedure]

Returns `#t` if the *fx2*th bit in the two's complement representation of *fx1* is 1, `#f` otherwise.

`fxcopy-bit` *fx1 fx2 fx3*   [Scheme Procedure]

Returns the result of setting the *fx2*th bit of *fx1* to the *fx2*th bit of *fx3*.

`fxbit-field` *fx1 fx2 fx3*   [Scheme Procedure]

Returns the integer representation of the contiguous sequence of bits in *fx1* that starts at position *fx2* (inclusive) and ends at position *fx3* (exclusive).

`fxcopy-bit-field` *fx1 fx2 fx3 fx4*   [Scheme Procedure]

Returns the result of replacing the bit field in *fx1* with start and end positions *fx2* and *fx3* with the corresponding bit field from *fx4*.

`fxarithmetic-shift` *fx1 fx2*   [Scheme Procedure]
`fxarithmetic-shift-left` *fx1 fx2*   [Scheme Procedure]
`fxarithmetic-shift-right` *fx1 fx2*   [Scheme Procedure]

Returns the result of shifting the bits of *fx1* right or left by the *fx2* positions. `fxarithmetic-shift` is identical to `fxarithmetic-shift-left`.

`fxrotate-bit-field` *fx1 fx2 fx3 fx4*   [Scheme Procedure]

Returns the result of cyclically permuting the bit field in *fx1* with start and end positions *fx2* and *fx3* by *fx4* bits in the direction of more significant bits.

`fxreverse-bit-field` *fx1 fx2 fx3*   [Scheme Procedure]

Returns the result of reversing the order of the bits of *fx1* between position *fx2* (inclusive) and position *fx3* (exclusive).

7.6.2.20 rnrs arithmetic flonums

The (rnrs arithmetic flonums (6)) library provides procedures for performing arithmetic operations on inexact representations of real numbers, which R6RS refers to as *flonums*.

Unless otherwise specified, all of the procedures below take flonums as arguments, and will raise an &assertion condition if passed a non-flonum argument.

flonum? *obj*   [Scheme Procedure]
    Returns #t if *obj* is a flonum, #f otherwise.

real->flonum *x*   [Scheme Procedure]
    Returns the flonum that is numerically closest to the real number *x*.

fl=? *fl1 fl2 fl3 ...*   [Scheme Procedure]
fl<? *fl1 fl2 fl3 ...*   [Scheme Procedure]
fl<=? *fl1 fl2 fl3 ...*   [Scheme Procedure]
fl>? *fl1 fl2 fl3 ...*   [Scheme Procedure]
fl>=? *fl1 fl2 fl3 ...*   [Scheme Procedure]
    These procedures return #t if their flonum arguments are (respectively): equal, monotonically increasing, monotonically decreasing, monotonically nondecreasing, or monotonically nonincreasing; #f otherwise.

flinteger? *fl*   [Scheme Procedure]
flzero? *fl*   [Scheme Procedure]
flpositive? *fl*   [Scheme Procedure]
flnegative? *fl*   [Scheme Procedure]
flodd? *fl*   [Scheme Procedure]
fleven? *fl*   [Scheme Procedure]
    These numerical predicates return #t if *fl* is, respectively, an integer, zero, greater than zero, less than zero, odd, even, #f otherwise. In the case of flodd? and fleven?, *fl* must be an integer-valued flonum.

flfinite? *fl*   [Scheme Procedure]
flinfinite? *fl*   [Scheme Procedure]
flnan? *fl*   [Scheme Procedure]
    These numerical predicates return #t if *fl* is, respectively, not infinite, infinite, or a NaN value.

flmax *fl1 fl2 ...*   [Scheme Procedure]
flmin *fl1 fl2 ...*   [Scheme Procedure]
    These procedures return the maximum or minimum of their arguments.

fl+ *fl1 ...*   [Scheme Procedure]
fl* *fl ...*   [Scheme Procedure]
    These procedures return the sum or product of their arguments.

fl- *fl1 fl2 ...*   [Scheme Procedure]
fl- *fl*   [Scheme Procedure]
fl/ *fl1 fl2 ...*   [Scheme Procedure]

`fl/` *fl*   [Scheme Procedure]

These procedures return, respectively, the difference or quotient of their arguments when called with two arguments; when called with a single argument, they return the additive or multiplicative inverse of *fl*.

`flabs` *fl*   [Scheme Procedure]

Returns the absolute value of *fl*.

`fldiv-and-mod` *fl1 fl2*   [Scheme Procedure]
`fldiv` *fl1 fl2*   [Scheme Procedure]
`fldmod` *fl1 fl2*   [Scheme Procedure]
`fldiv0-and-mod0` *fl1 fl2*   [Scheme Procedure]
`fldiv0` *fl1 fl2*   [Scheme Procedure]
`flmod0` *fl1 fl2*   [Scheme Procedure]

These procedures implement number-theoretic division on flonums; See ⟨undefined⟩ [(rnrs base)], page ⟨undefined⟩, for a description for their semantics.

`flnumerator` *fl*   [Scheme Procedure]
`fldenominator` *fl*   [Scheme Procedure]

These procedures return the numerator or denominator of *fl* as a flonum.

`flfloor` *fl1*   [Scheme Procedure]
`flceiling` *fl*   [Scheme Procedure]
`fltruncate` *fl*   [Scheme Procedure]
`flround` *fl*   [Scheme Procedure]

These procedures are identical to the `floor`, `ceiling`, `truncate`, and `round` procedures provided by Guile's core library. See Section 6.6.2.11 [Arithmetic], page 119, for documentation.

`flexp` *fl*   [Scheme Procedure]
`fllog` *fl*   [Scheme Procedure]
`fllog` *fl1 fl2*   [Scheme Procedure]
`flsin` *fl*   [Scheme Procedure]
`flcos` *fl*   [Scheme Procedure]
`fltan` *fl*   [Scheme Procedure]
`flasin` *fl*   [Scheme Procedure]
`flacos` *fl*   [Scheme Procedure]
`flatan` *fl*   [Scheme Procedure]
`flatan` *fl1 fl2*   [Scheme Procedure]

These procedures, which compute the usual transcendental functions, are the flonum variants of the procedures provided by the R6RS base library (see ⟨undefined⟩ [(rnrs base)], page ⟨undefined⟩).

`flsqrt` *fl*   [Scheme Procedure]

Returns the square root of *fl*. If *fl* is -0.0, -0.0 is returned; for other negative values, a NaN value is returned.

`flexpt` *fl1 fl2*   [Scheme Procedure]

Returns the value of *fl1* raised to the power of *fl2*.

The following condition types are provided to allow Scheme implementations that do not support infinities or NaN values to indicate that a computation resulted in such a value. Guile supports both of these, so these conditions will never be raised by Guile's standard libraries implementation.

&no-infinities   [Condition Type]
make-no-infinities-violation *obj*   [Scheme Procedure]
no-infinities-violation?   [Scheme Procedure]
> A condition type indicating that a computation resulted in an infinite value on a Scheme implementation incapable of representing infinities.

&no-nans   [Condition Type]
make-no-nans-violation *obj*   [Scheme Procedure]
no-nans-violation? *obj*   [Scheme Procedure]
> A condition type indicating that a computation resulted in a NaN value on a Scheme implementation incapable of representing NaNs.

fixnum->flonum *fx*   [Scheme Procedure]
> Returns the flonum that is numerically closest to the fixnum *fx*.

7.6.2.21 rnrs arithmetic bitwise

The (rnrs arithmetic bitwise (6)) library provides procedures for performing bitwise arithmetic operations on the two's complement representations of fixnums.

This library and the procedures it exports share functionality with SRFI-60, which provides support for bitwise manipulation of integers (see Section 7.5.33 [SRFI-60], page 616).

bitwise-not *ei*   [Scheme Procedure]
bitwise-and *ei1 ...*   [Scheme Procedure]
bitwise-ior *ei1 ...*   [Scheme Procedure]
bitwise-xor *ei1 ...*   [Scheme Procedure]
> These procedures are identical to the lognot, logand, logior, and logxor procedures provided by Guile's core library. See Section 6.6.2.13 [Bitwise Operations], page 125, for documentation.

bitwise-if *ei1 ei2 ei3*   [Scheme Procedure]
> Returns the bitwise "if" of its arguments. The bit at position i in the return value will be the ith bit from *ei2* if the ith bit of *ei1* is 1, the ith bit from *ei3*.

bitwise-bit-count *ei*   [Scheme Procedure]
> Returns the number of 1 bits in the two's complement representation of *ei*.

bitwise-length *ei*   [Scheme Procedure]
> Returns the number of bits necessary to represent *ei*.

bitwise-first-bit-set *ei*   [Scheme Procedure]
> Returns the index of the least significant 1 bit in the two's complement representation of *ei*.

bitwise-bit-set? *ei1 ei2*   [Scheme Procedure]
> Returns #t if the *ei2*th bit in the two's complement representation of *ei1* is 1, #f otherwise.

`bitwise-copy-bit` *ei1 ei2 ei3*   [Scheme Procedure]
> Returns the result of setting the *ei2*th bit of *ei1* to the *ei2*th bit of *ei3*.

`bitwise-bit-field` *ei1 ei2 ei3*   [Scheme Procedure]
> Returns the integer representation of the contiguous sequence of bits in *ei1* that starts at position *ei2* (inclusive) and ends at position *ei3* (exclusive).

`bitwise-copy-bit-field` *ei1 ei2 ei3 ei4*   [Scheme Procedure]
> Returns the result of replacing the bit field in *ei1* with start and end positions *ei2* and *ei3* with the corresponding bit field from *ei4*.

`bitwise-arithmetic-shift` *ei1 ei2*   [Scheme Procedure]
`bitwise-arithmetic-shift-left` *ei1 ei2*   [Scheme Procedure]
`bitwise-arithmetic-shift-right` *ei1 ei2*   [Scheme Procedure]
> Returns the result of shifting the bits of *ei1* right or left by the *ei2* positions. `bitwise-arithmetic-shift` is identical to `bitwise-arithmetic-shift-left`.

`bitwise-rotate-bit-field` *ei1 ei2 ei3 ei4*   [Scheme Procedure]
> Returns the result of cyclically permuting the bit field in *ei1* with start and end positions *ei2* and *ei3* by *ei4* bits in the direction of more significant bits.

`bitwise-reverse-bit-field` *ei1 ei2 ei3*   [Scheme Procedure]
> Returns the result of reversing the order of the bits of *ei1* between position *ei2* (inclusive) and position *ei3* (exclusive).

7.6.2.22 rnrs syntax-case

The (`rnrs syntax-case (6)`) library provides access to the `syntax-case` system for writing hygienic macros. With one exception, all of the forms and procedures exported by this library are "re-exports" of Guile's native support for `syntax-case`; See Section 6.10.3 [Syntax Case], page 263, for documentation, examples, and rationale.

`make-variable-transformer` *proc*   [Scheme Procedure]
> Creates a new variable transformer out of *proc*, a procedure that takes a syntax object as input and returns a syntax object. If an identifier to which the result of this procedure is bound appears on the left-hand side of a `set!` expression, *proc* will be called with a syntax object representing the entire `set!` expression, and its return value will replace that `set!` expression.

`syntax-case` *expression (literal ...) clause ...*   [Scheme Syntax]
> The `syntax-case` pattern matching form.

`syntax` *template*   [Scheme Syntax]
`quasisyntax` *template*   [Scheme Syntax]
`unsyntax` *template*   [Scheme Syntax]
`unsyntax-splicing` *template*   [Scheme Syntax]
> These forms allow references to be made in the body of a syntax-case output expression subform to datum and non-datum values. They are identical to the forms provided by Guile's core library; See Section 6.10.3 [Syntax Case], page 263, for documentation.

`identifier? `*obj*   [Scheme Procedure]
`bound-identifier=? `*id1 id2*   [Scheme Procedure]
`free-identifier=? `*id1 id2*   [Scheme Procedure]
>   These predicate procedures operate on syntax objects representing Scheme identi-
>   fiers. `identifier?` returns `#t` if *obj* represents an identifier, `#f` otherwise. `bound-`
>   `identifier=?` returns `#t` if and only if a binding for *id1* would capture a reference to
>   *id2* in the transformer's output, or vice-versa. `free-identifier=?` returns `#t` if and
>   only *id1* and *id2* would refer to the same binding in the output of the transformer,
>   independent of any bindings introduced by the transformer.

`generate-temporaries `*l*   [Scheme Procedure]
>   Returns a list, of the same length as *l*, which must be a list or a syntax object
>   representing a list, of globally unique symbols.

`syntax->datum `*syntax-object*   [Scheme Procedure]
`datum->syntax `*template-id datum*   [Scheme Procedure]
>   These procedures convert wrapped syntax objects to and from Scheme datum values.
>   The syntax object returned by `datum->syntax` shares contextual information with
>   the syntax object *template-id*.

`syntax-violation `*whom message form*   [Scheme Procedure]
`syntax-violation `*whom message form subform*   [Scheme Procedure]
>   Constructs a new compound condition that includes the following simple conditions:
>
>   - If *whom* is not `#f`, a `&who` condition with the *whom* as its field
>   - A `&message` condition with the specified *message*
>   - A `&syntax` condition with the specified *form* and optional *subform* fields

7.6.2.23 rnrs hashtables

The (`rnrs hashtables (6)`) library provides structures and procedures for creating and
accessing hash tables. The hash tables API defined by R6RS is substantially similar to
both Guile's native hash tables implementation as well as the one provided by SRFI-69; See
Section 6.7.14 [Hash Tables], page 236, and Section 7.5.38 [SRFI-69], page 618, respectively.
Note that you can write portable R6RS library code that manipulates SRFI-69 hash tables
(by importing the (`srfi :69`) library); however, hash tables created by one API cannot be
used by another.

   Like SRFI-69 hash tables—and unlike Guile's native ones—R6RS hash tables associate
hash and equality functions with a hash table at the time of its creation. Additionally,
R6RS allows for the creation (via `hashtable-copy`; see below) of immutable hash tables.

`make-eq-hashtable`   [Scheme Procedure]
`make-eq-hashtable `*k*   [Scheme Procedure]
>   Returns a new hash table that uses `eq?` to compare keys and Guile's `hashq` procedure
>   as a hash function. If *k* is given, it specifies the initial capacity of the hash table.

`make-eqv-hashtable`   [Scheme Procedure]
`make-eqv-hashtable `*k*   [Scheme Procedure]
>   Returns a new hash table that uses `eqv?` to compare keys and Guile's `hashv` procedure
>   as a hash function. If *k* is given, it specifies the initial capacity of the hash table.

make-hashtable *hash-function equiv*   [Scheme Procedure]
make-hashtable *hash-function equiv k*   [Scheme Procedure]
> Returns a new hash table that uses *equiv* to compare keys and *hash-function* as a
> hash function. *equiv* must be a procedure that accepts two arguments and returns
> a true value if they are equivalent, **#f** otherwise; *hash-function* must be a procedure
> that accepts one argument and returns a non-negative integer.
>
> If *k* is given, it specifies the initial capacity of the hash table.

hashtable? *obj*   [Scheme Procedure]
> Returns **#t** if *obj* is an R6RS hash table, **#f** otherwise.

hashtable-size *hashtable*   [Scheme Procedure]
> Returns the number of keys currently in the hash table *hashtable*.

hashtable-ref *hashtable key default*   [Scheme Procedure]
> Returns the value associated with *key* in the hash table *hashtable*, or *default* if none
> is found.

hashtable-set! *hashtable key obj*   [Scheme Procedure]
> Associates the key *key* with the value *obj* in the hash table *hashtable*, and returns
> an unspecified value. An **&assertion** condition is raised if *hashtable* is immutable.

hashtable-delete! *hashtable key*   [Scheme Procedure]
> Removes any association found for the key *key* in the hash table *hashtable*, and returns
> an unspecified value. An **&assertion** condition is raised if *hashtable* is immutable.

hashtable-contains? *hashtable key*   [Scheme Procedure]
> Returns **#t** if the hash table *hashtable* contains an association for the key *key*, **#f**
> otherwise.

hashtable-update! *hashtable key proc default*   [Scheme Procedure]
> Associates with *key* in the hash table *hashtable* the result of calling *proc*, which must
> be a procedure that takes one argument, on the value currently associated *key* in
> *hashtable*—or on *default* if no such association exists. An **&assertion** condition is
> raised if *hashtable* is immutable.

hashtable-copy *hashtable*   [Scheme Procedure]
hashtable-copy *hashtable mutable*   [Scheme Procedure]
> Returns a copy of the hash table *hashtable*. If the optional argument *mutable* is
> provided and is a true value, the new hash table will be mutable.

hashtable-clear! *hashtable*   [Scheme Procedure]
hashtable-clear! *hashtable k*   [Scheme Procedure]
> Removes all of the associations from the hash table *hashtable*. The optional argument
> *k*, which specifies a new capacity for the hash table, is accepted by Guile's (**rnrs
> hashtables**) implementation, but is ignored.

hashtable-keys *hashtable*   [Scheme Procedure]
> Returns a vector of the keys with associations in the hash table *hashtable*, in an
> unspecified order.

hashtable-entries *hashtable*   [Scheme Procedure]

> Return two values—a vector of the keys with associations in the hash table *hashtable*, and a vector of the values to which these keys are mapped, in corresponding but unspecified order.

hashtable-equivalence-function *hashtable*   [Scheme Procedure]

> Returns the equivalence predicated use by *hashtable*. This procedure returns `eq?` and `eqv?`, respectively, for hash tables created by `make-eq-hashtable` and `make-eqv-hashtable`.

hashtable-hash-function *hashtable*   [Scheme Procedure]

> Returns the hash function used by *hashtable*. For hash tables created by `make-eq-hashtable` or `make-eqv-hashtable`, `#f` is returned.

hashtable-mutable? *hashtable*   [Scheme Procedure]

> Returns `#t` if *hashtable* is mutable, `#f` otherwise.

A number of hash functions are provided for convenience:

equal-hash *obj*   [Scheme Procedure]

> Returns an integer hash value for *obj*, based on its structure and current contents. This hash function is suitable for use with `equal?` as an equivalence function.

string-hash *string*   [Scheme Procedure]
symbol-hash *symbol*   [Scheme Procedure]

> These procedures are identical to the ones provided by Guile's core library. See Section 6.7.14.2 [Hash Table Reference], page 237, for documentation.

string-ci-hash *string*   [Scheme Procedure]

> Returns an integer hash value for *string* based on its contents, ignoring case. This hash function is suitable for use with `string-ci=?` as an equivalence function.

7.6.2.24 rnrs enums

The (`rnrs enums (6)`) library provides structures and procedures for working with enumerable sets of symbols. Guile's implementation defines an *enum-set* record type that encapsulates a finite set of distinct symbols, the *universe*, and a subset of these symbols, which define the enumeration set.

The SRFI-1 list library provides a number of procedures for performing set operations on lists; Guile's (`rnrs enums`) implementation makes use of several of them. See Section 7.5.3.10 [SRFI-1 Set Operations], page 563, for more information.

make-enumeration *symbol-list*   [Scheme Procedure]

> Returns a new enum-set whose universe and enumeration set are both equal to *symbol-list*, a list of symbols.

enum-set-universe *enum-set*   [Scheme Procedure]

> Returns an enum-set representing the universe of *enum-set*, an enum-set.

enum-set-indexer *enum-set*   [Scheme Procedure]
> Returns a procedure that takes a single argument and returns the zero-indexed position of that argument in the universe of *enum-set*, or **#f** if its argument is not a member of that universe.

enum-set-constructor *enum-set*   [Scheme Procedure]
> Returns a procedure that takes a single argument, a list of symbols from the universe of *enum-set*, an enum-set, and returns a new enum-set with the same universe that represents a subset containing the specified symbols.

enum-set->list *enum-set*   [Scheme Procedure]
> Returns a list containing the symbols of the set represented by *enum-set*, an enum-set, in the order that they appear in the universe of *enum-set*.

enum-set-member? *symbol enum-set*   [Scheme Procedure]
enum-set-subset? *enum-set1 enum-set2*   [Scheme Procedure]
enum-set=? *enum-set1 enum-set2*   [Scheme Procedure]
> These procedures test for membership of symbols and enum-sets in other enum-sets. **enum-set-member?** returns **#t** if and only if *symbol* is a member of the subset specified by *enum-set*. **enum-set-subset?** returns **#t** if and only if the universe of *enum-set1* is a subset of the universe of *enum-set2* and every symbol in *enum-set1* is present in *enum-set2*. **enum-set=?** returns **#t** if and only if *enum-set1* is a subset, as per **enum-set-subset?** of *enum-set2* and vice versa.

enum-set-union *enum-set1 enum-set2*   [Scheme Procedure]
enum-set-intersection *enum-set1 enum-set2*   [Scheme Procedure]
enum-set-difference *enum-set1 enum-set2*   [Scheme Procedure]
> These procedures return, respectively, the union, intersection, and difference of their enum-set arguments.

enum-set-complement *enum-set*   [Scheme Procedure]
> Returns *enum-set*'s complement (an enum-set), with regard to its universe.

enum-set-projection *enum-set1 enum-set2*   [Scheme Procedure]
> Returns the projection of the enum-set *enum-set1* onto the universe of the enum-set *enum-set2*.

define-enumeration *type-name* (*symbol ...*) *constructor-syntax*   [Scheme Syntax]
> Evaluates to two new definitions: A constructor bound to *constructor-syntax* that behaves similarly to constructors created by **enum-set-constructor**, above, and creates new *enum-sets* in the universe specified by (**symbol ...**); and a "predicate macro" bound to *type-name*, which has the following form:
>
>   (type-name sym)
>
> If *sym* is a member of the universe specified by the *symbols* above, this form evaluates to *sym*. Otherwise, a **&syntax** condition is raised.

7.6.2.25 rnrs

The (rnrs (6)) library is a composite of all of the other R6RS standard libraries—it imports and re-exports all of their exported procedures and syntactic forms—with the exception of the following libraries:

- (rnrs eval (6))
- (rnrs mutable-pairs (6))
- (rnrs mutable-strings (6))
- (rnrs r5rs (6))

7.6.2.26 rnrs eval

The (rnrs eval (6) library provides procedures for performing "on-the-fly" evaluation of expressions.

eval *expression environment*   [Scheme Procedure]
> Evaluates *expression*, which must be a datum representation of a valid Scheme expression, in the environment specified by *environment*. This procedure is identical to the one provided by Guile's code library; See Section 6.17.4 [Fly Evaluation], page 362, for documentation.

environment *import-spec ...*   [Scheme Procedure]
> Constructs and returns a new environment based on the specified *import-spec*s, which must be datum representations of the import specifications used with the **import** form. See Section 6.19.6 [R6RS Libraries], page 388, for documentation.

7.6.2.27 rnrs mutable-pairs

The (rnrs mutable-pairs (6)) library provides the set-car! and set-cdr! procedures, which allow the car and cdr fields of a pair to be modified.

These procedures are identical to the ones provide by Guile's core library. See Section 6.7.1 [Pairs], page 185, for documentation. All pairs in Guile are mutable; consequently, these procedures will never throw the &assertion condition described in the R6RS libraries specification.

7.6.2.28 rnrs mutable-strings

The (rnrs mutable-strings (6)) library provides the string-set! and string-fill! procedures, which allow the content of strings to be modified "in-place."

These procedures are identical to the ones provided by Guile's core library. See Section 6.6.5.6 [String Modification], page 147, for documentation. All strings in Guile are mutable; consequently, these procedures will never throw the &assertion condition described in the R6RS libraries specification.

7.6.2.29 rnrs r5rs

The (rnrs r5rs (6)) library exports bindings for some procedures present in R5RS but omitted from the R6RS base library specification.

exact->inexact *z*   [Scheme Procedure]
inexact->exact *z*   [Scheme Procedure]
> These procedures are identical to the ones provided by Guile's core library. See
> Section 6.6.2.5 [Exactness], page 113, for documentation.

quotient *n1 n2*   [Scheme Procedure]
remainder *n1 n2*   [Scheme Procedure]
modulo *n1 n2*   [Scheme Procedure]
> These procedures are identical to the ones provided by Guile's core library. See
> Section 6.6.2.7 [Integer Operations], page 116, for documentation.

delay *expr*   [Scheme Syntax]
force *promise*   [Scheme Procedure]
> The delay form and the force procedure are identical to their counterparts in Guile's
> core library. See Section 6.17.9 [Delayed Evaluation], page 371, for documentation.

null-environment *n*   [Scheme Procedure]
scheme-report-environment *n*   [Scheme Procedure]
> These procedures are identical to the ones provided by the (ice-9 r5rs) Guile mod-
> ule. See Section 6.19.11 [Environments], page 395, for documentation.

7.7 Pattern Matching

The (ice-9 match) module provides a *pattern matcher*, written by Alex Shinn, and compatible with Andrew K. Wright's pattern matcher found in many Scheme implementations.

A pattern matcher can match an object against several patterns and extract the elements
that make it up. Patterns can represent any Scheme object: lists, strings, symbols, records,
etc. They can optionally contain *pattern variables*. When a matching pattern is found, an
expression associated with the pattern is evaluated, optionally with all pattern variables
bound to the corresponding elements of the object:

```
(let ((l '(hello (world))))
  (match l                ;; <- the input object
    (('hello (who))       ;; <- the pattern
     who)))               ;; <- the expression evaluated upon matching
⇒ world
```

In this example, list *l* matches the pattern ('hello (who)), because it is a two-element
list whose first element is the symbol hello and whose second element is a one-element list.
Here *who* is a pattern variable. match, the pattern matcher, locally binds *who* to the value
contained in this one-element list—i.e., the symbol world. An error would be raised if *l* did
not match the pattern.

The same object can be matched against a simpler pattern:

```
(let ((l '(hello (world))))
  (match l
    ((x y)
     (values x y))))
⇒ hello
⇒ (world)
```

Here pattern (x y) matches any two-element list, regardless of the types of these elements. Pattern variables *x* and *y* are bound to, respectively, the first and second element of *l*.

Patterns can be composed, and nested. For instance, ... (ellipsis) means that the previous pattern may be matched zero or more times in a list:

```
(match lst
  (((heads tails ...) ...)
   heads))
```

This expression returns the first element of each list within *lst*. For proper lists of proper lists, it is equivalent to (map car lst). However, it performs additional checks to make sure that *lst* and the lists therein are proper lists, as prescribed by the pattern, raising an error if they are not.

Compared to hand-written code, pattern matching noticeably improves clarity and conciseness—no need to resort to series of car and cdr calls when matching lists, for instance. It also improves robustness, by making sure the input *completely* matches the pattern—conversely, hand-written code often trades robustness for conciseness. And of course, match is a macro, and the code it expands to is just as efficient as equivalent hand-written code.

The pattern matcher is defined as follows:

match *exp clause1 clause2* ...   [Scheme Syntax]

Match object *exp* against the patterns in *clause1 clause2* ... in the order in which they appear. Return the value produced by the first matching clause. If no clause matches, throw an exception with key match-error.

Each clause has the form (pattern body1 body2 ...). Each *pattern* must follow the syntax described below. Each body is an arbitrary Scheme expression, possibly referring to pattern variables of *pattern*.

The syntax and interpretation of patterns is as follows:

```
        patterns:                         matches:


pat ::= identifier                        anything, and binds identifier
      | _                                 anything
      | ()                                the empty list
      | #t                                #t
      | #f                                #f
      | string                            a string
      | number                            a number
      | character                         a character
      | 'sexp                             an s-expression
      | 'symbol                           a symbol (special case of s-expr)
      | (pat_1 ... pat_n)                 list of n elements
      | (pat_1 ... pat_n . pat_{n+1})     list of n or more
      | (pat_1 ... pat_n pat_n+1 ooo)     list of n or more, each element
                                            of remainder must match pat_n+1
      | #(pat_1 ... pat_n)                vector of n elements
```

```
            | #(pat_1 ... pat_n pat_n+1 ooo)  vector of n or more, each element
                                                 of remainder must match pat_n+1
            | #&pat                          box
            | ($ record-name pat_1 ... pat_n) a record
            | (= field pat)                  a ''field'' of an object
            | (and pat_1 ... pat_n)          if all of pat_1 thru pat_n match
            | (or pat_1 ... pat_n)           if any of pat_1 thru pat_n match
            | (not pat_1 ... pat_n)          if all pat_1 thru pat_n don't match
            | (? predicate pat_1 ... pat_n)  if predicate true and all of
                                                 pat_1 thru pat_n match
            | (set! identifier)              anything, and binds setter
            | (get! identifier)              anything, and binds getter
            | `qp                            a quasi-pattern
            | (identifier *** pat)           matches pat in a tree and binds
                                             identifier to the path leading
                                             to the object that matches pat

ooo ::= ...                                  zero or more
     | ___                                   zero or more
     | ..1                                   1 or more

        quasi-patterns:                      matches:

qp  ::= ()                                   the empty list
     | #t                                    #t
     | #f                                    #f
     | string                                a string
     | number                                a number
     | character                             a character
     | identifier                            a symbol
     | (qp_1 ... qp_n)                       list of n elements
     | (qp_1 ... qp_n . qp_{n+1})            list of n or more
     | (qp_1 ... qp_n qp_n+1 ooo)            list of n or more, each element
                                                 of remainder must match qp_n+1
     | #(qp_1 ... qp_n)                      vector of n elements
     | #(qp_1 ... qp_n qp_n+1 ooo)           vector of n or more, each element
                                                 of remainder must match qp_n+1
     | #&qp                                  box
     | ,pat                                  a pattern
     | ,@pat                                 a pattern
```

The names quote, quasiquote, unquote, unquote-splicing, ?, _, $, and, or, not, set!, get!, ..., and ___ cannot be used as pattern variables.

Here is a more complex example:

```
(use-modules (srfi srfi-9))

(let ()
```

```
(define-record-type person
  (make-person name friends)
  person?
  (name      person-name)
  (friends person-friends))

(letrec ((alice (make-person "Alice" (delay (list bob))))
         (bob   (make-person "Bob" (delay (list alice)))))
  (match alice
    (($ person name (= force (($ person "Bob"))))
     (list 'friend-of-bob name))
    (_ #f))))
```

⇒ (friend-of-bob "Alice")

Here the $ pattern is used to match a SRFI-9 record of type *person* containing two or more slots. The value of the first slot is bound to *name*. The = pattern is used to apply force on the second slot, and then checking that the result matches the given pattern. In other words, the complete pattern matches any *person* whose second slot is a promise that evaluates to a one-element list containing a *person* whose first slot is "Bob".

Please refer to the ice-9/match.upstream.scm file in your Guile installation for more details.

Guile also comes with a pattern matcher specifically tailored to SXML trees, See Section 7.16 [sxml-match], page 687.

7.8 Readline Support

Guile comes with an interface module to the readline library (see *GNU Readline Library*). This makes interactive use much more convenient, because of the command-line editing features of readline. Using (ice-9 readline), you can navigate through the current input line with the cursor keys, retrieve older command lines from the input history and even search through the history entries.

7.8.1 Loading Readline Support

The module is not loaded by default and so has to be loaded and activated explicitly. This is done with two simple lines of code:

```
(use-modules (ice-9 readline))
(activate-readline)
```

The first line will load the necessary code, and the second will activate readline's features for the REPL. If you plan to use this module often, you should save these to lines to your .guile personal startup file.

You will notice that the REPL's behaviour changes a bit when you have loaded the readline module. For example, when you press Enter before typing in the closing parentheses of a list, you will see the *continuation* prompt, three dots: ... This gives you a nice visual feedback when trying to match parentheses. To make this even easier, *bouncing parentheses* are implemented. That means that when you type in a closing parentheses, the cursor will jump to the corresponding opening parenthesis for a short time, making it trivial to make them match.

Once the readline module is activated, all lines entered interactively will be stored in a history and can be recalled later using the cursor-up and -down keys. Readline also understands the Emacs keys for navigating through the command line and history.

When you quit your Guile session by evaluating (quit) or pressing Ctrl-D, the history will be saved to the file .guile_history and read in when you start Guile for the next time. Thus you can start a new Guile session and still have the (probably long-winded) definition expressions available.

You can specify a different history file by setting the environment variable GUILE_ HISTORY. And you can make Guile specific customizations to your .inputrc by testing for application 'Guile' (see Section "Conditional Init Constructs" in *GNU Readline Library*). For instance to define a key inserting a matched pair of parentheses,

```
$if Guile
  "\C-o": "()\C-b"
$endif
```

7.8.2 Readline Options

The readline interface module can be tweaked in a few ways to better suit the user's needs. Configuration is done via the readline module's options interface, in a similar way to the evaluator and debugging options (see Section 6.22.3 [Runtime Options], page 431).

readline-options	[Scheme Procedure]
readline-enable *option-name*	[Scheme Procedure]
readline-disable *option-name*	[Scheme Procedure]
readline-set! *option-name value*	[Scheme Syntax]

Accessors for the readline options. Note that unlike the enable/disable procedures, readline-set! is syntax, which expects an unquoted option name.

Here is the list of readline options generated by typing (readline-options 'help) in Guile. You can also see the default values.

```
history-file    yes    Use history file.
history-length  200    History length.
bounce-parens   500    Time (ms) to show matching opening parenthesis
                       (0 = off).
```

The readline options interface can only be used *after* loading the readline module, because it is defined in that module.

7.8.3 Readline Functions

The following functions are provided by

```
(use-modules (ice-9 readline))
```

There are two ways to use readline from Scheme code, either make calls to readline directly to get line by line input, or use the readline port below with all the usual reading functions.

`readline` [*prompt*]   [Function]
>   Read a line of input from the user and return it as a string (without a newline at the
>   end). *prompt* is the prompt to show, or the default is the string set in `set-readline-`
>   `prompt!` below.
>
>   (readline "Type something: ") ⇒ "hello"

`set-readline-input-port!` *port*   [Function]
`set-readline-output-port!` *port*   [Function]
>   Set the input and output port the readline function should read from and write to.
>   *port* must be a file port (see Section 6.14.9.1 [File Ports], page 326), and should
>   usually be a terminal.
>
>   The default is the `current-input-port` and `current-output-port` (see
>   Section 6.14.8 [Default Ports], page 325) when (`ice-9 readline`) loads, which in an
>   interactive user session means the Unix "standard input" and "standard output".

7.8.3.1 Readline Port

`readline-port`   [Function]
>   Return a buffered input port (see Section 7.14 [Buffered Input], page 684) which calls
>   the `readline` function above to get input. This port can be used with all the usual
>   reading functions (`read`, `read-char`, etc), and the user gets the interactive editing
>   features of readline.
>
>   There's only a single readline port created. `readline-port` creates it when first
>   called, and on subsequent calls just returns what it previously made.

`activate-readline`   [Function]
>   If the `current-input-port` is a terminal (see Section 7.2.9 [isatty?], page 499)
>   then enable readline for all reading from `current-input-port` (see Section 6.14.8
>   [Default Ports], page 325) and enable readline features in the interactive REPL (see
>   Section 3.3.3 [The REPL], page 25).
>
>   (activate-readline)
>   (read-char)
>
>   `activate-readline` enables readline on `current-input-port` simply by a
>   `set-current-input-port` to the `readline-port` above. An application can do that
>   directly if the extra REPL features that `activate-readline` adds are not wanted.

`set-readline-prompt!` *prompt1* [*prompt2*]   [Function]
>   Set the prompt string to print when reading input. This is used when reading through
>   `readline-port`, and is also the default prompt for the `readline` function above.
>
>   *prompt1* is the initial prompt shown. If a user might enter an expression across
>   multiple lines, then *prompt2* is a different prompt to show further input required. In
>   the Guile REPL for instance this is an ellipsis ('...').
>
>   See `set-buffered-input-continuation?!` (see Section 7.14 [Buffered Input],
>   page 684) for an application to indicate the boundaries of logical expressions
>   (assuming of course an application has such a notion).

7.8.3.2 Completion

`with-readline-completion-function` *completer thunk*   [Function]
> Call (`thunk`) with *completer* as the readline tab completion function to be used in
> any readline calls within that *thunk*. *completer* can be #f for no completion.
>
> *completer* will be called as (`completer` text state), as described in (see Section
> "How Completing Works" in *GNU Readline Library*). *text* is a partial word to be
> completed, and each *completer* call should return a possible completion string or #f
> when no more. *state* is #f for the first call asking about a new *text* then #t while
> getting further completions of that *text*.
>
> Here's an example *completer* for user login names from the password file
> (see Section 7.2.4 [User Information], page 483), much like readline's own
> `rl_username_completion_function`,

```
    (define (username-completer-function text state)
      (if (not state)
          (setpwent))  ;; new, go to start of database
      (let more ((pw (getpwent)))
        (if pw
            (if (string-prefix? text (passwd:name pw))
                (passwd:name pw)      ;; this name matches, return it
                (more (getpwent)))    ;; doesn't match, look at next
            (begin
              ;; end of database, close it and return #f
              (endpwent)
              #f))))
```

`apropos-completion-function` *text state*   [Function]
> A completion function offering completions for Guile functions and variables (all
> `define`s). This is the default completion function.

`filename-completion-function` *text state*   [Function]
> A completion function offering filename completions. This is readline's `rl_filename_`
> `completion_function` (see Section "Completion Functions" in *GNU Readline Li-*
> *brary*).

`make-completion-function` *string-list*   [Function]
> Return a completion function which offers completions from the possibilities in *string-*
> *list*. Matching is case-sensitive.

7.9 Pretty Printing

The module (`ice-9 pretty-print`) provides the procedure `pretty-print`, which provides
nicely formatted output of Scheme objects. This is especially useful for deeply nested or
complex data structures, such as lists and vectors.

The module is loaded by entering the following:

```
(use-modules (ice-9 pretty-print))
```

This makes the procedure `pretty-print` available. As an example how `pretty-print`
will format the output, see the following:

```
(pretty-print '(define (foo) (lambda (x)
(cond ((zero? x) #t) ((negative? x) -x) (else
(if (= x 1) 2 (* x x x)))))))
⊣
(define (foo)
  (lambda (x)
    (cond ((zero? x) #t)
          ((negative? x) -x)
          (else (if (= x 1) 2 (* x x x)))))))
```

pretty-print *obj* [*port*] [*keyword-options*]   [Scheme Procedure]
    Print the textual representation of the Scheme object *obj* to *port*. *port* defaults to
    the current output port, if not given.

    The further *keyword-options* are keywords and parameters as follows,

    #:display? *flag*
            If *flag* is true then print using **display**. The default is **#f** which means
            use **write** style. (see Section 6.14.3 [Writing], page 320)

    #:per-line-prefix *string*
            Print the given *string* as a prefix on each line. The default is no prefix.

    #:width *columns*
            Print within the given *columns*. The default is 79.

Also exported by the (ice-9 pretty-print) module is **truncated-print**, a procedure
to print Scheme datums, truncating the output to a certain number of characters. This is
useful when you need to present an arbitrary datum to the user, but you only have one line
in which to do so.

```
(define exp '(a b #(c d e) f . g))
(truncated-print exp #:width 10) (newline)
⊣ (a b . #)
(truncated-print exp #:width 15) (newline)
⊣ (a b # f . g)
(truncated-print exp #:width 18) (newline)
⊣ (a b #(c ...) . #)
(truncated-print exp #:width 20) (newline)
⊣ (a b #(c d e) f . g)
(truncated-print "The quick brown fox" #:width 20) (newline)
⊣ "The quick brown..."
(truncated-print (current-module) #:width 20) (newline)
⊣ #<directory (gui...>
```

truncated-print will not output a trailing newline. If an expression does not fit in the
given width, it will be truncated – possibly ellipsized[3], or in the worst case, displayed as **#**.

_____

[3] On Unicode-capable ports, the ellipsis is represented by character 'HORIZONTAL ELLIPSIS' (U+2026),
    otherwise it is represented by three dots.

`truncated-print` *obj* [*port*] [*keyword-options*]   [Scheme Procedure]

> Print *obj*, truncating the output, if necessary, to make it fit into *width* characters. By default, *obj* will be printed using `write`, though that behavior can be overridden via the *display?* keyword argument.
>
> The default behaviour is to print depth-first, meaning that the entire remaining width will be available to each sub-expression of *obj* – e.g., if *obj* is a vector, each member of *obj*. One can attempt to "ration" the available width, trying to allocate it equally to each sub-expression, via the *breadth-first?* keyword argument.
>
> The further *keyword-options* are keywords and parameters as follows,
>
> `#:display?` *flag*
>
> > If *flag* is true then print using `display`. The default is `#f` which means use `write` style. (see Section 6.14.3 [Writing], page 320)
>
> `#:width` *columns*
>
> > Print within the given *columns*. The default is 79.
>
> `#:breadth-first?` *flag*
>
> > If *flag* is true, then allocate the available width breadth-first among elements of a compound data structure (list, vector, pair, etc.). The default is `#f` which means that any element is allowed to consume all of the available width.

7.10 Formatted Output

The `format` function is a powerful way to print numbers, strings and other objects together with literal text under the control of a format string. This function is available from

        (use-modules (ice-9 format))

A format string is generally more compact and easier than using just the standard procedures like `display`, `write` and `newline`. Parameters in the output string allow various output styles, and parameters can be taken from the arguments for runtime flexibility.

`format` is similar to the Common Lisp procedure of the same name, but it's not identical and doesn't have quite all the features found in Common Lisp.

C programmers will note the similarity between `format` and `printf`, though escape sequences are marked with ~ instead of %, and are more powerful.

`format` *dest fmt arg . . .*   [Scheme Procedure]

> Write output specified by the *fmt* string to *dest*. *dest* can be an output port, `#t` for `current-output-port` (see Section 6.14.8 [Default Ports], page 325), or `#f` to return the output as a string.
>
> *fmt* can contain literal text to be output, and ~ escapes. Each escape has the form
>
> > ~ [param [, param...]] [:] [@] code
>
> `code` is a character determining the escape sequence. The : and @ characters are optional modifiers, one or both of which change the way various codes operate. Optional parameters are accepted by some codes too. Parameters have the following forms,
>
> `[+/-]number`
>
> > An integer, with optional + or -.

' (apostrophe)
> The following character in the format string, for instance 'z for z.

v
> The next function argument as the parameter. v stands for "variable", a parameter can be calculated at runtime and included in the arguments. Upper case V can be used too.

\#
> The number of arguments remaining. (See ~* below for some usages.)

Parameters are separated by commas (,). A parameter can be left empty to keep its default value when supplying later parameters.

The following escapes are available. The code letters are not case-sensitive, upper and lower case are the same.

~a

~s
> Object output. Parameters: *minwidth*, *padinc*, *minpad*, *padchar*.
>
> ~a outputs an argument like display, ~s outputs an argument like write (see Section 6.14.3 [Writing], page 320).
>
> ```
> (format #t "~a" "foo") ⊣ foo
> (format #t "~s" "foo") ⊣ "foo"
> ```
>
> ~:a and ~:s put objects that don't have an external representation in quotes like a string.
>
> ```
> (format #t "~:a" car) ⊣ "#<primitive-procedure car>"
> ```
>
> If the output is less than *minwidth* characters (default 0), it's padded on the right with *padchar* (default space). ~@a and ~@s put the padding on the left instead.
>
> ```
> (format #f "~5a" 'abc)          ⇒ "abc  "
> (format #f "~5,,,'-@a" 'abc) ⇒ "--abc"
> ```
>
> *minpad* is a minimum for the padding then plus a multiple of *padinc*. Ie. the padding is *minpad*+N∗*padinc*, where n is the smallest integer making the total object plus padding greater than or equal to *minwidth*. The default *minpad* is 0 and the default *padinc* is 1 (imposing no minimum or multiple).
>
> ```
> (format #f "~5,1,4a" 'abc) ⇒ "abc     "
> ```

~c
> Character. Parameter: *charnum*.
>
> Output a character. The default is to simply output, as per write-char (see Section 6.14.3 [Writing], page 320). ~@c prints in write style. ~:c prints control characters (ASCII 0 to 31) in ^X form.
>
> ```
> (format #t "~c" #\z)         ⊣ z
> (format #t "~@c" #\z)        ⊣ #\z
> (format #t "~:c" #\newline) ⊣ ^J
> ```
>
> If the *charnum* parameter is given then an argument is not taken but instead the character is (integer->char charnum) (see Section 6.6.3 [Characters], page 129). This can be used for instance to output characters given by their ASCII code.

```
        (format #t "~65c")   ⊣ A
```

~d
~x
~o
~b
Integer. Parameters: *minwidth*, *padchar*, *commachar*, *commawidth*.

Output an integer argument as a decimal, hexadecimal, octal or binary integer (respectively), in a locale-independent way.

```
        (format #t "~d" 123)  ⊣ 123
```

~@d etc shows a + sign is shown on positive numbers.

```
        (format #t "~@b" 12)  ⊣ +1100
```

If the output is less than the *minwidth* parameter (default no minimum), it's padded on the left with the *padchar* parameter (default space).

```
        (format #t "~5,'*d" 12)     ⊣ ***12
        (format #t "~5,'0d" 12)     ⊣ 00012
        (format #t "~3d"     1234)  ⊣ 1234
```

~:d adds commas (or the *commachar* parameter) every three digits (or the *commawidth* parameter many). However, when your intent is to write numbers in a way that follows typographical conventions, using ~h is recommended.

```
        (format #t "~:d" 1234567)          ⊣ 1,234,567
        (format #t "~10,'*,'/,2:d" 12345)  ⊣ ***1/23/45
```

Hexadecimal ~x output is in lower case, but the ~(and ~) case conversion directives described below can be used to get upper case.

```
        (format #t "~x"        65261)  ⊣ feed
        (format #t "~:@(~x~)"  65261)  ⊣ FEED
```

~r
Integer in words, roman numerals, or a specified radix. Parameters: *radix*, *minwidth*, *padchar*, *commachar*, *commawidth*.

With no parameters output is in words as a cardinal like "ten", or ~:r prints an ordinal like "tenth".

```
        (format #t "~r" 9)    ⊣ nine        ;; cardinal
        (format #t "~r" -9)   ⊣ minus nine  ;; cardinal
        (format #t "~:r" 9)   ⊣ ninth       ;; ordinal
```

And also with no parameters, ~@r gives roman numerals and ~:@r gives old roman numerals. In old roman numerals there's no "subtraction", so 9 is VIIII instead of IX. In both cases only positive numbers can be output.

```
        (format #t "~@r" 89)   ⊣ LXXXIX     ;; roman
        (format #t "~:@r" 89)  ⊣ LXXXVIIII  ;; old roman
```

When a parameter is given it means numeric output in the specified *radix*. The modifiers and parameters following the radix are the same as described for ~d etc above.

```
        (format #f "~3r" 27)    ⇒ "1000"   ;; base 3
        (format #f "~3,5r" 26)  ⇒ "  222"  ;; base 3 width 5
```

~f   Fixed-point float. Parameters: *width, decimals, scale, overflowchar, padchar.*

Output a number or number string in fixed-point format, ie. with a decimal point.

```
(format #t "~f" 5)        ⊣ 5.0
(format #t "~f" "123")    ⊣ 123.0
(format #t "~f" "1e-1")   ⊣ 0.1
```

`~@f` prints a + sign on positive numbers (including zero).

```
(format #t "~@f" 0)  ⊣ +0.0
```

If the output is less than *width* characters it's padded on the left with *padchar* (space by default). If the output equals or exceeds *width* then there's no padding. The default for *width* is no padding.

```
(format #f "~6f" -1.5)        ⇒ "  -1.5"
(format #f "~6,,,,'*f" 23)    ⇒ "**23.0"
(format #f "~6f" 1234567.0)   ⇒ "1234567.0"
```

decimals is how many digits to print after the decimal point, with the value rounded or padded with zeros as necessary. (The default is to output as many decimals as required.)

```
(format #t "~1,2f" 3.125)   ⊣ 3.13
(format #t "~1,2f" 1.5)     ⊣ 1.50
```

scale is a power of 10 applied to the value, moving the decimal point that many places. A positive *scale* increases the value shown, a negative decreases it.

```
(format #t "~,,2f" 1234)    ⊣ 123400.0
(format #t "~,,-2f" 1234)   ⊣ 12.34
```

If *overflowchar* and *width* are both given and if the output would exceed *width*, then that many *overflowchars* are printed instead of the value.

```
(format #t "~6,,,'xf" 12345)   ⊣ 12345.
(format #t "~5,,,'xf" 12345)   ⊣ xxxxx
```

~h   Localized number[4]. Parameters: *width, decimals, padchar.*

Like ~f, output an exact or floating point number, but do so according to the current locale, or according to the given locale object when the : modifier is used (see Section 6.24.4 [Number Input and Output], page 439).

```
(format #t "~h" 12345.5678)   ; with "C" as the current locale
⊣ 12345.5678

(format #t "~14,,'*:h" 12345.5678
      (make-locale LC_ALL "en_US"))
⊣ ***12,345.5678

(format #t "~,2:h" 12345.5678
```

---

[4] The ~h format specifier first appeared in Guile version 2.0.6.

```
                      (make-locale LC_NUMERIC "fr_FR"))
         ⊣ 12 345,56
```

~e   Exponential float. Parameters: *width*, *mantdigits*, *expdigits*, *intdigits*, *overflowchar*, *padchar*, *expchar*.

Output a number or number string in exponential notation.

```
(format #t "~e" 5000.25)  ⊣ 5.00025E+3
(format #t "~e" "123.4")  ⊣ 1.234E+2
(format #t "~e" "1e4")    ⊣ 1.0E+4
```

~@e prints a + sign on positive numbers (including zero). (This is for the mantissa, a + or - sign is always shown on the exponent.)

```
(format #t "~@e" 5000.0)  ⊣ +5.0E+3
```

If the output is less than *width* characters it's padded on the left with *padchar* (space by default). The default for *width* is to output with no padding.

```
(format #f "~10e" 1234.0)       ⇒ "  1.234E+3"
(format #f "~10,,,,,'*e" 0.5)   ⇒ "****5.0E-1"
```

mantdigits is the number of digits shown in the mantissa after the decimal point. The value is rounded or trailing zeros are added as necessary. The default *mantdigits* is to show as much as needed by the value.

```
(format #f "~,3e" 11111.0)  ⇒ "1.111E+4"
(format #f "~,8e" 123.0)    ⇒ "1.23000000E+2"
```

expdigits is the minimum number of digits shown for the exponent, with leading zeros added if necessary. The default for *expdigits* is to show only as many digits as required. At least 1 digit is always shown.

```
(format #f "~,,1e" 1.0e99)  ⇒ "1.0E+99"
(format #f "~,,6e" 1.0e99)  ⇒ "1.0E+000099"
```

intdigits (default 1) is the number of digits to show before the decimal point in the mantissa. *intdigits* can be zero, in which case the integer part is a single 0, or it can be negative, in which case leading zeros are shown after the decimal point.

```
(format #t "~,,,3e" 12345.0)   ⊣ 123.45E+2
(format #t "~,,,0e" 12345.0)   ⊣ 0.12345E+5
(format #t "~,,,-3e" 12345.0)  ⊣ 0.00012345E+8
```

If *overflowchar* is given then *width* is a hard limit. If the output would exceed *width* then instead that many *overflowchar*s are printed.

```
(format #f "~6,,,,'xe" 100.0)  ⇒ "1.0E+2"
(format #f "~3,,,,'xe" 100.0)  ⇒ "xxx"
```

expchar is the exponent marker character (default E).

```
(format #t "~,,,,,,'ee" 100.0)  ⊣ 1.0e+2
```

~g   General float. Parameters: *width*, *mantdigits*, *expdigits*, *intdigits*, *overflowchar*, *padchar*, *expchar*.

Output a number or number string in either exponential format the same as ~e, or fixed-point format like ~f but aligned where the mantissa would have been and followed by padding where the exponent would have been.

Fixed-point is used when the absolute value is 0.1 or more and it takes no more space than the mantissa in exponential format, ie. basically up to *mantdigits* digits.

```
(format #f "~12,4,2g" 999.0)     ⇒ "     999.0     "
(format #f "~12,4,2g" "100000") ⇒ "   1.0000E+05"
```

The parameters are interpreted as per ~e above. When fixed-point is used, the *decimals* parameter to ~f is established from *mantdigits*, so as to give a total *mantdigits* + 1 figures.

~$ Monetary style fixed-point float. Parameters: *decimals*, *intdigits*, *width*, *padchar*.

Output a number or number string in fixed-point format, ie. with a decimal point. *decimals* is the number of decimal places to show, default 2.

```
(format #t "~$" 5)          ⊣ 5.00
(format #t "~4$" "2.25")    ⊣ 2.2500
(format #t "~4$" "1e-2")    ⊣ 0.0100
```

~@$ prints a + sign on positive numbers (including zero).

```
(format #t "~@$" 0)  ⊣ +0.00
```

intdigits is a minimum number of digits to show in the integer part of the value (default 1).

```
(format #t "~,3$" 9.5)     ⊣ 009.50
(format #t "~,0$" 0.125)   ⊣ .13
```

If the output is less than *width* characters (default 0), it's padded on the left with *padchar* (default space). ~:$ puts the padding after the sign.

```
(format #f "~,,8$" -1.5)      ⇒ "   -1.50"
(format #f "~,,8:$" -1.5)     ⇒ "-   1.50"
(format #f "~,,8,'.:@$" 3)    ⇒ "+...3.00"
```

Note that floating point for dollar amounts is generally not a good idea, because a cent 0.01 cannot be represented exactly in the binary floating point Guile uses, which leads to slowly accumulating rounding errors. Keeping values as cents (or fractions of a cent) in integers then printing with the scale option in ~f may be a better approach.

~i   Complex fixed-point float.   Parameters: *width*, *decimals*, *scale*, *overflowchar*, *padchar*.

Output the argument as a complex number, with both real and imaginary part shown (even if one or both are zero).

The parameters and modifiers are the same as for fixed-point ~f described above. The real and imaginary parts are both output with the same given parameters and modifiers, except that for the imaginary part the @ modifier is always enabled, so as to print a + sign between the real and imaginary parts.

```
(format #t "~i" 1)   ⊣ 1.0+0.0i
```

~p   Plural. No parameters.

Output nothing if the argument is 1, or 's' for any other value.

```
(format #t "enter name~p" 1) ⊣ enter name
(format #t "enter name~p" 2) ⊣ enter names
```

~@p prints 'y' for 1 or 'ies' otherwise.

```
(format #t "pupp~@p" 1) ⊣ puppy
(format #t "pupp~@p" 2) ⊣ puppies
```

~:p re-uses the preceding argument instead of taking a new one, which can be convenient when printing some sort of count.

```
(format #t "~d cat~:p" 9)   ⊣ 9 cats
(format #t "~d pupp~:@p" 5) ⊣ 5 puppies
```

~p is designed for English plurals and there's no attempt to support other languages. ~[conditionals (below) may be able to help. When using **gettext** to translate messages **ngettext** is probably best though (see Section 6.24 [Internationalization], page 436).

~y   Structured printing. Parameters: *width*.

~y outputs an argument using **pretty-print** (see Section 7.9 [Pretty Printing], page 663). The result will be formatted to fit within *width* columns (79 by default), consuming multiple lines if necessary.

~@y outputs an argument using **truncated-print** (see Section 7.9 [Pretty Printing], page 663). The resulting code will be formatted to fit within *width* columns (79 by default), on a single line. The output will be truncated if necessary.

~:@y is like ~@y, except the *width* parameter is interpreted to be the maximum column to which to output. That is to say, if you are at column 10, and ~60:@y is seen, the datum will be truncated to 50 columns.

~? \
~k   Sub-format. No parameters.

Take a format string argument and a second argument which is a list of arguments for that string, and output the result.

```
(format #t "~?" "~d ~d" '(1 2))     ⊣ 1 2
```

~@? takes arguments for the sub-format directly rather than in a list.

```
(format #t "~@? ~s" "~d ~d" 1 2 "foo") ⊣ 1 2 "foo"
```

~? and ~k are the same, ~k is provided for T-Scheme compatibility.

~*   Argument jumping. Parameter: *N*.

Move forward *N* arguments (default 1) in the argument list. ~:* moves backwards. (*N* cannot be negative.)

```
(format #f "~d ~2*~d" 1 2 3 4) ⇒ "1 4"
(format #f "~d ~:*~d" 6)        ⇒ "6 6"
```

~@* moves to argument number *N*. The first argument is number 0 (and that's the default for *N*).

```
(format #f "~d~d again ~@*~d~d" 1 2)  ⇒ "12 again 12"
(format #f "~d~d~d ~1@*~d~d" 1 2 3)   ⇒ "123 23"
```

A # move to the end followed by a : modifier move back can be used for
an absolute position relative to the end of the argument list, a reverse of
what the @ modifier does.

```
(format #t "~#*~2:*~a" 'a 'b 'c 'd)     ⊣ c
```

At the end of the format string the current argument position doesn't
matter, any further arguments are ignored.

~t   Advance to a column position. Parameters: *colnum*, *colinc*, *padchar*.

          Output *padchar* (space by default) to move to the given *colnum* column.
          The start of the line is column 0, the default for *colnum* is 1.

```
(format #f "~tX")  ⇒ " X"
(format #f "~3tX") ⇒ "   X"
```

          If the current column is already past *colnum*, then the move is to there
          plus a multiple of *colinc*, ie. column $colnum + N * colinc$ for the smallest
          N which makes that value greater than or equal to the current column.
          The default *colinc* is 1 (which means no further move).

```
(format #f "abcd~2,5,'.tx") ⇒ "abcd...x"
```

          ~@t takes *colnum* as an offset from the current column. *colnum* many pad
          characters are output, then further padding to make the current column
          a multiple of *colinc*, if it isn't already so.

```
(format #f "a~3,5'*@tx") ⇒ "a****x"
```

          ~t is implemented using **port-column** (see Section 6.14.2 [Reading],
          page 318), so it works even there has been other output before **format**.

~~   Tilde character. Parameter: *n*.

          Output a tilde character ~, or *n* many if a parameter is given. Normally
          ~ introduces an escape sequence, ~~ is the way to output a literal tilde.

~%   Newline. Parameter: *n*.

          Output a newline character, or *n* many if a parameter is given. A newline
          (or a few newlines) can of course be output just by including them in the
          format string.

~&   Start a new line. Parameter: *n*.

          Output a newline if not already at the start of a line. With a parameter,
          output that many newlines, but with the first only if not already at the
          start of a line. So for instance 3 would be a newline if not already at the
          start of a line, and 2 further newlines.

~_   Space character. Parameter: *n*.

          Output a space character, or *n* many if a parameter is given.

          With a variable parameter this is one way to insert runtime calculated
          padding (~t or the various field widths can do similar things).

```
(format #f "~v_foo" 4) ⇒ "    foo"
```

~/   Tab character. Parameter: *n*.

           Output a tab character, or *n* many if a parameter is given.

~| Formfeed character. Parameter: *n*.

           Output a formfeed character, or *n* many if a parameter is given.

~!   Force output. No parameters.

           At the end of output, call `force-output` to flush any buffers on the destination (see Section 6.14.3 [Writing], page 320). ~! can occur anywhere in the format string, but the force is done at the end of output.

           When output is to a string (destination #f), ~! does nothing.

~newline (ie. newline character)
           Continuation line. No parameters.

           Skip this newline and any following whitespace in the format string, ie. don't send it to the output. This can be used to break up a long format string for readability, but not print the extra whitespace.

```
(format #f "abc~
        ~d def~
        ~d" 1 2) ⇒ "abc1 def2"
```

           ~:newline skips the newline but leaves any further whitespace to be printed normally.

           ~@newline prints the newline then skips following whitespace.

~(~)   Case conversion. No parameters.

           Between ~(and ~) the case of all output is changed. The modifiers on ~(control the conversion.

               ~(— lower case.

               ~:@(— upper case.

           For example,

```
(format #t "~(Hello~)")    ⊣ hello
(format #t "~:@(Hello~)")  ⊣ HELLO
```

           In the future it's intended the modifiers : and @ alone will capitalize the first letters of words, as per Common Lisp `format`, but the current implementation of this is flawed and not recommended for use.

           Case conversions do not nest, currently. This might change in the future, but if it does then it will be to Common Lisp style where the outermost conversion has priority, overriding inner ones (making those fairly pointless).

~{ ~}   Iteration. Parameter: *maxreps* (for ~{).

           The format between ~{ and ~} is iterated. The modifiers to ~{ determine how arguments are taken. The default is a list argument with each iteration successively consuming elements from it. This is a convenient way to output a whole list.

```
(format #t "~{~d~}"      '(1 2 3))          ⊣ 123
(format #t "~{~s=~d ~}" '("x" 1 "y" 2)) ⊣ "x"=1 "y"=2
```

`~:{` takes a single argument which is a list of lists, each of those contained lists gives the arguments for the iterated format.

```
(format #t "~:{~dx~d ~}" '((1 2) (3 4) (5 6)))
⊣ 1x2 3x4 5x6
```

`~@{` takes arguments directly, with each iteration successively consuming arguments.

```
(format #t "~@{~d~}"      1 2 3)          ⊣ 123
(format #t "~@{~s=~d ~}" "x" 1 "y" 2) ⊣ "x"=1 "y"=2
```

`~:@{` takes list arguments, one argument for each iteration, using that list for the format.

```
(format #t "~:@{~dx~d ~}" '(1 2) '(3 4) '(5 6))
⊣ 1x2 3x4 5x6
```

Iterating stops when there are no more arguments or when the *maxreps* parameter to `~{` is reached (default no maximum).

```
(format #t "~2{~d~}" '(1 2 3 4)) ⊣ 12
```

If the format between `~{` and `~}` is empty, then a format string argument is taken (before iteration argument(s)) and used instead. This allows a sub-format (like `~?` above) to be iterated.

```
(format #t "~{~}" "~d" '(1 2 3)) ⊣ 123
```

Iterations can be nested, an inner iteration operates in the same way as described, but of course on the arguments the outer iteration provides it. This can be used to work into nested list structures. For example in the following the inner `~{~d~}x` is applied to (1 2) then (3 4 5) etc.

```
(format #t "~{~{~d~}x~}" '((1 2) (3 4 5))) ⊣ 12x345x
```

See also `~^` below for escaping from iteration.

`~[ ~; ~]`   Conditional. Parameter: *selector*.

A conditional block is delimited by `~[` and `~]`, and `~;` separates clauses within the block. `~[` takes an integer argument and that number clause is used. The first clause is number 0.

```
(format #f "~[peach~;banana~;mango~]" 1)  ⇒ "banana"
```

The *selector* parameter can be used for the clause number, instead of taking an argument.

```
(format #f "~2[peach~;banana~;mango~]")  ⇒ "mango"
```

If the clause number is out of range then nothing is output. Or the last clause can be `~:;` to use that for a number out of range.

```
(format #f "~[banana~;mango~]"           99) ⇒ ""
(format #f "~[banana~;mango~:;fruit~]" 99) ⇒ "fruit"
```

`~:[` treats the argument as a flag, and expects two clauses. The first is used if the argument is `#f` or the second otherwise.

```
(format #f "~:[false~;not false~]" #f)   ⇒ "false"
(format #f "~:[false~;not false~]" 'abc) ⇒ "not false"

(let ((n 3))
  (format #t "~d gnu~:[s are~; is~] here" n (= 1 n)))
⊣ 3 gnus are here
```

~@[also treats the argument as a flag, and expects one clause. If the argument is #f then no output is produced and the argument is consumed, otherwise the clause is used and the argument is not consumed, it's left for the clause. This can be used for instance to suppress output if #f means something not available.

```
(format #f "~@[temperature=~d~]" 27) ⇒ "temperature=27"
(format #f "~@[temperature=~d~]" #f) ⇒ ""
```

~^   Escape. Parameters: *val1*, *val2*, *val3*.

Stop formatting if there are no more arguments. This can be used for instance to have a format string adapt to a variable number of arguments.

```
(format #t "~d~^ ~d" 1)    ⊣ 1
(format #t "~d~^ ~d" 1 2)  ⊣ 1 2
```

Within a ~{ ~} iteration, ~^ stops the current iteration step if there are no more arguments to that step, but continuing with possible further steps and the rest of the format. This can be used for instance to avoid a separator on the last iteration, or to adapt to variable length argument lists.

```
(format #f "~{~d~^/~} go"    '(1 2 3))      ⇒ "1/2/3 go"
(format #f "~:{ ~d~^~d~} go" '((1) (2 3))) ⇒ " 1 23 go"
```

Within a ~? sub-format, ~^ operates just on that sub-format. If it terminates the sub-format then the originating format will still continue.

```
(format #t "~? items" "~d~^ ~d" '(1))   ⊣ 1 items
(format #t "~? items" "~d~^ ~d" '(1 2)) ⊣ 1 2 items
```

The parameters to ~^ (which are numbers) change the condition used to terminate. For a single parameter, termination is when that value is zero (notice this makes plain ~^ equivalent to ~#^). For two parameters, termination is when those two are equal. For three parameters, termination is when *val1* ≤ *val2* and *val2* ≤ *val3*.

~q   Inquiry message. Insert a copyright message into the output.

         ~:q inserts the format implementation version.

It's an error if there are not enough arguments for the escapes in the format string, but any excess arguments are ignored.

Iterations ~{ ~} and conditionals ~[~; ~] can be nested, but must be properly nested, meaning the inner form must be entirely within the outer form. So it's not possible, for instance, to try to conditionalize the endpoint of an iteration.

```
(format #t "~{ ~[ ... ~] ~}" ...)        ;; good
(format #t "~{ ~[ ... ~} ... ~]" ...)    ;; bad
```

The same applies to case conversions ~(~), they must properly nest with respect to iterations and conditionals (though currently a case conversion cannot nest within another case conversion).

When a sub-format (~?) is used, that sub-format string must be self-contained. It cannot for instance give a ~{ to begin an iteration form and have the ~} up in the originating format, or similar.

Guile contains a `format` procedure even when the module (`ice-9 format`) is not loaded. The default `format` is `simple-format` (see Section 6.14.3 [Writing], page 320), it doesn't support all escape sequences documented in this section, and will signal an error if you try to use one of them. The reason for two versions is that the full `format` is fairly large and requires some time to load. `simple-format` is often adequate too.

7.11 File Tree Walk

The functions in this section traverse a tree of files and directories. They come in two flavors: the first one is a high-level functional interface, and the second one is similar to the C `ftw` and `nftw` routines (see Section "Working with Directory Trees" in *GNU C Library Reference Manual*).

```
(use-modules (ice-9 ftw))
```

file-system-tree *file-name* [*enter?* [*stat*]]   [Scheme Procedure]
    Return a tree of the form (`file-name stat children ...`) where *stat* is the result of (`stat file-name`) and *children* are similar structures for each file contained in *file-name* when it designates a directory.

    The optional *enter?* predicate is invoked as (`enter? name stat`) and should return true to allow recursion into directory *name*; the default value is a procedure that always returns `#t`. When a directory does not match *enter?*, it nonetheless appears in the resulting tree, only with zero children.

    The *stat* argument is optional and defaults to `lstat`, as for `file-system-fold` (see below.)

    The example below shows how to obtain a hierarchical listing of the files under the `module/language` directory in the Guile source tree, discarding their `stat` info:

```
(use-modules (ice-9 match))

(define remove-stat
  ;; Remove the 'stat' object the 'file-system-tree' provides
  ;; for each file in the tree.
  (match-lambda
    ((name stat)              ; flat file
     name)
    ((name stat children ...) ; directory
     (list name (map remove-stat children)))))
```

```
(let ((dir (string-append (assq-ref %guile-build-info 'top_srcdir)
                          "/module/language")))
  (remove-stat (file-system-tree dir)))

⇒
("language"
 (("value" ("spec.go" "spec.scm"))
  ("scheme"
   ("spec.go"
    "spec.scm"
    "compile-tree-il.scm"
    "decompile-tree-il.scm"
    "decompile-tree-il.go"
    "compile-tree-il.go"))
  ("tree-il"
   ("spec.go"
    "fix-letrec.go"
    "inline.go"
    "fix-letrec.scm"
    "compile-glil.go"
    "spec.scm"
    "optimize.scm"
    "primitives.scm"
    ...))
  ...))
```

It is often desirable to process directories entries directly, rather than building up a tree of entries in memory, like `file-system-tree` does. The following procedure, a *combinator*, is designed to allow directory entries to be processed directly as a directory tree is traversed; in fact, `file-system-tree` is implemented in terms of it.

`file-system-fold` *enter? leaf down up skip error init file-name*   [Scheme Procedure]
        [*stat*]

Traverse the directory at *file-name*, recursively, and return the result of the successive applications of the *leaf*, *down*, *up*, and *skip* procedures as described below.

Enter sub-directories only when (`enter? path stat result`) returns true. When a sub-directory is entered, call (`down path stat result`), where *path* is the path of the sub-directory and *stat* the result of (`false-if-exception (stat path)`); when it is left, call (`up path stat result`).

For each file in a directory, call (`leaf path stat result`).

When *enter?* returns #f, or when an unreadable directory is encountered, call (`skip path stat result`).

When *file-name* names a flat file, (`leaf path stat init`) is returned.

When an `opendir` or *stat* call fails, call (`error path stat errno result`), with *errno* being the operating system error number that was raised—e.g., EACCES—and *stat* either #f or the result of the *stat* call for that entry, when available.

The special . and .. entries are not passed to these procedures. The *path* argument to the procedures is a full file name—e.g., "../foo/bar/gnu"; if *file-name* is an absolute file name, then *path* is also an absolute file name. Files and directories, as identified by their device/inode number pair, are traversed only once.

The optional *stat* argument defaults to `lstat`, which means that symbolic links are not followed; the `stat` procedure can be used instead when symbolic links are to be followed (see Section 7.2.3 [File System], page 476).

The example below illustrates the use of `file-system-fold`:

```
(define (total-file-size file-name)
  "Return the size in bytes of the files under FILE-NAME (similar
to 'du --apparent-size' with GNU Coreutils.)"

  (define (enter? name stat result)
    ;; Skip version control directories.
    (not (member (basename name) '(".git" ".svn" "CVS"))))
  (define (leaf name stat result)
    ;; Return RESULT plus the size of the file at NAME.
    (+ result (stat:size stat)))

  ;; Count zero bytes for directories.
  (define (down name stat result) result)
  (define (up name stat result) result)

  ;; Likewise for skipped directories.
  (define (skip name stat result) result)

  ;; Ignore unreadable files/directories but warn the user.
  (define (error name stat errno result)
    (format (current-error-port) "warning: ~a: ~a~%"
            name (strerror errno))
    result)

  (file-system-fold enter? leaf down up skip error
                    0  ; initial counter is zero bytes
                    file-name))

(total-file-size ".")
⇒ 8217554

(total-file-size "/dev/null")
⇒ 0
```

The alternative C-like functions are described below.

scandir *name* [*select?* [*entry<?*]]   [Scheme Procedure]
Return the list of the names of files contained in directory *name* that match predicate *select?* (by default, all files). The returned list of file names is sorted according to

entry<?, which defaults to `string-locale<?` such that file names are sorted in the locale's alphabetical order (see Section 6.24.2 [Text Collation], page 437). Return `#f` when *name* is unreadable or is not a directory.

This procedure is modeled after the C library function of the same name (see Section "Scanning Directory Content" in *GNU C Library Reference Manual*).

`ftw` *startname proc* [*'hash-size n*]   [Scheme Procedure]
Walk the file system tree descending from *startname*, calling *proc* for each file and directory.

Hard links and symbolic links are followed. A file or directory is reported to *proc* only once, and skipped if seen again in another place. One consequence of this is that `ftw` is safe against circularly linked directory structures.

Each *proc* call is (`proc filename statinfo flag`) and it should return `#t` to continue, or any other value to stop.

filename is the item visited, being *startname* plus a further path and the name of the item. *statinfo* is the return from `stat` (see Section 7.2.3 [File System], page 476) on *filename*. *flag* is one of the following symbols,

`regular`   *filename* is a file, this includes special files like devices, named pipes, etc.

`directory`
              filename is a directory.

`invalid-stat`
              An error occurred when calling `stat`, so nothing is known. *statinfo* is `#f` in this case.

`directory-not-readable`
              filename is a directory, but one which cannot be read and hence won't be recursed into.

`symlink`   *filename* is a dangling symbolic link. Symbolic links are normally followed and their target reported, the link itself is reported if the target does not exist.

The return value from `ftw` is `#t` if it ran to completion, or otherwise the non-`#t` value from *proc* which caused the stop.

Optional argument symbol `hash-size` and an integer can be given to set the size of the hash table used to track items already visited. (see Section 6.7.14.2 [Hash Table Reference], page 237)

In the current implementation, returning non-`#t` from *proc* is the only valid way to terminate `ftw`. *proc* must not use `throw` or similar to escape.

`nftw` *startname proc* [*'chdir*] [*'depth*] [*'hash-size n*] [*'mount*]   [Scheme Procedure]
       [*'physical*]
Walk the file system tree starting at *startname*, calling *proc* for each file and directory. `nftw` has extra features over the basic `ftw` described above.

Like `ftw`, hard links and symbolic links are followed. A file or directory is reported to *proc* only once, and skipped if seen again in another place. One consequence of this is that `nftw` is safe against circular linked directory structures.

Each *proc* call is (`proc filename statinfo flag base level`) and it should return
`#t` to continue, or any other value to stop.

filename is the item visited, being *startname* plus a further path and the name of the
item. *statinfo* is the return from `stat` on *filename* (see Section 7.2.3 [File System],
page 476). *base* is an integer offset into *filename* which is where the basename for
this item begins. *level* is an integer giving the directory nesting level, starting from
0 for the contents of *startname* (or that item itself if it's a file). *flag* is one of the
following symbols,

`regular`   *filename* is a file, including special files like devices, named pipes, etc.

`directory`
                 filename is a directory.

`directory-processed`
                 filename is a directory, and its contents have all been visited. This flag is
                 given instead of `directory` when the `depth` option below is used.

`invalid-stat`
                 An error occurred when applying `stat` to *filename*, so nothing is known
                 about it. *statinfo* is `#f` in this case.

`directory-not-readable`
                 filename is a directory, but one which cannot be read and hence won't be
                 recursed into.

`stale-symlink`
                 filename is a dangling symbolic link. Links are normally followed and
                 their target reported, the link itself is reported if its target does not
                 exist.

`symlink`   When the `physical` option described below is used, this indicates *file-
                 name* is a symbolic link whose target exists (and is not being followed).

The following optional arguments can be given to modify the way `nftw` works. Each
is passed as a symbol (and `hash-size` takes a following integer value).

`chdir`   Change to the directory containing the item before calling *proc*. When
                 `nftw` returns the original current directory is restored.

                 Under this option, generally the *base* parameter to each *proc* call should
                 be used to pick out the base part of the *filename*. The *filename* is still a
                 path but with a changed directory it won't be valid (unless the *startname*
                 directory was absolute).

`depth`   Visit files "depth first", meaning *proc* is called for the contents of each
                 directory before it's called for the directory itself. Normally a directory
                 is reported first, then its contents.

                 Under this option, the *flag* to *proc* for a directory is `directory-`
                 `processed` instead of `directory`.

`hash-size` *n*
                 Set the size of the hash table used to track items already visited. (see
                 Section 6.7.14.2 [Hash Table Reference], page 237)

mount   Don't cross a mount point, meaning only visit items on the same file system as *startname* (ie. the same `stat:dev`).

physical   Don't follow symbolic links, instead report them to *proc* as `symlink`. Dangling links (those whose target doesn't exist) are still reported as `stale-symlink`.

The return value from `nftw` is `#t` if it ran to completion, or otherwise the non-`#t` value from *proc* which caused the stop.

In the current implementation, returning non-`#t` from *proc* is the only valid way to terminate `ftw`. *proc* must not use `throw` or similar to escape.

7.12 Queues

The functions in this section are provided by

     `(use-modules (ice-9 q))`

This module implements queues holding arbitrary scheme objects and designed for efficient first-in / first-out operations.

`make-q` creates a queue, and objects are entered and removed with `enq!` and `deq!`. `q-push!` and `q-pop!` can be used too, treating the front of the queue like a stack.

---

make-q   [Scheme Procedure]
> Return a new queue.

q? *obj*   [Scheme Procedure]
> Return `#t` if *obj* is a queue, or `#f` if not.
>
> Note that queues are not a distinct class of objects but are implemented with cons cells. For that reason certain list structures can get `#t` from `q?`.

enq! *q obj*   [Scheme Procedure]
> Add *obj* to the rear of *q*, and return *q*.

deq! *q*   [Scheme Procedure]
q-pop! *q*   [Scheme Procedure]
> Remove and return the front element from *q*. If *q* is empty, a `q-empty` exception is thrown.
>
> `deq!` and `q-pop!` are the same operation, the two names just let an application match `enq!` with `deq!`, or `q-push!` with `q-pop!`.

q-push! *q obj*   [Scheme Procedure]
> Add *obj* to the front of *q*, and return *q*.

q-length *q*   [Scheme Procedure]
> Return the number of elements in *q*.

q-empty? *q*   [Scheme Procedure]
> Return true if *q* is empty.

q-empty-check *q*   [Scheme Procedure]
> Throw a `q-empty` exception if *q* is empty.

q-front *q*   [Scheme Procedure]

> Return the first element of *q* (without removing it). If *q* is empty, a `q-empty` exception
> is thrown.

q-rear *q*   [Scheme Procedure]

> Return the last element of *q* (without removing it). If *q* is empty, a `q-empty` exception
> is thrown.

q-remove! *q obj*   [Scheme Procedure]

> Remove all occurrences of *obj* from *q*, and return *q*. *obj* is compared to queue elements
> using `eq?`.

The `q-empty` exceptions described above are thrown just as (`throw 'q-empty`), there's
no message etc like an error throw.

A queue is implemented as a cons cell, the `car` containing a list of queued elements, and
the `cdr` being the last cell in that list (for ease of enqueuing).

```
(list . last-cell)
```

If the queue is empty, *list* is the empty list and *last-cell* is `#f`.

An application can directly access the queue list if desired, for instance to search the
elements or to insert at a specific point.

sync-q! *q*   [Scheme Procedure]

> Recompute the *last-cell* field in *q*.
>
> All the operations above maintain *last-cell* as described, so normally there's no need
> for `sync-q!`. But if an application modifies the queue *list* then it must either maintain
> *last-cell* similarly, or call `sync-q!` to recompute it.

7.13 Streams

This section documents Guile's legacy stream module. For a more complete and portable
stream library, see Section 7.5.27 [SRFI-41], page 599.

A stream represents a sequence of values, each of which is calculated only when required.
This allows large or even infinite sequences to be represented and manipulated with familiar
operations like "car", "cdr", "map" or "fold". In such manipulations only as much as needed
is actually held in memory at any one time. The functions in this section are available from

```
(use-modules (ice-9 streams))
```

Streams are implemented using promises (see Section 6.17.9 [Delayed Evaluation],
page 371), which is how the underlying calculation of values is made only when needed,
and the values then retained so the calculation is not repeated.

Here is a simple example producing a stream of all odd numbers,

```
(define odds (make-stream (lambda (state)
                            (cons state (+ state 2)))
                          1))
(stream-car odds)            ⇒ 1
(stream-car (stream-cdr odds)) ⇒ 3
```

`stream-map` could be used to derive a stream of odd squares,

```
(define (square n) (* n n))
(define oddsquares (stream-map square odds))
```

These are infinite sequences, so it's not possible to convert them to a list, but they could be printed (infinitely) with for example

```
(stream-for-each (lambda (n sq)
                   (format #t "~a squared is ~a\n" n sq))
                 odds oddsquares)
⊣
1 squared is 1
3 squared is 9
5 squared is 25
7 squared is 49
...
```

make-stream *proc initial-state*   [Scheme Procedure]
  Return a new stream, formed by calling *proc* successively.

  Each call is (**proc state**), it should return a pair, the **car** being the value for the stream, and the **cdr** being the new *state* for the next call. For the first call *state* is the given *initial-state*. At the end of the stream, *proc* should return some non-pair object.

stream-car *stream*   [Scheme Procedure]
  Return the first element from *stream*. *stream* must not be empty.

stream-cdr *stream*   [Scheme Procedure]
  Return a stream which is the second and subsequent elements of *stream*. *stream* must not be empty.

stream-null? *stream*   [Scheme Procedure]
  Return true if *stream* is empty.

list->stream *list*   [Scheme Procedure]
vector->stream *vector*   [Scheme Procedure]
  Return a stream with the contents of *list* or *vector*.

  list or *vector* should not be modified subsequently, since it's unspecified whether changes there will be reflected in the stream returned.

port->stream *port readproc*   [Scheme Procedure]
  Return a stream which is the values obtained by reading from *port* using *readproc*. Each read call is (**readproc port**), and it should return an EOF object (see Section 6.14.2 [Reading], page 318) at the end of input.

  For example a stream of characters from a file,

```
(port->stream (open-input-file "/foo/bar.txt") read-char)
```

stream->list *stream*   [Scheme Procedure]
  Return a list which is the entire contents of *stream*.

stream->reversed-list *stream*   [Scheme Procedure]
> Return a list which is the entire contents of *stream*, but in reverse order.

stream->list&length *stream*   [Scheme Procedure]
> Return two values (see Section 6.13.7 [Multiple Values], page 301), being firstly a list
> which is the entire contents of *stream*, and secondly the number of elements in that
> list.

stream->reversed-list&length *stream*   [Scheme Procedure]
> Return two values (see Section 6.13.7 [Multiple Values], page 301) being firstly a list
> which is the entire contents of *stream*, but in reverse order, and secondly the number
> of elements in that list.

stream->vector *stream*   [Scheme Procedure]
> Return a vector which is the entire contents of *stream*.

stream-fold *proc init stream1 stream2 ...*   [Function]
> Apply *proc* successively over the elements of the given streams, from first to last until
> the end of the shortest stream is reached. Return the result from the last *proc* call.
>
> Each call is (*proc elem1 elem2 ... prev*), where each *elem* is from the corresponding
> *stream*. *prev* is the return from the previous *proc* call, or the given *init* for the first
> call.

stream-for-each *proc stream1 stream2 ...*   [Function]
> Call *proc* on the elements from the given *stream*s. The return value is unspecified.
>
> Each call is (*proc elem1 elem2 ...*), where each *elem* is from the corresponding
> *stream*. **stream-for-each** stops when it reaches the end of the shortest *stream*.

stream-map *proc stream1 stream2 ...*   [Function]
> Return a new stream which is the results of applying *proc* to the elements of the
> given *stream*s.
>
> Each call is (*proc elem1 elem2 ...*), where each *elem* is from the corresponding
> *stream*. The new stream ends when the end of the shortest given *stream* is reached.

7.14 Buffered Input

The following functions are provided by

```
(use-modules (ice-9 buffered-input))
```

A buffered input port allows a reader function to return chunks of characters which are
to be handed out on reading the port. A notion of further input for an application level
logical expression is maintained too, and passed through to the reader.

make-buffered-input-port *reader*   [Scheme Procedure]
> Create an input port which returns characters obtained from the given *reader* func-
> tion. *reader* is called (*reader cont*), and should return a string or an EOF object.
>
> The new port gives precisely the characters returned by *reader*, nothing is added, so
> if any newline characters or other separators are desired they must come from the
> reader function.

The *cont* parameter to *reader* is `#f` for initial input, or `#t` when continuing an expression. This is an application level notion, set with `set-buffered-input-continuation?!` below. If the user has entered a partial expression then it allows *reader* for instance to give a different prompt to show more is required.

`make-line-buffered-input-port` *reader*   [Scheme Procedure]

    Create an input port which returns characters obtained from the specified *reader* function, similar to `make-buffered-input-port` above, but where *reader* is expected to be a line-oriented.

    reader is called (*reader* cont), and should return a string or an EOF object as above. Each string is a line of input without a newline character, the port code inserts a newline after each string.

`set-buffered-input-continuation?!` *port cont*   [Scheme Procedure]

    Set the input continuation flag for a given buffered input *port*.

    An application uses this by calling with a *cont* flag of `#f` when beginning to read a new logical expression. For example with the Scheme `read` function (see Section 6.17.2 [Scheme Read], page 360),

```
(define my-port (make-buffered-input-port my-reader))


(set-buffered-input-continuation?! my-port #f)
(let ((obj (read my-port)))
    ...
```

7.15 Expect

The macros in this section are made available with:

```
(use-modules (ice-9 expect))
```

`expect` is a macro for selecting actions based on the output from a port. The name comes from a tool of similar functionality by Don Libes. Actions can be taken when a particular string is matched, when a timeout occurs, or when end-of-file is seen on the port. The `expect` macro is described below; `expect-strings` is a front-end to `expect` based on regexec (see the regular expression documentation).

`expect-strings` *clause* ...   [Macro]

    By default, `expect-strings` will read from the current input port. The first term in each clause consists of an expression evaluating to a string pattern (regular expression). As characters are read one-by-one from the port, they are accumulated in a buffer string which is matched against each of the patterns. When a pattern matches, the remaining expression(s) in the clause are evaluated and the value of the last is returned. For example:

```
(with-input-from-file "/etc/passwd"
  (lambda ()
    (expect-strings
      ("^nobody" (display "Got a nobody user.\n")
                 (display "That's no problem.\n"))
      ("^daemon" (display "Got a daemon user.\n")))))
```

The regular expression is compiled with the `REG_NEWLINE` flag, so that the ^ and $ anchors will match at any newline, not just at the start and end of the string.

There are two other ways to write a clause:

The expression(s) to evaluate can be omitted, in which case the result of the regular expression match (converted to strings, as obtained from regexec with match-pick set to `""`) will be returned if the pattern matches.

The symbol `=>` can be used to indicate that the expression is a procedure which will accept the result of a successful regular expression match. E.g.,

```
("^daemon" => write)
("^d(aemon)" => (lambda args (for-each write args)))
("^da(em)on" => (lambda (all sub)
                  (write all) (newline)
                  (write sub) (newline)))
```

The order of the substrings corresponds to the order in which the opening brackets occur.

A number of variables can be used to control the behaviour of **expect** (and **expect-strings**). Most have default top-level bindings to the value `#f`, which produces the default behaviour. They can be redefined at the top level or locally bound in a form enclosing the expect expression.

`expect-port`

> A port to read characters from, instead of the current input port.

`expect-timeout`

> **expect** will terminate after this number of seconds, returning `#f` or the value returned by expect-timeout-proc.

`expect-timeout-proc`

> A procedure called if timeout occurs. The procedure takes a single argument: the accumulated string.

`expect-eof-proc`

> A procedure called if end-of-file is detected on the input port. The procedure takes a single argument: the accumulated string.

`expect-char-proc`

> A procedure to be called every time a character is read from the port. The procedure takes a single argument: the character which was read.

`expect-strings-compile-flags`

> Flags to be used when compiling a regular expression, which are passed to **make-regexp** See Section 6.15.1 [Regexp Functions], page 350. The default value is `regexp/newline`.

`expect-strings-exec-flags`

> Flags to be used when executing a regular expression, which are passed to regexp-exec See Section 6.15.1 [Regexp Functions], page 350. The default value is `regexp/noteol`, which prevents $ from matching the end of the string while it is still accumulating, but still allows it to match after a line break or at the end of file.

Here's an example using all of the variables:

```
(let ((expect-port (open-input-file "/etc/passwd"))
      (expect-timeout 1)
      (expect-timeout-proc
        (lambda (s) (display "Times up!\n")))
      (expect-eof-proc
        (lambda (s) (display "Reached the end of the file!\n")))
      (expect-char-proc display)
      (expect-strings-compile-flags (logior regexp/newline regexp/icase))
      (expect-strings-exec-flags 0))
  (expect-strings
    ("^nobody"  (display "Got a nobody user\n"))))
```

expect *clause* ...   [Macro]

> **expect** is used in the same way as **expect-strings**, but tests are specified not as patterns, but as procedures. The procedures are called in turn after each character is read from the port, with two arguments: the value of the accumulated string and a flag to indicate whether end-of-file has been reached. The flag will usually be **#f**, but if end-of-file is reached, the procedures are called an additional time with the final accumulated string and **#t**.
>
> The test is successful if the procedure returns a non-false value.
>
> If the **=>** syntax is used, then if the test succeeds it must return a list containing the arguments to be provided to the corresponding expression.
>
> In the following example, a string will only be matched at the beginning of the file:
>
> ```
> (let ((expect-port (open-input-file "/etc/passwd")))
>   (expect
>     ((lambda (s eof?) (string=? s "fnord!"))
>       (display "Got a nobody user!\n"))))
> ```
>
> The control variables described for **expect-strings** also influence the behaviour of **expect**, with the exception of variables whose names begin with **expect-strings-**.

7.16 sxml-match: Pattern Matching of SXML

The (sxml match) module provides syntactic forms for pattern matching of SXML trees, in a "by example" style reminiscent of the pattern matching of the **syntax-rules** and **syntax-case** macro systems. See Section 7.22 [SXML], page 697, for more information on SXML.

The following example[5] provides a brief illustration, transforming a music album catalog language into HTML.

```
(define (album->html x)
  (sxml-match x
    [(album (@ (title ,t)) (catalog (num ,n) (fmt ,f)) ...)
     `(ul (li ,t)
          (li (b ,n) (i ,f)) ...)]))
```

Three macros are provided: sxml-match, sxml-match-let, and sxml-match-let*.

---

[5] This example is taken from a paper by Krishnamurthi et al. Their paper was the first to show the usefulness of the **syntax-rules** style of pattern matching for transformation of XML, though the language described, XT3D, is an XML language.

Compared to a standard s-expression pattern matcher (see Section 7.7 [Pattern Matching], page 657), `sxml-match` provides the following benefits:

- matching of SXML elements does not depend on any degree of normalization of the SXML;

- matching of SXML attributes (within an element) is under-ordered; the order of the attributes specified within the pattern need not match the ordering with the element being matched;

- all attributes specified in the pattern must be present in the element being matched; in the spirit that XML is 'extensible', the element being matched may include additional attributes not specified in the pattern.

The present module is a descendant of WebIt!, and was inspired by an s-expression pattern matcher developed by Erik Hilsdale, Dan Friedman, and Kent Dybvig at Indiana University.

Syntax

`sxml-match` provides `case`-like form for pattern matching of XML nodes.

`sxml-match` *input-expression clause1 clause2* ...   [Scheme Syntax]
    Match *input-expression*, an SXML tree, according to the given *clauses* (one or more), each consisting of a pattern and one or more expressions to be evaluated if the pattern match succeeds. Optionally, each *clause* within `sxml-match` may include a *guard expression*.

The pattern notation is based on that of Scheme's `syntax-rules` and `syntax-case` macro systems. The grammar for the `sxml-match` syntax is given below:

```
match-form ::= (sxml-match input-expression
                   clause+)

clause ::= [node-pattern action-expression+]
         | [node-pattern (guard expression*) action-expression+]

node-pattern ::= literal-pattern
               | pat-var-or-cata
               | element-pattern
               | list-pattern

literal-pattern ::= string
                  | character
                  | number
                  | #t
                  | #f

attr-list-pattern ::= (@ attribute-pattern*)
                    | (@ attribute-pattern* . pat-var-or-cata)

attribute-pattern ::= (tag-symbol attr-val-pattern)
```

```
attr-val-pattern ::= literal-pattern
                   | pat-var-or-cata
                   | (pat-var-or-cata default-value-expr)

element-pattern ::= (tag-symbol attr-list-pattern?)
                  | (tag-symbol attr-list-pattern? nodeset-pattern)
                  | (tag-symbol attr-list-pattern?
                          nodeset-pattern? . pat-var-or-cata)

list-pattern ::= (list nodeset-pattern)
               | (list nodeset-pattern? . pat-var-or-cata)
               | (list)

nodeset-pattern ::= node-pattern
                  | node-pattern ...
                  | node-pattern nodeset-pattern
                  | node-pattern ... nodeset-pattern

pat-var-or-cata ::= (unquote var-symbol)
                  | (unquote [var-symbol*])
                  | (unquote [cata-expression -> var-symbol*])
```

Within a list or element body pattern, ellipses may appear only once, but may be followed by zero or more node patterns.

Guard expressions cannot refer to the return values of catamorphisms.

Ellipses in the output expressions must appear only in an expression context; ellipses are not allowed in a syntactic form.

The sections below illustrate specific aspects of the `sxml-match` pattern matcher.

Matching XML Elements

The example below illustrates the pattern matching of an XML element:

```
(sxml-match '(e (@ (i 1)) 3 4 5)
  [(e (@ (i ,d)) ,a ,b ,c) (list d a b c)]
  [,otherwise #f])
```

Each clause in `sxml-match` contains two parts: a pattern and one or more expressions which are evaluated if the pattern is successfully match. The example above matches an element `e` with an attribute `i` and three children.

Pattern variables are must be "unquoted" in the pattern. The above expression binds d to 1, a to 3, b to 4, and c to 5.

Ellipses in Patterns

As in `syntax-rules`, ellipses may be used to specify a repeated pattern. Note that the pattern `item ...` specifies zero-or-more matches of the pattern `item`.

The use of ellipses in a pattern is illustrated in the code fragment below, where nested ellipses are used to match the children of repeated instances of an a element, within an element d.

```
(define x '(d (a 1 2 3) (a 4 5) (a 6 7 8) (a 9 10)))

(sxml-match x
  [(d (a ,b ...) ...)
   (list (list b ...) ...)])
```

The above expression returns a value of ((1 2 3) (4 5) (6 7 8) (9 10)).

Ellipses in Quasiquote'd Output

Within the body of an sxml-match form, a slightly extended version of quasiquote is provided, which allows the use of ellipses. This is illustrated in the example below.

```
(sxml-match '(e 3 4 5 6 7)
  [(e ,i ... 6 7) '("start" ,(list 'wrap i) ... "end")]
  [,otherwise #f])
```

The general pattern is that '(something ,i ...) is rewritten as '(something ,@i).

Matching Nodesets

A nodeset pattern is designated by a list in the pattern, beginning the identifier list. The example below illustrates matching a nodeset.

```
(sxml-match '("i" "j" "k" "l" "m")
  [(list ,a ,b ,c ,d ,e)
   '((p ,a) (p ,b) (p ,c) (p ,d) (p ,e))])
```

This example wraps each nodeset item in an HTML paragraph element. This example can be rewritten and simplified through using ellipsis:

```
(sxml-match '("i" "j" "k" "l" "m")
  [(list ,i ...)
   '((p ,i) ...)])
```

This version will match nodesets of any length, and wrap each item in the nodeset in an HTML paragraph element.

Matching the "Rest" of a Nodeset

Matching the "rest" of a nodeset is achieved by using a . rest) pattern at the end of an element or nodeset pattern.

This is illustrated in the example below:

```
(sxml-match '(e 3 (f 4 5 6) 7)
  [(e ,a (f . ,y) ,d)
   (list a y d)])
```

The above expression returns (3 (4 5 6) 7).

Matching the Unmatched Attributes

Sometimes it is useful to bind a list of attributes present in the element being matched, but which do not appear in the pattern. This is achieved by using a . rest) pattern at the end of the attribute list pattern. This is illustrated in the example below:

```
(sxml-match '(a (@ (z 1) (y 2) (x 3)) 4 5 6)
  [(a (@ (y ,www) . ,qqq) ,t ,u ,v)
   (list www qqq t u v)])
```

The above expression matches the attribute y and binds a list of the remaining attributes to the variable *qqq*. The result of the above expression is (2 ((z 1) (x 3)) 4 5 6).

This type of pattern also allows the binding of all attributes:

```
(sxml-match '(a (@ (z 1) (y 2) (x 3)))
  [(a (@ . ,qqq))
   qqq])
```

Default Values in Attribute Patterns

It is possible to specify a default value for an attribute which is used if the attribute is not present in the element being matched. This is illustrated in the following example:

```
(sxml-match '(e 3 4 5)
  [(e (@ (z (,d 1))) ,a ,b ,c) (list d a b c)])
```

The value 1 is used when the attribute z is absent from the element e.

Guards in Patterns

Guards may be added to a pattern clause via the **guard** keyword. A guard expression may include zero or more expressions which are evaluated only if the pattern is matched. The body of the clause is only evaluated if the guard expressions evaluate to #t.

The use of guard expressions is illustrated below:

```
(sxml-match '(a 2 3)
  ((a ,n) (guard (number? n)) n)
  ((a ,m ,n) (guard (number? m) (number? n)) (+ m n)))
```

Catamorphisms

The example below illustrates the use of explicit recursion within an sxml-match form. This example implements a simple calculator for the basic arithmetic operations, which are represented by the XML elements plus, minus, times, and div.

```
(define simple-eval
  (lambda (x)
    (sxml-match x
      [,i (guard (integer? i)) i]
      [(plus ,x ,y) (+ (simple-eval x) (simple-eval y))]
      [(times ,x ,y) (* (simple-eval x) (simple-eval y))]
      [(minus ,x ,y) (- (simple-eval x) (simple-eval y))]
      [(div ,x ,y) (/ (simple-eval x) (simple-eval y))]
      [,otherwise (error "simple-eval: invalid expression" x)])))
```

Using the catamorphism feature of sxml-match, a more concise version of simple-eval can be written. The pattern ,[x] recursively invokes the pattern matcher on the value bound in this position.

```
(define simple-eval
  (lambda (x)
```

```
(sxml-match x
  [,i (guard (integer? i)) i]
  [(plus ,[x] ,[y]) (+ x y)]
  [(times ,[x] ,[y]) (* x y)]
  [(minus ,[x] ,[y]) (- x y)]
  [(div ,[x] ,[y]) (/ x y)]
  [,otherwise (error "simple-eval: invalid expression" x)])))
```

Named-Catamorphisms

It is also possible to explicitly name the operator in the "cata" position. Where ,[id*] recurs to the top of the current sxml-match, ,[cata -> id*] recurs to cata. cata must evaluate to a procedure which takes one argument, and returns as many values as there are identifiers following ->.

Named catamorphism patterns allow processing to be split into multiple, mutually recursive procedures. This is illustrated in the example below: a transformation that formats a "TV Guide" into HTML.

```
(define (tv-guide->html g)
  (define (cast-list cl)
    (sxml-match cl
      [(CastList (CastMember (Character (Name ,ch)) (Actor (Name ,a))) ...)
       `(div (ul (li ,ch ": " ,a) ...))]))
  (define (prog p)
    (sxml-match p
      [(Program (Start ,start-time) (Duration ,dur) (Series ,series-title)
                (Description ,desc ...))
       `(div (p ,start-time
              (br) ,series-title
              (br) ,desc ...))]
      [(Program (Start ,start-time) (Duration ,dur) (Series ,series-title)
                (Description ,desc ...)
                ,[cast-list -> cl])
       `(div (p ,start-time
              (br) ,series-title
              (br) ,desc ...)
          ,cl)]))
  (sxml-match g
    [(TVGuide (@ (start ,start-date)
                 (end ,end-date))
              (Channel (Name ,nm) ,[prog -> p] ...) ...)
     `(html (head (title "TV Guide"))
            (body (h1 "TV Guide")
               (div (h2 ,nm) ,p ...) ...))]))
```

sxml-match-let and sxml-match-let*

sxml-match-let ((*pat expr*) ...) *expression0 expression* ...   [Scheme Syntax]

sxml-match-let* ((*pat expr*) ...) *expression0 expression* ...   [Scheme Syntax]
> These forms generalize the `let` and `let*` forms of Scheme to allow an XML pattern in the binding position, rather than a simple variable.

For example, the expression below:

```
(sxml-match-let ([(a ,i ,j) '(a 1 2)])
  (+ i j))
```

binds the variables *i* and *j* to 1 and 2 in the XML value given.

7.17 The Scheme shell (scsh)

An incomplete port of the Scheme shell (scsh) was once available for Guile as a separate package. However this code has bitrotten somewhat. The pieces are available in Guile's legacy CVS repository, which may be browsed at `http://cvs.savannah.gnu.org/viewvc/guile/guile-scsh/?root=guile`.

For information about scsh see `http://www.scsh.net/`.

This bitrotting is a bit of a shame, as there is a good deal of well-written Scheme code in scsh. Adopting this code and porting it to current Guile should be an educational experience, in addition to providing something of value to Guile folks.

7.18 Curried Definitions

The macros in this section are provided by

```
(use-modules (ice-9 curried-definitions))
```

and replace those provided by default.

Prior to Guile 2.0, Guile provided a type of definition known colloquially as a "curried definition". The idea is to extend the syntax of `define` so that you can conveniently define procedures that return procedures, up to any desired depth.

For example,

```
(define ((foo x) y)
  (list x y))
```

is a convenience form of

```
(define foo
  (lambda (x)
    (lambda (y)
      (list x y))))
```

define (... (*name args* ...) ...) *body* ...   [Scheme Syntax]
define* (... (*name args* ...) ...) *body* ...   [Scheme Syntax]
define-public (... (*name args* ...) ...) *body* ...   [Scheme Syntax]
> Create a top level variable *name* bound to the procedure with parameter list *args*. If *name* is itself a formal parameter list, then a higher order procedure is created using that formal-parameter list, and returning a procedure that has parameter list *args*. This nesting may occur to arbitrary depth.
>
> `define*` is similar but the formal parameter lists take additional options as described in Section 6.9.4.1 [lambda* and define*], page 248. For example,

```
(define* ((foo #:keys (bar 'baz) (quux 'zot)) frotz #:rest rest)
  (list bar quux frotz rest))

((foo #:quux 'foo) 1 2 3 4 5)
⇒ (baz foo 1 (2 3 4 5))
```

define-public is similar to define but it also adds *name* to the list of exported bindings of the current module.

7.19 Statprof

(statprof) is a fairly simple statistical profiler for Guile.

A simple use of statprof would look like this:

```
(statprof-reset 0 50000 #t)
(statprof-start)
(do-something)
(statprof-stop)
(statprof-display)
```

This would reset statprof, clearing all accumulated statistics, then start profiling, run some code, stop profiling, and finally display a gprof flat-style table of statistics which will look something like this:

```
  %    cumulative    self              self     total
 time   seconds     seconds   calls   ms/call  ms/call  name
35.29     0.23        0.23     2002     0.11     0.11    -
23.53     0.15        0.15     2001     0.08     0.08    positive?
23.53     0.15        0.15     2000     0.08     0.08    +
11.76     0.23        0.08     2000     0.04     0.11    do-nothing
 5.88     0.64        0.04     2001     0.02     0.32    loop
 0.00     0.15        0.00        1     0.00   150.59    do-something
 ...
```

All of the numerical data with the exception of the calls column is statistically approximate. In the following column descriptions, and in all of statprof, "time" refers to execution time (both user and system), not wall clock time.

% time   The percent of the time spent inside the procedure itself (not counting children).

cumulative seconds
          The total number of seconds spent in the procedure, including children.

self seconds
          The total number of seconds spent in the procedure itself (not counting children).

calls   The total number of times the procedure was called.

self ms/call
          The average time taken by the procedure itself on each call, in ms.

total ms/call
          The average time taken by each call to the procedure, including time spent in child functions.

name   The name of the procedure.

The profiler uses `eq?` and the procedure object itself to identify the procedures, so it won't confuse different procedures with the same name. They will show up as two different rows in the output.

Right now the profiler is quite simplistic. I cannot provide call-graphs or other higher level information. What you see in the table is pretty much all there is. Patches are welcome :-)

7.20 Implementation notes

The profiler works by setting the unix profiling signal `ITIMER_PROF` to go off after the interval you define in the call to `statprof-reset`. When the signal fires, a sampling routine is run which looks at the current procedure that's executing, and then crawls up the stack, and for each procedure encountered, increments that procedure's sample count. Note that if a procedure is encountered multiple times on a given stack, it is only counted once. After the sampling is complete, the profiler resets profiling timer to fire again after the appropriate interval.

Meanwhile, the profiler keeps track, via `get-internal-run-time`, how much CPU time (system and user – which is also what `ITIMER_PROF` tracks), has elapsed while code has been executing within a statprof-start/stop block.

The profiler also tries to avoid counting or timing its own code as much as possible.

7.21 Usage

`statprof-active?`   [Function]
  Returns `#t` if `statprof-start` has been called more times than `statprof-stop`, `#f` otherwise.

`statprof-start`   [Function]
  Start the profiler.

`statprof-stop`   [Function]
  Stop the profiler.

`statprof-reset` *sample-seconds sample-microseconds count-calls?*   [Function]
   [*full-stacks?*]
  Reset the statprof sampler interval to *sample-seconds* and *sample-microseconds*. If *count-calls?* is true, arrange to instrument procedure calls as well as collecting statistical profiling data. If *full-stacks?* is true, collect all sampled stacks into a list for later analysis.

  Enables traps and debugging as necessary.

`statprof-accumulated-time`   [Function]
  Returns the time accumulated during the last statprof run.

`statprof-sample-count`   [Function]
  Returns the number of samples taken during the last statprof run.

`statprof-fold-call-data` *proc init*   [Function]

Fold *proc* over the call-data accumulated by statprof. Cannot be called while statprof is active. *proc* should take two arguments, (`call-data prior-result`).

Note that a given proc-name may appear multiple times, but if it does, it represents different functions with the same name.

`statprof-proc-call-data` *proc*   [Function]

Returns the call-data associated with *proc*, or `#f` if none is available.

`statprof-call-data-name` *cd*   [Function]

`statprof-call-data-calls` *cd*   [Function]

`statprof-call-data-cum-samples` *cd*   [Function]

`statprof-call-data-self-samples` *cd*   [Function]

`statprof-call-data->stats` *call-data*   [Function]

Returns an object of type `statprof-stats`.

`statprof-stats-proc-name` *stats*   [Function]

`statprof-stats-%-time-in-proc` *stats*   [Function]

`statprof-stats-cum-secs-in-proc` *stats*   [Function]

`statprof-stats-self-secs-in-proc` *stats*   [Function]

`statprof-stats-calls` *stats*   [Function]

`statprof-stats-self-secs-per-call` *stats*   [Function]

`statprof-stats-cum-secs-per-call` *stats*   [Function]

`statprof-display` . _   [Function]

Displays a gprof-like summary of the statistics collected. Unless an optional *port* argument is passed, uses the current output port.

`statprof-display-anomolies`   [Function]

A sanity check that attempts to detect anomolies in statprof's statistics.

`statprof-fetch-stacks`   [Function]

Returns a list of stacks, as they were captured since the last call to `statprof-reset`.

Note that stacks are only collected if the *full-stacks?* argument to `statprof-reset` is true.

`statprof-fetch-call-tree`   [Function]

Return a call tree for the previous statprof run.

The return value is a list of nodes, each of which is of the type:
@@code
 node ::= (@@var@{proc@} @@var@{count@} . @@var@{nodes@})
@@end code

`statprof` *thunk* [*#:loop*] [*#:hz*] [*#:count-calls?*] [*#:full-stacks?*]   [Function]
> Profiles the execution of *thunk*.
>
> The stack will be sampled *hz* times per second, and the thunk itself will be called *loop* times.
>
> If *count-calls?* is true, all procedure calls will be recorded. This operation is somewhat expensive.
>
> If *full-stacks?* is true, at each sample, statprof will store away the whole call tree, for later analysis. Use `statprof-fetch-stacks` or `statprof-fetch-call-tree` to retrieve the last-stored stacks.

`with-statprof` *args*   [Special Form]
> Profiles the expressions in its body.
>
> Keyword arguments:
>
> `#:loop`   Execute the body *loop* number of times, or `#f` for no looping
>   default: `#f`
>
> `#:hz`   Sampling rate
>   default: 20
>
> `#:count-calls?`
>   Whether to instrument each function call (expensive)
>   default: `#f`
>
> `#:full-stacks?`
>   Whether to collect away all sampled stacks into a list
>   default: `#f`

`gcprof` *thunk* [*#:loop*] [*#:full-stacks?*]   [Function]
> Do an allocation profile of the execution of *thunk*.
>
> The stack will be sampled soon after every garbage collection, yielding an approximate idea of what is causing allocation in your program.
>
> Since GC does not occur very frequently, you may need to use the *loop* parameter, to cause *thunk* to be called *loop* times.
>
> If *full-stacks?* is true, at each sample, statprof will store away the whole call tree, for later analysis. Use `statprof-fetch-stacks` or `statprof-fetch-call-tree` to retrieve the last-stored stacks.

7.22 SXML

SXML is a native representation of XML in terms of standard Scheme data types: lists, symbols, and strings. For example, the simple XML fragment:

```
<parrot type="African Grey"><name>Alfie</name></parrot>
```

may be represented with the following SXML:

```
(parrot (@ (type "African Grey")) (name "Alfie"))
```

SXML is very general, and is capable of representing all of XML. Formally, this means that SXML is a conforming implementation of the http://www.w3.org/TR/xml-infoset/ standard.

Guile includes several facilities for working with XML and SXML: parsers, serializers, and transformers.

7.22.1 SXML Overview

(This section needs to be written; volunteers welcome.)

7.22.2 Reading and Writing XML

The (sxml simple) module presents a basic interface for parsing XML from a port into the Scheme SXML format, and for serializing it back to text.

```
(use-modules (sxml simple))
```

xml->sxml [*string-or-port*] [#:*namespaces*='()]   [Scheme Procedure]
      [#:*declare-namespaces?*=#t] [#:*trim-whitespace?*=#f] [#:*entities*='()]
      [#:*default-entity-handler*=#f] [#:*doctype-handler*=#f]
      Use SSAX to parse an XML document into SXML. Takes one optional argument, *string-or-port*, which defaults to the current input port. Returns the resulting SXML document. If *string-or-port* is a port, it will be left pointing at the next available character in the port.

As is normal in SXML, XML elements parse as tagged lists. Attributes, if any, are placed after the tag, within an @ element. The root of the resulting XML will be contained in a special tag, *TOP*. This tag will contain the root element of the XML, but also any prior processing instructions.

```
(xml->sxml "<foo/>")
⇒ (*TOP* (foo))
(xml->sxml "<foo>text</foo>")
⇒ (*TOP* (foo "text"))
(xml->sxml "<foo kind=\"bar\">text</foo>")
⇒ (*TOP* (foo (@ (kind "bar")) "text"))
(xml->sxml "<?xml version=\"1.0\"?><foo/>")
⇒ (*TOP* (*PI* xml "version=\"1.0\"") (foo))
```

All namespaces in the XML document must be declared, via xmlns attributes. SXML elements built from non-default namespaces will have their tags prefixed with their URI. Users can specify custom prefixes for certain namespaces with the #:namespaces keyword argument to xml->sxml.

```
(xml->sxml "<foo xmlns=\"http://example.org/ns1\">text</foo>")
⇒ (*TOP* (http://example.org/ns1:foo "text"))
(xml->sxml "<foo xmlns=\"http://example.org/ns1\">text</foo>"
           #:namespaces '((ns1 . "http://example.org/ns1")))
⇒ (*TOP* (ns1:foo "text"))
(xml->sxml "<foo xmlns:bar=\"http://example.org/ns2\"><bar:baz/></foo>"
           #:namespaces '((ns2 . "http://example.org/ns2")))
⇒ (*TOP* (foo (ns2:baz)))
```

By default, namespaces passed to xml->sxml are treated as if they were declared on the root element. Passing a false #:declare-namespaces? argument will disable this behavior, requiring in-document declarations of namespaces before use..

```
(xml->sxml "<foo><ns2:baz/></foo>"
           #:namespaces '((ns2 . "http://example.org/ns2")))
⇒ (*TOP* (foo (ns2:baz)))
(xml->sxml "<foo><ns2:baz/></foo>"
           #:namespaces '((ns2 . "http://example.org/ns2"))
           #:declare-namespaces? #f)
⇒ error: undeclared namespace: 'bar'
```

By default, all whitespace in XML is significant. Passing the #:trim-whitespace? keyword argument to xml->sxml will trim whitespace in front, behind and between elements, treating it as "unsignificant". Whitespace in text fragments is left alone.

```
(xml->sxml "<foo>\n<bar> Alfie the parrot! </bar>\n</foo>")
⇒ (*TOP* (foo "\n" (bar " Alfie the parrot! ") "\n"))
(xml->sxml "<foo>\n<bar> Alfie the parrot! </bar>\n</foo>"
           #:trim-whitespace? #t)
⇒ (*TOP* (foo (bar " Alfie the parrot! ")))
```

Parsed entities may be declared with the #:entities keyword argument, or handled with the #:default-entity-handler. By default, only the standard <, >, &, ' and " entities are defined, as well as the &#N; and &#xN; (decimal and hexadecimal) numeric character entities.

```
(xml->sxml "<foo>&amp;</foo>")
⇒ (*TOP* (foo "&"))
(xml->sxml "<foo> </foo>")
⇒ error: undefined entity: nbsp
(xml->sxml "<foo> </foo>")
⇒ (*TOP* (foo "\xa0"))
(xml->sxml "<foo> </foo>"
           #:entities '((nbsp . "\xa0")))
⇒ (*TOP* (foo "\xa0"))
(xml->sxml "<foo>  &foo;</foo>"
           #:default-entity-handler
           (lambda (port name)
             (case name
               ((nbsp) "\xa0")
               (else
                (format (current-warning-port)
                        "~a:~a:~a: undefined entity: ~a\n"
                        (or (port-filename port) "<unknown file>")
                        (port-line port) (port-column port)
                        name)
                (symbol->string name)))))
⊣ <unknown file>:0:17: undefined entity: foo
⇒ (*TOP* (foo "\xa0 foo"))
```

By default, xml->sxml skips over the <!DOCTYPE> declaration, if any. This behavior can be overridden with the #:doctype-handler argument, which should be a procedure of three arguments: the *docname* (a symbol), *systemid* (a string), and the internal doctype subset (as a string or #f if not present).

The handler should return keyword arguments as multiple values, as if it were calling its continuation with keyword arguments. The continuation accepts the `#:entities` and `#:namespaces` keyword arguments, in the same format that `xml->sxml` itself takes. These entities and namespaces will be prepended to those given to the `xml->sxml` invocation.

```
(define (handle-foo docname systemid internal-subset)
  (case docname
    ((foo)
     (values #:entities '((greets . "<i>Hello, world!</i>"))))
    (else
     (values))))

(xml->sxml "<!DOCTYPE foo><p>&greets;</p>"
           #:doctype-handler handle-foo)
⇒ (*TOP* (p (i "Hello, world!")))
```

If the document has no doctype declaration, the *doctype-handler* is invoked with `#f` for the three arguments.

In the future, the continuation may accept other keyword arguments, for example to validate the parsed SXML against the doctype.

sxml->xml *tree [port]*   [Scheme Procedure]
> Serialize the SXML tree *tree* as XML. The output will be written to the current output port, unless the optional argument *port* is present.

sxml->string *sxml*   [Scheme Procedure]
> Detag an sxml tree *sxml* into a string. Does not perform any formatting.

7.22.3 SSAX: A Functional XML Parsing Toolkit

Guile's XML parser is based on Oleg Kiselyov's powerful XML parsing toolkit, SSAX.

7.22.3.1 History

Back in the 1990s, when the world was young again and XML was the solution to all of its problems, there were basically two kinds of XML parsers out there: DOM parsers and SAX parsers.

A DOM parser reads through an entire XML document, building up a tree of "DOM objects" representing the document structure. They are very easy to use, but sometimes you don't actually want all of the information in a document; building an object tree is not necessary if all you want to do is to count word frequencies in a document, for example.

SAX parsers were created to give the programmer more control on the parsing process. A programmer gives the SAX parser a number of "callbacks": functions that will be called on various features of the XML stream as they are encountered. SAX parsers are more efficient, but much harder to user, as users typically have to manually maintain a stack of open elements.

Kiselyov realized that the SAX programming model could be made much simpler if the callbacks were formulated not as a linear fold across the features of the XML stream, but as a *tree fold* over the structure implicit in the XML. In this way, the user has a very convenient, functional-style interface that can still generate optimal parsers.

The `xml->sxml` interface from the (`sxml simple`) module is a DOM-style parser built
using SSAX, though it returns SXML instead of DOM objects.

7.22.3.2 Implementation

(`sxml ssax`) is a package of low-to-high level lexing and parsing procedures that can be
combined to yield a SAX, a DOM, a validating parser, or a parser intended for a particular
document type. The procedures in the package can be used separately to tokenize or
parse various pieces of XML documents. The package supports XML Namespaces, internal
and external parsed entities, user-controlled handling of whitespace, and validation. This
module therefore is intended to be a framework, a set of "Lego blocks" you can use to build
a parser following any discipline and performing validation to any degree. As an example
of the parser construction, this file includes a semi-validating SXML parser.

SSAX has a "sequential" feel of SAX yet a "functional style" of DOM. Like a SAX
parser, the framework scans the document only once and permits incremental processing.
An application that handles document elements in order can run as efficiently as possible.
Unlike a SAX parser, the framework does not require an application register stateful callbacks and surrender control to the parser. Rather, it is the application that can drive the
framework – calling its functions to get the current lexical or syntax element. These functions do not maintain or mutate any state save the input port. Therefore, the framework
permits parsing of XML in a pure functional style, with the input port being a monad (or
a linear, read-once parameter).

Besides the *port*, there is another monad – *seed*. Most of the middle- and high-level
parsers are single-threaded through the *seed*. The functions of this framework do not
process or affect the *seed* in any way: they simply pass it around as an instance of an
opaque datatype. User functions, on the other hand, can use the seed to maintain user's
state, to accumulate parsing results, etc. A user can freely mix his own functions with those
of the framework. On the other hand, the user may wish to instantiate a high-level parser:
`SSAX:make-elem-parser` or `SSAX:make-parser`. In the latter case, the user must provide
functions of specific signatures, which are called at predictable moments during the parsing:
to handle character data, element data, or processing instructions (PI). The functions are
always given the *seed*, among other parameters, and must return the new *seed*.

From a functional point of view, XML parsing is a combined pre-post-order traversal of
a "tree" that is the XML document itself. This down-and-up traversal tells the user about
an element when its start tag is encountered. The user is notified about the element once
more, after all element's children have been handled. The process of XML parsing therefore
is a fold over the raw XML document. Unlike a fold over trees defined in [1], the parser is
necessarily single-threaded – obviously as elements in a text XML document are laid down
sequentially. The parser therefore is a tree fold that has been transformed to accept an
accumulating parameter [1,2].

Formally, the denotational semantics of the parser can be expressed as

```
    parser:: (Start-tag -> Seed -> Seed) ->
      (Start-tag -> Seed -> Seed -> Seed) ->
      (Char-Data -> Seed -> Seed) ->
      XML-text-fragment -> Seed -> Seed
    parser fdown fup fchar "<elem attrs> content </elem>" seed
      = fup "<elem attrs>" seed
    (parser fdown fup fchar "content" (fdown "<elem attrs>" seed))
```

```
parser fdown fup fchar "char-data content" seed
 = parser fdown fup fchar "content" (fchar "char-data" seed)

parser fdown fup fchar "elem-content content" seed
 = parser fdown fup fchar "content" (
parser fdown fup fchar "elem-content" seed)
```

Compare the last two equations with the left fold

```
fold-left kons elem:list seed = fold-left kons list (kons elem seed)
```

The real parser created by `SSAX:make-parser` is slightly more complicated, to account for processing instructions, entity references, namespaces, processing of document type declaration, etc.

The XML standard document referred to in this module is `http://www.w3.org/TR/1998/REC-xml-19980210.html`

The present file also defines a procedure that parses the text of an XML document or of a separate element into SXML, an S-expression-based model of an XML Information Set. SXML is also an Abstract Syntax Tree of an XML document. SXML is similar but not identical to DOM; SXML is particularly suitable for Scheme-based XML/HTML authoring, SXPath queries, and tree transformations. See SXML.html for more details. SXML is a term implementation of evaluation of the XML document [3]. The other implementation is context-passing.

The present frameworks fully supports the XML Namespaces Recommendation: `http://www.w3.org/TR/REC-xml-names/`.

Other links:

[1]   Jeremy Gibbons, Geraint Jones, "The Under-appreciated Unfold," Proc. ICFP'98, 1998, pp. 273-279.

[2]   Richard S. Bird, The promotion and accumulation strategies in transformational programming, ACM Trans. Progr. Lang. Systems, 6(4):487-504, October 1984.

[3]   Ralf Hinze, "Deriving Backtracking Monad Transformers," Functional Pearl. Proc ICFP'00, pp. 186-197.

7.22.3.3 Usage

`current-ssax-error-port`   [Scheme Procedure]

`with-ssax-error-to-port` *port thunk*   [Scheme Procedure]

`xml-token?` _   [Scheme Procedure]
     -- Scheme Procedure: pair? x
          Return '#t' if X is a pair; otherwise return '#f'.

`xml-token-kind` *token*   [Scheme Syntax]

`xml-token-head` *token*   [Scheme Syntax]

`make-empty-attlist`   [Scheme Procedure] `attlist-add` *attlist name-value*   [Scheme Procedure]

`attlist-null?` *x*   [Scheme Procedure]
> Return `#t` if *x* is the empty list, else `#f`.

`attlist-remove-top` *attlist*   [Scheme Procedure]

`attlist->alist` *attlist*   [Scheme Procedure]

`attlist-fold` *kons knil lis1*   [Scheme Procedure]

`define-parsed-entity!` *entity str*   [Scheme Procedure]
> Define a new parsed entity. *entity* should be a symbol.
>
> Instances of &*entity*; in XML text will be replaced with the string *str*, which will then be parsed.

`reset-parsed-entity-definitions!`   [Scheme Procedure]
> Restore the set of parsed entity definitions to its initial state.

`ssax:uri-string->symbol` *uri-str*   [Scheme Procedure]

`ssax:skip-internal-dtd` *port*   [Scheme Procedure]

`ssax:read-pi-body-as-string` *port*   [Scheme Procedure]

`ssax:reverse-collect-str-drop-ws` *fragments*   [Scheme Procedure]

`ssax:read-markup-token` *port*   [Scheme Procedure]

`ssax:read-cdata-body` *port str-handler seed*   [Scheme Procedure]

`ssax:read-char-ref` *port*   [Scheme Procedure]

`ssax:read-attributes` *port entities*   [Scheme Procedure]

`ssax:complete-start-tag` *tag-head port elems entities*   [Scheme Procedure]
> *namespaces*

`ssax:read-external-id` *port*   [Scheme Procedure]

`ssax:read-char-data` *port expect-eof? str-handler seed*   [Scheme Procedure]

`ssax:xml->sxml` *port namespace-prefix-assig*   [Scheme Procedure]

`ssax:make-parser` . *kw-val-pairs*   [Scheme Syntax]

`ssax:make-pi-parser` *orig-handlers*   [Scheme Syntax]

`ssax:make-elem-parser` *my-new-level-seed my-finish-element*   [Scheme Syntax]
> *my-char-data-handler my-pi-handlers*

7.22.4 Transforming SXML

7.22.4.1 Overview

SXML expression tree transformers

Pre-Post-order traversal of a tree and creation of a new tree

```
pre-post-order:: <tree> x <bindings> -> <new-tree>
```

where

```
<bindings> ::= (<binding> ...)
<binding> ::= (<trigger-symbol> *preorder* . <handler>) |
              (<trigger-symbol> *macro* . <handler>) |
    (<trigger-symbol> <new-bindings> . <handler>) |
    (<trigger-symbol> . <handler>)
    <trigger-symbol> ::= XMLname | *text* | *default*
    <handler> :: <trigger-symbol> x [<tree>] -> <new-tree>
```

The pre-post-order function visits the nodes and nodelists pre-post-order (depth-first). For each <Node> of the form (*name* <Node> ...), it looks up an association with the given *name* among its <*bindings*>. If failed, pre-post-order tries to locate a *default* binding. It's an error if the latter attempt fails as well. Having found a binding, the pre-post-order function first checks to see if the binding is of the form

```
(<trigger-symbol> *preorder* . <handler>)
```

If it is, the handler is 'applied' to the current node. Otherwise, the pre-post-order function first calls itself recursively for each child of the current node, with <*new-bindings*> prepended to the <*bindings*> in effect. The result of these calls is passed to the <*handler*> (along with the head of the current <*Node*>). To be more precise, the handler is _applied_ to the head of the current node and its processed children. The result of the handler, which should also be a <tree>, replaces the current <*Node*>. If the current <*Node*> is a text string or other atom, a special binding with a symbol *text* is looked up.

A binding can also be of a form

```
(<trigger-symbol> *macro* . <handler>)
```

This is equivalent to *preorder* described above. However, the result is re-processed again, with the current stylesheet.

7.22.4.2 Usage

SRV:**send-reply** . *fragments*   [Scheme Procedure]
> Output the *fragments* to the current output port.
>
> The fragments are a list of strings, characters, numbers, thunks, #f, #t – and other fragments. The function traverses the tree depth-first, writes out strings and characters, executes thunks, and ignores #f and '(). The function returns #t if anything was written at all; otherwise the result is #f If #t occurs among the fragments, it is not written out but causes the result of SRV:send-reply to be #t.

foldts *fdown fup fhere seed tree*   [Scheme Procedure]

post-order *tree bindings*   [Scheme Procedure]

pre-post-order *tree bindings*   [Scheme Procedure]

replace-range *beg-pred end-pred forest*   [Scheme Procedure]

7.22.5 SXML Tree Fold

7.22.5.1 Overview

(sxml fold) defines a number of variants of the *fold* algorithm for use in transforming SXML trees. Additionally it defines the layout operator, fold-layout, which might be described as a context-passing variant of SSAX's pre-post-order.

7.22.5.2 Usage

foldt *fup fhere tree*   [Scheme Procedure]
> The standard multithreaded tree fold.
>
> *fup* is of type [a] -> a. *fhere* is of type object -> a.

foldts *fdown fup fhere seed tree*   [Scheme Procedure]
> The single-threaded tree fold originally defined in SSAX. See Section 7.22.3 [SSAX], page 700, for more information.

foldts* *fdown fup fhere seed tree*   [Scheme Procedure]
> A variant of foldts that allows pre-order tree rewrites. Originally defined in Andy Wingo's 2007 paper, *Applications of fold to XML transformation*.

fold-values *proc list . seeds*   [Scheme Procedure]
> A variant of fold that allows multi-valued seeds. Note that the order of the arguments differs from that of fold. See Section 7.5.3.5 [SRFI-1 Fold and Map], page 556.

foldts*-values *fdown fup fhere tree . seeds*   [Scheme Procedure]
> A variant of foldts* that allows multi-valued seeds. Originally defined in Andy Wingo's 2007 paper, *Applications of fold to XML transformation*.

fold-layout *tree bindings params layout stylesheet*   [Scheme Procedure]
> A traversal combinator in the spirit of pre-post-order. See Section 7.22.4 [Transforming SXML], page 703.
>
> fold-layout was originally presented in Andy Wingo's 2007 paper, *Applications of fold to XML transformation*.
>
> ```
>         bindings := (<binding>...)
>         binding  := (<tag> <bandler-pair>...)
>                   | (*default* . <post-handler>)
>                   | (*text* . <text-handler>)
>         tag        := <symbol>
>         handler-pair := (pre-layout . <pre-layout-handler>)
>                       | (post . <post-handler>)
>                       | (bindings . <bindings>)
>                       | (pre . <pre-handler>)
>                       | (macro . <macro-handler>)
> ```
>
> *pre-layout-handler*
>
> > A function of three arguments:
> >
> > | | |
> > |---|---|
> > | *kids* | the kids of the current node, before traversal |
> > | *params* | the params of the current node |

layout   the layout coming into this node

pre-layout-handler is expected to use this information to return a layout to pass to the kids. The default implementation returns the layout given in the arguments.

post-handler

A function of five arguments:

tag   the current tag being processed

params   the params of the current node

layout   the layout coming into the current node, before any kids were processed

klayout   the layout after processing all of the children

kids   the already-processed child nodes

post-handler should return two values, the layout to pass to the next node and the final tree.

text-handler

text-handler is a function of three arguments:

text   the string

params   the current params

layout   the current layout

text-handler should return two values, the layout to pass to the next node and the value to which the string should transform.

7.22.6 SXPath

7.22.6.1 Overview

SXPath: SXML Query Language

SXPath is a query language for SXML, an instance of XML Information set (Infoset) in the form of s-expressions. See (sxml ssax) for the definition of SXML and more details. SXPath is also a translation into Scheme of an XML Path Language, XPath. XPath and SXPath describe means of selecting a set of Infoset's items or their properties.

To facilitate queries, XPath maps the XML Infoset into an explicit tree, and introduces important notions of a location path and a current, context node. A location path denotes a selection of a set of nodes relative to a context node. Any XPath tree has a distinguished, root node – which serves as the context node for absolute location paths. Location path is recursively defined as a location step joined with a location path. A location step is a simple query of the database relative to a context node. A step may include expressions that further filter the selected set. Each node in the resulting set is used as a context node for the adjoining location path. The result of the step is a union of the sets returned by the latter location paths.

The SXML representation of the XML Infoset (see SSAX.scm) is rather suitable for querying as it is. Bowing to the XPath specification, we will refer to SXML information items as 'Nodes':

```
<Node> ::= <Element> | <attributes-coll> | <attrib>
      | "text string" | <PI>
```

This production can also be described as

```
<Node> ::= (name . <Nodeset>) | "text string"
```

An (ordered) set of nodes is just a list of the constituent nodes:

```
<Nodeset> ::= (<Node> ...)
```

Nodesets, and Nodes other than text strings are both lists. A <Nodeset> however is either an empty list, or a list whose head is not a symbol. A symbol at the head of a node is either an XML name (in which case it's a tag of an XML element), or an administrative name such as '@'. This uniform list representation makes processing rather simple and elegant, while avoiding confusion. The multi-branch tree structure formed by the mutually-recursive datatypes <Node> and <Nodeset> lends itself well to processing by functional languages.

A location path is in fact a composite query over an XPath tree or its branch. A singe step is a combination of a projection, selection or a transitive closure. Multiple steps are combined via join and union operations. This insight allows us to *elegantly* implement XPath as a sequence of projection and filtering primitives – converters – joined by *combinators*. Each converter takes a node and returns a nodeset which is the result of the corresponding query relative to that node. A converter can also be called on a set of nodes. In that case it returns a union of the corresponding queries over each node in the set. The union is easily implemented as a list append operation as all nodes in a SXML tree are considered distinct, by XPath conventions. We also preserve the order of the members in the union. Query combinators are high-order functions: they take converter(s) (which is a Node|Nodeset -> Nodeset function) and compose or otherwise combine them. We will be concerned with only relative location paths [XPath]: an absolute location path is a relative path applied to the root node.

Similarly to XPath, SXPath defines full and abbreviated notations for location paths. In both cases, the abbreviated notation can be mechanically expanded into the full form by simple rewriting rules. In case of SXPath the corresponding rules are given as comments to a sxpath function, below. The regression test suite at the end of this file shows a representative sample of SXPaths in both notations, juxtaposed with the corresponding XPath expressions. Most of the samples are borrowed literally from the XPath specification, while the others are adjusted for our running example, tree1.

7.22.6.2 Usage

nodeset? *x*   [Scheme Procedure]

node-typeof? *crit*   [Scheme Procedure]

node-eq? *other*   [Scheme Procedure]

node-equal? *other*   [Scheme Procedure]

node-pos *n*   [Scheme Procedure]

filter *pred?*   [Scheme Procedure]
    -- Scheme Procedure: filter pred list
        Return all the elements of 2nd arg LIST that satisfy predicate
        PRED. The list is not disordered - elements that appear in the
        result list occur in the same order as they occur in the argument
        list. The returned list may share a common tail with the argument
        list. The dynamic order in which the various applications of pred
        are made is not specified.

        (filter even? '(0 7 8 8 43 -4)) => (0 8 8 -4)

take-until *pred?*   [Scheme Procedure]

take-after *pred?*   [Scheme Procedure]

map-union *proc lst*   [Scheme Procedure]

node-reverse *node-or-nodeset*   [Scheme Procedure]

node-trace *title*   [Scheme Procedure]

select-kids *test-pred?*   [Scheme Procedure]

node-self *pred?*   [Scheme Procedure]
    -- Scheme Procedure: filter pred list
        Return all the elements of 2nd arg LIST that satisfy predicate
        PRED. The list is not disordered - elements that appear in the
        result list occur in the same order as they occur in the argument
        list. The returned list may share a common tail with the argument
        list. The dynamic order in which the various applications of pred
        are made is not specified.

        (filter even? '(0 7 8 8 43 -4)) => (0 8 8 -4)

node-join . *selectors*   [Scheme Procedure]

node-reduce . *converters*   [Scheme Procedure]

node-or . *converters*   [Scheme Procedure]

node-closure *test-pred?*   [Scheme Procedure]

node-parent *rootnode*   [Scheme Procedure]

sxpath *path*   [Scheme Procedure]

7.22.7 (sxml ssax input-parse)

7.22.7.1 Overview

A simple lexer.

The procedures in this module surprisingly often suffice to parse an input stream. They either skip, or build and return tokens, according to inclusion or delimiting semantics. The list of characters to expect, include, or to break at may vary from one invocation of a function to another. This allows the functions to easily parse even context-sensitive languages.

EOF is generally frowned on, and thrown up upon if encountered. Exceptions are mentioned specifically. The list of expected characters (characters to skip until, or break-characters) may include an EOF "character", which is to be coded as the symbol, *eof*.

The input stream to parse is specified as a *port*, which is usually the last (and optional) argument. It defaults to the current input port if omitted.

If the parser encounters an error, it will throw an exception to the key parser-error. The arguments will be of the form (*port message specialising-msg*).

The first argument is a port, which typically points to the offending character or its neighborhood. You can then use port-column and port-line to query the current position. *message* is the description of the error. Other arguments supply more details about the problem.

7.22.7.2 Usage

peek-next-char [*port*]   [Scheme Procedure]

assert-curr-char *expected-chars comment* [*port*]   [Scheme Procedure]

skip-until *arg* [*port*]   [Scheme Procedure]

skip-while *skip-chars* [*port*]   [Scheme Procedure]

next-token *prefix-skipped-chars break-chars* [*comment*] [*port*] [Scheme Procedure]

next-token-of *incl-list/pred* [*port*]   [Scheme Procedure]

read-text-line [*port*]   [Scheme Procedure]

read-string *n* [*port*]   [Scheme Procedure]

find-string-from-port? _ _ _ _   [Scheme Procedure]
  Looks for *str* in <input-port>, optionally within the first *max-no-char* characters.

7.22.8 (sxml apply-templates)

7.22.8.1 Overview

Pre-order traversal of a tree and creation of a new tree:

```
apply-templates:: tree x <templates> -> <new-tree>
```

where

```
<templates> ::= (<template> ...)
<template>  ::= (<node-test> <node-test> ... <node-test> . <handler>)
<node-test> ::= an argument to node-typeof? above
<handler>   ::= <tree> -> <new-tree>
```

This procedure does a *normal*, pre-order traversal of an SXML tree. It walks the tree, checking at each node against the list of matching templates.

If the match is found (which must be unique, i.e., unambiguous), the corresponding handler is invoked and given the current node as an argument. The result from the handler, which must be a `<tree>`, takes place of the current node in the resulting tree. The name of the function is not accidental: it resembles rather closely an `apply-templates` function of XSLT.

7.22.8.2 Usage

`apply-templates` *tree templates*   [Scheme Procedure]

7.23 Texinfo Processing

7.23.1 (texinfo)

7.23.1.1 Overview

Texinfo processing in scheme

This module parses texinfo into SXML. TeX will always be the processor of choice for print output, of course. However, although `makeinfo` works well for info, its output in other formats is not very customizable, and the program is not extensible as a whole. This module aims to provide an extensible framework for texinfo processing that integrates texinfo into the constellation of SXML processing tools.

Notes on the SXML vocabulary

Consider the following texinfo fragment:

```
@deffn Primitive set-car! pair value
This function...
@end deffn
```

Logically, the category (Primitive), name (set-car!), and arguments (pair value) are "attributes" of the deffn, with the description as the content. However, texinfo allows for @-commands within the arguments to an environment, like `@deffn`, which means that texinfo "attributes" are PCDATA. XML attributes, on the other hand, are CDATA. For this reason, "attributes" of texinfo @-commands are called "arguments", and are grouped under the special element, '%'.

Because '%' is not a valid NCName, stexinfo is a superset of SXML. In the interests of interoperability, this module provides a conversion function to replace the '%' with 'texinfo-arguments'.

7.23.1.2 Usage

`call-with-file-and-dir` *filename proc*   [Function]
> Call the one-argument procedure *proc* with an input port that reads from *filename*. During the dynamic extent of *proc*'s execution, the current directory will be `(dirname filename)`. This is useful for parsing documents that can include files by relative path name.

`texi-command-specs`   [Variable]

`texi-command-depth` *command max-depth*   [Function]

> Given the texinfo command *command*, return its nesting level, or `#f` if it nests too
> deep for *max-depth*.
>
> Examples:
>
> | | |
> |---|---|
> | `(texi-command-depth 'chapter 4)` | $\Rightarrow$ 1 |
> | `(texi-command-depth 'top 4)` | $\Rightarrow$ 0 |
> | `(texi-command-depth 'subsection 4)` | $\Rightarrow$ 3 |
> | `(texi-command-depth 'appendixsubsec 4)` | $\Rightarrow$ 3 |
> | `(texi-command-depth 'subsection 2)` | $\Rightarrow$ `#f` |

`texi-fragment->stexi` *string-or-port*   [Function]

> Parse the texinfo commands in *string-or-port*, and return the resultant stexi tree.
> The head of the tree will be the special command, `*fragment*`.

`texi->stexi` *port*   [Function]

> Read a full texinfo document from *port* and return the parsed stexi tree. The parsing
> will start at the `@settitle` and end at `@bye` or EOF.

`stexi->sxml` *tree*   [Function]

> Transform the stexi tree *tree* into sxml. This involves replacing the `%` element that
> keeps the texinfo arguments with an element for each argument.
>
> FIXME: right now it just changes `%` to `texinfo-arguments` – that doesn't hang with
> the idea of making a dtd at some point

7.23.2 (texinfo docbook)

7.23.2.1 Overview

This module exports procedures for transforming a limited subset of the SXML representation of docbook into stexi. It is not complete by any means. The intention is to gather a number of routines and stylesheets so that external modules can parse specific subsets of docbook, for example that set generated by certain tools.

7.23.2.2 Usage

`*sdocbook->stexi-rules*`   [Variable]

`*sdocbook-block-commands*`   [Variable]

`sdocbook-flatten` *sdocbook*   [Function]

> "Flatten" a fragment of sdocbook so that block elements do not nest inside each
> other.
>
> Docbook is a nested format, where e.g. a `refsect2` normally appears inside a
> `refsect1`. Logical divisions in the document are represented via the tree topology; a
> `refsect2` element *contains* all of the elements in its section.
>
> On the contrary, texinfo is a flat format, in which sections are marked off by standalone
> section headers like `@subsection`, and block elements do not nest inside each other.
>
> This function takes a nested sdocbook fragment *sdocbook* and flattens all of the
> sections, such that e.g.

```
(refsect1 (refsect2 (para "Hello")))
```

becomes

```
((refsect1) (refsect2) (para "Hello"))
```

Oftentimes (always?) sectioning elements have `<title>` as their first element child; users interested in processing the `refsect*` elements into proper sectioning elements like `chapter` might be interested in `replace-titles` and `filter-empty-elements`. See [replace-titles], page 712, and [filter-empty-elements], page 712.

Returns a nodeset; that is to say, an untagged list of stexi elements. See Section 7.22.6 [SXPath], page 706, for the definition of a nodeset.

filter-empty-elements *sdocbook*   [Function]
Filters out empty elements in an sdocbook nodeset. Mostly useful after running `sdocbook-flatten`.

replace-titles *sdocbook-fragment*   [Function]
Iterate over the sdocbook nodeset *sdocbook-fragment*, transforming contiguous `refsect` and `title` elements into the appropriate texinfo sectioning command. Most useful after having run `sdocbook-flatten`.

For example:

```
(replace-titles '((refsect1) (title "Foo") (para "Bar.")))
    ⇒ '((chapter "Foo") (para "Bar."))
```

7.23.3 (texinfo html)

7.23.3.1 Overview

This module implements transformation from `stexi` to HTML. Note that the output of `stexi->shtml` is actually SXML with the HTML vocabulary. This means that the output can be further processed, and that it must eventually be serialized by `sxml->xml`. See Section 7.22.2 [Reading and Writing XML], page 698.

References (i.e., the `@ref` family of commands) are resolved by a *ref-resolver*. See [texinfo html add-ref-resolver!], page 712.

7.23.3.2 Usage

add-ref-resolver! *proc*   [Function]
Add *proc* to the head of the list of ref-resolvers. *proc* will be expected to take the name of a node and the name of a manual and return the URL of the referent, or `#f` to pass control to the next ref-resolver in the list.

The default ref-resolver will return the concatenation of the manual name, `#`, and the node name.

stexi->shtml *tree*   [Function]
Transform the stexi *tree* into shtml, resolving references via ref-resolvers. See the module commentary for more details.

urlify *str*   [Function]

7.23.4 (texinfo indexing)

7.23.4.1 Overview

Given a piece of stexi, return an index of a specified variety.

Note that currently, `stexi-extract-index` doesn't differentiate between different kinds of index entries. That's a bug ;)

7.23.4.2 Usage

`stexi-extract-index` *tree manual-name kind*   [Function]

    Given an stexi tree *tree*, index all of the entries of type *kind*. *kind* can be one of the predefined texinfo indices (`concept`, `variable`, `function`, `key`, `program`, `type`) or one of the special symbols `auto` or `all`. `auto` will scan the stext for a (`printindex`) statement, and `all` will generate an index from all entries, regardless of type.

    The returned index is a list of pairs, the CAR of which is the entry (a string) and the CDR of which is a node name (a string).

7.23.5 (texinfo string-utils)

7.23.5.1 Overview

Module '(`texinfo string-utils`)' provides various string-related functions useful to Guile's texinfo support.

7.23.5.2 Usage

`escape-special-chars` *str special-chars escape-char*   [Function]

    Returns a copy of *str* with all given special characters preceded by the given *escape-char*.

    special-chars can either be a single character, or a string consisting of all the special characters.

```
;; make a string regexp-safe...
(escape-special-chars "***(Example String)***"
                      "[]()/*."
                      #\\)
=> "\\*\\*\\*\\(Example String\\)\\*\\*\\*"

;; also can escape a singe char...
(escape-special-chars "richardt@vzavenue.net"
                      #\@
                      #\@)
=> "richardt@@vzavenue.net"
```

`transform-string` *str match? replace* [*start*] [*end*]   [Function]

    Uses *match?* against each character in *str*, and performs a replacement on each character for which matches are found.

    match? may either be a function, a character, a string, or #t. If *match?* is a function, then it takes a single character as input, and should return '#t' for matches. *match?*

is a character, it is compared to each string character using `char=?`. If *match?* is a string, then any character in that string will be considered a match. `#t` will cause every character to be a match.

If *replace* is a function, it is called with the matched character as an argument, and the returned value is sent to the output string via '`display`'. If *replace* is anything else, it is sent through the output string via '`display`'.

Note that te replacement for the matched characters does not need to be a single character. That is what differentiates this function from '`string-map`', and what makes it useful for applications such as converting '`#\&`' to '"`&amp;`"' in web page text. Some other functions in this module are just wrappers around common uses of '`transform-string`'. Transformations not possible with this function should probably be done with regular expressions.

If *start* and *end* are given, they control which portion of the string undergoes transformation. The entire input string is still output, though. So, if *start* is '5', then the first five characters of *str* will still appear in the returned string.

```
; these two are equivalent...
(transform-string str #\space #\-) ; change all spaces to -'s
(transform-string str (lambda (c) (char=? #\space c)) #\-)
```

expand-tabs *str* [*tab-size*]   [Function]
    Returns a copy of *str* with all tabs expanded to spaces. *tab-size* defaults to 8.

    Assuming tab size of 8, this is equivalent to:

```
(transform-string str #\tab "        ")
```

center-string *str* [*width*] [*chr*] [*rchr*]   [Function]
    Returns a copy of *str* centered in a field of *width* characters. Any needed padding is done by character *chr*, which defaults to '`#\space`'. If *rchr* is provided, then the padding to the right will use it instead. See the examples below. left and *rchr* on the right. The default *width* is 80. The default *chr* and *rchr* is '`#\space`'. The string is never truncated.

```
(center-string "Richard Todd" 24)
=> "      Richard Todd      "

(center-string " Richard Todd " 24 #\=)
=> "===== Richard Todd ====="

(center-string " Richard Todd " 24 #\< #\>)
=> "<<<<< Richard Todd >>>>>"
```

left-justify-string *str* [*width*] [*chr*]   [Function]
    `left-justify-string str [width chr]`. Returns a copy of *str* padded with *chr* such that it is left justified in a field of *width* characters. The default *width* is 80. Unlike '`string-pad`' from srfi-13, the string is never truncated.

right-justify-string *str* [*width*] [*chr*]   [Function]
    Returns a copy of *str* padded with *chr* such that it is right justified in a field of *width* characters. The default *width* is 80. The default *chr* is '`#\space`'. Unlike '`string-pad`' from srfi-13, the string is never truncated.

`collapse-repeated-chars` *str* [*chr*] [*num*]   [Function]

> Returns a copy of *str* with all repeated instances of *chr* collapsed down to at most *num* instances. The default value for *chr* is '`#\space`', and the default value for *num* is 1.
>
> ```
> (collapse-repeated-chars "H  e  l  l  o")
> => "H e l l o"
> (collapse-repeated-chars "H--e--l--l--o" #\-)
> => "H-e-l-l-o"
> (collapse-repeated-chars "H-e--l---l----o" #\- 2)
> => "H-e--l--l--o"
> ```

`make-text-wrapper` [*#:line-width*] [*#:expand-tabs?*] [*#:tab-width*]   [Function]
        [*#:collapse-whitespace?*] [*#:subsequent-indent*] [*#:initial-indent*]
        [*#:break-long-words?*]

> Returns a procedure that will split a string into lines according to the given parameters.

> `#:line-width`
>
>> This is the target length used when deciding where to wrap lines. Default is 80.

> `#:expand-tabs?`
>
>> Boolean describing whether tabs in the input should be expanded. Default is #t.

> `#:tab-width`
>
>> If tabs are expanded, this will be the number of spaces to which they expand. Default is 8.

> `#:collapse-whitespace?`
>
>> Boolean describing whether the whitespace inside the existing text should be removed or not. Default is #t.
>>
>> If text is already well-formatted, and is just being wrapped to fit in a different width, then set this to '`#f`'. This way, many common text conventions (such as two spaces between sentences) can be preserved if in the original text. If the input text spacing cannot be trusted, then leave this setting at the default, and all repeated whitespace will be collapsed down to a single space.

> `#:initial-indent`
>
>> Defines a string that will be put in front of the first line of wrapped text. Default is the empty string, "".

> `#:subsequent-indent`
>
>> Defines a string that will be put in front of all lines of wrapped text, except the first one. Default is the empty string, "".

> `#:break-long-words?`
>
>> If a single word is too big to fit on a line, this setting tells the wrapper what to do. Defaults to #t, which will break up long words. When set

to #f, the line will be allowed, even though it is longer than the defined
`#:line-width`.

The return value is a procedure of one argument, the input string, which returns a list of strings, where each element of the list is one line.

fill-string *str* . *kwargs*   [Function]

Wraps the text given in string *str* according to the parameters provided in *kwargs*, or the default setting if they are not given. Returns a single string with the wrapped text. Valid keyword arguments are discussed in `make-text-wrapper`.

string->wrapped-lines *str* . *kwargs*   [Function]

`string->wrapped-lines str keywds ....` Wraps the text given in string *str* according to the parameters provided in *keywds*, or the default setting if they are not given. Returns a list of strings representing the formatted lines. Valid keyword arguments are discussed in `make-text-wrapper`.

7.23.6 (texinfo plain-text)

7.23.6.1 Overview

Transformation from stexi to plain-text. Strives to re-create the output from `info`; comes pretty damn close.

7.23.6.2 Usage

stexi->plain-text *tree*   [Function]

Transform *tree* into plain text. Returns a string.

7.23.7 (texinfo serialize)

7.23.7.1 Overview

Serialization of `stexi` to plain texinfo.

7.23.7.2 Usage

stexi->texi *tree*   [Function]

Serialize the stexi *tree* into plain texinfo.

7.23.8 (texinfo reflection)

7.23.8.1 Overview

Routines to generare `stexi` documentation for objects and modules.

Note that in this context, an *object* is just a value associated with a location. It has nothing to do with GOOPS.

7.23.8.2 Usage

module-stexi-documentation *sym-name* [*%docs-resolver*]   [Function]
[*#:docs-resolver*]

Return documentation for the module named *sym-name*. The documentation will be formatted as `stexi` (see Section 7.23.1 [texinfo], page 710).

script-stexi-documentation *scriptpath*   [Function]
> Return documentation for given script. The documentation will be taken from the
> script's commentary, and will be returned in the `stexi` format (see Section 7.23.1
> [texinfo], page 710).

object-stexi-documentation _ [_] [#:force]   [Function]

package-stexi-standard-copying *name version updated years*   [Function]
> *copyright-holder permissions*
> Create a standard texinfo `copying` section.
>
> *years* is a list of years (as integers) in which the modules being documented were
> released. All other arguments are strings.

package-stexi-standard-titlepage *name version updated authors*   [Function]
> Create a standard GNU title page.
>
> *authors* is a list of (`name . email`) pairs. All other arguments are strings.
>
> Here is an example of the usage of this procedure:
>
> ```
> (package-stexi-standard-titlepage
>  "Foolib"
>  "3.2"
>  "26 September 2006"
>  '(("Alyssa P Hacker" . "alyssa@example.com"))
>  '(2004 2005 2006)
>  "Free Software Foundation, Inc."
>  "Standard GPL permissions blurb goes here")
> ```

package-stexi-generic-menu *name entries*   [Function]
> Create a menu from a generic alist of entries, the car of which should be the node
> name, and the cdr the description. As an exception, an entry of `#f` will produce a
> separator.

package-stexi-standard-menu *name modules module-descriptions*   [Function]
> *extra-entries*
> Create a standard top node and menu, suitable for processing by makeinfo.

package-stexi-extended-menu *name module-pairs script-pairs*   [Function]
> *extra-entries*
> Create an "extended" menu, like the standard menu but with a section for scripts.

package-stexi-standard-prologue *name filename category*   [Function]
> *description copying titlepage menu*
> Create a standard prologue, suitable for later serialization to texinfo and .info creation
> with makeinfo.
>
> Returns a list of stexinfo forms suitable for passing to package-stexi-documentation as the prologue. See [texinfo reflection package-stexi-documentation], page 718, [texinfo reflection package-stexi-standard-titlepage], page 717, [texinfo reflection package-stexi-standard-copying], page 717, and [texinfo reflection package-stexi-standard-menu], page 717.

package-stexi-documentation *modules name filename prologue*   [Function]
       epilogue [*#:module-stexi-documentation-args*] [*#:scripts*]
    Create stexi documentation for a *package*, where a package is a set of modules that
    is released together.

    modules is expected to be a list of module names, where a module name is a list
    of symbols. The stexi that is returned will be titled *name* and a texinfo filename of
    filename.

    prologue and *epilogue* are lists of stexi forms that will be spliced into the output
    document before and after the generated modules documentation, respectively. See
    [texinfo reflection package-stexi-standard-prologue], page 717, to create a conventional
    GNU texinfo prologue.

    module-stexi-documentation-args is an optional argument that, if given, will be added
    to the argument list when `module-texi-documentation` is called. For example, it
    might be useful to define a `#:docs-resolver` argument.

package-stexi-documentation-for-include *modules*   [Function]
       module-descriptions [*#:module-stexi-documentation-args*]
    Create stexi documentation for a *package*, where a package is a set of modules that
    is released together.

    modules is expected to be a list of module names, where a module name is a list of
    symbols. Returns an stexinfo fragment.

    Unlike `package-stexi-documentation`, this function simply produces a menu and
    the module documentations instead of producing a full texinfo document. This can
    be useful if you write part of your manual by hand, and just use `@include` to pull in
    the automatically generated parts.

    module-stexi-documentation-args is an optional argument that, if given, will be added
    to the argument list when `module-texi-documentation` is called. For example, it
    might be useful to define a `#:docs-resolver` argument.

8 GOOPS

GOOPS is the object oriented extension to Guile. Its implementation is derived from STk-3.99.3 by Erick Gallesio and version 1.3 of Gregor Kiczales' *Tiny-Clos*. It is very close in spirit to CLOS, the Common Lisp Object System, but is adapted for the Scheme language.

GOOPS is a full object oriented system, with classes, objects, multiple inheritance, and generic functions with multi-method dispatch. Furthermore its implementation relies on a meta object protocol — which means that GOOPS's core operations are themselves defined as methods on relevant classes, and can be customised by overriding or redefining those methods.

To start using GOOPS you first need to import the (oop goops) module. You can do this at the Guile REPL by evaluating:

```
(use-modules (oop goops))
```

8.1 Copyright Notice

The material in this chapter is partly derived from the STk Reference Manual written by Erick Gallesio, whose copyright notice is as follows.

Copyright © 1993-1999 Erick Gallesio - I3S-CNRS/ESSI <eg@unice.fr> Permission to use, copy, modify, distribute,and license this software and its documentation for any purpose is hereby granted, provided that existing copyright notices are retained in all copies and that this notice is included verbatim in any distributions. No written agreement, license, or royalty fee is required for any of the authorized uses. This software is provided "AS IS" without express or implied warranty.

The material has been adapted for use in Guile, with the author's permission.

8.2 Class Definition

A new class is defined with the define-class syntax:

```
(define-class class (superclass ...)
   slot-description ...
   class-option ...)
```

class is the class being defined. The list of *superclasses* specifies which existing classes, if any, to inherit slots and properties from. *Slots* hold per-instance[1] data, for instances of that class — like "fields" or "member variables" in other object oriented systems. Each *slot-description* gives the name of a slot and optionally some "properties" of this slot; for example its initial value, the name of a function which will access its value, and so on. Class options, slot descriptions and inheritance are discussed more below.

define-class *name* (*super* ...) *slot-definition* ... *class-option* ...   [syntax]
    Define a class called *name* that inherits from *supers*, with direct slots defined by *slot-definitions* and *class-options*. The newly created class is bound to the variable name *name* in the current environment.

    Each *slot-definition* is either a symbol that names the slot or a list,

---

[1] Usually — but see also the #:allocation slot option.

```
(slot-name-symbol . slot-options)
```

where *slot-name-symbol* is a symbol and *slot-options* is a list with an even number of elements. The even-numbered elements of *slot-options* (counting from zero) are slot option keywords; the odd-numbered elements are the corresponding values for those keywords.

Each *class-option* is an option keyword and corresponding value.

As an example, let us define a type for representing a complex number in terms of two real numbers.[2] This can be done with the following class definition:

```
(define-class <my-complex> (<number>)
   r i)
```

This binds the variable `<my-complex>` to a new class whose instances will contain two slots. These slots are called `r` and `i` and will hold the real and imaginary parts of a complex number. Note that this class inherits from `<number>`, which is a predefined class.[3]

Slot options are described in the next section. The possible class options are as follows.

#:metaclass *metaclass*   [class option]

> The `#:metaclass` class option specifies the metaclass of the class being defined. *meta-class* must be a class that inherits from `<class>`. For the use of metaclasses, see Section 8.11.1 [Metaobjects and the Metaobject Protocol], page 743 and Section 8.11.2 [Metaclasses], page 745.
>
> If the `#:metaclass` option is absent, GOOPS reuses or constructs a metaclass for the new class by calling `ensure-metaclass` (see Section 8.11.5 [ensure-metaclass], page 747).

#:name *name*   [class option]

> The `#:name` class option specifies the new class's name. This name is used to identify the class whenever related objects - the class itself, its instances and its subclasses - are printed.
>
> If the `#:name` option is absent, GOOPS uses the first argument to `define-class` as the class name.

8.3 Instance Creation and Slot Access

An instance (or object) of a defined class can be created with `make`. `make` takes one mandatory parameter, which is the class of the instance to create, and a list of optional arguments that will be used to initialize the slots of the new instance. For instance the following form

```
(define c (make <my-complex>))
```

creates a new `<my-complex>` object and binds it to the Scheme variable `c`.

make   [generic]
make (*class* `<class>`) *initarg* . . .   [method]

> Create and return a new instance of class *class*, initialized using *initarg* . . . .

---

[2] Of course Guile already provides complex numbers, and `<complex>` is in fact a predefined class in GOOPS; but the definition here is still useful as an example.

[3] `<number>` is the direct superclass of the predefined class `<complex>`; `<complex>` is the superclass of `<real>`, and `<real>` is the superclass of `<integer>`.

In theory, *initarg* ... can have any structure that is understood by whatever methods get applied when the `initialize` generic function is applied to the newly allocated instance.

In practice, specialized `initialize` methods would normally call `(next-method)`, and so eventually the standard GOOPS `initialize` methods are applied. These methods expect *initargs* to be a list with an even number of elements, where even-numbered elements (counting from zero) are keywords and odd-numbered elements are the corresponding values.

GOOPS processes initialization argument keywords automatically for slots whose definition includes the `#:init-keyword` option (see Section 8.4 [init-keyword], page 721). Other keyword value pairs can only be processed by an `initialize` method that is specialized for the new instance's class. Any unprocessed keyword value pairs are ignored.

`make-instance`	[generic]
`make-instance` (*class* <*class*>) *initarg* ...	[method]

> `make-instance` is an alias for `make`.

The slots of the new complex number can be accessed using `slot-ref` and `slot-set!`. `slot-set!` sets the value of an object slot and `slot-ref` retrieves it.

```
(slot-set! c 'r 10)
(slot-set! c 'i 3)
(slot-ref c 'r) ⇒ 10
(slot-ref c 'i) ⇒ 3
```

The (oop goops describe) module provides a `describe` function that is useful for seeing all the slots of an object; it prints the slots and their values to standard output.

```
(describe c)
⊣
#<<my-complex> 401d8638> is an instance of class <my-complex>
Slots are:
     r = 10
     i = 3
```

8.4 Slot Options

When specifying a slot (in a (`define-class` ...) form), various options can be specified in addition to the slot's name. Each option is specified by a keyword. The list of possible keywords is as follows.

`#:init-value` *init-value*	[slot option]
`#:init-form` *init-form*	[slot option]
`#:init-thunk` *init-thunk*	[slot option]
`#:init-keyword` *init-keyword*	[slot option]

> These options provide various ways to specify how to initialize the slot's value at instance creation time.
>
> *init-value* specifies a fixed initial slot value (shared across all new instances of the class).

init-thunk specifies a thunk that will provide a default value for the slot. The thunk is called when a new instance is created and should return the desired initial slot value.

init-form specifies a form that, when evaluated, will return an initial value for the slot. The form is evaluated each time that an instance of the class is created, in the lexical environment of the containing `define-class` expression.

init-keyword specifies a keyword that can be used to pass an initial slot value to `make` when creating a new instance.

Note that, since an `init-value` value is shared across all instances of a class, you should only use it when the initial value is an immutable value, like a constant. If you want to initialize a slot with a fresh, independently mutable value, you should use `init-thunk` or `init-form` instead. Consider the following example.

```
(define-class <chbouib> ()
  (hashtab #:init-value (make-hash-table)))
```

Here only one hash table is created and all instances of `<chbouib>` have their `hashtab` slot refer to it. In order to have each instance of `<chbouib>` refer to a new hash table, you should instead write:

```
(define-class <chbouib> ()
  (hashtab #:init-thunk make-hash-table))
```

or:

```
(define-class <chbouib> ()
  (hashtab #:init-form (make-hash-table)))
```

If more than one of these options is specified for the same slot, the order of precedence, highest first is

- `#:init-keyword`, if *init-keyword* is present in the options passed to `make`
- `#:init-thunk`, `#:init-form` or `#:init-value`.

If the slot definition contains more than one initialization option of the same precedence, the later ones are ignored. If a slot is not initialized at all, its value is unbound.

In general, slots that are shared between more than one instance are only initialized at new instance creation time if the slot value is unbound at that time. However, if the new instance creation specifies a valid init keyword and value for a shared slot, the slot is re-initialized regardless of its previous value.

Note, however, that the power of GOOPS' metaobject protocol means that everything written here may be customized or overridden for particular classes! The slot initializations described here are performed by the least specialized method of the generic function `initialize`, whose signature is

```
(define-method (initialize (object <object>) initargs) ...)
```

The initialization of instances of any given class can be customized by defining a `initialize` method that is specialized for that class, and the author of the specialized method may decide to call `next-method` - which will result in a call to the next less specialized `initialize` method - at any point within the specialized code, or maybe not at all. In general, therefore, the initialization mechanisms described here may be modified or overridden by more specialized code, or may not be supported at all for particular classes.

#:getter *getter*   [slot option]
#:setter *setter*   [slot option]
#:accessor *accessor*   [slot option]

Given an object *obj* with slots named `foo` and `bar`, it is always possible to read and write those slots by calling `slot-ref` and `slot-set!` with the relevant slot name; for example:

```
(slot-ref obj 'foo)
(slot-set! obj 'bar 25)
```

The #:getter, #:setter and #:accessor options, if present, tell GOOPS to create generic function and method definitions that can be used to get and set the slot value more conveniently. *getter* specifies a generic function to which GOOPS will add a method for getting the slot value. *setter* specifies a generic function to which GOOPS will add a method for setting the slot value. *accessor* specifies an accessor to which GOOPS will add methods for both getting and setting the slot value.

So if a class includes a slot definition like this:

```
(c #:getter get-count #:setter set-count #:accessor count)
```

GOOPS defines generic function methods such that the slot value can be referenced using either the getter or the accessor -

```
(let ((current-count (get-count obj))) ...)
(let ((current-count (count obj))) ...)
```

- and set using either the setter or the accessor -

```
(set-count obj (+ 1 current-count))
(set! (count obj) (+ 1 current-count))
```

Note that

- with an accessor, the slot value is set using the generalized `set!` syntax

- in practice, it is unusual for a slot to use all three of these options: read-only, write-only and read-write slots would typically use only #:getter, #:setter and #:accessor options respectively.

The binding of the specified names is done in the environment of the **define-class** expression. If the names are already bound (in that environment) to values that cannot be upgraded to generic functions, those values are overwritten when the **define-class** expression is evaluated. For more detail, see Section 8.11.9 [ensure-generic], page 753.

#:allocation *allocation*   [slot option]

The #:allocation option tells GOOPS how to allocate storage for the slot. Possible values for *allocation* are

- #:instance

  Indicates that GOOPS should create separate storage for this slot in each new instance of the containing class (and its subclasses). This is the default.

- #:class

  Indicates that GOOPS should create storage for this slot that is shared by all instances of the containing class (and its subclasses). In other words, a slot in class C with allocation #:class is shared by all *instances* for which (is-a? *instance c*). This permits defining a kind of global variable which can be accessed only by (in)direct instances of the class which defines the slot.

- #:each-subclass

  Indicates that GOOPS should create storage for this slot that is shared by all *direct* instances of the containing class, and that whenever a subclass of the containing class is defined, GOOPS should create a new storage for the slot that is shared by all *direct* instances of the subclass. In other words, a slot with allocation #:each-subclass is shared by all instances with the same class-of.

- #:virtual

  Indicates that GOOPS should not allocate storage for this slot. The slot definition must also include the #:slot-ref and #:slot-set! options to specify how to reference and set the value for this slot. See the example below.

Slot allocation options are processed when defining a new class by the generic function compute-get-n-set, which is specialized by the class's metaclass. Hence new types of slot allocation can be implemented by defining a new metaclass and a method for compute-get-n-set that is specialized for the new metaclass. For an example of how to do this, see Section 8.11.6 [Customizing Class Definition], page 750.

#:slot-ref *getter*   [slot option]
#:slot-set! *setter*   [slot option]
    The #:slot-ref and #:slot-set! options must be specified if the slot allocation is #:virtual, and are ignored otherwise.

    getter should be a closure taking a single *instance* parameter that returns the current slot value. *setter* should be a closure taking two parameters - *instance* and *new-val* - that sets the slot value to *new-val*.

8.5 Illustrating Slot Description

To illustrate slot description, we can redefine the <my-complex> class seen before. A definition could be:

```
(define-class <my-complex> (<number>)
   (r #:init-value 0 #:getter get-r #:setter set-r! #:init-keyword #:r)
   (i #:init-value 0 #:getter get-i #:setter set-i! #:init-keyword #:i))
```

With this definition, the r and i slots are set to 0 by default, and can be initialised to other values by calling make with the #:r and #:i keywords. Also the generic functions get-r, set-r!, get-i and set-i! are automatically defined to read and write the slots.

```
(define c1 (make <my-complex> #:r 1 #:i 2))
(get-r c1) ⇒ 1
(set-r! c1 12)
(get-r c1) ⇒ 12
(define c2 (make <my-complex> #:r 2))
(get-r c2) ⇒ 2
(get-i c2) ⇒ 0
```

Accessors can both read and write a slot. So, another definition of the <my-complex> class, using the #:accessor option, could be:

```
(define-class <my-complex> (<number>)
   (r #:init-value 0 #:accessor real-part #:init-keyword #:r)
   (i #:init-value 0 #:accessor imag-part #:init-keyword #:i))
```

With this definition, the r slot can be read with:

```
(real-part c)
```

and set with:

```
(set! (real-part c) new-value)
```

Suppose now that we want to manipulate complex numbers with both rectangular and polar coordinates. One solution could be to have a definition of complex numbers which uses one particular representation and some conversion functions to pass from one representation to the other. A better solution is to use virtual slots, like this:

```
(define-class <my-complex> (<number>)
   ;; True slots use rectangular coordinates
   (r #:init-value 0 #:accessor real-part #:init-keyword #:r)
   (i #:init-value 0 #:accessor imag-part #:init-keyword #:i)
   ;; Virtual slots access do the conversion
   (m #:accessor magnitude #:init-keyword #:magn
      #:allocation #:virtual
      #:slot-ref (lambda (o)
                    (let ((r (slot-ref o 'r)) (i (slot-ref o 'i)))
                       (sqrt (+ (* r r) (* i i)))))
      #:slot-set! (lambda (o m)
                     (let ((a (slot-ref o 'a)))
                        (slot-set! o 'r (* m (cos a)))
                        (slot-set! o 'i (* m (sin a))))))
   (a #:accessor angle #:init-keyword #:angle
      #:allocation #:virtual
      #:slot-ref (lambda (o)
                    (atan (slot-ref o 'i) (slot-ref o 'r)))
      #:slot-set! (lambda(o a)
                     (let ((m (slot-ref o 'm)))
                        (slot-set! o 'r (* m (cos a)))
                        (slot-set! o 'i (* m (sin a)))))))
```

In this class definition, the magnitude m and angle a slots are virtual, and are calculated, when referenced, from the normal (i.e. #:allocation #:instance) slots r and i, by calling the function defined in the relevant #:slot-ref option. Correspondingly, writing m or a leads to calling the function defined in the #:slot-set! option. Thus the following expression

```
(slot-set! c 'a 3)
```

permits to set the angle of the c complex number.

```
(define c (make <my-complex> #:r 12 #:i 20))
(real-part c)  ⇒ 12
(angle c)  ⇒ 1.03037682652431
(slot-set! c 'i 10)
```

```
(set! (real-part c) 1)
(describe c)
⊣
#<<my-complex> 401e9b58> is an instance of class <my-complex>
Slots are:
     r = 1
     i = 10
     m = 10.0498756211209
     a = 1.47112767430373
```

Since initialization keywords have been defined for the four slots, we can now define the standard Scheme primitives `make-rectangular` and `make-polar`.

```
(define make-rectangular
    (lambda (x y) (make <my-complex> #:r x #:i y)))

(define make-polar
    (lambda (x y) (make <my-complex> #:magn x #:angle y)))
```

8.6 Methods and Generic Functions

A GOOPS method is like a Scheme procedure except that it is specialized for a particular set of argument classes, and will only be used when the actual arguments in a call match the classes in the method definition.

```
(define-method (+ (x <string>) (y <string>))
  (string-append x y))


(+ "abc" "de")  ⇒ "abcde"
```

A method is not formally associated with any single class (as it is in many other object oriented languages), because a method can be specialized for a combination of several classes. If you've studied object orientation in non-Lispy languages, you may remember discussions such as whether a method to stretch a graphical image around a surface should be a method of the image class, with a surface as a parameter, or a method of the surface class, with an image as a parameter. In GOOPS you'd just write

```
(define-method (stretch (im <image>) (sf <surface>))
    ...)
```

and the question of which class the method is more associated with does not need answering.

There can simultaneously be several methods with the same name but different sets of specializing argument classes; for example:

```
(define-method (+ (x <string>) (y <string>)) ...)
(define-method (+ (x <matrix>) (y <matrix>)) ...)
(define-method (+ (f <fish>) (b <bicycle>)) ...)
(define-method (+ (a <foo>) (b <bar>) (c <baz>)) ...)
```

A generic function is a container for the set of such methods that a program intends to use.

If you look at a program's source code, and see (+ x y) somewhere in it, conceptually what is happening is that the program at that point calls a generic function (in this case, the generic function bound to the identifier +). When that happens, Guile works out which of the generic function's methods is the most appropriate for the arguments that the function is being called with; then it evaluates the method's code with the arguments as formal parameters. This happens every time that a generic function call is evaluated — it isn't assumed that a given source code call will end up invoking the same method every time.

Defining an identifier as a generic function is done with the `define-generic` macro. Definition of a new method is done with the `define-method` macro. Note that `define-method` automatically does a `define-generic` if the identifier concerned is not already a generic function, so often an explicit `define-generic` call is not needed.

define-generic *symbol*   [syntax]

> Create a generic function with name *symbol* and bind it to the variable *symbol*. If *symbol* was previously bound to a Scheme procedure (or procedure-with-setter), the old procedure (and setter) is incorporated into the new generic function as its default procedure (and setter). Any other previous value, including an existing generic function, is discarded and replaced by a new, empty generic function.

define-method (*generic parameter ...*) *body ...*   [syntax]

> Define a method for the generic function or accessor *generic* with parameters *parameters* and body *body ....*
>
> *generic* is a generic function. If *generic* is a variable which is not yet bound to a generic function object, the expansion of `define-method` will include a call to `define-generic`. If *generic* is (`setter` *generic-with-setter*), where *generic-with-setter* is a variable which is not yet bound to a generic-with-setter object, the expansion will include a call to `define-accessor`.
>
> Each *parameter* must be either a symbol or a two-element list (`symbol class`). The symbols refer to variables in the body forms that will be bound to the parameters supplied by the caller when calling this method. The *classes*, if present, specify the possible combinations of parameters to which this method can be applied.
>
> *body ...* are the bodies of the method definition.

`define-method` expressions look a little like Scheme procedure definitions of the form

    (define (name formals ...) . body)

The important difference is that each formal parameter, apart from the possible "rest" argument, can be qualified by a class name: `formal` becomes (`formal class`). The meaning of this qualification is that the method being defined will only be applicable in a particular generic function invocation if the corresponding argument is an instance of `class` (or one of its subclasses). If more than one of the formal parameters is qualified in this way, then the method will only be applicable if each of the corresponding arguments is an instance of its respective qualifying class.

Note that unqualified formal parameters act as though they are qualified by the class `<top>`, which GOOPS uses to mean the superclass of all valid Scheme types, including both primitive types and GOOPS classes.

For example, if a generic function method is defined with *parameters* (s1 `<square>`) and (n `<number>`), that method is only applicable to invocations of its generic function that have two parameters where the first parameter is an instance of the `<square>` class and the second parameter is a number.

8.6.1 Accessors

An accessor is a generic function that can also be used with the generalized `set!` syntax (see Section 6.9.8 [Procedures with Setters], page 255). Guile will handle a call like

```
(set! (accessor args...) value)
```

by calling the most specialized method of `accessor` that matches the classes of `args` and `value`. `define-accessor` is used to bind an identifier to an accessor.

`define-accessor` *symbol*   [syntax]

> Create an accessor with name *symbol* and bind it to the variable *symbol*. If *symbol* was previously bound to a Scheme procedure (or procedure-with-setter), the old procedure (and setter) is incorporated into the new accessor as its default procedure (and setter). Any other previous value, including an existing generic function or accessor, is discarded and replaced by a new, empty accessor.

8.6.2 Extending Primitives

Many of Guile's primitive procedures can be extended by giving them a generic function definition that operates in conjunction with their normal C-coded implementation. When a primitive is extended in this way, it behaves like a generic function with the C-coded implementation as its default method.

This extension happens automatically if a method is defined (by a `define-method` call) for a variable whose current value is a primitive. But it can also be forced by calling `enable-primitive-generic!`.

`enable-primitive-generic!` *primitive*   [primitive procedure]

> Force the creation of a generic function definition for *primitive*.

Once the generic function definition for a primitive has been created, it can be retrieved using `primitive-generic-generic`.

`primitive-generic-generic` *primitive*   [primitive procedure]

> Return the generic function definition of *primitive*.
>
> `primitive-generic-generic` raises an error if *primitive* is not a primitive with generic capability.

8.6.3 Merging Generics

GOOPS generic functions and accessors often have short, generic names. For example, if a vector package provides an accessor for the X coordinate of a vector, that accessor may just be called `x`. It doesn't need to be called, for example, `vector:x`, because GOOPS will work out, when it sees code like (`x obj`), that the vector-specific method of `x` should be called if *obj* is a vector.

That raises the question, though, of what happens when different packages define a generic function with the same name. Suppose we work with a graphical package which needs to use two independent vector packages for 2D and 3D vectors respectively. If both packages export `x`, what does the code using those packages end up with?

Section 6.19.3 [duplicate binding handlers], page 383 explains how this is resolved for conflicting bindings in general. For generics, there is a special duplicates handler, `merge-`

generics, which tells the module system to merge generic functions with the same name. Here is an example:

```
(define-module (math 2D-vectors)
  #:use-module (oop goops)
  #:export (x y ...))

(define-module (math 3D-vectors)
  #:use-module (oop goops)
  #:export (x y z ...))

(define-module (my-module)
  #:use-module (oop goops)
  #:use-module (math 2D-vectors)
  #:use-module (math 3D-vectors)
  #:duplicates (merge-generics))
```

The generic function x in (my-module) will now incorporate all of the methods of x from both imported modules.

To be precise, there will now be three distinct generic functions named x: x in (math 2D-vectors), x in (math 3D-vectors), and x in (my-module); and these functions share their methods in an interesting and dynamic way.

To explain, let's call the imported generic functions (in (math 2D-vectors) and (math 3D-vectors)) the *ancestors*, and the merged generic function (in (my-module)), the *descendant*. The general rule is that for any generic function G, the applicable methods are selected from the union of the methods of G's descendant functions, the methods of G itself and the methods of G's ancestor functions.

Thus ancestor functions effectively share methods with their descendants, and vice versa. In the example above, x in (math 2D-vectors) will share the methods of x in (my-module) and vice versa.[4] Sharing is dynamic, so adding another new method to a descendant implies adding it to that descendant's ancestors too.

8.6.4 Next-method

When you call a generic function, with a particular set of arguments, GOOPS builds a list of all the methods that are applicable to those arguments and orders them by how closely the method definitions match the actual argument types. It then calls the method at the top of this list. If the selected method's code wants to call on to the next method in this list, it can do so by using next-method.

```
(define-method (Test (a <integer>)) (cons 'integer (next-method)))
(define-method (Test (a <number>))  (cons 'number  (next-method)))
(define-method (Test a)             (list 'top))
```

With these definitions,

```
(Test 1)   ⇒ (integer number top)
(Test 1.0) ⇒ (number top)
```

---

[4] But note that x in (math 2D-vectors) doesn't share methods with x in (math 3D-vectors), so modularity is still preserved.

```
(Test #t)  ⇒ (top)
```

`next-method` is always called as just `(next-method)`. The arguments for the next method call are always implicit, and always the same as for the original method call.

If you want to call on to a method with the same name but with a different set of arguments (as you might with overloaded methods in C++, for example), you do not use `next-method`, but instead simply write the new call as usual:

```
(define-method (Test (a <number>) min max)
  (if (and (>= a min) (<= a max))
      (display "Number is in range\n"))
  (Test a))


(Test 2 1 10)
⊣
Number is in range
⇒
(integer number top)
```

(You should be careful in this case that the `Test` calls do not lead to an infinite recursion, but this consideration is just the same as in Scheme code in general.)

8.6.5 Generic Function and Method Examples

Consider the following definitions:

```
(define-generic G)
(define-method (G (a <integer>) b) 'integer)
(define-method (G (a <real>) b) 'real)
(define-method (G a b) 'top)
```

The `define-generic` call defines G as a generic function. The three next lines define methods for G. Each method uses a sequence of *parameter specializers* that specify when the given method is applicable. A specializer permits to indicate the class a parameter must belong to (directly or indirectly) to be applicable. If no specializer is given, the system defaults it to `<top>`. Thus, the first method definition is equivalent to

```
(define-method (G (a <integer>) (b <top>)) 'integer)
```

Now, let's look at some possible calls to the generic function G:

```
(G 2 3)    ⇒ integer
(G 2 #t)   ⇒ integer
(G 1.2 'a) ⇒ real
(G #t #f)  ⇒ top
(G 1 2 3)  ⇒ error (since no method exists for 3 parameters)
```

The methods above use only one specializer per parameter list. But in general, any or all of a method's parameters may be specialized. Suppose we define now:

```
(define-method (G (a <integer>) (b <number>))  'integer-number)
(define-method (G (a <integer>) (b <real>))    'integer-real)
(define-method (G (a <integer>) (b <integer>)) 'integer-integer)
(define-method (G a (b <number>))              'top-number)
```

With these definitions:

```
(G 1 2)   ⇒ integer-integer
(G 1 1.0) ⇒ integer-real
(G 1 #t)  ⇒ integer
(G 'a 1)  ⇒ top-number
```

As a further example we shall continue to define operations on the <my-complex> class. Suppose that we want to use it to implement complex numbers completely. For instance a definition for the addition of two complex numbers could be

```
(define-method (new-+ (a <my-complex>) (b <my-complex>))
  (make-rectangular (+ (real-part a) (real-part b))
                    (+ (imag-part a) (imag-part b))))
```

To be sure that the + used in the method new-+ is the standard addition we can do:

```
(define-generic new-+)

(let ((+ +))
  (define-method (new-+ (a <my-complex>) (b <my-complex>))
    (make-rectangular (+ (real-part a) (real-part b))
                      (+ (imag-part a) (imag-part b)))))
```

The define-generic ensures here that new-+ will be defined in the global environment. Once this is done, we can add methods to the generic function new-+ which make a closure on the + symbol. A complete writing of the new-+ methods is shown in Figure 8.1.

```scheme
(define-generic new-+)

(let ((+ +))

  (define-method (new-+ (a <real>) (b <real>)) (+ a b))

  (define-method (new-+ (a <real>) (b <my-complex>))
    (make-rectangular (+ a (real-part b)) (imag-part b)))

  (define-method (new-+ (a <my-complex>) (b <real>))
    (make-rectangular (+ (real-part a) b) (imag-part a)))

  (define-method (new-+ (a <my-complex>) (b <my-complex>))
    (make-rectangular (+ (real-part a) (real-part b))
                      (+ (imag-part a) (imag-part b))))

  (define-method (new-+ (a <number>))  a)

  (define-method (new-+) 0)

  (define-method (new-+ . args)
    (new-+ (car args)
      (apply new-+ (cdr args)))))

(set! + new-+)
```
Figure 8.1: Extending + to handle complex numbers

We take advantage here of the fact that generic function are not obliged to have a fixed number of parameters. The four first methods implement dyadic addition. The fifth method says that the addition of a single element is this element itself. The sixth method says that using the addition with no parameter always return 0 (as is also true for the primitive +). The last method takes an arbitrary number of parameters[5]. This method acts as a kind of **reduce**: it calls the dyadic addition on the *car* of the list and on the result of applying it on its rest. To finish, the **set!** permits to redefine the + symbol to our extended addition.

To conclude our implementation (integration?) of complex numbers, we could redefine standard Scheme predicates in the following manner:

```scheme
(define-method (complex? c <my-complex>) #t)
(define-method (complex? c)            #f)

(define-method (number? n <number>) #t)
(define-method (number? n)          #f)
...
```

---

[5] The parameter list for a **define-method** follows the conventions used for Scheme procedures. In particular it can use the dot notation or a symbol to denote an arbitrary number of parameters

Standard primitives in which complex numbers are involved could also be redefined in the same manner.

8.6.6 Handling Invocation Errors

If a generic function is invoked with a combination of parameters for which there is no applicable method, GOOPS raises an error.

no-method   [generic]
no-method (*gf* <*generic*>) *args*   [method]
> When an application invokes a generic function, and no methods at all have been defined for that generic function, GOOPS calls the no-method generic function. The default method calls goops-error with an appropriate message.

no-applicable-method   [generic]
no-applicable-method (*gf* <*generic*>) *args*   [method]
> When an application applies a generic function to a set of arguments, and no methods have been defined for those argument types, GOOPS calls the no-applicable-method generic function. The default method calls goops-error with an appropriate message.

no-next-method   [generic]
no-next-method (*gf* <*generic*>) *args*   [method]
> When a generic function method calls (next-method) to invoke the next less specialized method for that generic function, and no less specialized methods have been defined for the current generic function arguments, GOOPS calls the no-next-method generic function. The default method calls goops-error with an appropriate message.

8.7 Inheritance

Here are some class definitions to help illustrate inheritance:

```
(define-class A () a)
(define-class B () b)
(define-class C () c)
(define-class D (A B) d a)
(define-class E (A C) e c)
(define-class F (D E) f)
```

A, B, C have a null list of superclasses. In this case, the system will replace the null list by a list which only contains <object>, the root of all the classes defined by define-class. D, E, F use multiple inheritance: each class inherits from two previously defined classes. Those class definitions define a hierarchy which is shown in Figure 8.2. In this figure, the class <top> is also shown; this class is the superclass of all Scheme objects. In particular, <top> is the superclass of all standard Scheme types.

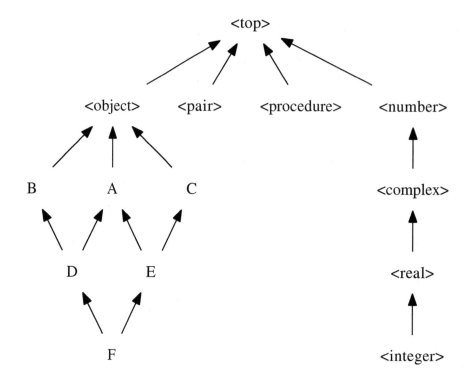

Figure 8.2: A class hierarchy.

When a class has superclasses, its set of slots is calculated by taking the union of its own slots and those of all its superclasses. Thus each instance of D will have three slots, a, b and d). The slots of a class can be discovered using the `class-slots` primitive. For instance,

```
(class-slots A) ⇒ ((a))
(class-slots E) ⇒ ((a) (e) (c))
(class-slots F) ⇒ ((e) (c) (b) (d) (a) (f))
```

The ordering of the returned slots is not significant.

8.7.1 Class Precedence List

What happens when a class inherits from two or more superclasses that have a slot with the same name but incompatible definitions — for example, different init values or slot allocations? We need a rule for deciding which slot definition the derived class ends up with, and this rule is provided by the class's *Class Precedence List*.[6]

Another problem arises when invoking a generic function, and there is more than one method that could apply to the call arguments. Here we need a way of ordering the applicable methods, so that Guile knows which method to use first, which to use next if that method calls `next-method`, and so on. One of the ingredients for this ordering

---

[6] This section is an adaptation of material from Jeff Dalton's (J.Dalton@ed.ac.uk) *Brief introduction to CLOS*

is determining, for each given call argument, which of the specializing classes, from each applicable method's definition, is the most specific for that argument; and here again the class precedence list helps.

If inheritance was restricted such that each class could only have one superclass — which is known as *single* inheritance — class ordering would be easy. The rule would be simply that a subclass is considered more specific than its superclass.

With multiple inheritance, ordering is less obvious, and we have to impose an arbitrary rule to determine precedence. Suppose we have

```
(define-class X ()
   (x #:init-value 1))

(define-class Y ()
   (x #:init-value 2))

(define-class Z (X Y)
   (...))
```

Clearly the Z class is more specific than X or Y, for instances of Z. But which is more specific out of X and Y — and hence, for the definitions above, which #:init-value will take effect when creating an instance of Z? The rule in GOOPS is that the superclasses listed earlier are more specific than those listed later. Hence X is more specific than Y, and the #:init-value for slot x in instances of Z will be 1.

Hence there is a linear ordering for a class and all its superclasses, from most specific to least specific, and this ordering is called the Class Precedence List of the class.

In fact the rules above are not quite enough to always determine a unique order, but they give an idea of how things work. For example, for the F class shown in Figure 8.2, the class precedence list is

```
(f d e a c b <object> <top>)
```

In cases where there is any ambiguity (like this one), it is a bad idea for programmers to rely on exactly what the order is. If the order for some superclasses is important, it can be expressed directly in the class definition.

The precedence list of a class can be obtained by calling `class-precedence-list`. This function returns a ordered list whose first element is the most specific class. For instance:

```
(class-precedence-list B)  ⇒  (#<<class> B 401b97c8>
                               #<<class> <object> 401e4a10>
                               #<<class> <top> 4026a9d8>)
```

Or for a more immediately readable result:

```
(map class-name (class-precedence-list B))  ⇒  (B <object> <top>)
```

8.7.2 Sorting Methods

Now, with the idea of the class precedence list, we can state precisely how the possible methods are sorted when more than one of the methods of a generic function are applicable to the call arguments.

The rules are that

- the applicable methods are sorted in order of specificity, and the most specific method is used first, then the next if that method calls `next-method`, and so on

- a method M1 is more specific than another method M2 if the first specializing class that differs, between the definitions of M1 and M2, is more specific, in M1's definition, for the corresponding actual call argument, than the specializing class in M2's definition

- a class C1 is more specific than another class C2, for an object of actual class C, if C1 comes before C2 in C's class precedence list.

8.8 Introspection

Introspection, or *reflection*, means being able to obtain information dynamically about GOOPS objects. It is perhaps best illustrated by considering an object oriented language that does not provide any introspection, namely C++.

Nothing in C++ allows a running program to obtain answers to the following types of question:

- What are the data members of this object or class?

- What classes does this class inherit from?

- Is this method call virtual or non-virtual?

- If I invoke `Employee::adjustHoliday()`, what class contains the `adjustHoliday()` method that will be applied?

In C++, answers to such questions can only be determined by looking at the source code, if you have access to it. GOOPS, on the other hand, includes procedures that allow answers to these questions — or their GOOPS equivalents — to be obtained dynamically, at run time.

8.8.1 Classes

A GOOPS class is itself an instance of the `<class>` class, or of a subclass of `<class>`. The definition of the `<class>` class has slots that are used to describe the properties of a class, including the following.

`class-name` *class*   [primitive procedure]
> Return the name of class *class*. This is the value of *class*'s `name` slot.

`class-direct-supers` *class*   [primitive procedure]
> Return a list containing the direct superclasses of *class*. This is the value of *class*'s `direct-supers` slot.

`class-direct-slots` *class*   [primitive procedure]
> Return a list containing the slot definitions of the direct slots of *class*. This is the value of *class*'s `direct-slots` slot.

`class-direct-subclasses` *class*   [primitive procedure]
> Return a list containing the direct subclasses of *class*. This is the value of *class*'s `direct-subclasses` slot.

`class-direct-methods` *class*   [primitive procedure]
> Return a list of all the generic function methods that use *class* as a formal parameter specializer. This is the value of *class*'s `direct-methods` slot.

`class-precedence-list` *class*   [primitive procedure]
>   Return the class precedence list for class *class* (see Section 8.7.1 [Class Precedence List], page 734). This is the value of *class*'s `cpl` slot.

`class-slots` *class*   [primitive procedure]
>   Return a list containing the slot definitions for all *class*'s slots, including any slots that are inherited from superclasses. This is the value of *class*'s `slots` slot.

`class-subclasses` *class*   [procedure]
>   Return a list of all subclasses of *class*.

`class-methods` *class*   [procedure]
>   Return a list of all methods that use *class* or a subclass of *class* as one of its formal parameter specializers.

8.8.2 Instances

`class-of` *value*   [primitive procedure]
>   Return the GOOPS class of any Scheme *value*.

`instance?` *object*   [primitive procedure]
>   Return `#t` if *object* is any GOOPS instance, otherwise `#f`.

`is-a?` *object class*   [procedure]
>   Return `#t` if *object* is an instance of *class* or one of its subclasses.

You can use the `is-a?` predicate to ask whether any given value belongs to a given class, or `class-of` to discover the class of a given value. Note that when GOOPS is loaded (by code using the `(oop goops)` module) built-in classes like `<string>`, `<list>` and `<number>` are automatically set up, corresponding to all Guile Scheme types.

```
(is-a? 2.3 <number>) ⇒ #t
(is-a? 2.3 <real>) ⇒ #t
(is-a? 2.3 <string>) ⇒ #f
(is-a? '("a" "b") <string>) ⇒ #f
(is-a? '("a" "b") <list>) ⇒ #t
(is-a? (car '("a" "b")) <string>) ⇒ #t
(is-a? <string> <class>) ⇒ #t
(is-a? <class> <string>) ⇒ #f

(class-of 2.3) ⇒ #<<class> <real> 908c708>
(class-of #(1 2 3)) ⇒ #<<class> <vector> 908cd20>
(class-of <string>) ⇒ #<<class> <class> 8bd3e10>
(class-of <class>) ⇒ #<<class> <class> 8bd3e10>
```

8.8.3 Slots

`class-slot-definition` *class slot-name*   [procedure]
>   Return the slot definition for the slot named *slot-name* in class *class*. *slot-name* should be a symbol.

`slot-definition-name` *slot-def*   [procedure]
Extract and return the slot name from *slot-def*.

`slot-definition-options` *slot-def*   [procedure]
Extract and return the slot options from *slot-def*.

`slot-definition-allocation` *slot-def*   [procedure]
Extract and return the slot allocation option from *slot-def*. This is the value of the
`#:allocation` keyword (see Section 8.4 [allocation], page 721), or `#:instance` if the
`#:allocation` keyword is absent.

`slot-definition-getter` *slot-def*   [procedure]
Extract and return the slot getter option from *slot-def*. This is the value of the
`#:getter` keyword (see Section 8.4 [getter], page 721), or `#f` if the `#:getter` keyword
is absent.

`slot-definition-setter` *slot-def*   [procedure]
Extract and return the slot setter option from *slot-def*. This is the value of the
`#:setter` keyword (see Section 8.4 [setter], page 721), or `#f` if the `#:setter` keyword
is absent.

`slot-definition-accessor` *slot-def*   [procedure]
Extract and return the slot accessor option from *slot-def*. This is the value of the
`#:accessor` keyword (see Section 8.4 [accessor], page 721), or `#f` if the `#:accessor`
keyword is absent.

`slot-definition-init-value` *slot-def*   [procedure]
Extract and return the slot init-value option from *slot-def*. This is the value of the
`#:init-value` keyword (see Section 8.4 [init-value], page 721), or the unbound value
if the `#:init-value` keyword is absent.

`slot-definition-init-form` *slot-def*   [procedure]
Extract and return the slot init-form option from *slot-def*. This is the value of the
`#:init-form` keyword (see Section 8.4 [init-form], page 721), or the unbound value if
the `#:init-form` keyword is absent.

`slot-definition-init-thunk` *slot-def*   [procedure]
Extract and return the slot init-thunk option from *slot-def*. This is the value of the
`#:init-thunk` keyword (see Section 8.4 [init-thunk], page 721), or `#f` if the `#:init-thunk` keyword is absent.

`slot-definition-init-keyword` *slot-def*   [procedure]
Extract and return the slot init-keyword option from *slot-def*. This is the value of
the `#:init-keyword` keyword (see Section 8.4 [init-keyword], page 721), or `#f` if the
`#:init-keyword` keyword is absent.

`slot-init-function` *class slot-name*   [procedure]
Return the initialization function for the slot named *slot-name* in class *class*. *slot-name* should be a symbol.

The returned initialization function incorporates the effects of the standard `#:init-thunk`, `#:init-form` and `#:init-value` slot options. These initializations can be overridden by the `#:init-keyword` slot option or by a specialized `initialize` method, so, in general, the function returned by **slot-init-function** may be irrelevant. For a fuller discussion, see Section 8.4 [init-value], page 721.

8.8.4 Generic Functions

A generic function is an instance of the `<generic>` class, or of a subclass of `<generic>`. The definition of the `<generic>` class has slots that are used to describe the properties of a generic function.

generic-function-name *gf*   [primitive procedure]
    Return the name of generic function *gf*.

generic-function-methods *gf*   [primitive procedure]
    Return a list of the methods of generic function *gf*. This is the value of *gf*'s **methods** slot.

Similarly, a method is an instance of the `<method>` class, or of a subclass of `<method>`; and the definition of the `<method>` class has slots that are used to describe the properties of a method.

method-generic-function *method*   [primitive procedure]
    Return the generic function that *method* belongs to. This is the value of *method*'s **generic-function** slot.

method-specializers *method*   [primitive procedure]
    Return a list of *method*'s formal parameter specializers . This is the value of *method*'s **specializers** slot.

method-procedure *method*   [primitive procedure]
    Return the procedure that implements *method*. This is the value of *method*'s **procedure** slot.

method-source   [generic]
method-source (*m* *<method>*)   [method]
    Return an expression that prints to show the definition of method *m*.

```
(define-generic cube)

(define-method (cube (n <number>))
  (* n n n))

(map method-source (generic-function-methods cube))
⇒
((method ((n <number>)) (* n n n)))
```

8.8.5 Accessing Slots

Any slot, regardless of its allocation, can be queried, referenced and set using the following four primitive procedures.

slot-exists? *obj slot-name*   [primitive procedure]
> Return #t if *obj* has a slot with name *slot-name*, otherwise #f.

slot-bound? *obj slot-name*   [primitive procedure]
> Return #t if the slot named *slot-name* in *obj* has a value, otherwise #f.
>
> **slot-bound?** calls the generic function **slot-missing** if *obj* does not have a slot called *slot-name* (see Section 8.8.5 [Accessing Slots], page 740).

slot-ref *obj slot-name*   [primitive procedure]
> Return the value of the slot named *slot-name* in *obj*.
>
> **slot-ref** calls the generic function **slot-missing** if *obj* does not have a slot called *slot-name* (see Section 8.8.5 [Accessing Slots], page 740).
>
> **slot-ref** calls the generic function **slot-unbound** if the named slot in *obj* does not have a value (see Section 8.8.5 [Accessing Slots], page 740).

slot-set! *obj slot-name value*   [primitive procedure]
> Set the value of the slot named *slot-name* in *obj* to *value*.
>
> **slot-set!** calls the generic function **slot-missing** if *obj* does not have a slot called *slot-name* (see Section 8.8.5 [Accessing Slots], page 740).

GOOPS stores information about slots in classes. Internally, all of these procedures work by looking up the slot definition for the slot named *slot-name* in the class (**class-of** *obj*), and then using the slot definition's "getter" and "setter" closures to get and set the slot value.

The next four procedures differ from the previous ones in that they take the class as an explicit argument, rather than assuming (**class-of** *obj*). Therefore they allow you to apply the "getter" and "setter" closures of a slot definition in one class to an instance of a different class.

slot-exists-using-class? *class obj slot-name*   [primitive procedure]
> Return #t if *class* has a slot definition for a slot with name *slot-name*, otherwise #f.

slot-bound-using-class? *class obj slot-name*   [primitive procedure]
> Return #t if applying **slot-ref-using-class** to the same arguments would call the generic function **slot-unbound**, otherwise #f.
>
> **slot-bound-using-class?** calls the generic function **slot-missing** if *class* does not have a slot definition for a slot called *slot-name* (see Section 8.8.5 [Accessing Slots], page 740).

slot-ref-using-class *class obj slot-name*   [primitive procedure]
> Apply the "getter" closure for the slot named *slot-name* in *class* to *obj*, and return its result.

> slot-ref-using-class calls the generic function slot-missing if *class* does not
> have a slot definition for a slot called *slot-name* (see Section 8.8.5 [Accessing Slots],
> page 740).
>
> slot-ref-using-class calls the generic function slot-unbound if the application of
> the "getter" closure to *obj* returns an unbound value (see Section 8.8.5 [Accessing
> Slots], page 740).

slot-set-using-class! *class obj slot-name value*   [primitive procedure]
> Apply the "setter" closure for the slot named *slot-name* in *class* to *obj* and *value*.
>
> slot-set-using-class! calls the generic function slot-missing if *class* does not
> have a slot definition for a slot called *slot-name* (see Section 8.8.5 [Accessing Slots],
> page 740).

Slots whose allocation is per-class rather than per-instance can be referenced and set without needing to specify any particular instance.

class-slot-ref *class slot-name*   [procedure]
> Return the value of the slot named *slot-name* in class *class*. The named slot must
> have #:class or #:each-subclass allocation (see Section 8.4 [allocation], page 721).
>
> If there is no such slot with #:class or #:each-subclass allocation, class-slot-
> ref calls the slot-missing generic function with arguments *class* and *slot-name*.
> Otherwise, if the slot value is unbound, class-slot-ref calls the slot-unbound
> generic function, with the same arguments.

class-slot-set! *class slot-name value*   [procedure]
> Set the value of the slot named *slot-name* in class *class* to *value*. The named slot must
> have #:class or #:each-subclass allocation (see Section 8.4 [allocation], page 721).
>
> If there is no such slot with #:class or #:each-subclass allocation, class-slot-ref
> calls the slot-missing generic function with arguments *class* and *slot-name*.

When a slot-ref or slot-set! call specifies a non-existent slot name, or tries to reference a slot whose value is unbound, GOOPS calls one of the following generic functions.

slot-missing   [generic]
slot-missing (*class <class>*) *slot-name*   [method]
slot-missing (*class <class>*) (*object <object>*) *slot-name*   [method]
slot-missing (*class <class>*) (*object <object>*) *slot-name value*   [method]
> When an application attempts to reference or set a class or instance slot by name,
> and the slot name is invalid for the specified *class* or *object*, GOOPS calls the slot-
> missing generic function.
>
> The default methods all call goops-error with an appropriate message.

slot-unbound   [generic]
slot-unbound (*object <object>*)   [method]
slot-unbound (*class <class>*) *slot-name*   [method]
slot-unbound (*class <class>*) (*object <object>*) *slot-name*   [method]
> When an application attempts to reference a class or instance slot, and the slot's
> value is unbound, GOOPS calls the slot-unbound generic function.
>
> The default methods all call goops-error with an appropriate message.

8.9 Error Handling

The procedure `goops-error` is called to raise an appropriate error by the default methods of the following generic functions:

- `slot-missing` (see Section 8.8.5 [slot-missing], page 740)
- `slot-unbound` (see Section 8.8.5 [slot-unbound], page 740)
- `no-method` (see Section 8.6.6 [no-method], page 733)
- `no-applicable-method` (see Section 8.6.6 [no-applicable-method], page 733)
- `no-next-method` (see Section 8.6.6 [no-next-method], page 733)

If you customize these functions for particular classes or metaclasses, you may still want to use `goops-error` to signal any error conditions that you detect.

`goops-error` *format-string arg . . .*   [procedure]
> Raise an error with key `goops-error` and error message constructed from *format-string* and *arg . . .*. Error message formatting is as done by `scm-error`.

8.10 GOOPS Object Miscellany

Here we cover some points about GOOPS objects that aren't substantial enough to merit sections on their own.

Object Equality

When GOOPS is loaded, `eqv?`, `equal?` and `=` become generic functions, and you can define methods for them, specialized for your own classes, so as to control what the various kinds of equality mean for your classes.

For example, the `assoc` procedure, for looking up an entry in an alist, is specified as using `equal?` to determine when the car of an entry in the alist is the same as the key parameter that `assoc` is called with. Hence, if you had defined a new class, and wanted to use instances of that class as the keys in an alist, you could define a method for `equal?`, for your class, to control `assoc`'s lookup precisely.

Cloning Objects

`shallow-clone`   [generic]
`shallow-clone` (*self* <*object*>)   [method]
> Return a "shallow" clone of *self*. The default method makes a shallow clone by allocating a new instance and copying slot values from self to the new instance. Each slot value is copied either as an immediate value or by reference.

`deep-clone`   [generic]
`deep-clone` (*self* <*object*>)   [method]
> Return a "deep" clone of *self*. The default method makes a deep clone by allocating a new instance and copying or cloning slot values from self to the new instance. If a slot value is an instance (satisfies `instance?`), it is cloned by calling `deep-clone` on that value. Other slot values are copied either as immediate values or by reference.

Write and Display

write *object port*   [primitive generic]
display *object port*   [primitive generic]

> When GOOPS is loaded, `write` and `display` become generic functions with special methods for printing
>
> - objects - instances of the class `<object>`
> - foreign objects - instances of the class `<foreign-object>`
> - classes - instances of the class `<class>`
> - generic functions - instances of the class `<generic>`
> - methods - instances of the class `<method>`.
>
> `write` and `display` print non-GOOPS values in the same way as the Guile primitive `write` and `display` functions.

In addition to the cases mentioned, you can of course define `write` and `display` methods for your own classes, to customize how instances of those classes are printed.

8.11 The Metaobject Protocol

At this point, we've said about as much as can be said about GOOPS without having to confront the idea of the metaobject protocol. There are a couple more topics that could be discussed in isolation first — class redefinition, and changing the class of existing instances — but in practice developers using them will be advanced enough to want to understand the metaobject protocol too, and will probably be using the protocol to customize exactly what happens during these events.

So let's plunge in. GOOPS is based on a "metaobject protocol" (aka "MOP") derived from the ones used in CLOS (the Common Lisp Object System), tiny-clos (a small Scheme implementation of a subset of CLOS functionality) and STKlos.

The MOP underlies many possible GOOPS customizations — such as defining an `initialize` method to customize the initialization of instances of an application-defined class — and an understanding of the MOP makes it much easier to explain such customizations in a precise way. And at a deeper level, understanding the MOP is a key part of understanding GOOPS, and of taking full advantage of GOOPS' power, by customizing the behaviour of GOOPS itself.

8.11.1 Metaobjects and the Metaobject Protocol

The building blocks of GOOPS are classes, slot definitions, instances, generic functions and methods. A class is a grouping of inheritance relations and slot definitions. An instance is an object with slots that are allocated following the rules implied by its class's superclasses and slot definitions. A generic function is a collection of methods and rules for determining which of those methods to apply when the generic function is invoked. A method is a procedure and a set of specializers that specify the type of arguments to which the procedure is applicable.

Of these entities, GOOPS represents classes, generic functions and methods as "metaobjects". In other words, the values in a GOOPS program that describe classes, generic functions and methods, are themselves instances (or "objects") of special GOOPS classes that encapsulate the behaviour, respectively, of classes, generic functions, and methods.

(The other two entities are slot definitions and instances. Slot definitions are not strictly instances, but every slot definition is associated with a GOOPS class that specifies the behaviour of the slot as regards accessibility and protection from garbage collection. Instances are of course objects in the usual sense, and there is no benefit from thinking of them as metaobjects.)

The "metaobject protocol" (or "MOP") is the specification of the generic functions which determine the behaviour of these metaobjects and the circumstances in which these generic functions are invoked.

For a concrete example of what this means, consider how GOOPS calculates the set of slots for a class that is being defined using `define-class`. The desired set of slots is the union of the new class's direct slots and the slots of all its superclasses. But `define-class` itself does not perform this calculation. Instead, there is a method of the `initialize` generic function that is specialized for instances of type `<class>`, and it is this method that performs the slot calculation.

`initialize` is a generic function which GOOPS calls whenever a new instance is created, immediately after allocating memory for a new instance, in order to initialize the new instance's slots. The sequence of steps is as follows.

- `define-class` uses `make` to make a new instance of the `<class>` class, passing as initialization arguments the superclasses, slot definitions and class options that were specified in the `define-class` form.

- `make` allocates memory for the new instance, and invokes the `initialize` generic function to initialize the new instance's slots.

- The `initialize` generic function applies the method that is specialized for instances of type `<class>`, and this method performs the slot calculation.

In other words, rather than being hardcoded in `define-class`, the default behaviour of class definition is encapsulated by generic function methods that are specialized for the class `<class>`.

It is possible to create a new class that inherits from `<class>`, which is called a "metaclass", and to write a new `initialize` method that is specialized for instances of the new metaclass. Then, if the `define-class` form includes a `#:metaclass` class option whose value is the new metaclass, the class that is defined by the `define-class` form will be an instance of the new metaclass rather than of the default `<class>`, and will be defined in accordance with the new `initialize` method. Thus the default slot calculation, as well as any other aspect of the new class's relationship with its superclasses, can be modified or overridden.

In a similar way, the behaviour of generic functions can be modified or overridden by creating a new class that inherits from the standard generic function class `<generic>`, writing appropriate methods that are specialized to the new class, and creating new generic functions that are instances of the new class.

The same is true for method metaobjects. And the same basic mechanism allows the application class author to write an `initialize` method that is specialized to their application class, to initialize instances of that class.

Such is the power of the MOP. Note that `initialize` is just one of a large number of generic functions that can be customized to modify the behaviour of application objects and classes and of GOOPS itself. Each following section covers a particular area of GOOPS functionality, and describes the generic functions that are relevant for customization of that area.

8.11.2 Metaclasses

A *metaclass* is the class of an object which represents a GOOPS class. Put more succinctly, a metaclass is a class's class.

Most GOOPS classes have the metaclass `<class>` and, by default, any new class that is created using `define-class` has the metaclass `<class>`.

But what does this really mean? To find out, let's look in more detail at what happens when a new class is created using `define-class`:

```
(define-class <my-class> (<object>) . slots)
```

Guile expands this to something like:

```
(define <my-class> (class (<object>) . slots))
```

which in turn expands to:

```
(define <my-class>
  (make <class> #:dsupers (list <object>) #:slots slots))
```

As this expansion makes clear, the resulting value of `<my-class>` is an instance of the class `<class>` with slot values specifying the superclasses and slot definitions for the class `<my-class>`. (`#:dsupers` and `#:slots` are initialization keywords for the `dsupers` and `dslots` slots of the `<class>` class.)

Now suppose that you want to define a new class with a metaclass other than the default `<class>`. This is done by writing:

```
(define-class <my-class2> (<object>)
    slot ...
    #:metaclass <my-metaclass>)
```

and Guile expands *this* to something like:

```
(define <my-class2>
    (make <my-metaclass> #:dsupers (list <object>) #:slots slots))
```

In this case, the value of `<my-class2>` is an instance of the more specialized class `<my-metaclass>`. Note that `<my-metaclass>` itself must previously have been defined as a subclass of `<class>`. For a full discussion of when and how it is useful to define new metaclasses, see Section 8.11.3 [MOP Specification], page 746.

Now let's make an instance of `<my-class2>`:

```
(define my-object (make <my-class2> ...))
```

All of the following statements are correct expressions of the relationships between `my-object`, `<my-class2>`, `<my-metaclass>` and `<class>`.

- `my-object` is an instance of the class `<my-class2>`.
- `<my-class2>` is an instance of the class `<my-metaclass>`.
- `<my-metaclass>` is an instance of the class `<class>`.

- The class of `my-object` is `<my-class2>`.
- The class of `<my-class2>` is `<my-metaclass>`.
- The class of `<my-metaclass>` is `<class>`.

8.11.3 MOP Specification

The aim of the MOP specification in this chapter is to specify all the customizable generic function invocations that can be made by the standard GOOPS syntax, procedures and methods, and to explain the protocol for customizing such invocations.

A generic function invocation is customizable if the types of the arguments to which it is applied are not completely determined by the lexical context in which the invocation appears. For example, the (`initialize` *instance initargs*) invocation in the default `make-instance` method is customizable, because the type of the *instance* argument is determined by the class that was passed to `make-instance`.

(Whereas — to give a counter-example — the (`make <generic>` `#:name` ',name) invocation in `define-generic` is not customizable, because all of its arguments have lexically determined types.)

When using this rule to decide whether a given generic function invocation is customizable, we ignore arguments that are expected to be handled in method definitions as a single "rest" list argument.

For each customizable generic function invocation, the *invocation protocol* is explained by specifying

- what, conceptually, the applied method is intended to do
- what assumptions, if any, the caller makes about the applied method's side effects
- what the caller expects to get as the applied method's return value.

8.11.4 Instance Creation Protocol

`make <class>` . *initargs* (method)

- `allocate-instance` *class initargs* (generic)

  The applied `allocate-instance` method should allocate storage for a new instance of class *class* and return the uninitialized instance.

- `initialize` *instance initargs* (generic)

  instance is the uninitialized instance returned by `allocate-instance`. The applied method should initialize the new instance in whatever sense is appropriate for its class. The method's return value is ignored.

`make` itself is a generic function. Hence the `make` invocation itself can be customized in the case where the new instance's metaclass is more specialized than the default `<class>`, by defining a `make` method that is specialized to that metaclass.

Normally, however, the method for classes with metaclass `<class>` will be applied. This method calls two generic functions:

- (allocate-instance *class* . *initargs*)
- (initialize *instance* . *initargs*)

`allocate-instance` allocates storage for and returns the new instance, uninitialized. You might customize `allocate-instance`, for example, if you wanted to provide a GOOPS wrapper around some other object programming system.

To do this, you would create a specialized metaclass, which would act as the metaclass for all classes and instances from the other system. Then define an `allocate-instance` method, specialized to that metaclass, which calls a Guile primitive C function (or FFI code), which in turn allocates the new instance using the interface of the other object system.

In this case, for a complete system, you would also need to customize a number of other generic functions like `make` and `initialize`, so that GOOPS knows how to make classes from the other system, access instance slots, and so on.

`initialize` initializes the instance that is returned by `allocate-instance`. The standard GOOPS methods perform initializations appropriate to the instance class.

- At the least specialized level, the method for instances of type `<object>` performs internal GOOPS instance initialization, and initializes the instance's slots according to the slot definitions and any slot initialization keywords that appear in *initargs*.

- The method for instances of type `<class>` calls `(next-method)`, then performs the class initializations described in Section 8.11.5 [Class Definition Protocol], page 747.

- and so on for generic functions, methods, operator classes ...

Similarly, you can customize the initialization of instances of any application-defined class by defining an `initialize` method specialized to that class.

Imagine a class whose instances' slots need to be initialized at instance creation time by querying a database. Although it might be possible to achieve this a combination of `#:init-thunk` keywords and closures in the slot definitions, it may be neater to write an `initialize` method for the class that queries the database once and initializes all the dependent slot values according to the results.

8.11.5 Class Definition Protocol

Here is a summary diagram of the syntax, procedures and generic functions that may be involved in class definition.

`define-class` (syntax)

- `class` (syntax)
    - `make-class` (procedure)
        - `ensure-metaclass` (procedure)
        - `make` *metaclass* ... (generic)
            - `allocate-instance` (generic)
            - `initialize` (generic)
                - `compute-cpl` (generic)
                    - `compute-std-cpl` (procedure)
                - `compute-slots` (generic)
                - `compute-get-n-set` (generic)
                - `compute-getter-method` (generic)

- • compute-setter-method (generic)
- • class-redefinition (generic)
  - • remove-class-accessors (generic)
  - • update-direct-method! (generic)
  - • update-direct-subclass! (generic)

Wherever a step above is marked as "generic", it can be customized, and the detail shown below it is only "correct" insofar as it describes what the default method of that generic function does. For example, if you write an `initialize` method, for some metaclass, that does not call `next-method` and does not call `compute-cpl`, then `compute-cpl` will not be called when a class is defined with that metaclass.

A (`define-class` ...) form (see Section 8.2 [Class Definition], page 719) expands to an expression which

- • checks that it is being evaluated only at top level
- • defines any accessors that are implied by the *slot-definitions*
- • uses `class` to create the new class
- • checks for a previous class definition for *name* and, if found, handles the redefinition by invoking `class-redefinition` (see Section 8.12 [Redefining a Class], page 755).

`class` *name* (*super* ...) *slot-definition* ... *class-option* ...   [syntax]
  Return a newly created class that inherits from *supers*, with direct slots defined by *slot-definitions* and *class-options*. For the format of *slot-definitions* and *class-options*, see Section 8.2 [define-class], page 719.

`class` expands to an expression which

- • processes the class and slot definition options to check that they are well-formed, to convert the `#:init-form` option to an `#:init-thunk` option, to supply a default environment parameter (the current top-level environment) and to evaluate all the bits that need to be evaluated
- • calls `make-class` to create the class with the processed and evaluated parameters.

`make-class` *supers* *slots* *class-option* ...   [procedure]
  Return a newly created class that inherits from *supers*, with direct slots defined by *slots* and *class-options*. For the format of *slots* and *class-options*, see Section 8.2 [define-class], page 719, except note that for `make-class`, *slots* is a separate list of slot definitions.

`make-class`

- • adds `<object>` to the *supers* list if *supers* is empty or if none of the classes in *supers* have `<object>` in their class precedence list
- • defaults the `#:environment`, `#:name` and `#:metaclass` options, if they are not specified by *options*, to the current top-level environment, the unbound value, and (`ensure-metaclass` *supers*) respectively
- • checks for duplicate classes in *supers* and duplicate slot names in *slots*, and signals an error if there are any duplicates
- • calls `make`, passing the metaclass as the first parameter and all other parameters as option keywords with values.

ensure-metaclass *supers env*   [procedure]

> Return a metaclass suitable for a class that inherits from the list of classes in *supers*. The returned metaclass is the union by inheritance of the metaclasses of the classes in *supers*.
>
> In the simplest case, where all the *supers* are straightforward classes with metaclass `<class>`, the returned metaclass is just `<class>`.
>
> For a more complex example, suppose that *supers* contained one class with metaclass `<operator-class>` and one with metaclass `<foreign-object-class>`. Then the returned metaclass would be a class that inherits from both `<operator-class>` and `<foreign-object-class>`.
>
> If *supers* is the empty list, `ensure-metaclass` returns the default GOOPS metaclass `<class>`.
>
> GOOPS keeps a list of the metaclasses created by `ensure-metaclass`, so that each required type of metaclass only has to be created once.
>
> The `env` parameter is ignored.

make *metaclass initarg* . . .   [generic]

> *metaclass* is the metaclass of the class being defined, either taken from the `#:metaclass` class option or computed by `ensure-metaclass`. The applied method must create and return the fully initialized class metaobject for the new class definition.

The (`make metaclass initarg` . . .) invocation is a particular case of the instance creation protocol covered in the previous section. It will create an class metaobject with metaclass *metaclass*. By default, this metaobject will be initialized by the `initialize` method that is specialized for instances of type `<class>`.

The `initialize` method for classes (signature (`initialize <class> initargs`)) calls the following generic functions.

- `compute-cpl` *class* (generic)

  The applied method should compute and return the class precedence list for *class* as a list of class metaobjects. When `compute-cpl` is called, the following *class* metaobject slots have all been initialized: `name`, `direct-supers`, `direct-slots`, `direct-subclasses` (empty), `direct-methods`. The value returned by `compute-cpl` will be stored in the `cpl` slot.

- `compute-slots` *class* (generic)

  The applied method should compute and return the slots (union of direct and inherited) for *class* as a list of slot definitions. When `compute-slots` is called, all the *class* metaobject slots mentioned for `compute-cpl` have been initialized, plus the following: `cpl`, `redefined` (#f), `environment`. The value returned by `compute-slots` will be stored in the `slots` slot.

- `compute-get-n-set` *class slot-def* (generic)

  `initialize` calls `compute-get-n-set` for each slot computed by `compute-slots`. The applied method should compute and return a pair of closures that, respectively, get and set the value of the specified slot. The get closure should have arity 1 and expect a single argument that is the instance whose slot value is to be retrieved. The set closure should have arity 2 and expect two arguments, where the first argument is the instance whose slot value is to be set and the second argument is the new value for that slot. The closures should be returned in a two element list: (list *get set*).

The closures returned by `compute-get-n-set` are stored as part of the value of the *class* metaobject's `getters-n-setters` slot. Specifically, the value of this slot is a list with the same number of elements as there are slots in the class, and each element looks either like

    (*slot-name-symbol init-function* . *index*)

or like

    (*slot-name-symbol init-function get set*)

Where the get and set closures are replaced by *index*, the slot is an instance slot and *index* is the slot's index in the underlying structure: GOOPS knows how to get and set the value of such slots and so does not need specially constructed get and set closures. Otherwise, *get* and *set* are the closures returned by `compute-get-n-set`.

The structure of the `getters-n-setters` slot value is important when understanding the next customizable generic functions that `initialize` calls...

- `compute-getter-method` *class gns* (generic)

    `initialize` calls `compute-getter-method` for each of the class's slots (as determined by `compute-slots`) that includes a #:`getter` or #:`accessor` slot option. *gns* is the element of the *class* metaobject's `getters-n-setters` slot that specifies how the slot in question is referenced and set, as described above under `compute-get-n-set`. The applied method should create and return a method that is specialized for instances of type *class* and uses the get closure to retrieve the slot's value. `initialize` uses `add-method!` to add the returned method to the generic function named by the slot definition's #:`getter` or #:`accessor` option.

- `compute-setter-method` *class gns* (generic)

    `compute-setter-method` is invoked with the same arguments as `compute-getter-method`, for each of the class's slots that includes a #:`setter` or #:`accessor` slot option. The applied method should create and return a method that is specialized for instances of type *class* and uses the set closure to set the slot's value. `initialize` then uses `add-method!` to add the returned method to the generic function named by the slot definition's #:`setter` or #:`accessor` option.

8.11.6 Customizing Class Definition

If the metaclass of the new class is something more specialized than the default `<class>`, then the type of *class* in the calls above is more specialized than `<class>`, and hence it becomes possible to define generic function methods, specialized for the new class's metaclass, that can modify or override the default behaviour of `initialize`, `compute-cpl` or `compute-get-n-set`.

`compute-cpl` computes the class precedence list ("CPL") for the new class (see Section 8.7.1 [Class Precedence List], page 734), and returns it as a list of class objects. The CPL is important because it defines a superclass ordering that is used, when a generic function is invoked upon an instance of the class, to decide which of the available generic function methods is the most specific. Hence `compute-cpl` could be customized in order to modify the CPL ordering algorithm for all classes with a special metaclass.

The default CPL algorithm is encapsulated by the `compute-std-cpl` procedure, which is called by the default `compute-cpl` method.

`compute-std-cpl` *class*   [procedure]
> Compute and return the class precedence list for *class* according to the algorithm described in Section 8.7.1 [Class Precedence List], page 734.

`compute-slots` computes and returns a list of all slot definitions for the new class. By default, this list includes the direct slot definitions from the `define-class` form, plus the slot definitions that are inherited from the new class's superclasses. The default `compute-slots` method uses the CPL computed by `compute-cpl` to calculate this union of slot definitions, with the rule that slots inherited from superclasses are shadowed by direct slots with the same name. One possible reason for customizing `compute-slots` would be to implement an alternative resolution strategy for slot name conflicts.

`compute-get-n-set` computes the low-level closures that will be used to get and set the value of a particular slot, and returns them in a list with two elements.

The closures returned depend on how storage for that slot is allocated. The standard `compute-get-n-set` method, specialized for classes of type `<class>`, handles the standard GOOPS values for the `#:allocation` slot option (see Section 8.4 [allocation], page 721). By defining a new `compute-get-n-set` method for a more specialized metaclass, it is possible to support new types of slot allocation.

Suppose you wanted to create a large number of instances of some class with a slot that should be shared between some but not all instances of that class - say every 10 instances should share the same slot storage. The following example shows how to implement and use a new type of slot allocation to do this.

```
(define-class <batched-allocation-metaclass> (<class>))


(let ((batch-allocation-count 0)
      (batch-get-n-set #f))
  (define-method (compute-get-n-set
                     (class <batched-allocation-metaclass>) s)
    (case (slot-definition-allocation s)
      ((#:batched)
       ;; If we've already used the same slot storage for 10 instances,
       ;; reset variables.
       (if (= batch-allocation-count 10)
           (begin
             (set! batch-allocation-count 0)
             (set! batch-get-n-set #f)))
       ;; If we don't have a current pair of get and set closures,
       ;; create one.  make-closure-variable returns a pair of closures
       ;; around a single Scheme variable - see goops.scm for details.
       (or batch-get-n-set
           (set! batch-get-n-set (make-closure-variable)))
       ;; Increment the batch allocation count.
       (set! batch-allocation-count (+ batch-allocation-count 1))
       batch-get-n-set)
```

```
      ;; Call next-method to handle standard allocation types.
      (else (next-method)))))))

  (define-class <class-using-batched-slot> ()
    ...
    (c #:allocation #:batched)
    ...
    #:metaclass <batched-allocation-metaclass>)
```

The usage of `compute-getter-method` and `compute-setter-method` is described in Section 8.11.5 [Class Definition Protocol], page 747.

`compute-cpl` and `compute-get-n-set` are called by the standard `initialize` method for classes whose metaclass is `<class>`. But `initialize` itself can also be modified, by defining an `initialize` method specialized to the new class's metaclass. Such a method could complete override the standard behaviour, by not calling (next-method) at all, but more typically it would perform additional class initialization steps before and/or after calling (next-method) for the standard behaviour.

8.11.7 Method Definition

define-method (syntax)

  - add-method! *target method* (generic)

`define-method` invokes the `add-method!` generic function to handle adding the new method to a variety of possible targets. GOOPS includes methods to handle *target* as

  - a generic function (the most common case)
  - a procedure
  - a primitive generic (see Section 8.6.2 [Extending Primitives], page 728)

By defining further methods for `add-method!`, you can theoretically handle adding methods to further types of target.

8.11.8 Method Definition Internals

define-method:

  - checks the form of the first parameter, and applies the following steps to the accessor's setter if it has the (setter ...) form
  - interpolates a call to `define-generic` or `define-accessor` if a generic function is not already defined with the supplied name
  - calls `method` with the *parameters* and *body*, to make a new method instance
  - calls `add-method!` to add this method to the relevant generic function.

method (*parameter ...*) *body ...*   [syntax]
      Make a method whose specializers are defined by the classes in *parameters* and whose procedure definition is constructed from the *parameter* symbols and *body* forms.

      The *parameter* and *body* parameters should be as for `define-method` (see Section 8.6 [define-method], page 726).

method:

- extracts formals and specializing classes from the *parameters*, defaulting the class for unspecialized parameters to `<top>`
- creates a closure using the formals and the *body* forms
- calls `make` with metaclass `<method>` and the specializers and closure using the `#:specializers` and `#:procedure` keywords.

`make-method` *specializers procedure*   [procedure]
>   Make a method using *specializers* and *procedure*.
>
>   *specializers* should be a list of classes that specifies the parameter combinations to which this method will be applicable.
>
>   *procedure* should be the closure that will applied to the generic function parameters when this method is invoked.

`make-method` is a simple wrapper around `make` with metaclass `<method>`.

`add-method!` *target method*   [generic]
>   Generic function for adding method *method* to *target*.

`add-method!` (*generic* <*generic*>) (*method* <*method*>)   [method]
>   Add method *method* to the generic function *generic*.

`add-method!` (*proc* <*procedure*>) (*method* <*method*>)   [method]
>   If *proc* is a procedure with generic capability (see Section 8.6.2 [generic-capability?], page 728), upgrade it to a primitive generic and add *method* to its generic function definition.

`add-method!` (*pg* <*primitive-generic*>) (*method* <*method*>)   [method]
>   Add method *method* to the generic function definition of *pg*.
>
>   Implementation: `(add-method! (primitive-generic-generic pg) method)`.

`add-method!` (*whatever* <*top*>) (*method* <*method*>)   [method]
>   Raise an error indicating that *whatever* is not a valid generic function.

8.11.9 Generic Function Internals

`define-generic` calls `ensure-generic` to upgrade a pre-existing procedure value, or `make` with metaclass `<generic>` to create a new generic function.

`define-accessor` calls `ensure-accessor` to upgrade a pre-existing procedure value, or `make-accessor` to create a new accessor.

`ensure-generic` *old-definition* [*name*]   [procedure]
>   Return a generic function with name *name*, if possible by using or upgrading *old-definition*. If unspecified, *name* defaults to `#f`.
>
>   If *old-definition* is already a generic function, it is returned unchanged.
>
>   If *old-definition* is a Scheme procedure or procedure-with-setter, `ensure-generic` returns a new generic function that uses *old-definition* for its default procedure and setter.
>
>   Otherwise `ensure-generic` returns a new generic function with no defaults and no methods.

make-generic [*name*]   [procedure]
> Return a new generic function with name (**car** **name**). If unspecified, *name* defaults to **#f**.

    ensure-generic calls **make** with metaclasses **<generic>** and **<generic-with-setter>**, depending on the previous value of the variable that it is trying to upgrade.

    make-generic is a simple wrapper for **make** with metaclass **<generic>**.

ensure-accessor *proc* [*name*]   [procedure]
> Return an accessor with name *name*, if possible by using or upgrading *proc*. If unspecified, *name* defaults to **#f**.
>
> If *proc* is already an accessor, it is returned unchanged.
>
> If *proc* is a Scheme procedure, procedure-with-setter or generic function, **ensure-accessor** returns an accessor that reuses the reusable elements of *proc*.
>
> Otherwise **ensure-accessor** returns a new accessor with no defaults and no methods.

make-accessor [*name*]   [procedure]
> Return a new accessor with name (**car** **name**). If unspecified, *name* defaults to **#f**.

    ensure-accessor calls **make** with metaclass **<generic-with-setter>**, as well as calls to **ensure-generic**, **make-accessor** and (tail recursively) **ensure-accessor**.

    make-accessor calls **make** twice, first with metaclass **<generic>** to create a generic function for the setter, then with metaclass **<generic-with-setter>** to create the accessor, passing the setter generic function as the value of the **#:setter** keyword.

8.11.10 Generic Function Invocation

There is a detailed and customizable protocol involved in the process of invoking a generic function — i.e., in the process of deciding which of the generic function's methods are applicable to the current arguments, and which one of those to apply. Here is a summary diagram of the generic functions involved.

apply-generic (generic)

- **no-method** (generic)
- **compute-applicable-methods** (generic)
- **sort-applicable-methods** (generic)
  - **method-more-specific?** (generic)
- **apply-methods** (generic)
  - **apply-method** (generic)
  - **no-next-method** (generic)
- **no-applicable-method**

    We do not yet have full documentation for these. Please refer to the code (**oop/goops.scm**) for details.

8.12 Redefining a Class

Suppose that a class <my-class> is defined using **define-class** (see Section 8.2 [define-class], page 719), with slots that have accessor functions, and that an application has created several instances of <my-class> using **make** (see Section 8.3 [make], page 720). What then happens if <my-class> is redefined by calling **define-class** again?

8.12.1 Default Class Redefinition Behaviour

GOOPS' default answer to this question is as follows.

- All existing direct instances of <my-class> are converted to be instances of the new class. This is achieved by preserving the values of slots that exist in both the old and new definitions, and initializing the values of new slots in the usual way (see Section 8.3 [make], page 720).

- All existing subclasses of <my-class> are redefined, as though the **define-class** expressions that defined them were re-evaluated following the redefinition of <my-class>, and the class redefinition process described here is applied recursively to the redefined subclasses.

- Once all of its instances and subclasses have been updated, the class metaobject previously bound to the variable <my-class> is no longer needed and so can be allowed to be garbage collected.

To keep things tidy, GOOPS also needs to do a little housekeeping on methods that are associated with the redefined class.

- Slot accessor methods for slots in the old definition should be removed from their generic functions. They will be replaced by accessor methods for the slots of the new class definition.

- Any generic function method that uses the old <my-class> metaobject as one of its formal parameter specializers must be updated to refer to the new <my-class> metaobject. (Whenever a new generic function method is defined, **define-method** adds the method to a list stored in the class metaobject for each class used as a formal parameter specializer, so it is easy to identify all the methods that must be updated when a class is redefined.)

If this class redefinition strategy strikes you as rather counter-intuitive, bear in mind that it is derived from similar behaviour in other object systems such as CLOS, and that experience in those systems has shown it to be very useful in practice.

Also bear in mind that, like most of GOOPS' default behaviour, it can be customized...

8.12.2 Customizing Class Redefinition

When **define-class** notices that a class is being redefined, it constructs the new class metaobject as usual, then invokes the **class-redefinition** generic function with the old and new classes as arguments. Therefore, if the old or new classes have metaclasses other than the default <class>, class redefinition behaviour can be customized by defining a **class-redefinition** method that is specialized for the relevant metaclasses.

class-redefinition   [generic]
> Handle the class redefinition from *old-class* to *new-class*, and return the new class metaobject that should be bound to the variable specified by `define-class`'s first argument.

class-redefinition (*old-class* <*class*>) (*new-class* <*class*>)   [method]
> Implements GOOPS' default class redefinition behaviour, as described in Section 8.12.1 [Default Class Redefinition Behaviour], page 755. Returns the metaobject for the new class definition.

The default `class-redefinition` method, for classes with the default metaclass `<class>`, calls the following generic functions, which could of course be individually customized.

remove-class-accessors! *old*   [generic]
> The default `remove-class-accessors!` method removes the accessor methods of the old class from all classes which they specialize.

update-direct-method! *method old new*   [generic]
> The default `update-direct-method!` method substitutes the new class for the old in all methods specialized to the old class.

update-direct-subclass! *subclass old new*   [generic]
> The default `update-direct-subclass!` method invokes `class-redefinition` recursively to handle the redefinition of subclasses.

An alternative class redefinition strategy could be to leave all existing instances as instances of the old class, but accepting that the old class is now "nameless", since its name has been taken over by the new definition. In this strategy, any existing subclasses could also be left as they are, on the understanding that they inherit from a nameless superclass.

This strategy is easily implemented in GOOPS, by defining a new metaclass, that will be used as the metaclass for all classes to which the strategy should apply, and then defining a `class-redefinition` method that is specialized for this metaclass:

```
(define-class <can-be-nameless> (<class>))

(define-method (class-redefinition (old <can-be-nameless>)
                                   (new <class>))
  new)
```

When customization can be as easy as this, aren't you glad that GOOPS implements the far more difficult strategy as its default!

8.13 Changing the Class of an Instance

When a class is redefined, any existing instance of the redefined class will be modified for the new class definition before the next time that any of the instance's slots is referenced or set. GOOPS modifies each instance by calling the generic function `change-class`.

More generally, you can change the class of an existing instance at any time by invoking the generic function `change-class` with two arguments: the instance and the new class.

The default method for `change-class` decides how to implement the change of class by looking at the slot definitions for the instance's existing class and for the new class. If the new class has slots with the same name as slots in the existing class, the values for those slots are preserved. Slots that are present only in the existing class are discarded. Slots that are present only in the new class are initialized using the corresponding slot definition's init function (see Section 8.8.1 [slot-init-function], page 736).

`change-class` *instance new-class*   [generic]

`change-class` (*obj* <*object*>) (*new* <*class*>)   [method]
> Modify instance *obj* to make it an instance of class *new*.
>
> The value of each of *obj*'s slots is preserved only if a similarly named slot exists in *new*; any other slot values are discarded.
>
> The slots in *new* that do not correspond to any of *obj*'s pre-existing slots are initialized according to *new*'s slot definitions' init functions.

The default `change-class` method also invokes another generic function, `update-instance-for-different-class`, as the last thing that it does before returning. The applied `update-instance-for-different-class` method can make any further adjustments to *new-instance* that are required to complete or modify the change of class. The return value from the applied method is ignored.

`update-instance-for-different-class` *old-instance new-instance*   [generic]
> A generic function that can be customized to put finishing touches to an instance whose class has just been changed. The default `update-instance-for-different-class` method does nothing.

Customized change of class behaviour can be implemented by defining `change-class` methods that are specialized either by the class of the instances to be modified or by the metaclass of the new class.

9 Guile Implementation

At some point, after one has been programming in Scheme for some time, another level of Scheme comes into view: its implementation. Knowledge of how Scheme can be implemented turns out to be necessary to become an expert hacker. As Peter Norvig notes in his retrospective on PAIP[1], "The expert Lisp programmer eventually develops a good 'efficiency model'."

By this Norvig means that over time, the Lisp hacker eventually develops an understanding of how much her code "costs" in terms of space and time.

This chapter describes Guile as an implementation of Scheme: its history, how it represents and evaluates its data, and its compiler. This knowledge can help you to make that step from being one who is merely familiar with Scheme to being a real hacker.

9.1 A Brief History of Guile

Guile is an artifact of historical processes, both as code and as a community of hackers. It is sometimes useful to know this history when hacking the source code, to know about past decisions and future directions.

Of course, the real history of Guile is written by the hackers hacking and not the writers writing, so we round up the section with a note on current status and future directions.

9.1.1 The Emacs Thesis

The story of Guile is the story of bringing the development experience of Emacs to the mass of programs on a GNU system.

Emacs, when it was first created in its GNU form in 1984, was a new take on the problem of "how to make a program". The Emacs thesis is that it is delightful to create composite programs based on an orthogonal kernel written in a low-level language together with a powerful, high-level extension language.

Extension languages foster extensible programs, programs which adapt readily to different users and to changing times. Proof of this can be seen in Emacs' current and continued existence, spanning more than a quarter-century.

Besides providing for modification of a program by others, extension languages are good for *intension* as well. Programs built in "the Emacs way" are pleasurable and easy for their authors to flesh out with the features that they need.

After the Emacs experience was appreciated more widely, a number of hackers started to consider how to spread this experience to the rest of the GNU system. It was clear that the easiest way to Emacsify a program would be to embed a shared language implementation into it.

9.1.2 Early Days

Tom Lord was the first to fully concentrate his efforts on an embeddable language runtime, which he named "GEL", the GNU Extension Language.

---

[1] PAIP is the common abbreviation for *Paradigms of Artificial Intelligence Programming*, an old but still useful text on Lisp. Norvig's retrospective sums up the lessons of PAIP, and can be found at http://norvig.com/Lisp-retro.html.

GEL was the product of converting SCM, Aubrey Jaffer's implementation of Scheme, into something more appropriate to embedding as a library. (SCM was itself based on an implementation by George Carrette, SIOD.)

Lord managed to convince Richard Stallman to dub GEL the official extension language for the GNU project. It was a natural fit, given that Scheme was a cleaner, more modern Lisp than Emacs Lisp. Part of the argument was that eventually when GEL became more capable, it could gain the ability to execute other languages, especially Emacs Lisp.

Due to a naming conflict with another programming language, Jim Blandy suggested a new name for GEL: "Guile". Besides being a recursive acronym, "Guile" craftily follows the naming of its ancestors, "Planner", "Conniver", and "Schemer". (The latter was truncated to "Scheme" due to a 6-character file name limit on an old operating system.) Finally, "Guile" suggests "guy-ell", or "Guy L. Steele", who, together with Gerald Sussman, originally discovered Scheme.

Around the same time that Guile (then GEL) was readying itself for public release, another extension language was gaining in popularity, Tcl. Many developers found advantages in Tcl because of its shell-like syntax and its well-developed graphical widgets library, Tk. Also, at the time there was a large marketing push promoting Tcl as a "universal extension language".

Richard Stallman, as the primary author of GNU Emacs, had a particular vision of what extension languages should be, and Tcl did not seem to him to be as capable as Emacs Lisp. He posted a criticism to the comp.lang.tcl newsgroup, sparking one of the internet's legendary flamewars. As part of these discussions, retrospectively dubbed the "Tcl Wars", he announced the Free Software Foundation's intent to promote Guile as the extension language for the GNU project.

It is a common misconception that Guile was created as a reaction to Tcl. While it is true that the public announcement of Guile happened at the same time as the "Tcl wars", Guile was created out of a condition that existed outside the polemic. Indeed, the need for a powerful language to bridge the gap between extension of existing applications and a more fully dynamic programming environment is still with us today.

9.1.3 A Scheme of Many Maintainers

Surveying the field, it seems that Scheme implementations correspond with their maintainers on an N-to-1 relationship. That is to say, that those people that implement Schemes might do so on a number of occasions, but that the lifetime of a given Scheme is tied to the maintainership of one individual.

Guile is atypical in this regard.

Tom Lord maintained Guile for its first year and a half or so, corresponding to the end of 1994 through the middle of 1996. The releases made in this time constitute an arc from SCM as a standalone program to Guile as a reusable, embeddable library, but passing through a explosion of features: embedded Tcl and Tk, a toolchain for compiling and disassembling Java, addition of a C-like syntax, creation of a module system, and a start at a rich POSIX interface.

Only some of those features remain in Guile. There were ongoing tensions between providing a small, embeddable language, and one which had all of the features (e.g. a graphical toolkit) that a modern Emacs might need. In the end, as Guile gained in uptake, the development team decided to focus on depth, documentation and orthogonality rather than on breadth. This has been the focus of Guile ever since, although there is a wide range of third-party libraries for Guile.

Jim Blandy presided over that period of stabilization, in the three years until the end of 1999, when he too moved on to other projects. Since then, Guile has had a group maintainership. The first group was Maciej Stachowiak, Mikael Djurfeldt, and Marius Vollmer, with Vollmer staying on the longest. By late 2007, Vollmer had mostly moved on to other things, so Neil Jerram and Ludovic Courtès stepped up to take on the primary maintenance responsibility. Jerram and Courtès were joined by Andy Wingo in late 2009.

Of course, a large part of the actual work on Guile has come from other contributors too numerous to mention, but without whom the world would be a poorer place.

9.1.4 A Timeline of Selected Guile Releases

guile-i — 4 February 1995
>   SCM, turned into a library.

guile-ii — 6 April 1995
>   A low-level module system was added. Tcl/Tk support was added, allowing extension of Scheme by Tcl or vice versa. POSIX support was improved, and there was an experimental stab at Java integration.

guile-iii — 18 August 1995
>   The C-like syntax, ctax, was improved, but mostly this release featured a start at the task of breaking Guile into pieces.

1.0 — 5 January 1997
>   `#f` was distinguished from `'()`. User-level, cooperative multi-threading was added. Source-level debugging became more useful, and programmer's and user's manuals were begun. The module system gained a high-level interface, which is still used today in more or less the same form.

1.1 — 16 May 1997
1.2 — 24 June 1997
>   Support for Tcl/Tk and ctax were split off as separate packages, and have remained there since. Guile became more compatible with SCSH, and more useful as a UNIX scripting language. Libguile could now be built as a shared library, and third-party extensions written in C became loadable via dynamic linking.

1.3.0 — 19 October 1998
>   Command-line editing became much more pleasant through the use of the readline library. The initial support for internationalization via multi-byte strings was removed; 10 years were to pass before proper internationalization would land again. Initial Emacs Lisp support landed, ports gained better support for file descriptors, and fluids were added.

1.3.2 — 20 August 1999

1.3.4 — 25 September 1999

1.4 — 21 June 2000

> A long list of lispy features were added: hooks, Common Lisp's `format`, optional and keyword procedure arguments, `getopt-long`, sorting, random numbers, and many other fixes and enhancements. Guile also gained an interactive debugger, interactive help, and better backtraces.

1.6 — 6 September 2002

> Guile gained support for the R5RS standard, and added a number of SRFI modules. The module system was expanded with programmatic support for identifier selection and renaming. The GOOPS object system was merged into Guile core.

1.8 — 20 February 2006

> Guile's arbitrary-precision arithmetic switched to use the GMP library, and added support for exact rationals. Guile's embedded user-space threading was removed in favor of POSIX pre-emptive threads, providing true multiprocessing. Gettext support was added, and Guile's C API was cleaned up and orthogonalized in a massive way.

2.0 — 16 February 2010

> A virtual machine was added to Guile, along with the associated compiler and toolchain. Support for internationalization was finally reimplemented, in terms of unicode, locales, and libunistring. Running Guile instances became controllable and debuggable from within Emacs, via Geiser. Guile caught up to features found in a number of other Schemes: SRFI-18 threads, module-hygienic macros, a profiler, tracer, and debugger, SSAX XML integration, bytevectors, a dynamic FFI, delimited continuations, module versions, and partial support for R6RS.

9.1.5 Status, or: Your Help Needed

Guile has achieved much of what it set out to achieve, but there is much remaining to do.

There is still the old problem of bringing existing applications into a more Emacs-like experience. Guile has had some successes in this respect, but still most applications in the GNU system are without Guile integration.

Getting Guile to those applications takes an investment, the "hacktivation energy" needed to wire Guile into a program that only pays off once it is good enough to enable new kinds of behavior. This would be a great way for new hackers to contribute: take an application that you use and that you know well, think of something that it can't yet do, and figure out a way to integrate Guile and implement that task in Guile.

With time, perhaps this exposure can reverse itself, whereby programs can run under Guile instead of vice versa, eventually resulting in the Emacsification of the entire GNU system. Indeed, this is the reason for the naming of the many Guile modules that live in the `ice-9` namespace, a nod to the fictional substance in Kurt Vonnegut's novel, Cat's Cradle, capable of acting as a seed crystal to crystallize the mass of software.

Implicit to this whole discussion is the idea that dynamic languages are somehow better than languages like C. While languages like C have their place, Guile's take on this question is that yes, Scheme is more expressive than C, and more fun to write. This realization carries an imperative with it to write as much code in Scheme as possible rather than in other languages.

These days it is possible to write extensible applications almost entirely from high-level languages, through byte-code and native compilation, speed gains in the underlying hardware, and foreign call interfaces in the high-level language. Smalltalk systems are like this, as are Common Lisp-based systems. While there already are a number of pure-Guile applications out there, users still need to drop down to C for some tasks: interfacing to system libraries that don't have prebuilt Guile interfaces, and for some tasks requiring high performance.

The addition of the virtual machine in Guile 2.0, together with the compiler infrastructure, should go a long way to addressing the speed issues. But there is much optimization to be done. Interested contributors will find lots of delightful low-hanging fruit, from simple profile-driven optimization to hacking a just-in-time compiler from VM bytecode to native code.

Still, even with an all-Guile application, sometimes you want to provide an opportunity for users to extend your program from a language with a syntax that is closer to C, or to Python. Another interesting idea to consider is compiling e.g. Python to Guile. It's not that far-fetched of an idea: see for example IronPython or JRuby.

And then there's Emacs itself. Though there is a somewhat-working Emacs Lisp language frontend for Guile, it cannot yet execute all of Emacs Lisp. A serious integration of Guile with Emacs would replace the Elisp virtual machine with Guile, and provide the necessary C shims so that Guile could emulate Emacs' C API. This would give lots of exciting things to Emacs: native threads, a real object system, more sophisticated types, cleaner syntax, and access to all of the Guile extensions.

Finally, there is another axis of crystallization, the axis between different Scheme implementations. Guile does not yet support the latest Scheme standard, R6RS, and should do so. Like all standards, R6RS is imperfect, but supporting it will allow more code to run on Guile without modification, and will allow Guile hackers to produce code compatible with other schemes. Help in this regard would be much appreciated.

9.2 Data Representation

Scheme is a latently-typed language; this means that the system cannot, in general, determine the type of a given expression at compile time. Types only become apparent at run time. Variables do not have fixed types; a variable may hold a pair at one point, an integer at the next, and a thousand-element vector later. Instead, values, not variables, have fixed types.

In order to implement standard Scheme functions like `pair?` and `string?` and provide garbage collection, the representation of every value must contain enough information to accurately determine its type at run time. Often, Scheme systems also use this information to determine whether a program has attempted to apply an operation to an inappropriately typed value (such as taking the `car` of a string).

Because variables, pairs, and vectors may hold values of any type, Scheme implementations use a uniform representation for values — a single type large enough to hold either a complete value or a pointer to a complete value, along with the necessary typing information.

The following sections will present a simple typing system, and then make some refinements to correct its major weaknesses. We then conclude with a discussion of specific choices that Guile has made regarding garbage collection and data representation.

9.2.1 A Simple Representation

The simplest way to represent Scheme values in C would be to represent each value as a pointer to a structure containing a type indicator, followed by a union carrying the real value. Assuming that SCM is the name of our universal type, we can write:

```
enum type { integer, pair, string, vector, ... };

typedef struct value *SCM;

struct value {
  enum type type;
  union {
    int integer;
    struct { SCM car, cdr; } pair;
    struct { int length; char *elts; } string;
    struct { int length; SCM  *elts; } vector;
    ...
  } value;
};
```

with the ellipses replaced with code for the remaining Scheme types.

This representation is sufficient to implement all of Scheme's semantics. If x is an SCM value:

- To test if x is an integer, we can write x->type == integer.
- To find its value, we can write x->value.integer.
- To test if x is a vector, we can write x->type == vector.
- If we know x is a vector, we can write x->value.vector.elts[0] to refer to its first element.
- If we know x is a pair, we can write x->value.pair.car to extract its car.

9.2.2 Faster Integers

Unfortunately, the above representation has a serious disadvantage. In order to return an integer, an expression must allocate a struct value, initialize it to represent that integer, and return a pointer to it. Furthermore, fetching an integer's value requires a memory reference, which is much slower than a register reference on most processors. Since integers are extremely common, this representation is too costly, in both time and space. Integers should be very cheap to create and manipulate.

One possible solution comes from the observation that, on many architectures, heap-allocated data (i.e., what you get when you call malloc) must be aligned on an eight-byte boundary. (Whether or not the machine actually requires it, we can write our own allocator for `struct value` objects that assures this is true.) In this case, the lower three bits of the structure's address are known to be zero.

This gives us the room we need to provide an improved representation for integers. We make the following rules:

- If the lower three bits of an SCM value are zero, then the SCM value is a pointer to a `struct value`, and everything proceeds as before.

- Otherwise, the SCM value represents an integer, whose value appears in its upper bits.

Here is C code implementing this convention:

```
enum type { pair, string, vector, ... };

typedef struct value *SCM;

struct value {
  enum type type;
  union {
    struct { SCM car, cdr; } pair;
    struct { int length; char *elts; } string;
    struct { int length; SCM  *elts; } vector;
    ...
  } value;
};

#define POINTER_P(x) (((int) (x) & 7) == 0)
#define INTEGER_P(x) (! POINTER_P (x))

#define GET_INTEGER(x)  ((int) (x) >> 3)
#define MAKE_INTEGER(x) ((SCM) (((x) << 3) | 1))
```

Notice that `integer` no longer appears as an element of `enum type`, and the union has lost its `integer` member. Instead, we use the `POINTER_P` and `INTEGER_P` macros to make a coarse classification of values into integers and non-integers, and do further type testing as before.

Here's how we would answer the questions posed above (again, assume x is an SCM value):

- To test if x is an integer, we can write `INTEGER_P` (x).

- To find its value, we can write `GET_INTEGER` (x).

- To test if x is a vector, we can write:

```
POINTER_P (x) && x->type == vector
```

Given the new representation, we must make sure x is truly a pointer before we dereference it to determine its complete type.

- If we know x is a vector, we can write `x->value.vector.elts[0]` to refer to its first element, as before.

- If we know x is a pair, we can write `x->value.pair.car` to extract its car, just as before.

This representation allows us to operate more efficiently on integers than the first. For example, if x and y are known to be integers, we can compute their sum as follows:

```
MAKE_INTEGER (GET_INTEGER (x) + GET_INTEGER (y))
```

Now, integer math requires no allocation or memory references. Most real Scheme systems actually implement addition and other operations using an even more efficient algorithm, but this essay isn't about bit-twiddling. (Hint: how do you decide when to overflow to a bignum? How would you do it in assembly?)

9.2.3 Cheaper Pairs

However, there is yet another issue to confront. Most Scheme heaps contain more pairs than any other type of object; Jonathan Rees said at one point that pairs occupy 45% of the heap in his Scheme implementation, Scheme 48. However, our representation above spends three SCM-sized words per pair — one for the type, and two for the CAR and CDR. Is there any way to represent pairs using only two words?

Let us refine the convention we established earlier. Let us assert that:

- If the bottom three bits of an SCM value are #b000, then it is a pointer, as before.
- If the bottom three bits are #b001, then the upper bits are an integer. This is a bit more restrictive than before.
- If the bottom two bits are #b010, then the value, with the bottom three bits masked out, is the address of a pair.

Here is the new C code:

```
enum type { string, vector, ... };

typedef struct value *SCM;

struct value {
  enum type type;
  union {
    struct { int length; char *elts; } string;
    struct { int length; SCM  *elts; } vector;
    ...
  } value;
};

struct pair {
  SCM car, cdr;
};

#define POINTER_P(x) (((int) (x) & 7) == 0)

#define INTEGER_P(x)  (((int) (x) & 7) == 1)
#define GET_INTEGER(x)  ((int) (x) >> 3)
#define MAKE_INTEGER(x) ((SCM) (((x) << 3) | 1))

#define PAIR_P(x) (((int) (x) & 7) == 2)
#define GET_PAIR(x) ((struct pair *) ((int) (x) & ~7))
```

Notice that `enum type` and `struct value` now only contain provisions for vectors and strings; both integers and pairs have become special cases. The code above also assumes that an `int` is large enough to hold a pointer, which isn't generally true.

Our list of examples is now as follows:

- To test if x is an integer, we can write `INTEGER_P (x)`; this is as before.

- To find its value, we can write `GET_INTEGER (x)`, as before.

- To test if x is a vector, we can write:

    `POINTER_P (x) && x->type == vector`

    We must still make sure that x is a pointer to a `struct value` before dereferencing it to find its type.

- If we know x is a vector, we can write `x->value.vector.elts[0]` to refer to its first element, as before.

- We can write `PAIR_P (x)` to determine if x is a pair, and then write `GET_PAIR (x)->car` to refer to its car.

This change in representation reduces our heap size by 15%. It also makes it cheaper to decide if a value is a pair, because no memory references are necessary; it suffices to check the bottom two bits of the `SCM` value. This may be significant when traversing lists, a common activity in a Scheme system.

Again, most real Scheme systems use a slightly different implementation; for example, if GET_PAIR subtracts off the low bits of `x`, instead of masking them off, the optimizer will often be able to combine that subtraction with the addition of the offset of the structure member we are referencing, making a modified pointer as fast to use as an unmodified pointer.

9.2.4 Conservative Garbage Collection

Aside from the latent typing, the major source of constraints on a Scheme implementation's data representation is the garbage collector. The collector must be able to traverse every live object in the heap, to determine which objects are not live, and thus collectable.

There are many ways to implement this. Guile's garbage collection is built on a library, the Boehm-Demers-Weiser conservative garbage collector (BDW-GC). The BDW-GC "just works", for the most part. But since it is interesting to know how these things work, we include here a high-level description of what the BDW-GC does.

Garbage collection has two logical phases: a *mark* phase, in which the set of live objects is enumerated, and a *sweep* phase, in which objects not traversed in the mark phase are collected. Correct functioning of the collector depends on being able to traverse the entire set of live objects.

In the mark phase, the collector scans the system's global variables and the local variables on the stack to determine which objects are immediately accessible by the C code. It then scans those objects to find the objects they point to, and so on. The collector logically sets a *mark bit* on each object it finds, so each object is traversed only once.

When the collector can find no unmarked objects pointed to by marked objects, it assumes that any objects that are still unmarked will never be used by the program (since there is no path of dereferences from any global or local variable that reaches them) and deallocates them.

In the above paragraphs, we did not specify how the garbage collector finds the global and local variables; as usual, there are many different approaches. Frequently, the programmer must maintain a list of pointers to all global variables that refer to the heap, and another list (adjusted upon entry to and exit from each function) of local variables, for the collector's benefit.

The list of global variables is usually not too difficult to maintain, since global variables are relatively rare. However, an explicitly maintained list of local variables (in the author's personal experience) is a nightmare to maintain. Thus, the BDW-GC uses a technique called *conservative garbage collection*, to make the local variable list unnecessary.

The trick to conservative collection is to treat the stack as an ordinary range of memory, and assume that *every* word on the stack is a pointer into the heap. Thus, the collector marks all objects whose addresses appear anywhere in the stack, without knowing for sure how that word is meant to be interpreted.

In addition to the stack, the BDW-GC will also scan static data sections. This means that global variables are also scanned when looking for live Scheme objects.

Obviously, such a system will occasionally retain objects that are actually garbage, and should be freed. In practice, this is not a problem. The alternative, an explicitly maintained list of local variable addresses, is effectively much less reliable, due to programmer error. Interested readers should see the BDW-GC web page at `http://www.hpl.hp.com/personal/Hans_Boehm/gc`, for more information.

9.2.5 The SCM Type in Guile

Guile classifies Scheme objects into two kinds: those that fit entirely within an SCM, and those that require heap storage.

The former class are called *immediates*. The class of immediates includes small integers, characters, boolean values, the empty list, the mysterious end-of-file object, and some others.

The remaining types are called, not surprisingly, *non-immediates*. They include pairs, procedures, strings, vectors, and all other data types in Guile. For non-immediates, the SCM word contains a pointer to data on the heap, with further information about the object in question is stored in that data.

This section describes how the SCM type is actually represented and used at the C level. Interested readers should see `libguile/tags.h` for an exposition of how Guile stores type information.

In fact, there are two basic C data types to represent objects in Guile: SCM and `scm_t_bits`.

9.2.5.1 Relationship between SCM and `scm_t_bits`

A variable of type SCM is guaranteed to hold a valid Scheme object. A variable of type `scm_t_bits`, on the other hand, may hold a representation of a SCM value as a C integral type, but may also hold any C value, even if it does not correspond to a valid Scheme object.

For a variable x of type SCM, the Scheme object's type information is stored in a form that is not directly usable. To be able to work on the type encoding of the scheme value, the SCM variable has to be transformed into the corresponding representation as a `scm_t_bits` variable y by using the SCM_UNPACK macro. Once this has been done, the type of the scheme object x can be derived from the content of the bits of the `scm_t_bits` value y, in the way illustrated by the example earlier in this chapter (see Section 9.2.3 [Cheaper Pairs], page 766). Conversely, a valid bit encoding of a Scheme value as a `scm_t_bits` variable can be transformed into the corresponding SCM value using the `SCM_PACK` macro.

9.2.5.2 Immediate objects

A Scheme object may either be an immediate, i.e. carrying all necessary information by itself, or it may contain a reference to a *cell* with additional information on the heap. Although in general it should be irrelevant for user code whether an object is an immediate or not, within Guile's own code the distinction is sometimes of importance. Thus, the following low level macro is provided:

int SCM_IMP (*SCM x*)   [Macro]
> A Scheme object is an immediate if it fulfills the `SCM_IMP` predicate, otherwise it holds an encoded reference to a heap cell. The result of the predicate is delivered as a C style boolean value. User code and code that extends Guile should normally not be required to use this macro.

Summary:

- Given a Scheme object *x* of unknown type, check first with `SCM_IMP` (*x*) if it is an immediate object.

- If so, all of the type and value information can be determined from the `scm_t_bits` value that is delivered by `SCM_UNPACK` (*x*).

There are a number of special values in Scheme, most of them documented elsewhere in this manual. It's not quite the right place to put them, but for now, here's a list of the C names given to some of these values:

SCM SCM_EOL   [Macro]
> The Scheme empty list object, or "End Of List" object, usually written in Scheme as `'()`.

SCM SCM_EOF_VAL   [Macro]
> The Scheme end-of-file value. It has no standard written representation, for obvious reasons.

SCM SCM_UNSPECIFIED   [Macro]
> The value returned by some (but not all) expressions that the Scheme standard says return an "unspecified" value.
>
> This is sort of a weirdly literal way to take things, but the standard read-eval-print loop prints nothing when the expression returns this value, so it's not a bad idea to return this when you can't think of anything else helpful.

SCM SCM_UNDEFINED   [Macro]
> The "undefined" value. Its most important property is that is not equal to any valid Scheme value. This is put to various internal uses by C code interacting with Guile.
>
> For example, when you write a C function that is callable from Scheme and which takes optional arguments, the interpreter passes `SCM_UNDEFINED` for any arguments you did not receive.
>
> We also use this to mark unbound variables.

`int SCM_UNBNDP` (*SCM x*)   [Macro]
> Return true if *x* is `SCM_UNDEFINED`. Note that this is not a check to see if *x* is `SCM_UNBOUND`. History will not be kind to us.

9.2.5.3 Non-immediate objects

A Scheme object of type SCM that does not fulfill the `SCM_IMP` predicate holds an encoded reference to a heap cell. This reference can be decoded to a C pointer to a heap cell using the SCM2PTR macro. The encoding of a pointer to a heap cell into a SCM value is done using the PTR2SCM macro.

`scm_t_cell * SCM2PTR` (*SCM x*)   [Macro]
> Extract and return the heap cell pointer from a non-immediate SCM object *x*.

`SCM PTR2SCM` (*scm_t_cell * x*)   [Macro]
> Return a SCM value that encodes a reference to the heap cell pointer *x*.

Note that it is also possible to transform a non-immediate SCM value by using `SCM_UNPACK` into a `scm_t_bits` variable. However, the result of `SCM_UNPACK` may not be used as a pointer to a `scm_t_cell`: only SCM2PTR is guaranteed to transform a SCM object into a valid pointer to a heap cell. Also, it is not allowed to apply PTR2SCM to anything that is not a valid pointer to a heap cell.

Summary:

- Only use SCM2PTR on SCM values for which `SCM_IMP` is false!
- Don't use `(scm_t_cell *) SCM_UNPACK (x)`! Use `SCM2PTR (x)` instead!
- Don't use PTR2SCM for anything but a cell pointer!

9.2.5.4 Allocating Cells

Guile provides both ordinary cells with two slots, and double cells with four slots. The following two function are the most primitive way to allocate such cells.

If the caller intends to use it as a header for some other type, she must pass an appropriate magic value in *word_0*, to mark it as a member of that type, and pass whatever value as *word_1*, etc that the type expects. You should generally not need these functions, unless you are implementing a new datatype, and thoroughly understand the code in `<libguile/tags.h>`.

If you just want to allocate pairs, use `scm_cons`.

`SCM scm_cell` (*scm_t_bits word_0, scm_t_bits word_1*)   [Function]
> Allocate a new cell, initialize the two slots with *word_0* and *word_1*, and return it.
>
> Note that *word_0* and *word_1* are of type `scm_t_bits`. If you want to pass a SCM object, you need to use `SCM_UNPACK`.

`SCM scm_double_cell` (*scm_t_bits word_0, scm_t_bits word_1, scm_t_bits*   [Function]
> *word_2, scm_t_bits word_3*)
> Like `scm_cell`, but allocates a double cell with four slots.

9.2.5.5 Heap Cell Type Information

Heap cells contain a number of entries, each of which is either a scheme object of type `SCM` or a raw C value of type `scm_t_bits`. Which of the cell entries contain Scheme objects and which contain raw C values is determined by the first entry of the cell, which holds the cell type information.

`scm_t_bits SCM_CELL_TYPE` (*SCM x*)   [Macro]

> For a non-immediate Scheme object *x*, deliver the content of the first entry of the heap cell referenced by *x*. This value holds the information about the cell type.

`void SCM_SET_CELL_TYPE` (*SCM x, scm_t_bits t*)   [Macro]

> For a non-immediate Scheme object *x*, write the value *t* into the first entry of the heap cell referenced by *x*. The value *t* must hold a valid cell type.

9.2.5.6 Accessing Cell Entries

For a non-immediate Scheme object *x*, the object type can be determined by reading the cell type entry using the `SCM_CELL_TYPE` macro. For each different type of cell it is known which cell entries hold Scheme objects and which cell entries hold raw C data. To access the different cell entries appropriately, the following macros are provided.

`scm_t_bits SCM_CELL_WORD` (*SCM x, unsigned int n*)   [Macro]

> Deliver the cell entry *n* of the heap cell referenced by the non-immediate Scheme object *x* as raw data. It is illegal, to access cell entries that hold Scheme objects by using these macros. For convenience, the following macros are also provided.
>
> - SCM_CELL_WORD_0 $(x) \Rightarrow$ SCM_CELL_WORD $(x, 0)$
> - SCM_CELL_WORD_1 $(x) \Rightarrow$ SCM_CELL_WORD $(x, 1)$
> - ...
> - SCM_CELL_WORD_n $(x) \Rightarrow$ SCM_CELL_WORD (x, n)

`SCM SCM_CELL_OBJECT` (*SCM x, unsigned int n*)   [Macro]

> Deliver the cell entry *n* of the heap cell referenced by the non-immediate Scheme object *x* as a Scheme object. It is illegal, to access cell entries that do not hold Scheme objects by using these macros. For convenience, the following macros are also provided.
>
> - SCM_CELL_OBJECT_0 $(x) \Rightarrow$ SCM_CELL_OBJECT $(x, 0)$
> - SCM_CELL_OBJECT_1 $(x) \Rightarrow$ SCM_CELL_OBJECT $(x, 1)$
> - ...
> - SCM_CELL_OBJECT_n $(x) \Rightarrow$ SCM_CELL_OBJECT (x, n)

`void SCM_SET_CELL_WORD` (*SCM x, unsigned int n, scm_t_bits w*)   [Macro]

> Write the raw C value *w* into entry number *n* of the heap cell referenced by the non-immediate Scheme value *x*. Values that are written into cells this way may only be read from the cells using the `SCM_CELL_WORD` macros or, in case cell entry 0 is written, using the `SCM_CELL_TYPE` macro. For the special case of cell entry 0 it has to be made sure that *w* contains a cell type information which does not describe a Scheme object. For convenience, the following macros are also provided.

- SCM_SET_CELL_WORD_0 $(x, w) \Rightarrow$ SCM_SET_CELL_WORD $(x, 0, w)$
- SCM_SET_CELL_WORD_1 $(x, w) \Rightarrow$ SCM_SET_CELL_WORD $(x, 1, w)$
- ...
- SCM_SET_CELL_WORD_n $(x, w) \Rightarrow$ SCM_SET_CELL_WORD (x, n, w)

`void SCM_SET_CELL_OBJECT` (*SCM* `x`, *unsigned int* `n`, *SCM* `o`)   [Macro]

Write the Scheme object *o* into entry number *n* of the heap cell referenced by the non-immediate Scheme value *x*. Values that are written into cells this way may only be read from the cells using the `SCM_CELL_OBJECT` macros or, in case cell entry 0 is written, using the `SCM_CELL_TYPE` macro. For the special case of cell entry 0 the writing of a Scheme object into this cell is only allowed if the cell forms a Scheme pair. For convenience, the following macros are also provided.

- SCM_SET_CELL_OBJECT_0 $(x, o) \Rightarrow$ SCM_SET_CELL_OBJECT $(x, 0, o)$
- SCM_SET_CELL_OBJECT_1 $(x, o) \Rightarrow$ SCM_SET_CELL_OBJECT $(x, 1, o)$
- ...
- SCM_SET_CELL_OBJECT_n $(x, o) \Rightarrow$ SCM_SET_CELL_OBJECT (x, n, o)

Summary:

- For a non-immediate Scheme object *x* of unknown type, get the type information by using `SCM_CELL_TYPE` (`x`).

- As soon as the cell type information is available, only use the appropriate access methods to read and write data to the different cell entries.

9.3 A Virtual Machine for Guile

Guile has both an interpreter and a compiler. To a user, the difference is transparent—interpreted and compiled procedures can call each other as they please.

The difference is that the compiler creates and interprets bytecode for a custom virtual machine, instead of interpreting the S-expressions directly. Loading and running compiled code is faster than loading and running source code.

The virtual machine that does the bytecode interpretation is a part of Guile itself. This section describes the nature of Guile's virtual machine.

9.3.1 Why a VM?

For a long time, Guile only had an interpreter. Guile's interpreter operated directly on the S-expression representation of Scheme source code.

But while the interpreter was highly optimized and hand-tuned, it still performs many needless computations during the course of evaluating an expression. For example, application of a function to arguments needlessly consed up the arguments in a list. Evaluation of an expression always had to figure out what the car of the expression is – a procedure, a memoized form, or something else. All values have to be allocated on the heap. Et cetera.

The solution to this problem was to compile the higher-level language, Scheme, into a lower-level language for which all of the checks and dispatching have already been done—the code is instead stripped to the bare minimum needed to "do the job".

The question becomes then, what low-level language to choose? There are many options. We could compile to native code directly, but that poses portability problems for Guile, as it is a highly cross-platform project.

So we want the performance gains that compilation provides, but we also want to maintain the portability benefits of a single code path. The obvious solution is to compile to a virtual machine that is present on all Guile installations.

The easiest (and most fun) way to depend on a virtual machine is to implement the virtual machine within Guile itself. This way the virtual machine provides what Scheme needs (tail calls, multiple values, `call/cc`) and can provide optimized inline instructions for Guile (`cons`, `struct-ref`, etc.).

So this is what Guile does. The rest of this section describes that VM that Guile implements, and the compiled procedures that run on it.

Before moving on, though, we should note that though we spoke of the interpreter in the past tense, Guile still has an interpreter. The difference is that before, it was Guile's main evaluator, and so was implemented in highly optimized C; now, it is actually implemented in Scheme, and compiled down to VM bytecode, just like any other program. (There is still a C interpreter around, used to bootstrap the compiler, but it is not normally used at runtime.)

The upside of implementing the interpreter in Scheme is that we preserve tail calls and multiple-value handling between interpreted and compiled code. The downside is that the interpreter in Guile 2.0 is slower than the interpreter in 1.8. We hope the that the compiler's speed makes up for the loss!

Also note that this decision to implement a bytecode compiler does not preclude native compilation. We can compile from bytecode to native code at runtime, or even do ahead of time compilation. More possibilities are discussed in Section 9.4.8 [Extending the Compiler], page 804.

9.3.2 VM Concepts

Compiled code is run by a virtual machine (VM). Each thread has its own VM. When a compiled procedure is run, Guile looks up the virtual machine for the current thread and executes the procedure using that VM.

Guile's virtual machine is a stack machine—that is, it has few registers, and the instructions defined in the VM operate by pushing and popping values from a stack.

Stack memory is exclusive to the virtual machine that owns it. In addition to their stacks, virtual machines also have access to the global memory (modules, global bindings, etc) that is shared among other parts of Guile, including other VMs.

A VM has generic instructions, such as those to reference local variables, and instructions designed to support Guile's languages – mathematical instructions that support the entire numerical tower, an inlined implementation of `cons`, etc.

The registers that a VM has are as follows:

- ip - Instruction pointer
- sp - Stack pointer
- fp - Frame pointer

In other architectures, the instruction pointer is sometimes called the "program counter" (pc). This set of registers is pretty typical for stack machines; their exact meanings in the context of Guile's VM are described in the next section.

9.3.3 Stack Layout

While not strictly necessary to understand how to work with the VM, it is instructive and sometimes entertaining to consider the structure of the VM stack.

Logically speaking, a VM stack is composed of "frames". Each frame corresponds to the application of one compiled procedure, and contains storage space for arguments, local variables, intermediate values, and some bookkeeping information (such as what to do after the frame computes its value).

While the compiler is free to do whatever it wants to, as long as the semantics of a computation are preserved, in practice every time you call a function, a new frame is created. (The notable exception of course is the tail call case, see Section 3.3.2 [Tail Calls], page 24.)

Within a frame, you have the data associated with the function application itself, which is of a fixed size, and the stack space for intermediate values. Sometimes only the former is referred to as the "frame", and the latter is the "stack", although all pending application frames can have some intermediate computations interleaved on the stack.

The structure of the fixed part of an application frame is as follows:

```
          Stack
| ...                |
| Intermed. val. 0   | <- fp + bp->nargs + bp->nlocs = SCM_FRAME_UPPER_ADDRESS (
+===================+
| Local variable 1   |
| Local variable 0   | <- fp + bp->nargs
| Argument 1         |
| Argument 0         | <- fp
| Program            | <- fp - 1
+-------------------+
| Return address     |
| MV return address  |
| Dynamic link       | <- fp - 4 = SCM_FRAME_DATA_ADDRESS (fp) = SCM_FRAME_LOWER
+===================+
|                    |
```

In the above drawing, the stack grows upward. The intermediate values stored in the application of this frame are stored above SCM_FRAME_UPPER_ADDRESS (fp). bp refers to the struct scm_objcode data associated with the program at fp - 1. nargs and nlocs are properties of the compiled procedure, which will be discussed later.

The individual fields of the frame are as follows:

Return address

> The ip that was in effect before this program was applied. When we return from this activation frame, we will jump back to this ip.

MV return address

> The `ip` to return to if this application returns multiple values. For continuations that only accept one value, this value will be `NULL`; for others, it will be an `ip` that points to a multiple-value return address in the calling code. That code will expect the top value on the stack to be an integer—the number of values being returned—and that below that integer there are the values being returned.

Dynamic link

> This is the `fp` in effect before this program was applied. In effect, this and the return address are the registers that are always "saved". The dynamic link links the current frame to the previous frame; computing a stack trace involves traversing these frames.

Local variable *n*

> Lambda-local variables that are all allocated as part of the frame. This makes access to variables very cheap.

Argument *n*

> The calling convention of the VM requires arguments of a function application to be pushed on the stack, and here they are. References to arguments dispatch to these locations on the stack.

Program This is the program being applied. For more information on how programs are implemented, See Section 9.3.5 [VM Programs], page 776.

9.3.4 Variables and the VM

Consider the following Scheme code as an example:

```
(define (foo a)
  (lambda (b) (list foo a b)))
```

Within the lambda expression, `foo` is a top-level variable, `a` is a lexically captured variable, and `b` is a local variable.

Another way to refer to `a` and `b` is to say that `a` is a "free" variable, since it is not defined within the lambda, and `b` is a "bound" variable. These are the terms used in the *lambda calculus*, a mathematical notation for describing functions. The lambda calculus is useful because it allows one to prove statements about functions. It is especially good at describing scope relations, and it is for that reason that we mention it here.

Guile allocates all variables on the stack. When a lexically enclosed procedure with free variables—a *closure*—is created, it copies those variables into its free variable vector. References to free variables are then redirected through the free variable vector.

If a variable is ever `set!`, however, it will need to be heap-allocated instead of stack-allocated, so that different closures that capture the same variable can see the same value. Also, this allows continuations to capture a reference to the variable, instead of to its value at one point in time. For these reasons, `set!` variables are allocated in "boxes"—actually, in variable cells. See Section 6.19.7 [Variables], page 390, for more information. References to `set!` variables are indirected through the boxes.

Thus perhaps counterintuitively, what would seem "closer to the metal", viz `set!`, actually forces an extra memory allocation and indirection.

Going back to our example, b may be allocated on the stack, as it is never mutated.

a may also be allocated on the stack, as it too is never mutated. Within the enclosed lambda, its value will be copied into (and referenced from) the free variables vector.

foo is a top-level variable, because foo is not lexically bound in this example.

9.3.5 Compiled Procedures are VM Programs

By default, when you enter in expressions at Guile's REPL, they are first compiled to VM object code, then that VM object code is executed to produce a value. If the expression evaluates to a procedure, the result of this process is a compiled procedure.

A compiled procedure is a compound object, consisting of its bytecode, a reference to any captured lexical variables, an object array, and some metadata such as the procedure's arity, name, and documentation. You can pick apart these pieces with the accessors in (system vm program). See Section 6.9.3 [Compiled Procedures], page 245, for a full API reference.

The object array of a compiled procedure, also known as the *object table*, holds all Scheme objects whose values are known not to change across invocations of the procedure: constant strings, symbols, etc. The object table of a program is initialized right before a program is loaded with load-program. See Section 9.3.6.8 [Loading Instructions], page 786, for more information.

Variable objects are one such type of constant object: when a global binding is defined, a variable object is associated to it and that object will remain constant over time, even if the value bound to it changes. Therefore, toplevel bindings only need to be looked up once. Thereafter, references to the corresponding toplevel variables from within the program are then performed via the toplevel-ref instruction, which uses the object vector, and are almost as fast as local variable references.

We can see how these concepts tie together by disassembling the foo function we defined earlier to see what is going on:

```
scheme@(guile-user)> (define (foo a) (lambda (b) (list foo a b)))
scheme@(guile-user)> ,x foo
   0    (assert-nargs-ee/locals 1)
   2    (object-ref 1)                    ;; #<procedure 8ebec20 at <current input>:0:17 (b)>
   4    (local-ref 0)                     ;; 'a'
   6    (make-closure 0 1)
   9    (return)


----------------------------------------

Disassembly of #<procedure 8ebec20 at <current input>:0:17 (b)>:

   0    (assert-nargs-ee/locals 1)
   2    (toplevel-ref 1)                  ;; 'foo'
   4    (free-ref 0)                      ;; (closure variable)
   6    (local-ref 0)                     ;; 'b'
   8    (list 0 3)                        ;; 3 elements        at (unknown file):0:29
  11    (return)
```

First there's some prelude, where foo checks that it was called with only 1 argument. Then at ip 2, we load up the compiled lambda. Ip 4 loads up 'a', so that it can be captured into a closure by at ip 6—binding code (from the compiled lambda) with data (the free-variable vector). Finally we return the closure.

The second stanza disassembles the compiled lambda. After the prelude, we note that toplevel variables are resolved relative to the module that was current when the procedure was created. This lookup occurs lazily, at the first time the variable is actually referenced, and the location of the lookup is cached so that future references are very cheap. See Section 9.3.6.2 [Top-Level Environment Instructions], page 779, for more details.

Then we see a reference to a free variable, corresponding to a. The disassembler doesn't have enough information to give a name to that variable, so it just marks it as being a "closure variable". Finally we see the reference to b, then the list opcode, an inline implementation of the list scheme routine.

9.3.6 Instruction Set

There are about 180 instructions in Guile's virtual machine. These instructions represent atomic units of a program's execution. Ideally, they perform one task without conditional branches, then dispatch to the next instruction in the stream.

Instructions themselves are one byte long. Some instructions take parameters, which follow the instruction byte in the instruction stream.

Sometimes the compiler can figure out that it is compiling a special case that can be run more efficiently. So, for example, while Guile offers a generic test-and-branch instruction, it also offers specific instructions for special cases, so that the following cases all have their own test-and-branch instructions:

```
(if pred then else)
(if (not pred) then else)
(if (null? l) then else)
(if (not (null? l)) then else)
```

In addition, some Scheme primitives have their own inline implementations, e.g. cons, and list, as we saw in the previous section.

So Guile's instruction set is a *complete* instruction set, in that it provides the instructions that are suited to the problem, and is not concerned with making a minimal, orthogonal set of instructions. More instructions may be added over time.

9.3.6.1 Lexical Environment Instructions

These instructions access and mutate the lexical environment of a compiled procedure—its free and bound variables.

Some of these instructions have long- variants, the difference being that they take 16-bit arguments, encoded in big-endianness, instead of the normal 8-bit range.

See Section 9.3.3 [Stack Layout], page 774, for more information on the format of stack frames.

local-ref *index*   [Instruction]
long-local-ref *index*   [Instruction]

    Push onto the stack the value of the local variable located at *index* within the current stack frame.

    Note that arguments and local variables are all in one block. Thus the first argument, if any, is at index 0, and local bindings follow the arguments.

`local-set` *index*   [Instruction]
`long-local-set` *index*   [Instruction]
> Pop the Scheme object located on top of the stack and make it the new value of the local variable located at *index* within the current stack frame.

`box` *index*   [Instruction]
> Pop a value off the stack, and set the *index*nth local variable to a box containing that value. A shortcut for `make-variable` then `local-set`, used when binding boxed variables.

`empty-box` *index*   [Instruction]
> Set the *index*th local variable to a box containing a variable whose value is unbound. Used when compiling some `letrec` expressions.

`local-boxed-ref` *index*   [Instruction]
`local-boxed-set` *index*   [Instruction]
> Get or set the value of the variable located at *index* within the current stack frame. A shortcut for `local-ref` then `variable-ref` or `variable-set`, respectively.

`free-ref` *index*   [Instruction]
> Push the value of the captured variable located at position *index* within the program's vector of captured variables.

`free-boxed-ref` *index*   [Instruction]
`free-boxed-set` *index*   [Instruction]
> Get or set a boxed free variable. A shortcut for `free-ref` then `variable-ref` or `variable-set`, respectively.
>
> Note that there is no `free-set` instruction, as variables that are `set!` must be boxed.

`make-closure` *num-free-vars*   [Instruction]
> Pop *num-free-vars* values and a program object off the stack in that order, and push a new program object closing over the given free variables. *num-free-vars* is encoded as a two-byte big-endian value.
>
> The free variables are stored in an array, inline to the new program object, in the order that they were on the stack (not the order they are popped off). The new closure shares state with the original program. At the time of this writing, the space overhead of closures is 3 words, plus one word for each free variable.

`fix-closure` *index*   [Instruction]
> Fix up the free variables array of the closure stored in the *index*th local variable. *index* is a two-byte big-endian integer.
>
> This instruction will pop as many values from the stack as are in the corresponding closure's free variables array. The topmost value on the stack will be stored as the closure's last free variable, with other values filling in free variable slots in order.
>
> `fix-closure` is part of a hack for allocating mutually recursive procedures. The hack is to store the procedures in their corresponding local variable slots, with space already allocated for free variables. Then once they are all in place, this instruction fixes up their procedures' free variable bindings in place. This allows most `letrec`-bound procedures to be allocated unboxed on the stack.

`local-bound?` *index*   [Instruction]

`long-local-bound?` *index*   [Instruction]

> Push #t on the stack if the `index`th local variable has been assigned, or #f otherwise.
> Mostly useful for handling optional arguments in procedure prologues.

9.3.6.2 Top-Level Environment Instructions

These instructions access values in the top-level environment: bindings that were not lexically apparent at the time that the code in question was compiled.

The location in which a toplevel binding is stored can be looked up once and cached for later. The binding itself may change over time, but its location will stay constant.

Currently only toplevel references within procedures are cached, as only procedures have a place to cache them, in their object tables.

`toplevel-ref` *index*   [Instruction]

`long-toplevel-ref` *index*   [Instruction]

> Push the value of the toplevel binding whose location is stored in at position *index* in the current procedure's object table. The `long-` variant encodes the index over two bytes.
>
> Initially, a cell in a procedure's object table that is used by `toplevel-ref` is initialized to one of two forms. The normal case is that the cell holds a symbol, whose binding will be looked up relative to the module that was current when the current program was created.
>
> Alternately, the lookup may be performed relative to a particular module, determined at compile-time (e.g. via @ or @@). In that case, the cell in the object table holds a list: (*modname sym public?*). The symbol *sym* will be looked up in the module named *modname* (a list of symbols). The lookup will be performed against the module's public interface, unless *public?* is #f, which it is for example when compiling @@.
>
> In any case, if the symbol is unbound, an error is signalled. Otherwise the initial form is replaced with the looked-up variable, an in-place mutation of the object table. This mechanism provides for lazy variable resolution, and an important cached fast-path once the variable has been successfully resolved.
>
> This instruction pushes the value of the variable onto the stack.

`toplevel-set` *index*   [Instruction]

`long-toplevel-set` *index*   [Instruction]

> Pop a value off the stack, and set it as the value of the toplevel variable stored at *index* in the object table. If the variable has not yet been looked up, we do the lookup as in `toplevel-ref`.

`define`   [Instruction]

> Pop a symbol and a value from the stack, in that order. Look up its binding in the current toplevel environment, creating the binding if necessary. Set the variable to the value.

`link-now`   [Instruction]

> Pop a value, *x*, from the stack. Look up the binding for *x*, according to the rules for `toplevel-ref`, and push that variable on the stack. If the lookup fails, an error will be signalled.

This instruction is mostly used when loading programs, because it can do toplevel variable lookups without an object table.

`variable-ref`   [Instruction]

Dereference the variable object which is on top of the stack and replace it by the value of the variable it represents.

`variable-set`   [Instruction]

Pop off two objects from the stack, a variable and a value, and set the variable to the value.

`variable-bound?`   [Instruction]

Pop off the variable object from top of the stack and push `#t` if it is bound, or `#f` otherwise. Mostly useful in procedure prologues for defining default values for boxed optional variables.

`make-variable`   [Instruction]

Replace the top object on the stack with a variable containing it. Used in some circumstances when compiling `letrec` expressions.

9.3.6.3 Procedure Call and Return Instructions

`new-frame`   [Instruction]

Push a new frame on the stack, reserving space for the dynamic link, return address, and the multiple-values return address. The frame pointer is not yet updated, because the frame is not yet active – it has to be patched by a `call` instruction to get the return address.

`call` *nargs*   [Instruction]

Call the procedure located at `sp[-nargs]` with the *nargs* arguments located from `sp[-nargs + 1]` to `sp[0]`.

This instruction requires that a new frame be pushed on the stack before the procedure, via **new-frame**. See Section 9.3.3 [Stack Layout], page 774, for more information. It patches up that frame with the current `ip` as the return address, then dispatches to the first instruction in the called procedure, relying on the called procedure to return one value to the newly-created continuation. Because the new frame pointer will point to `sp[-nargs + 1]`, the arguments don't have to be shuffled around – they are already in place.

`tail-call` *nargs*   [Instruction]

Transfer control to the procedure located at `sp[-nargs]` with the *nargs* arguments located from `sp[-nargs + 1]` to `sp[0]`.

Unlike `call`, which requires a new frame to be pushed onto the stack, `tail-call` simply shuffles down the procedure and arguments to the current stack frame. This instruction implements tail calls as required by RnRS.

`apply` *nargs*   [Instruction]
`tail-apply` *nargs*   [Instruction]

Like `call` and `tail-call`, except that the top item on the stack must be a list. The elements of that list are then pushed on the stack and treated as additional arguments, replacing the list itself, then the procedure is invoked as usual.

call/nargs   [Instruction]
tail-call/nargs   [Instruction]

These are like call and tail-call, except they take the number of arguments from the stack instead of the instruction stream. These instructions are used in the implementation of multiple value returns, where the actual number of values is pushed on the stack.

mv-call *nargs offset*   [Instruction]

Like call, except that a multiple-value continuation is created in addition to a single-value continuation.

The offset (a three-byte value) is an offset within the instruction stream; the multiple-value return address in the new frame (see Section 9.3.3 [Stack Layout], page 774) will be set to the normal return address plus this offset. Instructions at that offset will expect the top value of the stack to be the number of values, and below that values themselves, pushed separately.

return   [Instruction]

Free the program's frame, returning the top value from the stack to the current continuation. (The stack should have exactly one value on it.)

Specifically, the sp is decremented to one below the current fp, the ip is reset to the current return address, the fp is reset to the value of the current dynamic link, and then the returned value is pushed on the stack.

return/values *nvalues*   [Instruction]
return/nvalues   [Instruction]

Return the top *nvalues* to the current continuation. In the case of return/nvalues, *nvalues* itself is first popped from the top of the stack.

If the current continuation is a multiple-value continuation, return/values pushes the number of values on the stack, then returns as in return, but to the multiple-value return address.

Otherwise if the current continuation accepts only one value, i.e. the multiple-value return address is NULL, then we assume the user only wants one value, and we give them the first one. If there are no values, an error is signaled.

return/values* *nvalues*   [Instruction]

Like a combination of apply and return/values, in which the top value on the stack is interpreted as a list of additional values. This is an optimization for the common (apply values ...) case.

truncate-values *nbinds nrest*   [Instruction]

Used in multiple-value continuations, this instruction takes the values that are on the stack (including the number-of-values marker) and truncates them for a binding construct.

For example, a call to (receive (x y . z) (foo) ...) would, logically speaking, pop off the values returned from (foo) and push them as three values, corresponding to x, y, and z. In that case, *nbinds* would be 3, and *nrest* would be 1 (to indicate that one of the bindings was a rest argument).

Signals an error if there is an insufficient number of values.

`call/cc`   [Instruction]

`tail-call/cc`   [Instruction]

> Capture the current continuation, and then call (or tail-call) the procedure on the top of the stack, with the continuation as the argument.
>
> `call/cc` does not require a `new-frame` to be pushed on the stack, as `call` does, because it needs to capture the stack before the frame is pushed.
>
> Both the VM continuation and the C continuation are captured.

9.3.6.4 Function Prologue Instructions

A function call in Guile is very cheap: the VM simply hands control to the procedure. The procedure itself is responsible for asserting that it has been passed an appropriate number of arguments. This strategy allows arbitrarily complex argument parsing idioms to be developed, without harming the common case.

For example, only calls to keyword-argument procedures "pay" for the cost of parsing keyword arguments. (At the time of this writing, calling procedures with keyword arguments is typically two to four times as costly as calling procedures with a fixed set of arguments.)

`assert-nargs-ee` *n*   [Instruction]

`assert-nargs-ge` *n*   [Instruction]

> Assert that the current procedure has been passed exactly *n* arguments, for the `-ee` case, or *n* or more arguments, for the `-ge` case. *n* is encoded over two bytes.
>
> The number of arguments is determined by subtracting the frame pointer from the stack pointer (`sp - (fp -1)`). See Section 9.3.3 [Stack Layout], page 774, for more details on stack frames.

`br-if-nargs-ne` *n offset*   [Instruction]

`br-if-nargs-gt` *n offset*   [Instruction]

`br-if-nargs-lt` *n offset*   [Instruction]

> Jump to *offset* if the number of arguments is not equal to, greater than, or less than *n*. *n* is encoded over two bytes, and *offset* has the normal three-byte encoding.
>
> These instructions are used to implement multiple arities, as in `case-lambda`. See Section 6.9.5 [Case-lambda], page 251, for more information.

`bind-optionals` *n*   [Instruction]

> If the procedure has been called with fewer than *n* arguments, fill in the remaining arguments with an unbound value (`SCM_UNDEFINED`). *n* is encoded over two bytes.
>
> The optionals can be later initialized conditionally via the `local-bound?` instruction.

`push-rest` *n*   [Instruction]

> Pop off excess arguments (more than *n*), collecting them into a list, and push that list. Used to bind a rest argument, if the procedure has no keyword arguments. Procedures with keyword arguments use `bind-rest` instead.

`bind-rest` *n idx*   [Instruction]

> Pop off excess arguments (more than *n*), collecting them into a list. The list is then assigned to the *idx*th local variable.

`bind-optionals/shuffle` *nreq nreq-and-opt ntotal*   [Instruction]

`bind-optionals/shuffle-or-br` *nreq nreq-and-opt ntotal offset*   [Instruction]

Shuffle keyword arguments to the top of the stack, filling in the holes with `SCM_UNDEFINED`. Each argument is encoded over two bytes.

This instruction is used by procedures with keyword arguments. *nreq* is the number of required arguments to the procedure, and *nreq-and-opt* is the total number of positional arguments (required plus optional). `bind-optionals/shuffle` will scan the stack from the *nreq*th argument up to the *nreq-and-opt*th, and start shuffling when it sees the first keyword argument or runs out of positional arguments.

`bind-optionals/shuffle-or-br` does the same, except that it checks if there are too many positional arguments before shuffling. If this is the case, it jumps to *offset*, encoded using the normal three-byte encoding.

Shuffling simply moves the keyword arguments past the total number of arguments, *ntotal*, which includes keyword and rest arguments. The free slots created by the shuffle are filled in with `SCM_UNDEFINED`, so they may be conditionally initialized later in the function's prologue.

`bind-kwargs` *idx ntotal flags*   [Instruction]

Parse keyword arguments, assigning their values to the corresponding local variables. The keyword arguments should already have been shuffled above the *ntotal*th stack slot by `bind-optionals/shuffle`.

The parsing is driven by a keyword arguments association list, looked up from the *idx*th element of the procedures object array. The alist is a list of pairs of the form (`kw` . `index`), mapping keyword arguments to their local variable indices.

There are two bitflags that affect the parser, `allow-other-keys?` (0x1) and `rest?` (0x2). Unless `allow-other-keys?` is set, the parser will signal an error if an unknown key is found. If `rest?` is set, errors parsing the keyword arguments will be ignored, as a later `bind-rest` instruction will collect all of the tail arguments, including the keywords, into a list. Otherwise if the keyword arguments are invalid, an error is signalled.

idx and *ntotal* are encoded over two bytes each, and *flags* is encoded over one byte.

`reserve-locals` *n*   [Instruction]

Resets the stack pointer to have space for *n* local variables, including the arguments. If this operation increments the stack pointer, as in a push, the new slots are filled with `SCM_UNBOUND`. If this operation decrements the stack pointer, any excess values are dropped.

`reserve-locals` is typically used after argument parsing to reserve space for local variables.

`assert-nargs-ee/locals` *n*   [Instruction]

`assert-nargs-ge/locals` *n*   [Instruction]

A combination of `assert-nargs-ee` and `reserve-locals`. The number of arguments is encoded in the lower three bits of *n*, a one-byte value. The number of additional local variables is take from the upper 5 bits of *n*.

9.3.6.5 Trampoline Instructions

Though most applicable objects in Guile are procedures implemented in bytecode, not all are. There are primitives, continuations, and other procedure-like objects that have their own calling convention. Instead of adding special cases to the `call` instruction, Guile wraps these other applicable objects in VM trampoline procedures, then provides special support for these objects in bytecode.

Trampoline procedures are typically generated by Guile at runtime, for example in response to a call to `scm_c_make_gsubr`. As such, a compiler probably shouldn't emit code with these instructions. However, it's still interesting to know how these things work, so we document these trampoline instructions here.

subr-call *nargs* [Instruction]

> Pop off a foreign pointer (which should have been pushed on by the trampoline), and call it directly, with the *nargs* arguments from the stack. Return the resulting value or values to the calling procedure.

foreign-call *nargs* [Instruction]

> Pop off an internal foreign object (which should have been pushed on by the trampoline), and call that foreign function with the *nargs* arguments from the stack. Return the resulting value to the calling procedure.

continuation-call [Instruction]

> Pop off an internal continuation object (which should have been pushed on by the trampoline), and reinstate that continuation. All of the procedure's arguments are passed to the continuation. Does not return.

partial-cont-call [Instruction]

> Pop off two objects from the stack: the dynamic winds associated with the partial continuation, and the VM continuation object. Unroll the continuation onto the stack, rewinding the dynamic environment and overwriting the current frame, and pass all arguments to the continuation. Control flow proceeds where the continuation was captured.

9.3.6.6 Branch Instructions

All the conditional branch instructions described below work in the same way:

- They pop off Scheme object(s) located on the stack for use in the branch condition
- If the condition is true, then the instruction pointer is increased by the offset passed as an argument to the branch instruction;
- Program execution proceeds with the next instruction (that is, the one to which the instruction pointer points).

Note that the offset passed to the instruction is encoded as three 8-bit integers, in big-endian order, effectively giving Guile a 24-bit relative address space.

br *offset* [Instruction]

> Jump to *offset*. No values are popped.

br-if *offset* [Instruction]

> Jump to *offset* if the object on the stack is not false.

br-if-not *offset*   [Instruction]

    Jump to *offset* if the object on the stack is false.

br-if-eq *offset*   [Instruction]

    Jump to *offset* if the two objects located on the stack are equal in the sense of **eq?**.
    Note that, for this instruction, the stack pointer is decremented by two Scheme objects
    instead of only one.

br-if-not-eq *offset*   [Instruction]

    Same as **br-if-eq** for non-**eq?** objects.

br-if-null *offset*   [Instruction]

    Jump to *offset* if the object on the stack is '().

br-if-not-null *offset*   [Instruction]

    Jump to *offset* if the object on the stack is not '().

9.3.6.7 Data Constructor Instructions

These instructions push simple immediate values onto the stack, or construct compound
data structures from values on the stack.

make-int8 *value*   [Instruction]

    Push *value*, an 8-bit integer, onto the stack.

make-int8:0   [Instruction]

    Push the immediate value 0 onto the stack.

make-int8:1   [Instruction]

    Push the immediate value 1 onto the stack.

make-int16 *value*   [Instruction]

    Push *value*, a 16-bit integer, onto the stack.

make-uint64 *value*   [Instruction]

    Push *value*, an unsigned 64-bit integer, onto the stack. The value is encoded in 8
    bytes, most significant byte first (big-endian).

make-int64 *value*   [Instruction]

    Push *value*, a signed 64-bit integer, onto the stack. The value is encoded in 8 bytes,
    most significant byte first (big-endian), in twos-complement arithmetic.

make-false   [Instruction]

    Push #f onto the stack.

make-true   [Instruction]

    Push #t onto the stack.

make-nil   [Instruction]

    Push #nil onto the stack.

make-eol   [Instruction]

    Push '() onto the stack.

make-char8 *value*   [Instruction]

    Push *value*, an 8-bit character, onto the stack.

make-char32 *value*   [Instruction]

    Push *value*, an 32-bit character, onto the stack. The value is encoded in big-endian order.

make-symbol   [Instruction]

    Pops a string off the stack, and pushes a symbol.

make-keyword *value*   [Instruction]

    Pops a symbol off the stack, and pushes a keyword.

list *n*   [Instruction]

    Pops off the top *n* values off of the stack, consing them up into a list, then pushes that list on the stack. What was the topmost value will be the last element in the list. *n* is a two-byte value, most significant byte first.

vector *n*   [Instruction]

    Create and fill a vector with the top *n* values from the stack, popping off those values and pushing on the resulting vector. *n* is a two-byte value, like in **vector**.

make-struct *n*   [Instruction]

    Make a new struct from the top *n* values on the stack. The values are popped, and the new struct is pushed.

    The deepest value is used as the vtable for the struct, and the rest are used in order as the field initializers. Tail arrays are not supported by this instruction.

make-array *n*   [Instruction]

    Pop an array shape from the stack, then pop the remaining *n* values, pushing a new array. *n* is encoded over three bytes.

    The array shape should be appropriate to store *n* values. See Section 6.7.5.2 [Array Procedures], page 202, for more information on array shapes.

    Many of these data structures are constant, never changing over the course of the different invocations of the procedure. In that case it is often advantageous to make them once when the procedure is created, and just reference them from the object table thereafter. See Section 9.3.4 [Variables and the VM], page 775, for more information on the object table.

object-ref *n*   [Instruction]
long-object-ref *n*   [Instruction]

    Push *n*th value from the current program's object vector. The "long" variant has a 16-bit index instead of an 8-bit index.

9.3.6.8 Loading Instructions

In addition to VM instructions, an instruction stream may contain variable-length data embedded within it. This data is always preceded by special loading instructions, which interpret the data and advance the instruction pointer to the next VM instruction.

    All of these loading instructions have a **length** parameter, indicating the size of the embedded data, in bytes. The length itself is encoded in 3 bytes.

`load-number` *length* [Instruction]

> Load an arbitrary number from the instruction stream. The number is embedded in the stream as a string.

`load-string` *length* [Instruction]

> Load a string from the instruction stream. The string is assumed to be encoded in the "latin1" locale.

`load-wide-string` *length* [Instruction]

> Load a UTF-32 string from the instruction stream. *length* is the length in bytes, not in codepoints.

`load-symbol` *length* [Instruction]

> Load a symbol from the instruction stream. The symbol is assumed to be encoded in the "latin1" locale. Symbols backed by wide strings may be loaded via `load-wide-string` then `make-symbol`.

`load-array` *length* [Instruction]

> Load a uniform array from the instruction stream. The shape and type of the array are popped off the stack, in that order.

`load-program` [Instruction]

> Load bytecode from the instruction stream, and push a compiled procedure.
>
> This instruction pops one value from the stack: the program's object table, as a vector, or `#f` in the case that the program has no object table. A program that does not reference toplevel bindings and does not use `object-ref` does not need an object table.
>
> This instruction is unlike the rest of the loading instructions, because instead of parsing its data, it directly maps the instruction stream onto a C structure, `struct scm_objcode`. See Section 9.4.6 [Bytecode and Objcode], page 803, for more information.
>
> The resulting compiled procedure will not have any free variables captured, so it may be loaded only once but used many times to create closures.

9.3.6.9 Dynamic Environment Instructions

Guile's virtual machine has low-level support for `dynamic-wind`, dynamic binding, and composable prompts and aborts.

`wind` [Instruction]

> Pop an unwind thunk and a wind thunk from the stack, in that order, and push them onto the "dynamic stack". The unwind thunk will be called on nonlocal exits, and the wind thunk on reentries. Used to implement `dynamic-wind`.
>
> Note that neither thunk is actually called; the compiler should emit calls to wind and unwind for the normal dynamic-wind control flow. See Section 6.13.10 [Dynamic Wind], page 309.

`unwind` [Instruction]

> Pop off the top entry from the "dynamic stack", for example, a wind/unwind thunk pair. `unwind` instructions should be properly paired with their winding instructions, like `wind`.

wind-fluids *n*   [Instruction]

    Pop off *n* values and *n* fluids from the stack, in that order. Set the fluids to the values by creating a with-fluids object and pushing that object on the dynamic stack. See Section 6.21.7 [Fluids and Dynamic States], page 419.

unwind-fluids   [Instruction]

    Pop a with-fluids object from the dynamic stack, and swap the current values of its fluids with the saved values of its fluids. In this way, the dynamic environment is left as it was before the corresponding **wind-fluids** instruction was processed.

fluid-ref   [Instruction]

    Pop a fluid from the stack, and push its current value.

fluid-set   [Instruction]

    Pop a value and a fluid from the stack, in that order, and set the fluid to the value.

prompt *escape-only? offset*   [Instruction]

    Establish a dynamic prompt. See Section 6.13.5 [Prompts], page 296, for more information on prompts.

    The prompt will be pushed on the dynamic stack. The normal control flow should ensure that the prompt is popped off at the end, via **unwind**.

    If an abort is made to this prompt, control will jump to *offset*, a three-byte relative address. The continuation and all arguments to the abort will be pushed on the stack, along with the total number of arguments (including the continuation. If control returns to the handler, the prompt is already popped off by the abort mechanism. (Guile's **prompt** implements Felleisen's –F– operator.)

    If *escape-only?* is nonzero, the prompt will be marked as escape-only, which allows an abort to this prompt to avoid reifying the continuation.

abort *n*   [Instruction]

    Abort to a dynamic prompt.

    This instruction pops one tail argument list, *n* arguments, and a prompt tag from the stack. The dynamic environment is then searched for a prompt having the given tag. If none is found, an error is signalled. Otherwise all arguments are passed to the prompt's handler, along with the captured continuation, if necessary.

    If the prompt's handler can be proven to not reference the captured continuation, no continuation is allocated. This decision happens dynamically, at run-time; the general case is that the continuation may be captured, and thus resumed. A reinstated continuation will have its arguments pushed on the stack, along with the number of arguments, as in the multiple-value return convention. Therefore an **abort** instruction should be followed by code ready to handle the equivalent of a multiply-valued return.

9.3.6.10 Miscellaneous Instructions

nop   [Instruction]

    Does nothing! Used for padding other instructions to certain alignments.

halt   [Instruction]

> Exits the VM, returning a SCM value. Normally, this instruction is only part of the "bootstrap program", a program run when a virtual machine is first entered; compiled Scheme procedures will not contain this instruction.
>
> If multiple values have been returned, the SCM value will be a multiple-values object (see Section 6.13.7 [Multiple Values], page 301).

break   [Instruction]

> Does nothing, but invokes the break hook.

drop   [Instruction]

> Pops off the top value from the stack, throwing it away.

dup   [Instruction]

> Re-pushes the top value onto the stack.

void   [Instruction]

> Pushes "the unspecified value" onto the stack.

9.3.6.11 Inlined Scheme Instructions

The Scheme compiler can recognize the application of standard Scheme procedures. It tries to inline these small operations to avoid the overhead of creating new stack frames.

Since most of these operations are historically implemented as C primitives, not inlining them would entail constantly calling out from the VM to the interpreter, which has some costs—registers must be saved, the interpreter has to dispatch, called procedures have to do much type checking, etc. It's much more efficient to inline these operations in the virtual machine itself.

All of these instructions pop their arguments from the stack and push their results, and take no parameters from the instruction stream. Thus, unlike in the previous sections, these instruction definitions show stack parameters instead of parameters from the instruction stream.

not x [Instruction]
not-not x [Instruction]
eq? $x\,y$ [Instruction]
not-eq? $x\,y$ [Instruction]
null?   [Instruction]
not-null?   [Instruction]
eqv? $x\,y$ [Instruction]
equal? $x\,y$ [Instruction]
pair? $x\,y$ [Instruction]
list? x [Instruction]
set-car! *pair x*   [Instruction]
set-cdr! *pair x*   [Instruction]
cons $x\,y$ [Instruction]
car x [Instruction]
cdr x [Instruction]
vector-ref $x\,y$ [Instruction]

`vector-set` *x* n *y*	[Instruction]
`struct?` *x*	[Instruction]
`struct-ref` *x* n	[Instruction]
`struct-set` *x* n *v*	[Instruction]
`struct-vtable` *x*	[Instruction]
`class-of` *x*	[Instruction]
`slot-ref` *struct* n	[Instruction]
`slot-set` *struct* n *x*	[Instruction]

Inlined implementations of their Scheme equivalents.

Note that `caddr` and friends compile to a series of `car` and `cdr` instructions.

9.3.6.12 Inlined Mathematical Instructions

Inlining mathematical operations has the obvious advantage of handling fixnums without function calls or allocations. The trick, of course, is knowing when the result of an operation will be a fixnum, and there might be a couple bugs here.

More instructions could be added here over time.

As in the previous section, the definitions below show stack parameters instead of instruction stream parameters.

`add` *x y*	[Instruction]
`add1` *x*	[Instruction]
`sub` *x y*	[Instruction]
`sub1` *x*	[Instruction]
`mul` *x y*	[Instruction]
`div` *x y*	[Instruction]
`quo` *x y*	[Instruction]
`rem` *x y*	[Instruction]
`mod` *x y*	[Instruction]
`ee?` *x y*	[Instruction]
`lt?` *x y*	[Instruction]
`gt?` *x y*	[Instruction]
`le?` *x y*	[Instruction]
`ge?` *x y*	[Instruction]
`ash` *x* n	[Instruction]
`logand` *x y*	[Instruction]
`logior` *x y*	[Instruction]
`logxor` *x y*	[Instruction]

Inlined implementations of the corresponding mathematical operations.

9.3.6.13 Inlined Bytevector Instructions

Bytevector operations correspond closely to what the current hardware can do, so it makes sense to inline them to VM instructions, providing a clear path for eventual native compilation. Without this, Scheme programs would need other primitives for accessing raw bytes – but these primitives are as good as any.

As in the previous section, the definitions below show stack parameters instead of instruction stream parameters.

The multibyte formats (`u16`, `f64`, etc) take an extra endianness argument. Only aligned native accesses are currently fast-pathed in Guile's VM.

`bv-u8-ref` *bv n*	[Instruction]
`bv-s8-ref` *bv n*	[Instruction]
`bv-u16-native-ref` *bv n*	[Instruction]
`bv-s16-native-ref` *bv n*	[Instruction]
`bv-u32-native-ref` *bv n*	[Instruction]
`bv-s32-native-ref` *bv n*	[Instruction]
`bv-u64-native-ref` *bv n*	[Instruction]
`bv-s64-native-ref` *bv n*	[Instruction]
`bv-f32-native-ref` *bv n*	[Instruction]
`bv-f64-native-ref` *bv n*	[Instruction]
`bv-u16-ref` *bv n endianness*	[Instruction]
`bv-s16-ref` *bv n endianness*	[Instruction]
`bv-u32-ref` *bv n endianness*	[Instruction]
`bv-s32-ref` *bv n endianness*	[Instruction]
`bv-u64-ref` *bv n endianness*	[Instruction]
`bv-s64-ref` *bv n endianness*	[Instruction]
`bv-f32-ref` *bv n endianness*	[Instruction]
`bv-f64-ref` *bv n endianness*	[Instruction]
`bv-u8-set` *bv n val*	[Instruction]
`bv-s8-set` *bv n val*	[Instruction]
`bv-u16-native-set` *bv n val*	[Instruction]
`bv-s16-native-set` *bv n val*	[Instruction]
`bv-u32-native-set` *bv n val*	[Instruction]
`bv-s32-native-set` *bv n val*	[Instruction]
`bv-u64-native-set` *bv n val*	[Instruction]
`bv-s64-native-set` *bv n val*	[Instruction]
`bv-f32-native-set` *bv n val*	[Instruction]
`bv-f64-native-set` *bv n val*	[Instruction]
`bv-u16-set` *bv n val endianness*	[Instruction]
`bv-s16-set` *bv n val endianness*	[Instruction]
`bv-u32-set` *bv n val endianness*	[Instruction]
`bv-s32-set` *bv n val endianness*	[Instruction]
`bv-u64-set` *bv n val endianness*	[Instruction]
`bv-s64-set` *bv n val endianness*	[Instruction]
`bv-f32-set` *bv n val endianness*	[Instruction]
`bv-f64-set` *bv n val endianness*	[Instruction]

Inlined implementations of the corresponding bytevector operations.

9.4 Compiling to the Virtual Machine

Compilers have a mystique about them that is attractive and off-putting at the same time. They are attractive because they are magical – they transform inert text into live results, like throwing the switch on Frankenstein's monster. However, this magic is perceived by many to be impenetrable.

This section aims to pay attention to the small man behind the curtain.

See Section 6.17 [Read/Load/Eval/Compile], page 357, if you're lost and you just wanted to know how to compile your `.scm` file.

9.4.1 Compiler Tower

Guile's compiler is quite simple, actually – its *compilers*, to put it more accurately. Guile defines a tower of languages, starting at Scheme and progressively simplifying down to languages that resemble the VM instruction set (see Section 9.3.6 [Instruction Set], page 777).

Each language knows how to compile to the next, so each step is simple and understandable. Furthermore, this set of languages is not hardcoded into Guile, so it is possible for the user to add new high-level languages, new passes, or even different compilation targets.

Languages are registered in the module, (`system base language`):

```
(use-modules (system base language))
```

They are registered with the `define-language` form.

define-language [*#:name*] [*#:title*] [*#:reader*] [*#:printer*]   [Scheme Syntax]
      [*#:parser=#f*] [*#:compilers='()*] [*#:decompilers='()*] [*#:evaluator=#f*]
      [*#:joiner=#f*] [*#:for-humans?=#t*]
      [*#:make-default-environment=make-fresh-user-module*]
> Define a language.
>
> This syntax defines a `#<language>` object, bound to *name* in the current environment. In addition, the language will be added to the global language set. For example, this is the language definition for Scheme:
>
> ```
> (define-language scheme
>   #:title "Scheme"
>   #:reader      (lambda (port env) ...)
>   #:compilers   '((tree-il . ,compile-tree-il))
>   #:decompilers '((tree-il . ,decompile-tree-il))
>   #:evaluator (lambda (x module) (primitive-eval x))
>   #:printer write
>   #:make-default-environment (lambda () ...))
> ```

The interesting thing about having languages defined this way is that they present a uniform interface to the read-eval-print loop. This allows the user to change the current language of the REPL:

```
scheme@(guile-user)> ,language tree-il
Happy hacking with Tree Intermediate Language!  To switch back, type ',L scheme'
tree-il@(guile-user)> ,L scheme
Happy hacking with Scheme!  To switch back, type ',L tree-il'.
scheme@(guile-user)>
```

Languages can be looked up by name, as they were above.

lookup-language *name*   [Scheme Procedure]
> Looks up a language named *name*, autoloading it if necessary.
>
> Languages are autoloaded by looking for a variable named *name* in a module named (`language` *name* `spec`).

The language object will be returned, or #f if there does not exist a language with that name.

Defining languages this way allows us to programmatically determine the necessary steps for compiling code from one language to another.

`lookup-compilation-order` *from to*   [Scheme Procedure]
   Recursively traverses the set of languages to which *from* can compile, depth-first, and return the first path that can transform *from* to *to*. Returns #f if no path is found.

   This function memoizes its results in a cache that is invalidated by subsequent calls to `define-language`, so it should be quite fast.

There is a notion of a "current language", which is maintained in the `current-language` parameter, defined in the core (`guile`) module. This language is normally Scheme, and may be rebound by the user. The run-time compilation interfaces (see Section 6.17 [Read/Load/Eval/Compile], page 357) also allow you to choose other source and target languages.

The normal tower of languages when compiling Scheme goes like this:

- Scheme

- Tree Intermediate Language (Tree-IL)

- Guile Lowlevel Intermediate Language (GLIL)

- Assembly

- Bytecode

- Objcode

Object code may be serialized to disk directly, though it has a cookie and version prepended to the front. But when compiling Scheme at run time, you want a Scheme value: for example, a compiled procedure. For this reason, so as not to break the abstraction, Guile defines a fake language at the bottom of the tower:

- Value

Compiling to `value` loads the object code into a procedure, and wakes the sleeping giant.

Perhaps this strangeness can be explained by example: `compile-file` defaults to compiling to object code, because it produces object code that has to live in the barren world outside the Guile runtime; but `compile` defaults to compiling to `value`, as its product re-enters the Guile world.

Indeed, the process of compilation can circulate through these different worlds indefinitely, as shown by the following quine:

```
((lambda (x) ((compile x) x)) '(lambda (x) ((compile x) x)))
```

9.4.2 The Scheme Compiler

The job of the Scheme compiler is to expand all macros and all of Scheme to its most primitive expressions. The definition of "primitive" is given by the inventory of constructs provided by Tree-IL, the target language of the Scheme compiler: procedure applications, conditionals, lexical references, etc. This is described more fully in the next section.

The tricky and amusing thing about the Scheme-to-Tree-IL compiler is that it is completely implemented by the macro expander. Since the macro expander has to run over all of the source code already in order to expand macros, it might as well do the analysis at the same time, producing Tree-IL expressions directly.

Because this compiler is actually the macro expander, it is extensible. Any macro which the user writes becomes part of the compiler.

The Scheme-to-Tree-IL expander may be invoked using the generic `compile` procedure:

```
(compile '(+ 1 2) #:from 'scheme #:to 'tree-il)
⇒
 #<<application> src: #f
                 proc: #<<toplevel-ref> src: #f name: +>
                 args: (#<<const> src: #f exp: 1>
                        #<<const> src: #f exp: 2>)>
```

Or, since Tree-IL is so close to Scheme, it is often useful to expand Scheme to Tree-IL, then translate back to Scheme. For that reason the expander provides two interfaces. The former is equivalent to calling `(macroexpand '(+ 1 2) 'c)`, where the `'c` is for "compile". With `'e` (the default), the result is translated back to Scheme:

```
(macroexpand '(+ 1 2))
⇒ (+ 1 2)
(macroexpand '(let ((x 10)) (* x x)))
⇒ (let ((x84 10)) (* x84 x84))
```

The second example shows that as part of its job, the macro expander renames lexically-bound variables. The original names are preserved when compiling to Tree-IL, but can't be represented in Scheme: a lexical binding only has one name. It is for this reason that the *native* output of the expander is *not* Scheme. There's too much information we would lose if we translated to Scheme directly: lexical variable names, source locations, and module hygiene.

Note however that `macroexpand` does not have the same signature as `compile-tree-il`. `compile-tree-il` is a small wrapper around `macroexpand`, to make it conform to the general form of compiler procedures in Guile's language tower.

Compiler procedures take three arguments: an expression, an environment, and a keyword list of options. They return three values: the compiled expression, the corresponding environment for the target language, and a "continuation environment". The compiled expression and environment will serve as input to the next language's compiler. The "continuation environment" can be used to compile another expression from the same source language within the same module.

For example, you might compile the expression, `(define-module (foo))`. This will result in a Tree-IL expression and environment. But if you compiled a second expression, you would want to take into account the compile-time effect of compiling the previous expression, which puts the user in the `(foo)` module. That is purpose of the "continuation environment"; you would pass it as the environment when compiling the subsequent expression.

For Scheme, an environment is a module. By default, the `compile` and `compile-file` procedures compile in a fresh module, such that bindings and macros introduced by the expression being compiled are isolated:

```
(eq? (current-module) (compile '(current-module)))
⇒ #f

(compile '(define hello 'world))
(defined? 'hello)
⇒ #f

(define / *)
(eq? (compile '/) /)
⇒ #f
```

Similarly, changes to the **current-reader** fluid (see Section 6.17.6 [Loading], page 366) are isolated:

```
(compile '(fluid-set! current-reader (lambda args 'fail)))
(fluid-ref current-reader)
⇒ #f
```

Nevertheless, having the compiler and *compilee* share the same name space can be achieved by explicitly passing (**current-module**) as the compilation environment:

```
(define hello 'world)
(compile 'hello #:env (current-module))
⇒ world
```

9.4.3 Tree-IL

Tree Intermediate Language (Tree-IL) is a structured intermediate language that is close in expressive power to Scheme. It is an expanded, pre-analyzed Scheme.

Tree-IL is "structured" in the sense that its representation is based on records, not S-expressions. This gives a rigidity to the language that ensures that compiling to a lower-level language only requires a limited set of transformations. For example, the Tree-IL type <const> is a record type with two fields, **src** and **exp**. Instances of this type are created via **make-const**. Fields of this type are accessed via the **const-src** and **const-exp** procedures. There is also a predicate, **const?**. See Section 6.7.9 [Records], page 219, for more information on records.

All Tree-IL types have a **src** slot, which holds source location information for the expression. This information, if present, will be residualized into the compiled object code, allowing backtraces to show source information. The format of **src** is the same as that returned by Guile's **source-properties** function. See Section 6.25.2 [Source Properties], page 447, for more information.

Although Tree-IL objects are represented internally using records, there is also an equivalent S-expression external representation for each kind of Tree-IL. For example, the S-expression representation of #<const src: #f exp: 3> expression would be:

```
(const 3)
```

Users may program with this format directly at the REPL:

```
scheme@(guile-user)> ,language tree-il
Happy hacking with Tree Intermediate Language!  To switch back, type ',L scheme'.
tree-il@(guile-user)> (apply (primitive +) (const 32) (const 10))
```

⇒ 42

The `src` fields are left out of the external representation.

One may create Tree-IL objects from their external representations via calling `parse-tree-il`, the reader for Tree-IL. If any source information is attached to the input S-expression, it will be propagated to the resulting Tree-IL expressions. This is probably the easiest way to compile to Tree-IL: just make the appropriate external representations in S-expression format, and let `parse-tree-il` take care of the rest.

`<void>` *src*   [Scheme Variable]
`(void)`   [External Representation]
    An empty expression. In practice, equivalent to Scheme's (`if #f #f`).

`<const>` *src exp*   [Scheme Variable]
`(const exp)`   [External Representation]
    A constant.

`<primitive-ref>` *src name*   [Scheme Variable]
`(primitive name)`   [External Representation]
    A reference to a "primitive". A primitive is a procedure that, when compiled, may be open-coded. For example, `cons` is usually recognized as a primitive, so that it compiles down to a single instruction.

    Compilation of Tree-IL usually begins with a pass that resolves some `<module-ref>` and `<toplevel-ref>` expressions to `<primitive-ref>` expressions. The actual compilation pass has special cases for applications of certain primitives, like `apply` or `cons`.

`<lexical-ref>` *src name gensym*   [Scheme Variable]
`(lexical name gensym)`   [External Representation]
    A reference to a lexically-bound variable. The *name* is the original name of the variable in the source program. *gensym* is a unique identifier for this variable.

`<lexical-set>` *src name gensym exp*   [Scheme Variable]
`(set!` (*lexical* `name gensym`) `exp`)   [External Representation]
    Sets a lexically-bound variable.

`<module-ref>` *src mod name public?*   [Scheme Variable]
`(@ mod name)`   [External Representation]
`(@@ mod name)`   [External Representation]
    A reference to a variable in a specific module. *mod* should be the name of the module, e.g. (`guile-user`).

    If *public?* is true, the variable named *name* will be looked up in *mod*'s public interface, and serialized with `@`; otherwise it will be looked up among the module's private bindings, and is serialized with `@@`.

`<module-set>` *src mod name public? exp*   [Scheme Variable]
`(set! (@ mod name) exp)`   [External Representation]
`(set! (@@ mod name) exp)`   [External Representation]
    Sets a variable in a specific module.

`<toplevel-ref>` *src name*   [Scheme Variable]
(`toplevel` *name*)   [External Representation]
> References a variable from the current procedure's module.

`<toplevel-set>` *src name exp*   [Scheme Variable]
(`set!` (*toplevel* *name*) *exp*)   [External Representation]
> Sets a variable in the current procedure's module.

`<toplevel-define>` *src name exp*   [Scheme Variable]
(`define` (*toplevel* *name*) *exp*)   [External Representation]
> Defines a new top-level variable in the current procedure's module.

`<conditional>` *src test then else*   [Scheme Variable]
(`if` *test then else*)   [External Representation]
> A conditional. Note that *else* is not optional.

`<application>` *src proc args*   [Scheme Variable]
(`apply` *proc . args*)   [External Representation]
> A procedure call.

`<sequence>` *src exps*   [Scheme Variable]
(`begin . exps`)   [External Representation]
> Like Scheme's `begin`.

`<lambda>` *src meta body*   [Scheme Variable]
(`lambda` *meta body*)   [External Representation]
> A closure. *meta* is an association list of properties for the procedure. *body* is a single Tree-IL expression of type `<lambda-case>`. As the `<lambda-case>` clause can chain to an alternate clause, this makes Tree-IL's `<lambda>` have the expressiveness of Scheme's `case-lambda`.

`<lambda-case>` *req opt rest kw inits gensyms body alternate*   [Scheme Variable]
(`lambda-case` ((*req opt rest kw inits gensyms*)   [External Representation]
        body) [*alternate*])
> One clause of a `case-lambda`. A `lambda` expression in Scheme is treated as a `case-lambda` with one clause.
>
> *req* is a list of the procedure's required arguments, as symbols. *opt* is a list of the optional arguments, or `#f` if there are no optional arguments. *rest* is the name of the rest argument, or `#f`.
>
> *kw* is a list of the form, (`allow-other-keys?` (*keyword name var*) ...), where *keyword* is the keyword corresponding to the argument named *name*, and whose corresponding gensym is *var*. *inits* are tree-il expressions corresponding to all of the optional and keyword arguments, evaluated to bind variables whose value is not supplied by the procedure caller. Each *init* expression is evaluated in the lexical context of previously bound variables, from left to right.
>
> *gensyms* is a list of gensyms corresponding to all arguments: first all of the required arguments, then the optional arguments if any, then the rest argument if any, then all of the keyword arguments.

body is the body of the clause. If the procedure is called with an appropriate number of arguments, *body* is evaluated in tail position. Otherwise, if there is an *alternate*, it should be a `<lambda-case>` expression, representing the next clause to try. If there is no *alternate*, a wrong-number-of-arguments error is signaled.

`<let>` *src names gensyms vals exp*   [Scheme Variable]
`(let names gensyms vals exp)`   [External Representation]
> Lexical binding, like Scheme's `let`. *names* are the original binding names, *gensyms* are gensyms corresponding to the *names*, and *vals* are Tree-IL expressions for the values. *exp* is a single Tree-IL expression.

`<letrec>` *in-order? src names gensyms vals exp*   [Scheme Variable]
`(letrec names gensyms vals exp)`   [External Representation]
`(letrec* names gensyms vals exp)`   [External Representation]
> A version of `<let>` that creates recursive bindings, like Scheme's `letrec`, or `letrec*` if *in-order?* is true.

`<dynlet>` *fluids vals body*   [Scheme Variable]
`(dynlet fluids vals body)`   [External Representation]
> Dynamic binding; the equivalent of Scheme's `with-fluids`. *fluids* should be a list of Tree-IL expressions that will evaluate to fluids, and *vals* a corresponding list of expressions to bind to the fluids during the dynamic extent of the evaluation of *body*.

`<dynref>` *fluid*   [Scheme Variable]
`(dynref fluid)`   [External Representation]
> A dynamic variable reference. *fluid* should be a Tree-IL expression evaluating to a fluid.

`<dynset>` *fluid exp*   [Scheme Variable]
`(dynset fluid exp)`   [External Representation]
> A dynamic variable set. *fluid*, a Tree-IL expression evaluating to a fluid, will be set to the result of evaluating *exp*.

`<dynwind>` *winder body unwinder*   [Scheme Variable]
`(dynwind winder body unwinder)`   [External Representation]
> A `dynamic-wind`. *winder* and *unwinder* should both evaluate to thunks. Ensure that the winder and the unwinder are called before entering and after leaving *body*. Note that *body* is an expression, without a thunk wrapper.

`<prompt>` *tag body handler*   [Scheme Variable]
`(prompt tag body handler)`   [External Representation]
> A dynamic prompt. Instates a prompt named *tag*, an expression, during the dynamic extent of the execution of *body*, also an expression. If an abort occurs to this prompt, control will be passed to *handler*, a `<lambda-case>` expression with no optional or keyword arguments, and no alternate. The first argument to the `<lambda-case>` will be the captured continuation, and then all of the values passed to the abort. See Section 6.13.5 [Prompts], page 296, for more information.

`<abort>` *tag args tail*   [Scheme Variable]

`(abort tag args tail)`   [External Representation]

> An abort to the nearest prompt with the name *tag*, an expression. *args* should be a
> list of expressions to pass to the prompt's handler, and *tail* should be an expression
> that will evaluate to a list of additional arguments. An abort will save the partial
> continuation, which may later be reinstated, resulting in the `<abort>` expression
> evaluating to some number of values.

There are two Tree-IL constructs that are not normally produced by higher-level compilers, but instead are generated during the source-to-source optimization and analysis passes that the Tree-IL compiler does. Users should not generate these expressions directly, unless they feel very clever, as the default analysis pass will generate them as necessary.

`<let-values>` *src names gensyms exp body*   [Scheme Variable]

`(let-values names gensyms exp body)`   [External Representation]

> Like Scheme's `receive` – binds the values returned by evaluating `exp` to the `lambda`-
> like bindings described by *gensyms*. That is to say, *gensyms* may be an improper
> list.
>
> `<let-values>` is an optimization of `<application>` of the primitive, `call-with-`
> `values`.

`<fix>` *src names gensyms vals body*   [Scheme Variable]

`(fix names gensyms vals body)`   [External Representation]

> Like `<letrec>`, but only for *vals* that are unset `lambda` expressions.
>
> `fix` is an optimization of `letrec` (and `let`).

Tree-IL implements a compiler to GLIL that recursively traverses Tree-IL expressions, writing out GLIL expressions into a linear list. The compiler also keeps some state as to whether the current expression is in tail context, and whether its value will be used in future computations. This state allows the compiler not to emit code for constant expressions that will not be used (e.g. docstrings), and to perform tail calls when in tail position.

Most optimization, such as it currently is, is performed on Tree-IL expressions as source-to-source transformations. There will be more optimizations added in the future.

Interested readers are encouraged to read the implementation in `(language tree-il compile-glil)` for more details.

9.4.4 GLIL

Guile Lowlevel Intermediate Language (GLIL) is a structured intermediate language whose expressions more closely approximate Guile's VM instruction set. Its expression types are defined in `(language glil)`.

`<glil-program>` *meta . body*   [Scheme Variable]

> A unit of code that at run-time will correspond to a compiled procedure. *meta* should
> be an alist of properties, as in Tree-IL's `<lambda>`. *body* is an ordered list of GLIL
> expressions.

`<glil-std-prelude>` *nreq nlocs else-label*   [Scheme Variable]

> A prologue for a function with no optional, keyword, or rest arguments. *nreq* is the
> number of required arguments. *nlocs* the total number of local variables, including

the arguments. If the procedure was not given exactly *nreq* arguments, control will jump to *else-label*, if given, or otherwise signal an error.

`<glil-opt-prelude>` *nreq nopt rest nlocs else-label*   [Scheme Variable]
    A prologue for a function with optional or rest arguments. Like `<glil-std-prelude>`, with the addition that *nopt* is the number of optional arguments (possibly zero) and *rest* is an index of a local variable at which to bind a rest argument, or `#f` if there is no rest argument.

`<glil-kw-prelude>` *nreq nopt rest kw allow-other-keys? nlocs*   [Scheme Variable]
        else-label
    A prologue for a function with keyword arguments. Like `<glil-opt-prelude>`, with the addition that *kw* is a list of keyword arguments, and *allow-other-keys?* is a flag indicating whether to allow unknown keys. See Section 9.3.6.4 [Function Prologue Instructions], page 782, for details on the format of *kw*.

`<glil-bind>` . *vars*   [Scheme Variable]
    An advisory expression that notes a liveness extent for a set of variables. *vars* is a list of (`name type index`), where *type* should be either `argument`, `local`, or `external`.

    `<glil-bind>` expressions end up being serialized as part of a program's metadata and do not form part of a program's code path.

`<glil-mv-bind>` *vars rest*   [Scheme Variable]
    A multiple-value binding of the values on the stack to *vars*. If *rest* is true, the last element of *vars* will be treated as a rest argument.

    In addition to pushing a binding annotation on the stack, like `<glil-bind>`, an expression is emitted at compilation time to make sure that there are enough values available to bind. See the notes on `truncate-values` in Section 9.3.6.3 [Procedure Call and Return Instructions], page 780, for more information.

`<glil-unbind>`   [Scheme Variable]
    Closes the liveness extent of the most recently encountered `<glil-bind>` or `<glil-mv-bind>` expression. As GLIL expressions are compiled, a parallel stack of live bindings is maintained; this expression pops off the top element from that stack.

    Bindings are written into the program's metadata so that debuggers and other tools can determine the set of live local variables at a given offset within a VM program.

`<glil-source>` *loc*   [Scheme Variable]
    Records source information for the preceding expression. *loc* should be an association list of containing `line column`, and `filename` keys, e.g. as returned by `source-properties`.

`<glil-void>`   [Scheme Variable]
    Pushes "the unspecified value" on the stack.

`<glil-const>` *obj*   [Scheme Variable]
    Pushes a constant value onto the stack. *obj* must be a number, string, symbol, keyword, boolean, character, uniform array, the empty list, or a pair or vector of constants.

`<glil-lexical>` *local? boxed? op index*   [Scheme Variable]

> Accesses a lexically bound variable. If the variable is not *local?* it is free. All variables may have `ref`, `set`, and `bound?` as their *op*. Boxed variables may also have the *ops* `box`, `empty-box`, and `fix`, which correspond in semantics to the VM instructions `box`, `empty-box`, and `fix-closure`. See Section 9.3.3 [Stack Layout], page 774, for more information.

`<glil-toplevel>` *op name*   [Scheme Variable]

> Accesses a toplevel variable. *op* may be `ref`, `set`, or `define`.

`<glil-module>` *op mod name public?*   [Scheme Variable]

> Accesses a variable within a specific module. See Tree-IL's `<module-ref>`, for more information.

`<glil-label>` *label*   [Scheme Variable]

> Creates a new label. *label* can be any Scheme value, and should be unique.

`<glil-branch>` *inst label*   [Scheme Variable]

> Branch to a label. *label* should be a `<ghil-label>`. `inst` is a branching instruction: `br-if`, `br`, etc.

`<glil-call>` *inst nargs*   [Scheme Variable]

> This expression is probably misnamed, as it does not correspond to function calls. `<glil-call>` invokes the VM instruction named *inst*, noting that it is called with *nargs* stack arguments. The arguments should be pushed on the stack already. What happens to the stack afterwards depends on the instruction.

`<glil-mv-call>` *nargs ra*   [Scheme Variable]

> Performs a multiple-value call. *ra* is a `<glil-label>` corresponding to the multiple-value return address for the call. See the notes on `mv-call` in Section 9.3.6.3 [Procedure Call and Return Instructions], page 780, for more information.

`<glil-prompt>` *label escape-only?*   [Scheme Variable]

> Push a dynamic prompt into the stack, with a handler at *label*. *escape-only?* is a flag that is propagated to the prompt, allowing an abort to avoid capturing a continuation in some cases. See Section 6.13.5 [Prompts], page 296, for more information.

Users may enter in GLIL at the REPL as well, though there is a bit more bookkeeping to do:

```
scheme@(guile-user)> ,language glil
Happy hacking with Guile Lowlevel Intermediate Language (GLIL)!
To switch back, type ',L scheme'.
glil@(guile-user)> (program () (std-prelude 0 0 #f)
                       (const 3) (call return 1))
⇒ 3
```

Just as in all of Guile's compilers, an environment is passed to the GLIL-to-object code compiler, and one is returned as well, along with the object code.

9.4.5 Assembly

Assembly is an S-expression-based, human-readable representation of the actual bytecodes that will be emitted for the VM. As such, it is a useful intermediate language both for compilation and for decompilation.

Besides the fact that it is not a record-based language, assembly differs from GLIL in four main ways:

- Labels have been resolved to byte offsets in the program.

- Constants inside procedures have either been expressed as inline instructions or cached in object arrays.

- Procedures with metadata (source location information, liveness extents, procedure names, generic properties, etc) have had their metadata serialized out to thunks.

- All expressions correspond directly to VM instructions – i.e., there is no <glil-lexical> which can be a ref or a set.

Assembly is isomorphic to the bytecode that it compiles to. You can compile to bytecode, then decompile back to assembly, and you have the same assembly code.

The general form of assembly instructions is the following:

```
(inst arg ...)
```

The *inst* names a VM instruction, and its *args* will be embedded in the instruction stream. The easiest way to see assembly is to play around with it at the REPL, as can be seen in this annotated example:

```
scheme@(guile-user)> ,pp (compile '(+ 32 10) #:to 'assembly)
(load-program
  ((:LCASE16 . 2))      ; Labels, unused in this case.
  8                     ; Length of the thunk that was compiled.
  (load-program         ; Metadata thunk.
    ()
    17
    #f                  ; No metadata thunk for the metadata thunk.
    (make-eol)
    (make-eol)
    (make-int8 2)       ; Liveness extents, source info, and arities,
    (make-int8 8)       ; in a format that Guile knows how to parse.
    (make-int8:0)
    (list 0 3)
    (list 0 1)
    (list 0 3)
    (return))
  (assert-nargs-ee/locals 0)  ; Prologue.
  (make-int8 32)     ; Actual code starts here.
  (make-int8 10)
  (add)
  (return))
```

Of course you can switch the REPL to assembly and enter in assembly S-expressions directly, like with other languages, though it is more difficult, given that the length fields have to be correct.

9.4.6 Bytecode and Objcode

Finally, the raw bytes. There are actually two different "languages" here, corresponding to two different ways to represent the bytes.

"Bytecode" represents code as uniform byte vectors, useful for structuring and destructuring code on the Scheme level. Bytecode is the next step down from assembly:

```
scheme@(guile-user)> (compile '(+ 32 10) #:to 'bytecode)
⇒ #vu8(8 0 0 0 25 0 0 0          ; Header.
       95 0                      ; Prologue.
       10 32 10 10 148 66 17     ; Actual code.
       0 0 0 0 0 0 9             ; Metadata thunk.
       9 10 2 10 8 11 18 0 3 18 0 1 18 0 3 66)
```

"Objcode" is bytecode, but mapped directly to a C structure, struct scm_objcode:

```
struct scm_objcode {
  scm_t_uint32 len;
  scm_t_uint32 metalen;
  scm_t_uint8 base[0];
};
```

As one might imagine, objcode imposes a minimum length on the bytecode. Also, the len and metalen fields are in native endianness, which makes objcode (and bytecode) system-dependent.

Objcode also has a couple of important efficiency hacks. First, objcode may be mapped directly from disk, allowing compiled code to be loaded quickly, often from the system's disk cache, and shared among multiple processes. Secondly, objcode may be embedded in other objcode, allowing procedures to have the text of other procedures inlined into their bodies, without the need for separate allocation of the code. Of course, the objcode object itself does need to be allocated.

Procedures related to objcode are defined in the (system vm objcode) module.

objcode? *obj*   [Scheme Procedure]
scm_objcode_p (*obj*)   [C Function]
     Returns #f if *obj* is object code, #f otherwise.

bytecode->objcode *bytecode*   [Scheme Procedure]
scm_bytecode_to_objcode (*bytecode*)   [C Function]
     Makes a bytecode object from *bytecode*, which should be a bytevector. See Section 6.6.6 [Bytevectors], page 163.

load-objcode *file*   [Scheme Variable]
scm_load_objcode (*file*)   [C Function]
     Load object code from a file named *file*. The file will be mapped into memory via mmap, so this is a very fast operation.

     On disk, object code has an sixteen-byte cookie prepended to it, to prevent accidental loading of arbitrary garbage.

`write-objcode` *objcode file*   [Scheme Variable]
`scm_write_objcode` (*objcode*)   [C Function]
    Write object code out to a file, prepending the sixteen-byte cookie.

`objcode->bytecode` *objcode*   [Scheme Variable]
`scm_objcode_to_bytecode` (*objcode*)   [C Function]
    Copy object code out to a bytevector for analysis by Scheme.

The following procedure is actually in (`system vm program`), but we'll mention it here:

`make-program` *objcode objtable* [*free-vars=#f*]   [Scheme Variable]
`scm_make_program` (*objcode, objtable, free_vars*)   [C Function]
    Load up object code into a Scheme program. The resulting program will have *objtable* as its object table, which should be a vector or `#f`, and will capture the free variables from *free-vars*.

Object code from a file may be disassembled at the REPL via the meta-command `,disassemble-file`, abbreviated as `,xx`. Programs may be disassembled via `,disassemble`, abbreviated as `,x`.

Compiling object code to the fake language, `value`, is performed via loading objcode into a program, then executing that thunk with respect to the compilation environment. Normally the environment propagates through the compiler transparently, but users may specify the compilation environment manually as well, as a module.

9.4.7 Writing New High-Level Languages

In order to integrate a new language *lang* into Guile's compiler system, one has to create the module (`language lang spec`) containing the language definition and referencing the parser, compiler and other routines processing it. The module hierarchy in (`language brainfuck`) defines a very basic Brainfuck implementation meant to serve as easy-to-understand example on how to do this. See for instance `http://en.wikipedia.org/wiki/Brainfuck` for more information about the Brainfuck language itself.

9.4.8 Extending the Compiler

At this point we take a detour from the impersonal tone of the rest of the manual. Admit it: if you've read this far into the compiler internals manual, you are a junkie. Perhaps a course at your university left you unsated, or perhaps you've always harbored a desire to hack the holy of computer science holies: a compiler. Well you're in good company, and in a good position. Guile's compiler needs your help.

There are many possible avenues for improving Guile's compiler. Probably the most important improvement, speed-wise, will be some form of native compilation, both just-in-time and ahead-of-time. This could be done in many ways. Probably the easiest strategy would be to extend the compiled procedure structure to include a pointer to a native code vector, and compile from bytecode to native code at run-time after a procedure is called a certain number of times.

The name of the game is a profiling-based harvest of the low-hanging fruit, running programs of interest under a system-level profiler and determining which improvements would give the most bang for the buck. It's really getting to the point though that native compilation is the next step.

The compiler also needs help at the top end, enhancing the Scheme that it knows to also understand R6RS, and adding new high-level compilers. We have JavaScript and Emacs Lisp mostly complete, but they could use some love; Lua would be nice as well, but whatever language it is that strikes your fancy would be welcome too.

Compilers are for hacking, not for admiring or for complaining about. Get to it!

Appendix A GNU Free Documentation License

Version 1.3, 3 November 2008

Copyright © 2000, 2001, 2002, 2007, 2008 Free Software Foundation, Inc.
http://fsf.org/

0. PREAMBLE

The purpose of this License is to make a manual, textbook, or other functional and useful document *free* in the sense of freedom: to assure everyone the effective freedom to copy and redistribute it, with or without modifying it, either commercially or noncommercially. Secondarily, this License preserves for the author and publisher a way to get credit for their work, while not being considered responsible for modifications made by others.

This License is a kind of "copyleft", which means that derivative works of the document must themselves be free in the same sense. It complements the GNU General Public License, which is a copyleft license designed for free software.

We have designed this License in order to use it for manuals for free software, because free software needs free documentation: a free program should come with manuals providing the same freedoms that the software does. But this License is not limited to software manuals; it can be used for any textual work, regardless of subject matter or whether it is published as a printed book. We recommend this License principally for works whose purpose is instruction or reference.

1. APPLICABILITY AND DEFINITIONS

This License applies to any manual or other work, in any medium, that contains a notice placed by the copyright holder saying it can be distributed under the terms of this License. Such a notice grants a world-wide, royalty-free license, unlimited in duration, to use that work under the conditions stated herein. The "Document", below, refers to any such manual or work. Any member of the public is a licensee, and is addressed as "you". You accept the license if you copy, modify or distribute the work in a way requiring permission under copyright law.

A "Modified Version" of the Document means any work containing the Document or a portion of it, either copied verbatim, or with modifications and/or translated into another language.

A "Secondary Section" is a named appendix or a front-matter section of the Document that deals exclusively with the relationship of the publishers or authors of the Document to the Document's overall subject (or to related matters) and contains nothing that could fall directly within that overall subject. (Thus, if the Document is in part a textbook of mathematics, a Secondary Section may not explain any mathematics.) The relationship could be a matter of historical connection with the subject or with related matters, or of legal, commercial, philosophical, ethical or political position regarding them.

The "Invariant Sections" are certain Secondary Sections whose titles are designated, as being those of Invariant Sections, in the notice that says that the Document is released under this License. If a section does not fit the above definition of Secondary then it is not allowed to be designated as Invariant. The Document may contain zero Invariant Sections. If the Document does not identify any Invariant Sections then there are none.

The "Cover Texts" are certain short passages of text that are listed, as Front-Cover Texts or Back-Cover Texts, in the notice that says that the Document is released under this License. A Front-Cover Text may be at most 5 words, and a Back-Cover Text may be at most 25 words.

A "Transparent" copy of the Document means a machine-readable copy, represented in a format whose specification is available to the general public, that is suitable for revising the document straightforwardly with generic text editors or (for images composed of pixels) generic paint programs or (for drawings) some widely available drawing editor, and that is suitable for input to text formatters or for automatic translation to a variety of formats suitable for input to text formatters. A copy made in an otherwise Transparent file format whose markup, or absence of markup, has been arranged to thwart or discourage subsequent modification by readers is not Transparent. An image format is not Transparent if used for any substantial amount of text. A copy that is not "Transparent" is called "Opaque".

Examples of suitable formats for Transparent copies include plain ASCII without markup, Texinfo input format, LaTeX input format, SGML or XML using a publicly available DTD, and standard-conforming simple HTML, PostScript or PDF designed for human modification. Examples of transparent image formats include PNG, XCF and JPG. Opaque formats include proprietary formats that can be read and edited only by proprietary word processors, SGML or XML for which the DTD and/or processing tools are not generally available, and the machine-generated HTML, PostScript or PDF produced by some word processors for output purposes only.

The "Title Page" means, for a printed book, the title page itself, plus such following pages as are needed to hold, legibly, the material this License requires to appear in the title page. For works in formats which do not have any title page as such, "Title Page" means the text near the most prominent appearance of the work's title, preceding the beginning of the body of the text.

The "publisher" means any person or entity that distributes copies of the Document to the public.

A section "Entitled XYZ" means a named subunit of the Document whose title either is precisely XYZ or contains XYZ in parentheses following text that translates XYZ in another language. (Here XYZ stands for a specific section name mentioned below, such as "Acknowledgements", "Dedications", "Endorsements", or "History".) To "Preserve the Title" of such a section when you modify the Document means that it remains a section "Entitled XYZ" according to this definition.

The Document may include Warranty Disclaimers next to the notice which states that this License applies to the Document. These Warranty Disclaimers are considered to be included by reference in this License, but only as regards disclaiming warranties: any other implication that these Warranty Disclaimers may have is void and has no effect on the meaning of this License.

2. VERBATIM COPYING

You may copy and distribute the Document in any medium, either commercially or noncommercially, provided that this License, the copyright notices, and the license notice saying this License applies to the Document are reproduced in all copies, and that you add no other conditions whatsoever to those of this License. You may not use technical measures to obstruct or control the reading or further copying of the copies you make or distribute. However, you may accept compensation in exchange for copies. If you distribute a large enough number of copies you must also follow the conditions in section 3.

You may also lend copies, under the same conditions stated above, and you may publicly display copies.

3. COPYING IN QUANTITY

    If you publish printed copies (or copies in media that commonly have printed covers) of the Document, numbering more than 100, and the Document's license notice requires Cover Texts, you must enclose the copies in covers that carry, clearly and legibly, all these Cover Texts: Front-Cover Texts on the front cover, and Back-Cover Texts on the back cover. Both covers must also clearly and legibly identify you as the publisher of these copies. The front cover must present the full title with all words of the title equally prominent and visible. You may add other material on the covers in addition. Copying with changes limited to the covers, as long as they preserve the title of the Document and satisfy these conditions, can be treated as verbatim copying in other respects.

    If the required texts for either cover are too voluminous to fit legibly, you should put the first ones listed (as many as fit reasonably) on the actual cover, and continue the rest onto adjacent pages.

    If you publish or distribute Opaque copies of the Document numbering more than 100, you must either include a machine-readable Transparent copy along with each Opaque copy, or state in or with each Opaque copy a computer-network location from which the general network-using public has access to download using public-standard network protocols a complete Transparent copy of the Document, free of added material. If you use the latter option, you must take reasonably prudent steps, when you begin distribution of Opaque copies in quantity, to ensure that this Transparent copy will remain thus accessible at the stated location until at least one year after the last time you distribute an Opaque copy (directly or through your agents or retailers) of that edition to the public.

    It is requested, but not required, that you contact the authors of the Document well before redistributing any large number of copies, to give them a chance to provide you with an updated version of the Document.

4. MODIFICATIONS

    You may copy and distribute a Modified Version of the Document under the conditions of sections 2 and 3 above, provided that you release the Modified Version under precisely this License, with the Modified Version filling the role of the Document, thus licensing distribution and modification of the Modified Version to whoever possesses a copy of it. In addition, you must do these things in the Modified Version:

    A. Use in the Title Page (and on the covers, if any) a title distinct from that of the Document, and from those of previous versions (which should, if there were any, be listed in the History section of the Document). You may use the same title as a previous version if the original publisher of that version gives permission.

B. List on the Title Page, as authors, one or more persons or entities responsible for authorship of the modifications in the Modified Version, together with at least five of the principal authors of the Document (all of its principal authors, if it has fewer than five), unless they release you from this requirement.

C. State on the Title page the name of the publisher of the Modified Version, as the publisher.

D. Preserve all the copyright notices of the Document.

E. Add an appropriate copyright notice for your modifications adjacent to the other copyright notices.

F. Include, immediately after the copyright notices, a license notice giving the public permission to use the Modified Version under the terms of this License, in the form shown in the Addendum below.

G. Preserve in that license notice the full lists of Invariant Sections and required Cover Texts given in the Document's license notice.

H. Include an unaltered copy of this License.

I. Preserve the section Entitled "History", Preserve its Title, and add to it an item stating at least the title, year, new authors, and publisher of the Modified Version as given on the Title Page. If there is no section Entitled "History" in the Document, create one stating the title, year, authors, and publisher of the Document as given on its Title Page, then add an item describing the Modified Version as stated in the previous sentence.

J. Preserve the network location, if any, given in the Document for public access to a Transparent copy of the Document, and likewise the network locations given in the Document for previous versions it was based on. These may be placed in the "History" section. You may omit a network location for a work that was published at least four years before the Document itself, or if the original publisher of the version it refers to gives permission.

K. For any section Entitled "Acknowledgements" or "Dedications", Preserve the Title of the section, and preserve in the section all the substance and tone of each of the contributor acknowledgements and/or dedications given therein.

L. Preserve all the Invariant Sections of the Document, unaltered in their text and in their titles. Section numbers or the equivalent are not considered part of the section titles.

M. Delete any section Entitled "Endorsements". Such a section may not be included in the Modified Version.

N. Do not retitle any existing section to be Entitled "Endorsements" or to conflict in title with any Invariant Section.

O. Preserve any Warranty Disclaimers.

If the Modified Version includes new front-matter sections or appendices that qualify as Secondary Sections and contain no material copied from the Document, you may at your option designate some or all of these sections as invariant. To do this, add their titles to the list of Invariant Sections in the Modified Version's license notice. These titles must be distinct from any other section titles.

You may add a section Entitled "Endorsements", provided it contains nothing but endorsements of your Modified Version by various parties—for example, statements of peer review or that the text has been approved by an organization as the authoritative definition of a standard.

You may add a passage of up to five words as a Front-Cover Text, and a passage of up to 25 words as a Back-Cover Text, to the end of the list of Cover Texts in the Modified Version. Only one passage of Front-Cover Text and one of Back-Cover Text may be added by (or through arrangements made by) any one entity. If the Document already includes a cover text for the same cover, previously added by you or by arrangement made by the same entity you are acting on behalf of, you may not add another; but you may replace the old one, on explicit permission from the previous publisher that added the old one.

The author(s) and publisher(s) of the Document do not by this License give permission to use their names for publicity for or to assert or imply endorsement of any Modified Version.

5. COMBINING DOCUMENTS

You may combine the Document with other documents released under this License, under the terms defined in section 4 above for modified versions, provided that you include in the combination all of the Invariant Sections of all of the original documents, unmodified, and list them all as Invariant Sections of your combined work in its license notice, and that you preserve all their Warranty Disclaimers.

The combined work need only contain one copy of this License, and multiple identical Invariant Sections may be replaced with a single copy. If there are multiple Invariant Sections with the same name but different contents, make the title of each such section unique by adding at the end of it, in parentheses, the name of the original author or publisher of that section if known, or else a unique number. Make the same adjustment to the section titles in the list of Invariant Sections in the license notice of the combined work.

In the combination, you must combine any sections Entitled "History" in the various original documents, forming one section Entitled "History"; likewise combine any sections Entitled "Acknowledgements", and any sections Entitled "Dedications". You must delete all sections Entitled "Endorsements."

6. COLLECTIONS OF DOCUMENTS

You may make a collection consisting of the Document and other documents released under this License, and replace the individual copies of this License in the various documents with a single copy that is included in the collection, provided that you follow the rules of this License for verbatim copying of each of the documents in all other respects.

You may extract a single document from such a collection, and distribute it individually under this License, provided you insert a copy of this License into the extracted document, and follow this License in all other respects regarding verbatim copying of that document.

7. AGGREGATION WITH INDEPENDENT WORKS

A compilation of the Document or its derivatives with other separate and independent documents or works, in or on a volume of a storage or distribution medium, is called an "aggregate" if the copyright resulting from the compilation is not used to limit the legal rights of the compilation's users beyond what the individual works permit. When the Document is included in an aggregate, this License does not apply to the other works in the aggregate which are not themselves derivative works of the Document.

If the Cover Text requirement of section 3 is applicable to these copies of the Document, then if the Document is less than one half of the entire aggregate, the Document's Cover Texts may be placed on covers that bracket the Document within the aggregate, or the electronic equivalent of covers if the Document is in electronic form. Otherwise they must appear on printed covers that bracket the whole aggregate.

8. TRANSLATION

Translation is considered a kind of modification, so you may distribute translations of the Document under the terms of section 4. Replacing Invariant Sections with translations requires special permission from their copyright holders, but you may include translations of some or all Invariant Sections in addition to the original versions of these Invariant Sections. You may include a translation of this License, and all the license notices in the Document, and any Warranty Disclaimers, provided that you also include the original English version of this License and the original versions of those notices and disclaimers. In case of a disagreement between the translation and the original version of this License or a notice or disclaimer, the original version will prevail.

If a section in the Document is Entitled "Acknowledgements", "Dedications", or "History", the requirement (section 4) to Preserve its Title (section 1) will typically require changing the actual title.

9. TERMINATION

You may not copy, modify, sublicense, or distribute the Document except as expressly provided under this License. Any attempt otherwise to copy, modify, sublicense, or distribute it is void, and will automatically terminate your rights under this License.

However, if you cease all violation of this License, then your license from a particular copyright holder is reinstated (a) provisionally, unless and until the copyright holder explicitly and finally terminates your license, and (b) permanently, if the copyright holder fails to notify you of the violation by some reasonable means prior to 60 days after the cessation.

Moreover, your license from a particular copyright holder is reinstated permanently if the copyright holder notifies you of the violation by some reasonable means, this is the first time you have received notice of violation of this License (for any work) from that copyright holder, and you cure the violation prior to 30 days after your receipt of the notice.

Termination of your rights under this section does not terminate the licenses of parties who have received copies or rights from you under this License. If your rights have been terminated and not permanently reinstated, receipt of a copy of some or all of the same material does not give you any rights to use it.

10. FUTURE REVISIONS OF THIS LICENSE

The Free Software Foundation may publish new, revised versions of the GNU Free Documentation License from time to time. Such new versions will be similar in spirit to the present version, but may differ in detail to address new problems or concerns. See http://www.gnu.org/copyleft/.

Each version of the License is given a distinguishing version number. If the Document specifies that a particular numbered version of this License "or any later version" applies to it, you have the option of following the terms and conditions either of that specified version or of any later version that has been published (not as a draft) by the Free Software Foundation. If the Document does not specify a version number of this License, you may choose any version ever published (not as a draft) by the Free Software Foundation. If the Document specifies that a proxy can decide which future versions of this License can be used, that proxy's public statement of acceptance of a version permanently authorizes you to choose that version for the Document.

11. RELICENSING

"Massive Multiauthor Collaboration Site" (or "MMC Site") means any World Wide Web server that publishes copyrightable works and also provides prominent facilities for anybody to edit those works. A public wiki that anybody can edit is an example of such a server. A "Massive Multiauthor Collaboration" (or "MMC") contained in the site means any set of copyrightable works thus published on the MMC site.

"CC-BY-SA" means the Creative Commons Attribution-Share Alike 3.0 license published by Creative Commons Corporation, a not-for-profit corporation with a principal place of business in San Francisco, California, as well as future copyleft versions of that license published by that same organization.

"Incorporate" means to publish or republish a Document, in whole or in part, as part of another Document.

An MMC is "eligible for relicensing" if it is licensed under this License, and if all works that were first published under this License somewhere other than this MMC, and subsequently incorporated in whole or in part into the MMC, (1) had no cover texts or invariant sections, and (2) were thus incorporated prior to November 1, 2008.

The operator of an MMC Site may republish an MMC contained in the site under CC-BY-SA on the same site at any time before August 1, 2009, provided the MMC is eligible for relicensing.

ADDENDUM: How to use this License for your documents

To use this License in a document you have written, include a copy of the License in the document and put the following copyright and license notices just after the title page:

```
Copyright (C)  year  your name.
Permission is granted to copy, distribute and/or modify this document
under the terms of the GNU Free Documentation License, Version 1.3
or any later version published by the Free Software Foundation;
with no Invariant Sections, no Front-Cover Texts, and no Back-Cover
Texts.  A copy of the license is included in the section entitled ``GNU
Free Documentation License''.
```

If you have Invariant Sections, Front-Cover Texts and Back-Cover Texts, replace the "with...Texts." line with this:

```
with the Invariant Sections being list their titles, with
the Front-Cover Texts being list, and with the Back-Cover Texts
being list.
```

If you have Invariant Sections without Cover Texts, or some other combination of the three, merge those two alternatives to suit the situation.

If your document contains nontrivial examples of program code, we recommend releasing these examples in parallel under your choice of free software license, such as the GNU General Public License, to permit their use in free software.

Concept Index

This index contains concepts, keywords and non-Schemey names for several features, to make it easier to locate the desired sections.

Procedure Index

This is an alphabetical list of all the procedures and macros in Guile. It also includes Guile's Autoconf macros.

When looking for a particular procedure, please look under its Scheme name as well as under its C name. The C name can be constructed from the Scheme names by a simple transformation described in the section See Section 6.1 [API Overview], page 99.

C

H

O

P

Q

S

Variable Index

This is an alphabetical list of all the important variables and constants in Guile.

When looking for a particular variable or constant, please look under its Scheme name as well as under its C name. The C name can be constructed from the Scheme names by a simple transformation described in the section See Section 6.1 [API Overview], page 99.

Type Index

This is an alphabetical list of all the important data types defined in the Guile Programmers Manual.

R5RS Index